The Political Development of Modern Thailand

Based on extensive empirical research, *The Political Development of Modern Thailand* analyses the country's political history from the late nineteenth century to the present day. Long known for political instability, Thailand was thrust into a deep state of crisis by a royalist military coup staged in 2006. Since then, conservative royalists have overthrown more elected governments after violent street protests, while equally disruptive demonstrations staged by supporters of electoral democracy were crushed by military force. Federico Ferrara traces the roots of the crisis to unresolved struggles regarding the content of Thailand's national identity, dating back to the abolition of absolute monarchy in 1932. He explains the conflict's re-intensification with reference to a growing chasm between the hierarchical world view of Thailand's hegemonic 'royal nationalism' and the aspirations that millions of ordinary people have come to harbour as a result of modernization.

FEDERICO FERRARA is Assistant Professor in the Department of Asian and International Studies at the City University of Hong Kong.

The Political Development of Modern Thailand

Federico Ferrara
City University of Hong Kong

CAMBRIDGE
UNIVERSITY PRESS

CAMBRIDGE
UNIVERSITY PRESS

University Printing House, Cambridge CB2 8BS, United Kingdom

One Liberty Plaza, 20th Floor, New York, NY 10006, USA

477 Williamstown Road, Port Melbourne, VIC 3207, Australia

4843/24, 2nd Floor, Ansari Road, Daryaganj, Delhi - 110002, India

79 Anson Road, #06-04/06, Singapore 079906

Cambridge University Press is part of the University of Cambridge.

It furthers the University's mission by disseminating knowledge in the pursuit of education, learning and research at the highest international levels of excellence.

www.cambridge.org
Information on this title: www.cambridge.org/9781107657298

First published 2015
First paperback edition 2017

A catalogue record for this publication is available from the British Library

Library of Congress Cataloging in Publication data
Ferrara, Federico.
The political development of modern Thailand / Federico Ferrara.
pages cm
Includes bibliographical references and index.
1. Thailand – Politics and government. I. Title.
JQ1745.F47 2015
320.9593 – dc23 2014038238

ISBN 978-1-107-06181-1 Hardback
ISBN 978-1-107-65729-8 Paperback

Ai miei.

It is a good working rule to be suspicious about political and intellectual leaders who talk mainly about moral virtues; many poor devils are liable to be badly hurt.

– Barrington Moore

Contents

Figures and tables

Figures

Tables

Map The Kingdom of Thailand
Based on original design by Daniel Dalet (http://d-maps.com).

Preface

On the evening of 11 October 1933, troops of the Royal Thai Army based in Nakhon Ratchasima and Ayutthaya marched into the northern outskirts of the city of Bangkok. The rebels struck just as Siam's first legislative elections, staggered over several weeks, were being held throughout the country. The 'National Salvation Council' (*Khana Ku Ban Mueang*), featuring well-known conservative officials led by the former Minister of War, Prince Boworadet Kridakorn, had acted with the covert backing of senior members of the royal family, whose previous efforts to dislodge the new constitutional regime – established with the overthrow of the absolute monarchy on 24 June 1932 – had met with failure. After seizing the aerodrome at Don Muang on 12 October, the rebels issued an ultimatum to the Prime Minister, Colonel Phraya Phahon Phonphayuhasena, intimating that he resign within an hour. The rebels' missive and first public pronouncement (reproduced in Thamrongsak 2007: 109–13), printed on leaflets airdropped into the city, declared that the government had lost the trust of 'the people' and the legitimacy to rule. Chief among the administration's alleged misdeeds were encouraging public criticism of the monarchy, inviting civilian revolutionist Pridi Banomyong to return from exile, and reopening the legislature, which King Prajadhipok had prorogued in April 1933 to forestall passage of Pridi's 'communist' economic policies. The rebels further explained that the government planned to exploit its stranglehold over the legislature to usurp the King's powers, using the constitution only as a 'cover' (*khrueang kambang*) for its self-serving designs. While professing respect for the constitution, they stated that the government's behaviour had left them with no choice but to temporarily seize the country's administration through extra-constitutional means. They would relinquish power upon the installation of a royally appointed government, tasked with undertaking 'reforms' necessary to the establishment of a genuine constitutional monarchy, free of the influence of Pridi and his allies.

Eight decades on, Thailand is mired in much the same fight. On 24 November 2013, almost exactly 80 years after the crushing of Prince

Boworadet's 'Blue Army' (see Nattapoll 2013: 27), a royalist crowd of 150,000 people demonstrated in Bangkok to demand the removal of Yingluck Shinawatra's elected government. With an assist by the Constitutional Court – days earlier, the Court had struck down an amendment to the constitution, ruling that parliament's attempt to institute a fully elected Senate amounted to an act of sedition against 'Democracy with the King as Head of State' – protest leaders called for a 'People's Revolution' (*patiwat prachachon*) to 'defend the constitution'. They also presented the success of their seizure of power as the only way to prevent parliament from reviving an amnesty bill that would permit billionaire former Prime Minister Thaksin Shinawatra to return from exile without serving a 2-year prison sentence, imposed after a military coup forcibly removed him in 2006. Fronting the protests this time were the scions of some of Thailand's richest families, like beer heiress Chitpas Kridakorn, and high-ranking officials of the Democrat Party – an organization whose founders in 1946 included veterans of the royalist counter-revolution of the 1930s. Like Prince Boworadet before them, the leaders of a party that had not managed a plurality of the vote since 1992, despite the financial backing of some of the country's largest business conglomerates, arrogated the right to speak for all 'the people' in declaring the elected government 'null and void' (*mokha*) and in stating their intent to overthrow the 'Thaksin System' – shorthand for 'the dictatorship of capitalist political parties through the parliamentary system' (*phadetkan doi phak kan mueang nai thun nai rabop ratthasapha*). Taking another page from Prince Boworadet's playbook, protest leader Suthep Thaugsuban complemented his call to 'protect the constitution' with the demand that its provisions be set aside for the sake of allowing 'good people' (*khon di*) to run the government. Rejecting the electoral process as irremediably tainted by the participation of corruptible provincial voters, Suthep and his supporters demanded that power be transferred to an unelected 'People's Council', which would be tasked with uprooting Thaksin's influence as well as enacting 'reforms' designed to usher in an 'absolute' (*sombun*) version of 'Democracy with the King as Head of State'.

Thaksin Shinawatra, to be clear, is not Pridi Banomyong. For if Pridi was himself no saint, Thaksin's egocentrism and opportunism are in a league of their own. Even so, the reason why royalists have sought to make them into enemies of the state is one and the same: both men, for all their actual failings, are above all guilty of upsetting the 'natural' order of things, Thaksin having come as close as anyone to subverting the royalist order established upon the rollback of Pridi's 1932 revolution. Indeed, as profoundly as Thailand has changed since the mid 1930s, the country has yet conclusively to settle a dispute first occasioned by its transformation into a bounded, absolutist kingdom at the turn of the last century, having failed to reach a basic consensus over just who 'the people' are, how the will of 'the people' is expressed, whether self-styled 'good people' are bound by the same rules as everyone else, and what rights and responsibilities, if any, different constituencies can legitimately claim for themselves. The unending succession of coups, constitutions, armed rebellions, and popular uprisings the country has experienced since 1932 is but the most visible manifestation of the unresolved nature of this conflict, rooted in the juxtaposition of fundamentally different conceptions of the Thai nation.

Beyond its leaders and the nature of their private agendas, the fight over the content of Thailand's national identity – and, therefore, over the formal and informal institutions, constitutive of alternative political regimes, through which the nation exercises its sovereignty – has changed in three major respects over the intervening eight decades. First, and perhaps most obviously, the alignments have shifted. For if the small commoner bourgeoisie and its representatives in the armed forces and the civil service presented the most serious challenge to the power of the aristocracy back in the 1930s, these groups are now overwhelmingly (albeit not unanimously) in the royalist camp. In 2014, the task of removing an elected government that had shown uncommon resilience against the onslaught mounted by royalists in the streets, the courts, and the bureaucracy eventually fell upon the Commander-in-Chief of the Royal Thai Army, General Prayuth Chan-ocha. The suspension of the constitution and the wave of summons, searches, seizures, and arbitrary detentions that followed the military's illegal seizure of power on 22 May were justified in the old royalist rhetoric of replacing 'parliamentary dictatorship' with 'genuine democracy'. Second, the fight has broadened far beyond its original participants among urban elites, as ordinary citizens have become increasingly active on *both sides* of the ongoing struggle for the nation's soul and future – in the words of E.E. Schattschneider, the conflict has been 'nationalized' (Schattschneider (1988[1960]: 10–11). Finally, the 'nationalization' of the fight between populist (egalitarian) and royalist (hierarchical) world views has resulted in its merger with regional cleavages that were also formed as a consequence of Thailand's process of state formation, concerning the place that different regions and their ethnic populations have in the nation that was first imagined for them in Bangkok in the late nineteenth century. Today, royalist positions, political parties, and social movements draw much of their support from the Bangkok metropolitan area and the relatively affluent southern region, whose ethno-cultural heritage and political history are most closely intertwined with the kingdom's core in central Thailand. More populist, egalitarian positions with regard to the form of government and the state's involvement in the economy, by contrast, have often since resonated in regions whose integration into Thailand's national territory was more recent and a great deal more problematic – above all, those northern and northeastern provinces inhabited, in their largest part, by peoples whom the authorities in Bangkok once collectively referred to as 'Lao'.

This book offers an explanation for Thailand's decades-long history of political instability, one that seeks to illuminate the elements of continuity and change instantiated in its ongoing political crisis. While much of the time it took to write it – a task on which I have focused almost single-mindedly since September 2011 – was spent in something of a self-imposed solitary confinement, I cannot fail to acknowledge the contributions many people have made, sometimes unwittingly, to making it a reality.

I came to the Thai Studies field relatively late and largely unaware of its unwelcoming reputation. Given that reputation, I am in retrospect even more grateful for the encouragement and support I almost invariably received from academics and writers more experienced than myself. I also wish to express my appreciation for the scholars, journalists, bloggers, activists, students, artists, novelists, and others in Bangkok and elsewhere who took the time to read, share, and comment on some of my earlier writings on Thailand. At the City University of Hong Kong, I have benefited from the assistance and guidance of a number of colleagues in the Department of Asian and International Studies, where I have worked since 2010. But for the insistence of Nick Thomas, risk averseness would likely have caused me to set my sights on a lesser publisher. Mark Thompson and Bill Case provided comments on parts of an earlier draft. Having put himself through the entire manuscript, James Buchanan offered a long list of valuable suggestions. Kyaw Yin Hlaing, Brad Williams, Jonathan London, and Chiara Formichi made frequent enquiries as to its progress, indulging my need to vent on whatever I was stuck on at the time. Our Department Head, Paul Cammack, went so far as to volunteer to teach one of my courses in early 2013, freeing up time I was able to dedicate to the book's completion. Most of all, I am indebted to my editor at Cambridge University Press for the thoughtfulness and care in handling my submission, as well as to the anonymous readers who reviewed the manuscript in as timely and as rigorous a fashion. It goes without saying that I bear sole responsibility for any errors.

Introducing a book that will likely define my professional reputation for some time to come also gives me a chance to properly acknowledge the teachers and mentors who helped me get this far. At the University of Kansas – where I spent some of the best years of my life after leaving my hometown of Venice, Italy – Ronald Francisco first inspired me to embark on an academic career; with Paul Johnson and Erik Herron, he provided me with the skills and opportunities to pursue it to the best of my abilities. Just as valuable as the first-rate education I received upon venturing out of my comfort zone on Mt. Oread were the sobering life lessons I learned at Harvard University, a place where one is soon confronted with the limits of one's potential. The group of students who entered the Department of Government's doctoral programme in the summer of 2003 remains far and away the smartest bunch of people I have ever been around. Certainly, I learned more from them than I ever did in any classroom. At Harvard University, I was also fortunate to find a fantastic dissertation advisor in Peter Hall, whose dedication and wisdom I can only aspire vaguely to approximate. Judging from the outcome, the other members of my dissertation committee, Torben Iversen and Yoshiko Herrera, convincingly vouched for me with prospective employers when I first stepped into a tough job market. While the corroborating evidence may come in somewhat past its due date, I hope that this book's publication will go some distance towards justifying the investment of trust, time, and trouble each of these people – Ron, Erik, and Peter especially – have made in me.

Finally, an apology is owed to friends and family for the distance and aloofness I have often exhibited over the course of writing this book. All of you, no doubt, deserved better.

17 June 2014

1 Unfinished business

Coups d'état work by the law of the jungle, not the law of the land. For this much is true everywhere: an illegal seizure of power is only truly illegal if it is unsuccessful. More unique to Thailand is the fact that a military coup has little chance of being successful in the first place, but for the endorsement of the world's richest and longest-serving monarch, King Bhumibol Adulyadej. It stands to reason that the Commander-in-Chief of the Royal Thai Army at the time, General Sonthi Boonyaratglin, would be photographed on his knees at Chitralada Palace, just over an hour after announcing that the military had seized power on the evening of 19 September 2006. By then, the generals' every move had been choreographed to impress upon the public that the coup had been staged in the King's name, if not at his behest. Yellow ribbons and flowers adorned tanks, uniforms, and assault rifles. Giant portraits of the King and Queen served as the background for major announcements. The junta's studiously verbose name, the Council for Democratic Reform under the King as Head of State (CDRM) was officially changed 12 days after the coup,[1] but not before making sure that the people had heard the message loud and clear. Thailand had seen royalist coups before, to be sure, but none as awash in royal symbolism. Then again, the military had never removed a Prime Minister as popular as Thaksin Shinawatra. As life quickly returned to normal, it was evident that royal sanction alone could have muted public opposition to the coup, or staved off the possibility that the deposed Prime Minister might put up any resistance.

As the junta deployed its arsenal of royal symbols to forestall active opposition in the streets, the central role played by King Bhumibol in the pseudo-legal process that governed the transition thwarted any attempt Thaksin could otherwise have made to challenge the legality of the coup and continue to present himself as Thailand's rightful, *de jure* Prime

[1] The junta's title was changed to 'Council for National Security' with the promulgation of the interim constitution on 1 October 2006. Its official English name had been shortened to 'Council for Democratic Reform' (CDR) days earlier.

Minister. By any meaningful legal standard, the generals had no authority to abrogate Thailand's 1997 constitution. In turn, in the absence of a constitution specifying the scope of his powers, King Bhumibol had no real legal standing to endorse the generals' actions, grant them immunity from prosecution, or promulgate an interim charter on 1 October 2006. Still, Thaksin could not possibly have dared to point out the obvious lack of legal foundations besetting the process – challenging the legality of his replacement would have required him not only to argue that the King's signature was inconsequential to the validity of documents that sanctioned the transition, but also effectively to assert, blasphemously, that King Bhumibol had enabled an illegal act. Instead, Thaksin and his supporters were forced to argue against the *merits* of staging the coup, a subject where the deposed Prime Minister stood on much shakier ground, given the skeletons crammed in his closet.

Quite aside from the strategic import of the monarchy's endorsement to the junta's public relations campaign, the broad-based acceptance of the legality of measures imposed in the coup's immediate aftermath laid bare what sets Thailand apart from the average constitutional monarchy. In Thailand, the monarchy's authority exists independently of what the constitution provides. And while each of the country's constitutions has made variously worded references to the concept of popular sovereignty, the fact that the King conserves his authority even after the constitution is abrogated indicates that His Majesty reigns by something more akin to natural right than positive law. A noted royalist stated as much in a best-selling book published before the coup (see Pramuan 2005), where he argued – correctly, as a matter of empirical observation – that 'the constitution is not above the King in any way [. . .] the status of the King does not come under the constitution' (see Pasuk and Baker 2009: 255–6). Decade after decade, royalist judges and jurists have more generally gone to extraordinary lengths to sanction the authority of select individuals periodically to brandish the law of the jungle, should constitutions fail to produce the desired outcomes (see Streckfuss 2011: 118–35; Connors 2008: 148–51; Nattapoll 2013: 126). Whereas the stated intent of the revolution that overthrew the absolute monarchy on 24 June 1932 had been to place the King 'under the law of the land', King Bhumibol's 68-year reign coincided with the emergence of a system of government that effectively elevates the King – and his self-appointed defenders – *above* the constitution.

The years since Thaksin's downfall have exposed the fatal flaws of a system of government royalists like to call 'Democracy with the King as Head of State'. The coup set in motion a series of events that plunged the country into a situation of deep political instability – in the intervening time, Thailand's 'slow-burn civil war' (Montesano 2012) has repeatedly seemed on the verge of raging out of control. What is more, the series of actions royalists have seen fit to take since 2006 against Thaksin, his supporters, and his proxies have given rise to a severe crisis of legitimacy marked by a hitherto unseen measure of resentment for the royal family, complete with expressions of public disgust for the monarchy that would have been unthinkable just a few years ago (for instance, see Ünaldi 2014).

Indeed, the historic significance of Thailand's political crisis is that the 2006 coup has reignited a foundational struggle, carried over from the days of the absolute monarchy, between alternative conceptions of the country's nationhood. This basic dispute has crucial implications for some of the most pressing questions defining Thailand's ongoing political conflict. Most crucially, perhaps, does sovereignty ultimately rest with 'the people' or the King? Put differently, whether or not sovereignty is vested in 'the people' in an abstract sense, is the will of 'the people' expressed most authoritatively by the electorate as a whole, or by a minority of 'good' men and women whose claims to superior morality and wisdom are grounded in their professed ontological proximity to the monarchy? In turn, to the extent that 'the people' have rights, *de facto* as well as *de jure*, do they enjoy such rights as citizens – that is, as full members of the national community, 'equal with respect to the rights and duties with which the status is endowed' (Marshall 1964 [1949]: 84) – or as subjects to whom certain freedoms are delegated by a higher (sovereign) power, perhaps in measures commensurate with social status? Should the King – as well as the multiplicity of individuals, organizations, and institutions claiming to speak for, or act in the interest of, the monarchy – be any way constrained by the constitution, or effectively above it? And do these actors have the authority to undo, through extra-constitutional means, the results of participatory processes conducted in accordance with the constitution? Establishing what John Adams referred to as 'a government of laws, and not one of men' (Adams 1851 [1777]: 106), is the unfinished business of Thailand's 1932 revolution.

The purpose of this book is to build an explanation for Thailand's trajectory of political development from 1932 to the present day – one that accounts for the period's unending succession of coups and constitutions. Thailand's chronic regime instability, as well as its current crisis, is traced back to the failure of its transformation into a modern nation-state – its 'National Revolution' (see Lipset and Rokkan 1967: 13) – to give rise to an idea of 'the nation' qua 'deep, horizontal comradeship' (see Anderson 1991 [1983]: 15) between collectively sovereign citizens who are equal with respect to their rights, their treatment under the law, and their legitimate political role. For reasons that have to do with the timing, sequencing, and tempo of Thailand's processes of state and nation building, as well as the contingent outcomes of a continuous process of struggle, the removal of the absolute monarchy did not settle the conflict between the royalist (hierarchical) and the more populist (egalitarian) conceptions of the nation that had emerged upon the founding of an absolutist state in the late nineteenth century (see Copeland 1993). Rather, the events that followed aggravated the constitutional regime's internal contradictions, its deficit of legitimacy, and its resulting instability, creating an opening royalists would later exploit to regain their ascendancy in the 1940s and 1950s. When Thailand's constitutional regime was ultimately put to the sword by a pair of coups staged by Field Marshal Sarit Thanarat in 1957 and 1958, it was in an adaptation of the 'royal nationalism' (*rachachatniyom*; see Thongchai 2001), first elaborated in defence of the absolute monarchy, that the new alliance of the palace, the military, and the bureaucracy grounded its repudiation of the 1932 revolution's founding principles – principles of popular sovereignty, individual equality, constitutionalism, and democracy.

In the time since, the resilience of Thailand's royal nationalism and the enduring strength of institutions responsible for its production and propagation, even in the face of growing popular demands for political and economic empowerment, are explained with reference to mechanisms of institutional reproduction (see Mahoney 2000) accounting for the persistence of asymmetries of power and legitimacy between elected and non-elected institutions. Emphasis is also placed on the strategic adaptations that have allowed the monarchy, the military, and the bureaucracy – the coalition's scarce internal cohesiveness notwithstanding – to respond to a continuous process of change, as well as occasional exogenous shocks, in such a way as to preserve their ability to circumscribe and periodically dismantle political regimes that threatened their prerogatives. It is, conversely, their recent failure to adapt to critical aspects of the thorough transformation of Thai society, as well as the part-structural, part-contingent rise of forces capable of exploiting the opportunities these transformations engendered, that explains the re-emergence of conflict over issues left unsettled by the country's unfinished National Revolution.

This chapter systematically assembles the components of the book's basic argument. The account begins with a historical overview of Thailand's protracted state of crisis, identifying in its elements of continuity and discontinuity the study's *explananda*. The exposition continues with a brief discussion of the genesis and content of Thailand's 'royal nationalism', as well as its significance to the country's history of instability and conflict. Considerations made about the relationship between nationalism and democracy subsequently emerge as a crucial building block in the specification of a dynamic theory of Thailand's regime instability, one that relies heavily on analytical tools drawn from the general literature on political development and historical institutionalism. A final section outlines the book's structure and research design.

Past and prologue

The absolute monarchy came to an end in Thailand, known at the time as Siam, with a coup d'état staged on 24 June 1932 by a group of mostly young, foreign-educated military officers and civil servants, who had organized themselves in the clandestine People's Party (*Khana Ratsadon*). Upon seizing power, the 'Promoters' (*phu ko kan,* short for *phu ko kan plian plaeng kan pokkhrong*, literally, 'initiators of the change of government'), as they have since been known, mapped out a 10-year transition to representative democracy. The coup, however, had been less about 'democracy' than it had been about 'constitutionalism', or the ambition to limit royal authority and place the King under the law. The six principles spelled out in the incendiary 'First Announcement of the People's Party' included 'freedom' (*seriphap*) and 'individual autonomy' (*khwam pen itsara*) as well as the provision of 'equal rights' (*sitthi samoe phak kan*), such that 'the royal class does not have more rights than the people' (*mai chai phuak chao mi sitthi ying kwa ratsadon*). Crucially, the Promoters declared, 'the country belongs to the people, not to the King, as he fraudulently claims' (*prathet rao ni pen khong ratsadon mai chai khong kasat tam thi khao lok luang*).

Seventy-four years later, the claim the Promoters had dismissed as fraudulent was decidedly back in fashion, to the point of serving as the centrepiece of the public case made by royalists to justify the removal of an elected government and the disposal of a democratic constitution in 2006. Nowhere was the fight against Thaksin Shinawatra defined in more memorable terms than in a speech delivered by General Prem Tinsulanond – a former Prime Minister (1980–8) and President of King Bhumibol's Privy Council – at the Chulachomklao Royal Military Academy 2 months before the coup. Prem famously likened the military to a 'horse', adding that governments, unlike the horse's actual 'owner', come and go like mere 'jockeys'. Then, as if to dispel any doubt, Prem reminded his audience: 'You belong to the Nation and His Majesty the King' (*The Nation*, 15 July 2006). The simple imagery invoked by the old general offers a measure of the journey Thailand has travelled over King Bhumibol's long reign. In Prem's formulation, sovereignty rests with the

King, as well as an idea of 'the nation' quite distinct from the electorate that selected the 'jockey' – twice, and by crushing margins. Elections, after all, weigh each person's vote equally, thereby distorting the will of a nation whose very essence, whose main claim to exceptionalism and uniqueness, is a hierarchy of karmic merit, status, and power atop which sits His Majesty the King.

The elevation of the King above the constitution, and the 'royal nationalism' that substituted 'hierarchical' for 'egalitarian' understandings of the nation, are legacies of the dictatorship of Field Marshal Sarit Thanarat (1958–63). Having suffered considerable erosion in the quarter-century that followed the 1932 revolution, it was during this time that the principles spelled out in the 'First Announcement of the People's Party' came to be subverted entirely. With the backing of the United States government, Sarit committed his regime to the re-sacralization of the monarchy and the glorification of King Bhumibol – an irrelevance at the time he had ascended the throne, in tragic circumstances, in 1946. Meanwhile, Sarit's ideologues conceived a model of governance – sometimes referred to as 'Thai-style democracy' – that might be described as a form of 'Platonic guardianship with Buddhist characteristics'.[2] At first only figuratively, the polymath 'philosopher-king' was hoisted to the top of a hierarchy of 'natural' (but, just in case, aggressively state-enforced) inequalities of wealth, power, and status – legitimized, in place of Plato's 'Noble Lie', by Buddhist superstitions of karma, merit (*bun*), and charismatic authority (*barami*). In exchange, the King's uniformed auxiliaries were entrusted with running the country and effectively placed beyond the law. What the system demanded of 'the people' – now, as in the days of Siamese absolutism, equated with 'children', not citizens – was reverence and obedience.

Since Sarit's death in 1963, Thailand has been governed by a series of political regimes reflecting various combinations of democratic and non-democratic rule. Figure 1.1, which plots the country's Freedom House scores on measures of 'political rights' and 'civil liberties' for as long as such scores have been assigned, offers a visual representation of its tangled trajectory of political development. Over the last half-century, the military has alternated periods of outright dictatorship (1958–68, 1971–3, 1976–8, 1991–2, 2006–7, 2014–) with periods of pseudo-democracy in which unelected generals (active duty or retired) served as the Prime Minister but cohabitated with an elected legislature (1969–71, 1979–88, and parts of 1992), as well as periods in which the armed forces allowed the formation of fully civilian governments (1973–6, 1988–91,

[2] The concept of 'guardianship' is contrasted with 'democracy' in Dahl (1991: 52–64).

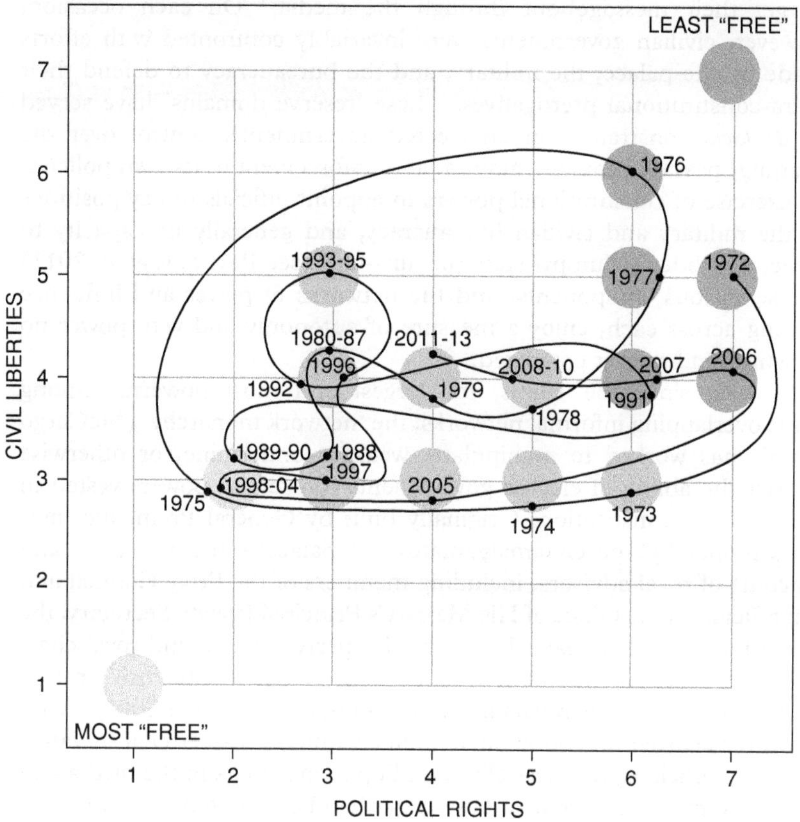

Figure 1.1 Thailand's Freedom House ratings, 1972–2013.
Note: Freedom House scores range from 1 (best) to 7 (worst). Because Freedom House publishes its scores in January of each year, its assessment refers to the previous year (e.g., scores issued in 2014 refer to 2013). For the purposes of this graph, each data point describes Thailand's performance during the year the Freedom House scores cover, not the year in which the scores were published. Colour shadings reflect overall ratings of 'Free' (light grey), 'Partly Free' (darker grey), and 'Not Free' (darkest grey).

1992–2006, 2008–14). In four instances, Thailand was permitted to transition to 'electoral democracy' (1975–6, 1988–91, 1992–2006, 2011–14) – as Freedom House defines it, a system where governments are chosen through regular elections that are free of systematic violence, intimidation, and fraud as well as minimally competitive, thanks to a multiparty system, open campaigning, and opportunities for parties to get their message out through the media.[3] On each occasion, however, civilian governments were invariably confronted with efforts made by the palace, the military, and the bureaucracy to defend their extra-constitutional prerogatives. These 'reserve domains' have served as *de facto* constraints on an elected government's control over the drafting, passage, implementation, and enforcement of its own policies, its exercise of constitutional powers to appoint officials to key positions in the military and civilian bureaucracy, and generally its capacity to direct a decidedly 'lumpy' state (or 'un-state'; see Reynolds *et al.* 2011) whose various components, and the networks of power and influence cutting across each, enjoy a measure of autonomy and veto power no constitution has ever envisaged.

At least since the 1980s, the largest and most powerful among these overlapping informal networks, the 'network monarchy' (McCargo 2005), has worked to manipulate, weaken, undermine, or otherwise restrict the ability of elected governments to exercise powers vested in them by the constitution. Originally built by General Prem, the 'network monarchy' loosely amalgamates 'the palace' – the monarchy and its court of royal advisors, including members of the Privy Council and top officials in the Office of His Majesty's Principal Private Secretary, the Royal Household Bureau, the Crown Property Bureau, and royal charitable foundations, organized in competing 'circles of influence' around senior members of the royal family (see John, 23 November 2009) – with networks centred on conservative military officers, career civil servants, judges, politicians, business elites, and opinion leaders in the media and the academy. Until recently, its strength had been rooted, even more so than its powers of coercion and patronage, in the 'cultural hegemony' of its official ideology (among others, see Connors 2007 [2003]; Streckfuss 2011; Glassman 2011), sustained through schooling and aggressive legal enforcement, as well as a massive, taxpayer-funded propaganda campaign that built for King Bhumibol a cult of personality quite uncharacteristic of a society as modern. Indeed, while a degree of political pluralism has generally been tolerated, often even in the wake of military coups, the

[3] Since the adoption of this classification in 1989, Freedom House has identified Thailand as an 'electoral democracy' for 1989–90 and 1990–1, qualifying its rating by noting 'military influence' over Thailand's parliamentary democracy. Having dropped out in the 1991–2 ratings, owing to the military coup staged in 1991, Thailand was continuously classified as an 'electoral democracy' between 1992–3 and 2006. Beginning with its ratings for 1999–2000, Freedom House dropped the qualification of 'military influence'. Thailand did not recover its classification as an 'electoral democracy' after the 2006 coup despite its return to civilian rule a year later, because Freedom House (2008) reasoned that the elections held on 23 December 2007 were not sufficiently competitive, given the junta's activities against the Thaksin-backed People Power Party. Thailand re-joined the ranks of 'electoral democracies', per Freedom House, after the 2011 elections.

only subject whose discussion has always been truly off-limits since the late 1950s is the monarchy, protected by one of the world's harshest and most vigorously enforced *lèse majesté* laws. It is no surprise, in this sense, that arrests and prosecutions for *lèse majesté* skyrocketed after the 2006 coup,[4] considering the extent to which Thaksin Shinawatra's enemies have relied on the need to 'protect the monarchy' to justify his removal and rationalize the smorgasbord of illiberal measures taken since then to prevent his return.

There is, of course, considerable merit to the allegation that Thaksin had sought to establish something of an 'elected dictatorship' during his 5 years in office, because the administration had parlayed its unprecedented electoral strength into policies that compromised key aspects of the country's democracy. The rule of law was openly flouted in the wave of state violence unleashed pursuant to the government's 'War on Drugs' in 2003 and its response to the outbreak of the southern insurgency in 2004. Accountability was undermined by the efforts made to secure the subservience of state agencies that had been designed as a check on the government's power. And freedom of the press declined sharply as a result of legal measures taken against critics, as well as the informal pressure placed on the print and broadcast media to provide favourable coverage. After the 2005 elections, in which Thaksin's political party Thai Rak Thai took three-quarters of the lower-house seats, Thailand was well on its way to developing a form of 'democracy' with a much stronger 'delegative' (see O'Donnell 1994: 59) than 'liberal' flavour.

Characteristically, Thaksin's removal from office had far less to do with his pronounced illiberal tendencies than his attempt to neutralize the 'network monarchy' and project the power of his government deep into institutions, such as the bureaucracy and the military, traditionally off-limits to elected officials (see Thitinan 2008). Aside from the likelihood that Thaksin might be in office long enough to preside over the dreaded royal succession (see Marshall 2014), by then the network monarchy's affiliates in both the state and civil society understood that the former Prime Minister had already begun, in the space of a few years, to muscle the palace out of its central position in the political, social, and economic life of the country. Such fears were rendered particularly acute by the recognition

[4] Thailand's courts used to accept around ten new cases of *lèse majesté* per year between the mid 1980s and the mid 2000s. The year 2005 set what was at the time a record of thirty-three cases, but the number almost quadrupled to 126 cases in 2007. After a 1-year drop to seventy-seven cases in 2008, after the country's formal return to civilian rule, a new record was set in 2009, with 164 new cases reaching the lower courts (see Streckfuss 2011: 195, 205). David Streckfuss (cited in Prachatai, 28 June 2011) reported that the number rose to 478 cases in 2010. Thailand's ratings on international measures of freedom of the press and freedom of expression cratered as a result.

that Thaksin's vision of 'capitalist revolution' was decidedly more in step with the provincial electorate's aspirations than the King's retrograde economic ideas – and that, in turn, the ambitions of upward mobility even the poorest Thais were now encouraged to embrace threatened to scramble the social hierarchies upon which 'Thai-style democracy' had once been founded (see Hewison and Kengkij 2010: 194–6).

The agencies and institutions set up by the generals in the aftermath of the coup initiated Thaksin's criminal prosecution, froze his assets, disbanded his political party, and dismantled the constitutional provisions that had facilitated the entrenchment of his legislative and executive dominance. All that, however, did not stop the Thaksin-backed People Power Party from winning a comfortable plurality of votes and seats in the general elections held on 23 December 2007. Within months, the royalist 'Yellow Shirts' of the People's Alliance for Democracy (PAD) returned to the streets to wage an aggressive campaign against the new government, featuring a long-running occupation of the Government House as well as the seizure of Bangkok's international airports in late November 2008. The manufactured crisis of governability was brought to an end by the Constitutional Court, whose decision to dissolve the People Power Party and two of its coalition partners has often since been referred to as a 'judicial coup'. Shortly thereafter, Democrat Party leader Abhisit Vejjajiva became Prime Minister, at the head of a ragtag legislative coalition patched together with assistance from the military and the palace.

Abhisit Vejjajiva's swearing in as Prime Minister marked the opening of one of the most tumultuous periods in King Bhumibol's entire reign. It was only then that the street movement founded by Thaksin's loyalists after the coup came into its own, stepping up mobilization efforts that led to the emergence of a social movement organization unprecedented for its size, its territorial coverage, and its staying power. Channelling the anger and frustration that much of the electorate felt, especially in the country's North and Northeast, over the undoing of successive election results, the 'Red Shirts' of the United Front for Democracy Against Dictatorship (UDD) took to demanding the establishment of a form of 'democracy' that would recognize ordinary people as 'the nation's rightful owners' (*chao khong prathet thi thae ching*) and true sovereign power, end the 'double standards' (*song matrathan*) responsible for perpetuating inequalities in *de facto* citizenship status, and dispense with the authority that Thailand's royal nationalism vests in 'good people' to act outside the constitution, often for the purposes of substituting their will for the electorate's. Eventually, faced with large, disruptive, and at times violent protests staged in the heart of Bangkok beginning on 12 March 2010, Abhisit Vejjajiva's administration authorized dispersal operations that resulted in possibly the bloodiest in a string of military crackdowns carried out against street demonstrations since the 1970s. By the time it was all over, on 19 May 2010, the crackdown had claimed the lives of nearly a hundred people.

As much as Thaksin himself, it was thanks to royalists like General Prem that the fight became about the unfinished business of the 1932 revolution. Several years on, the decision made by royalists to frame the fight as a choice between Thaksin and the King, grounding Thaksin's removal in the denial of popular sovereignty, the repudiation of majority rule, and the advocacy of hierarchical over egalitarian conceptions of the nation, might seem reckless and shortsighted. Aside from bringing back to the foreground a century-old cleavage they had struggled to suppress over the past several decades, royalists disregarded the dangers of pitting the institution of the monarchy against a popular Prime Minister, to say nothing of the millions who elected him. Indeed, while the conspicuous use of royal symbolism helped the generals outmanoeuvre Thaksin on the night of 19 September 2006, the challenge before royalists was far more complex than the Prime Minister's removal from office. The complexity of the task, and the determination with which Thaksin and his supporters eventually fought back, transformed the attempt to stamp out his influence into something of a bottomless pit, down which the monarchy flushed much of the considerable political capital it had accumulated over decades.

It was the military that physically wrested the reins of power out of Thaksin's hands. The King, however, loomed large in the rationale the generals concocted for the operation, the theatrics designed to secure the public's acquiescence, and the coup's veneer of legality. Worse, Thaksin's comeback forced his enemies to fall back on the need to 'protect the monarchy' so often, and to justify measures so distasteful, that they not only diminished the power of the argument, but also effectively damaged the institution itself. The airport occupations, the censorship of the media, the hundreds of arrests for *lèse majesté*, the recourse to emergency powers, and even the killing of Red Shirt protesters were all justified on the pretext of defending the King from a tenebrous conspiracy. Whatever the extent, if any, of King Bhumibol's involvement in the coup, the massacre, and the intervening manipulations of Thailand's judicial system, the fact that none of it could have happened but for legitimacy borrowed from the throne inevitably turned the monarchy into a focal point for the anger and frustration of many, among those whose choices had been rubbished so contemptuously.

General elections held on 3 July 2011 added to the growing body of evidence suggesting that royalists cannot win the fight they helped define in these terms. Brushing off instructions issued by the Commander-in-Chief of the Army, among others, to elect 'good people' in order to 'protect the monarchy' (see Bangkok Post, 15 June 2011), voters showed Abhisit Vejjajiva's incumbent administration the door. Instead, the elections ushered in a government led by Yingluck Shinawatra, who had been selected weeks earlier to stand in for her elder brother at the head of the Pheu Thai Party. In winning a comfortable majority in the House of Representatives, Pheu Thai actually went some distance towards replicating Thai Rak Thai's success in the 2005 elections, regaining the support of many voters in Bangkok and elsewhere who appeared to have deserted Thaksin in the wake of the coup.

Even so, while Yingluck's election was followed by 2 years of apparent stability and calm, it became obvious by the end of 2013 that royalists by and large still refuse to accept their defeats at the ballot box for what they are – a symptom of the decline of a political order that has failed to keep pace with the aspirations of a changing electorate. On the contrary, many among them reverted back to the position that democracy must once again be suspended, in order to rectify the failure of the 2006 coup to eradicate the 'Thaksin System' and install an uncorrupted form of 'Democracy with the King as Head of State' – a 'democracy' where elections do not matter, dissent is crushed in the name of 'unity', and everyone loves the King. The military junta that seized power on 22 May 2014, an event followed by the muscular repression of Thaksin allies and pro-democracy activists, appears to have made this vision its own. Just how far, or at what cost, the dictatorial regime installed by General Prayuth Chan-ocha is willing to pursue the royalist restoration demanded by its conservative backers remains unclear as this book goes into production. Somewhat less venturesome is the prediction that the latest suspension of electoral democracy will do more to hasten than to prevent the destruction of Thailand's royalist order.

Continuities and change

The political crisis set in motion by Thaksin Shinawatra's rise to power features elements of both continuity and discontinuity with Thailand's recent history. On the one hand, the events of the past several years epitomize the fragility that the country's formal political regimes have exhibited since 1932. Beginning with the abolishment of the absolute monarchy, Thailand has experienced (by a conservative count) thirteen successful coups – in 1932, 1933 (twice), 1947, 1951, 1957, 1958, 1971, 1976, 1977, 1991, 2006, and 2014 – and at least an equal number of aborted, thwarted, or failed rebellions. During this time, it has been governed by a succession of nineteen constitutions. On the other hand, there appears to be a growing consensus among scholars and observers that the events since the military coup of 19 September 2006 harbour something of the end of an era, especially in light of the looming royal succession. In fact, it is increasingly commonplace for journalistic and scholarly accounts to describe the significance of these events through metaphors that conjure up images of death and dramatic breaks with the past – to cite but a few, the 'death of deference' (Chang Noi, 22 March 2010), the 'death of Thai-style democracy' (Ferrara 2011), the 'death of Thainess' (Streckfuss 2011), a 'moment of truth' (Marshall 2011), 'walls crumbling down' (Connors 2011), and 'the last gasp of Thai dynastic paternalism' (McCargo, 19 December 2013).

While these assessments refer to somewhat different aspects of the crisis, three elements could be said to account for the *fin-de-siècle* air of Thailand's current political situation. The first is the politicization of constituencies that had not been especially active in previous political fights – indeed, constituencies whose 'acquiescence' and 'indifference' had once been regarded as essential to the stability of Thailand's political order (see Wilson 1962: 57–8). The second is the likely fatal decline in the legitimacy accorded by much of the population to the extra-constitutional role played by unelected institutions. The third is the increased questioning of an official ideology that emphasizes 'unity in hierarchy', as reflected in the concepts of 'Thainess' and 'Thai-style democracy', evidenced in the growing demands for equality under the law, the dwindling effectiveness of royalist propaganda, and the scrutiny, criticism, and ridicule responsible for piercing the sacral inviolateness of the monarchy. To the extent that this world view once served as a substitute for reality itself, the discontinuity in question constitutes a 'cultural' as well as an ideological shift.

The profound significance of these developments notwithstanding, one cannot fail to note that the workings of Thailand's political system have continued to exhibit very little change. Even after the humiliation suffered in the 2011 elections, royalists have employed a variety of means, backed by the threat of military intervention, routinely to enforce limitations on the activities of elected governments well in excess of those contemplated by the constitution. Even so, while Thailand's royalist establishment still has the power to circumscribe, undermine, and suspend electoral democracy, it appears to have now lost the *authority* that once allowed it to impose its will legitimately, in a way that minimized both the need for physical coercion and the risks of incurring a public backlash. The aggressiveness with which the military has repressed all expressions of dissent after the 2014 coup, going so far as to criminalize symbolic hand gestures flashed by small crowds of protesters, reflects the junta's anxiety to deny any oxygen to the faintest flame of resistance, rooted in its well-founded insecurity about the usual rationalizations' capacity to secure the public's acquiescence. Having already antagonized much of the country's electorate, Thailand's royalist order threatens definitively to unravel as a result of the succession of the ailing King, born in 1927, and his likely replacement with a man, Crown Prince Vajiralongkorn, disliked by the staunchest royalists. Whether or not a liberal democracy will emerge as a result remains to be seen. But the search for new sources of legitimacy or, conversely, the choice exclusively to rely on coercion, will perforce render future non-democratic regimes, however stringent, quite dissimilar from the forms of rule to which Thailand has been accustomed.

This book puts forth an explanation for Thailand's present political crisis – one designed to account for its elements of continuity and change. As illustrated by the previous discussion, Thailand's political development is not just a story of oscillations between democracy and dictatorship, but also one of continuous struggle between the state and parts of the citizenry, not to mention ongoing conflict between social groups as well as intramural fights within both state and non-state elites. It is this continuous process of conflict that has, at different times, ushered in different combinations of democratic and non-democratic rule. The current crisis, in this sense, underscores not just the impermanence of democratic institutions, but also the instability that has characterized political regimes writ large since the absolute monarchy was fully established in the late nineteenth century (see Anderson 1978). This study's *explanandum*, therefore, is not just the country's failure to consolidate a functioning democracy, but more broadly the development of Thailand's political regimes, defined as the set of formal and informal institutions that govern relations between the state and the citizenry as well as regulating interactions between major political actors. In turn, this approach calls for a strategy of inquiry concerned less with the identification of variables or 'factors' that 'influence whether, once created, democracy is likely to survive' (Acemoglu and Robinson 2006: xiv) than the specification of dynamic 'processes, moving in opposite directions, that produce democratization and de-democratization' (Tilly 2007: xi).

While the events since the military coup of 19 September 2006 were singled out for their element of discontinuity with Thailand's recent past, these developments become perhaps less jarring when analysed through the prism of a continuous process of change. In his study of Siam's 1932 revolution, for instance, Charnvit (2000: 34) argued that a decisive factor in the removal of the absolute monarchy was the emergence of 'new leaders' (*phu nam mai*), particularly within the bureaucracy, predisposed by their education and life experience to 'adopt views that questioned the fundamental beliefs of the old system, customs and traditions based on birthright or notions of karmic merit and charismatic authority' (*mi khwam hen thi tang kham tham to khwam chuea nai rabop kao tam charit prapheni thi wa duai chat kamnoet rue bun barami*). While, as noted, those very ideas were repackaged into the country's official ideology in the late 1950s, it is the rejection of this belief system by an unprecedented number of ordinary people that gives the present the feel of the end of an era. On this score, it should be pointed out that the cultural and ideological transformation Thailand is currently undergoing is not at all unforeseen. Almost four decades ago, Anderson (1977: 24) spoke of an acceleration in the 'secular demystification of Thai politics' and ventured a prediction that 'direct and open attacks on the monarchy loom imminently'. What is remarkable about the developments since the 2006 coup, then, is possibly the fact that it has taken so long for 'secular demystification of Thai politics' to endanger the legitimacy of the country's royalist order. The questions this book takes on are why now, and why in a manner so explosive after the 2006 coup.

Having defined the study's *explananda*, it may be worth expending a few words on the character of the explanation, before moving on to describe the substance of the argument and highlight the contribution it purports to make. This is a study in 'political development', an expression used in this context in much the same manner it is employed in the bourgeoning field of 'American Political Development'. More a work of political science than one of history or area studies, this book is neither a 'political history' of Thailand, nor does it simply treat the country's history as a source of data to test general theories. It is rather a study of the 'historical construction' of the present, conducted with a view to building an explanation 'more attentive than others available to specifically historical processes of change' (see Orren and Skowronek 2004: 6) – one accounting for the temporal dynamics that contribute to continuity as well as change, whether of a sudden or incremental nature (see Mahoney and Thelen 2010). The resulting approach is at once keenly contextual and self-consciously comparative, marrying a healthy scepticism of grand theories with pretensions of universal validity with a continuing interest in 'grasping processes of change conceptually, in general terms' (see Orren and Skowronek 2004: 6).

As Elster (2007: 13) pointed out, explanations in the social sciences should refer only to individuals. In other words, while references to 'supra-individual' entities like families, social classes, or nations may be acceptable as 'harmless shorthand' or 'second best', explanations of collective behaviour require, at least in principle, explanations of the behaviour of individuals within the group. Ideally, then, 'causal explanation' – a statement explaining an event or a state of the world (the *explanandum*) by citing an earlier phenomenon that caused it (the *explanans*) – requires a mechanism accounting for the manner in which a particular event or state of the world influences the behaviour of individuals, as well as the process by which the aggregation of individual actions gives rise to the *explanandum* (see also Elster 1990 [1983]: 84). In turn, the antecedent desires and beliefs that motivate individual action should also be subject to explanation, as opposed to being assumed or inferred based on the agent's choices. On the one hand, the focus on the intentionality of individuals is what separates 'causal explanation' from the statements about 'necessitation' typical of structuralist, non-voluntaristic accounts (for example, see Skocpol 1979: 14–18), which are less concerned with explaining something as it happened than with explaining why it 'had to happen', and 'would have happened some other way had it not happened the way it did' (Elster 2007: 23). On the other hand, the focus on explaining desires and beliefs distinguishes 'causal explanation' from rationalist 'just-so stories' that rely on unverified assumptions about the motivations of individuals to provide a conjectural account for what happened, 'as it *might* have happened' (Elster 2007: 24).

The explanation offered in this study for Thailand's trajectory of political development seeks to stick as close as possible to Elster's recommendations. While, that is, the explanation could be characterized as 'historical institutionalist' (see Hall and Taylor 1996; Thelen 1999) because of its emphasis on the temporal dynamics of institutional reproduction and change, wherever possible the account treats 'macro-states' such as political regimes as the aggregation of individual behaviour, and examines their importance in terms of their effect on individual behaviour. Consistent with much of the recent work on democratization, the explanation offered in these pages centres on the dynamics of strategic interactions, albeit in a manner that takes into account a multiplicity of motivations beyond the maximization of expected utility, and considers the tendency of actors to fail to anticipate the consequences of their actions (see Pierson 2004: 105–22). Attention is also paid to the effects of ideology, culture, and the emotions on the formation of preferences and beliefs, in an effort to infer the motives behind the actions of key players.

'Nationness' and democracy

In a landmark study of democratic transitions, Linz and Stepan (1996) identified in the imperfect correspondence between the outcomes produced by its processes of state and nation building a major hindrance to a country's democratization. 'A modern democratic state', Linz and Stepan (1996: 16) explained, 'is based on the participation of the *demos* (the population), and nationalism provides one possible definition of the *demos*, which may or may not coincide with the *demos* of the state'. As Anderson (1991 [1983]: 6) defines them, nations are 'political communities' that are 'imagined as both inherently limited and sovereign'. Consequently, the establishment and consolidation of a democratic regime may be threatened by the incongruence between the boundaries (or 'limits') of the state and the nation – a challenge all too common in countries that undertake democratic transitions in the developing world. Perhaps most saliently, conflicts over the requirements of full citizenship, and hence over the composition of the *demos*, can undermine lasting agreement over 'political procedures to produce an elected government' as well as the legitimacy of electoral consultations, however 'democratic', that either exclude or include groups whose citizenship is contested.

Under these circumstances, the consolidation of a democratic regime is complicated in each of the requirements Linz and Stepan (1996: 6) maintain must be satisfied before democracy is considered 'the only game in town'. *Behaviourally*, the exclusion or inclusion of the 'wrong' groups may give rise to attempts either to establish a non-democratic regime or violently secede from the state. *Attitudinally*, the scarce legitimacy of the democratic process may render some constituencies available to support non-democratic change, especially in situations of crisis. *Constitutionally*, the 'subjection' and 'habituation' of major political actors to 'the resolution of conflict within specific laws, procedures, and institutions sanctioned by the new democratic process' (Linz and Stepan 1996: 6) may be compromised if various 'governmental and non-governmental forces' either do not submit to playing by the rules, or can exploit the public's scarce attachment to democracy to impose desired outcomes through undemocratic means.

Linz and Stepan's (1996) analysis of the problems of 'stateness' is limited to instances in which a state is inhabited by more than one 'nation' or does not fully encompass the nation that inhabits it. In Thailand, the challenges posed by the inconsonance between the boundaries of state and nation are most severe in its three Muslim-majority southern provinces, where one of the world's bloodiest insurgencies has been raging since 2004 (see McCargo 2008). On the one hand, the insurgency represents a violent attempt to win autonomy or independence from the Thai state through extra-democratic means. On the other hand, as Linz and Stepan (1996: 25) predicted, Thailand's 'nationalizing state policies' have themselves proven at odds with principles of liberal democracy, even at times when the country was ruled by an elected government. Thaksin Shinawatra's authoritarian response to the insurgency's outbreak in 2004 did not seriously dent the government's popularity, even among sections of the public otherwise supportive of 'democracy'.

While the vicissitudes in the South have played an important role in the political crisis Thailand has experienced over the past several years,[5] to say nothing of the thousands of deaths the insurgency has caused, outside the provinces of Pattani, Yala, and Narathiwat, Thailand exhibits a relatively high degree of 'nation-state homogeneity' in a territorial sense (see Thongchai 2004 [1994]: 129–35). Ethnic minorities, variously defined, inhabit most parts of the national territory; despite their less than full or equal inclusion in the country's political life (see McCargo 2012a; Anderson 1978: 211–15), none exhibits serious 'national' aspirations. At the same time, although the discourse of 'lost territories' (see Bowie 1997: 199–201; Thongchai 2004 [1994]: 150–6) is still popular among ultra-royalists, irredentist impulses of the kind that led the Thai government to annex parts of Cambodia, Laos, Malaysia, and Burma's Shan State during World War II have since died down considerably. Even Thailand's ongoing territorial dispute with Cambodia, which recently featured exchanges of artillery fire between the two countries, only centres on 4.6 km^2 of land surrounding the Preah Vihear Temple complex.

This study's contention is that Thailand's political instability, as well as its recent crisis of legitimacy and attendant 'moral panic' (see Cohen 2002 [1972]), is rooted in an aspect of the relationship between state formation, nationalism, and democracy that Linz and Stepan (1996) did not specifically address – what could be said to be an issue of 'nationness' rather than one of 'stateness'. In brief, the hierarchical world view of the country's 'official nationalism' (see Anderson 1991 [1983]: Ch. 6) has, perhaps not surprisingly, proven to be incompatible with the workings of a modern democratic regime, while the enduring strength, within the state, of forces that have styled themselves as either the embodiment or defenders of this conception of 'the nation' is responsible for much of Thailand's political instability. Over the past decade, conversely, it is the re-emergence of a more 'popular' form of nationalism that accounts for the declining legitimacy of the non-democratic component of Thailand's political regime, grounded in the social hierarchies sanctioned by the country's 'royal nationalism'.

[5] McCargo (2007: 64–7) argues that the insurgency contributed to the 2006 coup by undermining Thaksin's personal authority and by bringing to the fore the conflict between the Prime Minister and the palace, which eventually induced the 'network monarchy' to 'mobilize formidable moral resources to harass and discredit the Thaksin government'.

Few casual observers would consider Thailand a country whose sense of 'nation' is weak. Schoolchildren are taught to make conspicuous public displays of respect for national symbols such as the monarchy and the tricolour flag. Millions of people pause every day, at 8 a.m. and 6 p.m., when the notes of the national anthem are played on every radio station, every television channel, and on loudspeakers in public places. Billions of Thai baht have been spent on institutions like the National Culture Commission, the National Identity Board, and the Subcommittee for the Propagation of National Identity to define and disseminate what it means to be 'Thai' (see Connors 2007 [2003]: 142–7 and 233–5; Reynolds 2002: 11–15). 'Nation, Religion, King' has long served as a 'fighting political slogan' (Anderson 1977: 22) against enemies foreign and, especially, domestic – to this day, dissidents are routinely portrayed as 'un-Thai'. In the 1970s, state-sanctioned civilian groups often described as 'ultra-royalist' and 'ultra-nationalist' targeted students, rural activists, and leftist politicians in bombings, assassinations, and mob lynchings. More recently, the so-called 'People's Alliance for Democracy' (PAD) and its various spin-offs – including Suthep Thaugsuban's 'People's Committee to Change Thailand into an Absolute Democracy with the King as Head of State' (PCAD) – have made heavy use of national symbols, slogans, and songs to campaign *against* electoral democracy and urge the arrest of the monarchy's critics. Meanwhile, it remains socially acceptable in public debates to speak of foreigners and ethnic minorities in racist and dehumanizing terms. All this accounts for the common perception that Thailand's sense of nation is, if anything, vastly overblown.

Reactionary and deeply ingrained though it may be, Thailand's brand of 'official nationalism' differs from what Anderson (1991 [1983]) refers to as 'authentic' or 'popular' nationalism. Nationalism of the 'popular' or 'authentic' variety emerges from below and conceives of the nation, however exploitative or unequal its social structure, as a 'deep, horizontal comradeship' (Anderson 1991 [1983]: 15) of equal citizens. 'Official nationalism', by contrast, is an 'anticipatory strategy adopted by dominant groups which are threatened with marginalization or exclusion from an emerging nationally-imagined community' (Anderson 1991 [1983]: 101), typically designed to defeat challenges to dynastic rule presented by the 'fraternizing' qualities of nationalism. Just as the surviving 'dynastic realms' in Europe increasingly came to ground their legitimacy in 'nationalist' discourse, so were the foundations of Siam's 'official nationalism' laid a century ago by King Chulalongkorn (r. 1868–1910) and King Vajiravudh (r. 1910–25), as a reaction to the popular nationalism emerging within the ranks of the country's officialdom and urban intelligentsia. Crafted as a defence of royal absolutism, from the very beginning 'official nationalism' stressed the identification of 'nation' and 'king', and conceived the nation in organic, hierarchical terms. It is on these foundations that Thailand's official ideology still rests (see Murashima 1988).

What makes Thailand's historical experience distinctive is neither the genesis nor the content of its official nationalist ideology, but rather its extraordinary longevity. Most visibly, the persistence of this form of nationalism is reflected in the continuing conflation of 'monarchy' and 'nation', the unremitting failure to conceive of the nation as more than just the monopoly of a single ethno-cultural group (see Anderson 1978: 211–15), and the enduring hegemony of a 'pre-nationalist' cosmological hierarchy (see Anderson 1991 [1983]: 15), typical of old 'sacral cultures' and 'dynastic realms', where social groups are conceived of as 'centripetal and hierarchical', organized around a 'high centre' – the King, or as he is literally referred to in Thai, 'the lord (god) upon our heads' (*Phra Chao Yu Hua*). The King's legitimacy, in turn, derives in part from his stock of karmic merit, presumed to be the highest in the land in keeping with pre-nationalist tradition, and in part from a more modern, state-sanctioned ideology presenting the King as the embodiment of the nation, and conferring upon him the ability to represent the interests of 'the people' far better than its individual members could through the free exercise of their political rights – a state of affairs often equated with utter chaos.

On that basis, while all Thai nationals are formally guaranteed the same legal rights of citizenship, individuals are understood to have legitimate claims to rights, prerogatives, and powers that vary with their respective distance, in terms of the merit and purity revealed by social status, from the country's sacral monarchy (for a visual representation, see Streckfuss 2011: 216). Arranged hierarchically between the 'earth' and the 'sky' – metaphors commonly used in Thailand to describe, respectively, ordinary people and the monarchy – are the Buddhist clergy, the aristocracy, high-ranking state officials, business elites, and Bangkok's middle and upper-middle class, while a hierarchy of 'informal citizenship' distinguishes between the legitimate political role reserved for members of ethno-regional groups based on the degree to which their language and culture deviate from Central Thai standards (see McCargo 2012b). Whatever their status or provenance, people whose actions or words threaten the 'natural' order prescribed by the country's royal nationalism are banished, sometimes more than just rhetorically, to the netherworld of traitors and folk demons.

Writing in the wake of one of the most shameful episodes in Thailand's modern history, as well as one of its most dramatic authoritarian reversals, Anderson (1978: 216–17) explained the 'great instability' of the 40 years since the end of the absolute monarchy with reference to the 'stunted and incomplete transition from kingdom to modern nation-state'. Anderson (1978: 226–7) argued that the absence of a 'decisive break with "absolutism", fuelled by social radicalism and indeed mass nationalism', was behind the instability that Siam/Thailand experienced after the 1932 revolution: 'Suspended between royalist absolutism and popular nationalism, the modern "bureaucratic polity" was both deeply conservative and highly unstable – not because it was "uniquely Thai", but because it contained within itself no real foundation of or criteria for internal and external legitimation.'

This reasoning could be taken a few steps further to provide some perspective on the instability that Thailand has experienced after the 1970s and the failure of the experiments with electoral democracy the country has conducted since. On the one hand, the masses' gradual entry into Thailand's historical stage, as well as the growing complexity of Thai society (see Thak 2007 [1979]: xv) – both of which resulted from the rapid modernization the country has undergone since the 1960s – has made it far more difficult for the military to run the country directly for any meaningful period of time. On the other hand, while the 1973 mass protests seemed to have brought the era of indefinite military dictatorship to a close, the palace and the military were extremely successful in stemming the tide of the new 'popular nationalism' Anderson (1977: 24) had credited for the acceleration in the 'secular demystification of Thai politics'. The cultural hegemony of Thailand's 'official nationalism', in turn, facilitated efforts to undermine democracy, and occasionally suspend it via military coup, by legitimizing the extra-constitutional role of unelected officials and institutions deputized to protect the monarchy and 'the nation'. What is more, the continuing cachet commanded by the hierarchical world view of Thailand's royal nationalism has prevented, within the electorate, the achievement of a basic consensus on the procedures by which governments are selected and (perhaps especially) removed, which is necessary for democracy to assert itself as 'the only game in town'. Although challenged by increasingly large segments of the population, in recent years this world view has been repeatedly affirmed by royalists, whether as justification for the undoing of election results or as the ideological underpinnings of proposals, like the PAD's 'New Politics' (see Connors, 7 July 2008), designed to move the country away from the principle of 'one person, one vote'.

Once again, in this instance the problem is not, as in Linz and Stepan's (1996) treatment, that the state includes more (or less) than one 'nation', but rather that competing ways of imagining the same nation define the *demos* very differently – as Benito Mussolini (2001 [1932]: 85) once put it, one in 'quantitative' (i.e., egalitarian) terms, the other in 'qualitative' (i.e., hierarchical) terms. Still, Thailand's political development suggests that the issue of 'nationness' presents much the same challenges for democratic consolidation as those posed by the problem of 'stateness' identified by Linz and Stepan (1996): *behaviourally*, the continuing strength of institutions and social constituencies that reject the legitimacy of the democratic process, and have periodically sought to subvert the outcomes it tends to produce; *attitudinally*, the availability of significant segments of the population to support authoritarian reversals in times of crisis; *constitutionally*, the persistence of extra-constitutional, unaccountable powers exercised by the palace, the military, and parts of the civilian bureaucracy, as well as the scarce habituation of major political actors to 'the resolution of conflict within specific laws, procedures, and institutions sanctioned by the new democratic process'. More generally, Thailand's royal nationalism continues to legitimize practices that violate two of the conditions Tilly (2007: 74–6) deems necessary to democratization: 1) 'the weakening of autonomous centres of power', like Thailand's 'network monarchy'; and 2) the reduction in the extent to which socio-economic disparities coincide with inequalities in the enjoyment of civil and political rights.[6]

The notion that the Thai *demos* should either exclude much of the country's working class and its provincial population, or otherwise confer upon the majority of the electorate less than full voting rights and citizenship status, remains popular with the privileged in Bangkok and elsewhere. Just as important, while the crucial swing constituency, the urban middle class, is less invested in this world view's anti-democratic features, it has nonetheless oscillated back and forth between backing pro-democratic movements (in 1973 and 1992) and tolerating major authoritarian reversals (in 1976, 1991, 2006 and 2014). Status insecurities, and an intense but constantly threatened sense of moral superiority, have at different times led this constituency to offer at least situational support for actions designed to protect the *demos* from the entry of the 'great unwashed', to borrow an expression from Democrat Party stalwart Korn Chatikavanij (see Chang Noi, 19 April 2010). Even to this constituency, Thailand's royal nationalism offers an argument for the

[6] Rueschemeyer *et al.* (1992: 41) also identify, as a 'minimal condition of democracy', the existence of 'a fairly strong institutional separation [. . .] of the realm of politics from the overall system of inequality in society', for 'only then is it even conceivable that those who stand at the bottom of the scales of power, wealth, and cultural participation will – by themselves or through their representatives – significantly shape collective decisions that are binding for all'.

basic fairness of social and political hierarchies, as well as a mask for motivations driven by interest or emotions like resentment and fear.

Accounts of the political crisis into which Thailand descended with the military coup of 19 September 2006 have emphasized different aspects of the crisis – intra-elite struggle (see Lintner, 15 April 2009), class conflict (see Giles 2010), economic inequality (see Hewison 2012), urban–rural cleavages (see Glassman 2010), political culture and socio-economic change (see Walker 2012), ethnicity (see Streckfuss, 24 May 2010), elite aversion to democracy (see Thongchai 2008a), ' royal liberalism' and its suspicion of majoritarianism (see Connors 2008), opposition to global capitalism (see Kasian 2006), and various combinations thereof. This study seeks to build an explanation that can do justice to the complexity and multidimensionality of the conflict. Perhaps most crucially, while acknowledging the significance of a power struggle taking place at the elite level, where private concerns trump the ideals in which both sides couch their appeals for public support, this treatment portrays the ongoing crisis as more than a 'conflict between different elements of the Thai elite, who have mobilized rival patronage-based networks of supporters' (McCargo 2010: 9; see also Crispin 2012). Like most political fights, private and public motives are far from mutually exclusive, as movements or causes most often amalgamate a multiplicity of motivations. As Lipset and Rokkan (1967: 10) once put it, the fact that, on some level, political cleavages 'might be nothing more than direct struggles among competing elites for central power' in no way precludes the possibility that 'they might also reflect deeper differences in conceptions of nationhood, over domestic priorities, and over external strategies'.

Beyond the elite dimension, Thailand's political crisis is best described as a conflict over identity, one that has its roots in the process of state formation that led to the establishment of the absolute monarchy in the late nineteenth century. Fearon (1999: 14) usefully describes 'identity politics' as a form of contestation over the membership rules, the content, and the 'moral valuation' or 'political treatment' of certain social constituencies. Thailand's crisis is an identity conflict in each of these three ways: 1) a conflict over the *membership rules* of full citizenship; 2) a conflict over the *content* of 'Thainess'; and 3) a conflict over the *moral valuation* and the *political treatment* of the groups Thailand's royal nationalism relegates to a subaltern social status, whether on account of their socio-economic status, ethno-regional background, or anti-establishment ideas. The struggle is also an 'identity conflict' in the sense that the actions of individual participants can only be understood with reference to the role that socially constructed collective identities play in shaping motivations and beliefs – on one side, the desire to affirm the sense of pride and self-respect individuals derive from their identification as 'citizen' (*prachachon*), 'commoner' (*samanchon*), 'ordinary person' (*khon thammada*), or even *phrai* (an archaic term for commoners once subject to *corvée*, the forced provision of unpaid labour in lieu of taxes); on the other side, the desire to affirm the sense of pride and self-respect individuals derive from their identification as defenders of the monarchy, as guardians of the nation's traditions, or as 'good people' born (or otherwise most qualified) to rule.

Dynamics of regime instability

Thailand's trajectory of political development may not seem all that extraordinary when it is matched up against what is known more generally about the 'mechanics' of regime instability. Przeworski (2009: 21) introduces two 'general facts' to make sense of why countries where democracy is established early may end up enjoying it less frequently, or may indeed have trouble consolidating a stable regime of any kind. First, 'the probability that, once in place, a democracy survives increases steeply in per capita income, converging to certainty when income is sufficiently high' (Przeworski 2009: 21; see also Przeworski and Limongi 1997). Second, both democracy and non-democracy tend to be more unstable in countries that previously experienced at least one episode of failed democratization. Putting the two together, democracy is said to be at a high risk of collapsing when it is established in conditions of underdevelopment. If it does fail, all else being equal, future regimes, whether democracies or non-democracies, will also be less likely to survive. When income levels remain flat, therefore, the country in question might experience multiple democratic transitions and authoritarian reversals, each of them rendering future regimes more unstable. As incomes rise, however, spells of democracy become longer in duration, until income crosses a threshold whereupon democracy, once established, becomes 'impregnable' (see Przeworski 2009: 23).[7]

While both 'general facts' are supported by a robust body of evidence, Przeworski (2009: 6) concedes that the establishment of empirical regularities does not amount to an explanation. Aside from the recognition that regime instability is not entirely a matter of 'mechanics', what accounts for such regularities remains an open question. As for the reason why democracy would be more stable at higher levels of development,

[7] Tilly's (2007: xi) point that democratization should be conceived of as a process that 'always remains incomplete and perpetually runs the risk of reversal – of de-democratization' is well taken. Przeworski (2009: 19–20), however, only refers to a limited form of democracy, similar to Freedom House's concept of 'electoral democracy'.

Przeworski (2009: 27–9; see also Przeworski 2006) suggests that, as a society grows wealthier, democracy's redistributive tendencies become less threatening to elites, while dictatorship simultaneously becomes less appealing to those with the means to overthrow the existing regime.[8] At some point, the benefits of dictatorship become smaller than the disutility incurred, even by elites, from the loss of individual freedoms; moreover, consenting to democracy, even one where elites support perennial losers at the ballot box, becomes more attractive than risking the violence that might result from its suspension. As for why both democracy and non-democracy would be rendered more unstable by previous failures of democracy, Przeworski (2009: 27) notes that authoritarian reversals most frequently take place as a result of military intervention. While military dictatorship tends to be more short-lived than other forms of dictatorship, one military intervention makes future interventions more likely – perhaps by creating stronger militaries, by crippling forces capable of resisting future reversals, and/or by increasing the public's habituation to coups.

On the whole, Thailand fits rather comfortably in Przeworski's (2009) framework. Its first attempt to establish a semblance of democracy came early, not just relatively to other countries in the region, but also given its levels of development *circa* 1932. While its failure was not unavoidable, the democratic potential of the 1932 revolution evaporated within months of the constitutional regime's founding. As illustrated in Figure 1.2, moreover, the regimes established thereafter have been characterized by considerable instability.[9] Still, although Thailand never overcame the legacy of successive military interventions, its experiments with 'electoral democracy' have become longer as incomes have risen – the one concluded in 2006 lasted 14 years. Thailand's income per capita is now fast approaching a level beyond which there are no examples of authoritarian reversals.[10]

[8] Redistribution in a context of plenty damages elites less than in one of scarcity. Because of the decreasing marginal utility of income and consumption, moreover, the potential benefits of dictatorship will also be valued lower as overall incomes rise.

[9] In Figure 1.2, the designation 'dictatorship' is reserved for periods of royal absolutism or military rule. The classification of regimes as 'electoral democracies' from 1989 onwards is based on data by Freedom House; before that time, it is based on the author's application of Freedom House's definition. Regimes labelled 'pseudo-democracy' are distinguished from electoral democracy because, even though at least a partially elected legislature was in place, elections were either not sufficiently competitive or ultimately not relevant to the Prime Minister's selection.

[10] The highest case is Argentina in 1975. At the time, its GDP per capita, estimated in constant 2005 dollars adjusted for PPP was USD 9,766 (approximately USD 6,000 in 1985 dollars adjusted for PPP). In 2012, Thailand's GDP per capita, estimated in constant 2005 dollars adjusted for PPP, was USD 8,451 (see Lindgren 2013).

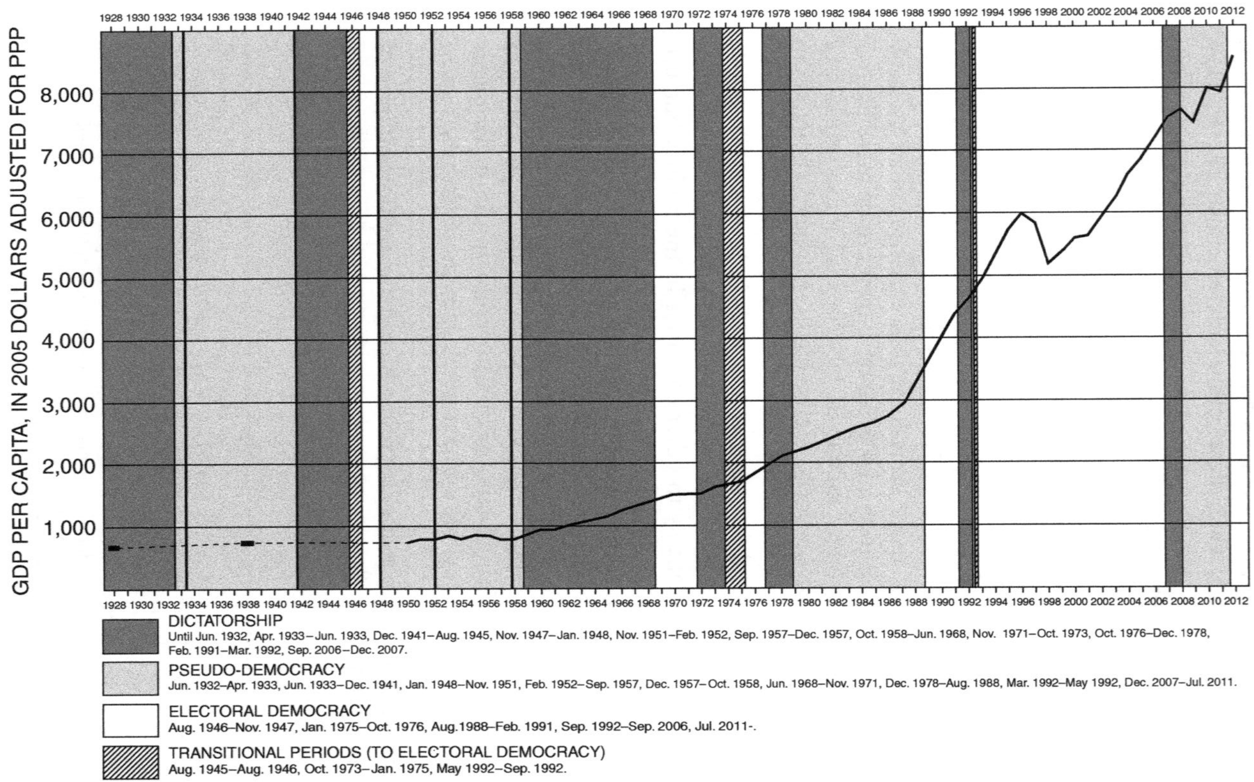

Figure 1.2 Thai regimes and income per capita, 1929–2012

Note: Estimates of GDP per capita are from Lindgren (2013); dashed lines indicate interpolation.

In this study, Thailand's history of political development serves as a laboratory in which a more fully fledged, dynamic theory of regime instability is designed and assessed. More precisely, the aim is to build a 'middle-range theory' (see George and Bennett 2005) – one that explains Thailand's trajectory of political development in terms that are sufficiently general to have implications beyond the case at hand, but too specific and contingent to warrant ambitions of universal validity.

Perhaps a good place to start in the specification of the said dynamic theory is the concept of 'path dependence'. Often central to explanations based on path dependence is the notion that in its early stages – or indeed during 'critical junctures' that may happen at various points in the sequence, when 'the structural (that is, economic, cultural, ideological, organizational) influences on political action are significantly relaxed' (see Capoccia and Keleman 2007: 343) – a developmental process is open to a wide range of alternative paths. In these circumstances, small, random events can have disproportionately large effects on the outcome. Historical institutionalist accounts generally conceive of the selection of institutions at 'critical junctures' as a contingent event – an outcome whose specific features are not predictable by theory (see Mahoney 2000: 513–15). Once established, institutions may be subject to 'increasing returns' and 'positive feedback' (see Pierson 2004), benefiting from mechanisms of institutional reproduction that make it increasingly difficult to change or reverse course.

The account presented in this study makes extensive reference to mechanisms based on the dynamics of 'power' and 'legitimation' (see Mahoney 2000: 521–5) to make sense of path-dependent processes characterized by the reproduction of certain institutional arrangements over time. Explanations based on the logic of *power* generally take the following form: 'The institution initially empowers a certain group at the expense of other groups; the advantaged group uses its additional power to expand the institution further; the expansion of the institution increases the power of the advantaged group; and the advantaged group encourages additional institutional expansion' (Mahoney 2000: 521; see also Pierson 2004: 36–7). Explanations based on the logic of *legitimation*, instead, take the following form: 'The institution that is initially favoured sets a standard for legitimacy; this institution is reproduced because it is seen as legitimate; and the reproduction of the institution reinforces its legitimacy' (Mahoney 2000: 524). The logics of power and legitimation can be mutually reinforcing, because power comes with resources with which an advantaged group may entrench a particular standard of legitimacy, which in turn becomes the source of more power.

When mechanisms of institutional reproduction are too weak, are triggered too slowly, or set in motion countervailing processes that result in the mobilization of constituencies disadvantaged by the status quo, the establishment of one set of institutions may lead to effective reactions against it. The result could be processes that, while not distinguished by the self-reinforcement and eventual 'lock in' of any particular set of institutions, are still 'path dependent' insofar as the outcomes at any one stage are affected by outcomes at previous stages as well as their temporal ordering (see Page 2006: 97). Examples include: 1) processes marked by the cycling between two or more alternatives; and 2) processes where a particular outcome, though subject to periodic disruptions, is a recurrent equilibrium, thanks to 'negative' (as opposed to 'positive') feedback mechanisms (see Bennett and Elman 2006: 259).

Accounts that reference path dependence have at times been criticized for presenting processes that are excessively open or contingent at the outset and excessively closed or deterministic downstream (see Pierson 2004: 51–3; Thelen 1999). Fending off the first such threat requires a focus on how different sets of 'initial conditions', to which subsequent outcomes are 'related stochastically' (see Goldstone 1998: 834), assign different probabilities to a range of alternative outcomes. Averting the second requires an explanation accounting for shifts that occur downstream. Of course, it is often reasonable to attribute any such shift downstream to 'exogenous shocks', given the history-making impact of events such as a foreign invasion, an economic depression, or a natural disaster. The focus on 'exogenous shocks', however, should not come at the cost of ignoring more endogenous, continuous, and incremental forms of change, brought about by conflict and competition between major political actors (see Mahoney and Thelen 2010). This consideration applies to both variants of path-dependent temporal sequences. On the one hand, cyclical processes where groups are ensnared in historical battles marked by mutual adaptations, frequent reversals of fortunes, and periodic institutional change may come to be disrupted if one group manages to gain the upper hand. On the other hand, while institutions may be subject to positive feedback or increasing returns, it is in their features that are often found the seeds of future instability, in the form of vulnerabilities that offer those disadvantaged by the status quo opportunities to gradually undermine the source of their competitors' strength.

Indeed, Mahoney (2000) points out that each of two mechanisms of institutional reproduction described earlier comes with a built-in dynamic of potential change. With regard to the dynamics of power, a mechanism of change frequently observed over the course of Thailand's contemporary political development is one where 'the very process through which an institution empowers an elite group may eventually become a source of division for this elite group, which in turn can facilitate a transformation of existing arrangements' (Mahoney 2000: 523). In Thailand, this dynamic has most frequently been accompanied by the unintended consequences of other measures taken to maximize the stability of the status quo by securing the loyalty of subordinate groups, particularly through the promotion of economic development. With regard to the dynamics of legitimation, when 'institutional reproduction is grounded in actors' subjective orientations and beliefs about what is appropriate or morally correct', the mechanism can be disrupted when the emergence of an alternative 'cognitive framework' leads to a 'breakdown in consensual beliefs regarding the reproduction of an institution' (see Mahoney 2000: 524–5). While declines in legitimacy may be brought about by a variety of factors, perhaps most consequential are those disruptions that result from 'the introduction of new ideas by political leaders' (Mahoney 2000: 524–5). After all, as Przeworski (1991: 54–5) has put it, non-democratic regimes generally fear 'not the breakdown of legitimacy but the organization of counterhegemony: collective projects for an alternative future'. Once again, these dynamics of change can be related, because, if a breakdown in the status quo's legitimacy undermines the effectiveness with which power can be wielded without force, the unpopularity of the use of force can provoke divisions within an elite group and encourage further challenges – from the inside as well as from below – to a political order's legitimacy and power.

While never referred to in quite these terms, Przeworski's (2009) framework has both 'path-dependent' and 'path-independent' dimensions. The expectation that the failure to establish a stable democratic regime makes future democratic regimes more unstable is justified with reference to a 'military legacy' that could be said to reproduce itself through the tendency of asymmetries of power to become larger over time (see also Pierson 2004: 36–7). Each military intervention strengthens militaries and weakens oppositions targeted for repression, making future military interventions more likely. In Przeworski's (2009) account, however, the trend towards ever-growing military power is tempered by the armed forces' own propensity for withdrawing, once a minimum set of objectives is accomplished, instead of taking advantage of the situation by establishing regimes intended to rule indefinitely. The implication is that when democracy is established 'early' – that is, in the presence of low levels of income – the process is open to a broad range of alternative developmental courses. Przeworski (1988) himself argued that democracy, when it emerges as 'the contingent outcome of conflicts', can succeed at any income level; while its chances of success rise in income, low income is never determinative of its failure, as many other factors intervene to determine its fate. If democracy does fail, however, Przeworski (2009) suggests that a country might set out on a path towards ever greater regime instability – all else being equal, the failure of each democratic regime makes future democratic regimes, re-established periodically as the military returns to the barracks, more unstable.

In Przeworski's (2009) framework, rising income levels gradually weaken the tendency of regime instability to become more intractable over time. Indeed, the argument that democracy becomes 'impregnable' beyond some level of income suggests that, ultimately, economic development allows countries to shake off the influence of their past, converging to a 'unique, globally stable equilibrium configuration regardless of where they started, or how they approached that eventual outcome' (David 2007: 97). This equilibrium – stable democracy – is not independent of history, at least insofar as levels of income are determined by history. However, it is 'path independent' in that previous outcomes, and their sequencing, are ultimately irrelevant: when democracy is established at high levels of income, it remains stable regardless of how many transitions and reversals have occurred in the past. As is typical of rational choice approaches (see Thelen 1999: 381–2), moreover, Przeworski takes the stability of democracy to hinge not on the elimination of alternatives, accomplished through a historical process that renders their adoption effectively unimaginable, but on the capacity of democratic institutions to coordinate and structure behaviour. Once certain levels of income are achieved, democracy is 'self-enforcing' because it becomes more effective at inducing compliance – it is in the interest of losers to accept the results, while it is also in the interest of winners to refrain from exploiting victories at the ballot box to make themselves dictators.

Thailand's political development exhibits both these 'path-dependent' and 'path-independent' dynamics. Its vicissitudes, however, call into question aspects of Przeworski's tentative explanation. First, while democracy has, indeed, become more resilient as incomes have risen, this study contends that authoritarian reversals have been rendered more difficult not by the reduction in the threat that democracy presents to Thailand's royalist establishment, parts of which fear it more than ever, but rather by the increased costs of overthrowing a democratic regime and governing the country dictatorially. In keeping with recent work on the social and cultural transformations resulting from (post-industrial) economic development (see Inglehart and Welzel 2005), such costs have risen over time as modernization produced a more resourceful, politically conscious populace desirous of greater equality, self-expression, and emancipation from authority, and as political entrepreneurs have emerged to mobilize the population in such a way as to both weaken the legitimacy of military interventions and increase the costs of repression.

Thailand, moreover, exemplifies why failed attempts to establish democratic regimes make future regimes more unstable. As for non-democracy, however, it could be argued that instability is not owed to the inherently provisional nature of military regimes. Between 1932 and 1958, non-democratic regimes were unstable not because the military frequently withdrew from power, but rather because it failed to sustain and legitimize its more permanent aspirations of power. Since the late 1960s, spells of military rule have become increasingly short-lived, but only as a result of the military's increased discomfort with running a more complex society, as well as the threat, when not the actual manifestation, of mass mobilization. That is to say that Thai military regimes are not short-lived by nature; rather, they have become increasingly short-lived as a result of a process of struggle, fuelled in part by modernization, that has weakened the public's tolerance for military rule, increased its capacity to fight back against it, and instituted more stringent checks on the military's ambitions of power. As for democracy, likewise, while the legacy of military rule has been no doubt very damaging, it is by no means the only reason for the fragility of Thailand's democratic institutions. Indeed, the instability of democratic regimes has at least as much to do with the presence of a strong and interventionist military as it does with the role played by the monarchy in directing and/or legitimizing the informal networks of power responsible for limiting, undermining, and periodically overthrowing elected governments. Each successive failure of democracy, in turn, made future reversals more likely, not only by strengthening the military but also by elevating the monarchy above the country's ever-changing, disposable constitutions.

As noted, the strength of Thailand's royalist establishment, at least as much as its powers of coercion and patronage, has been the cultural hegemony of its official nationalist ideology, which has earned it loyalty and compliance above and beyond its capacity to punish defections or provide material inducements, and has led a great many people from all walks of life to make spontaneous contributions to the reproduction of institutions widely perceived as legitimate. As E.E. Schattschneider (1988 [1960]: 66) pointed out, 'the definition of alternatives is the supreme instrument of power'. In the specific case, royalists have effectively exercised their control of the definition of what it means to be Thai – backed up by law, money, and live ammunition – in such a way as to restrict the scope of political contestation, setting the boundaries of acceptable political debate in accordance with official definitions of the values and beliefs a 'real Thai' does and does not hold. Most significantly, the elevation of the monarchy 'above politics' (see Thongchai 2008a) and its placement outside the bounds of legitimate political debate insulated the palace from public scrutiny, allowing the state's exaltation of the monarchy's status to go almost entirely unanswered. In turn, insofar as the extra-constitutional authority of unelected institutions over the past five decades has been derived from the political and moral imperative to 'protect the monarchy', the monarchy's towering, untouchable status favoured the reproduction of the networks of power presided over by the palace, as well as its capacity to interfere with the workings of the democratic process. The resulting political instability further sharpened the contrast between the constancy of the monarchy and the chaotic nature of representative democracy, just as prophesied by the country's official ideology.

Overall, the explanation of Thailand's sequence of political development offered in this study may be characterized as follows. In the heyday of the 'bureaucratic polity' (see Riggs 1966), which emerged from the rubble of the 1932 revolution's more idealistic, democratic aspirations, regime instability was largely a matter of elite conflict, marked by factional competition between rival cliques within the military and civilian bureaucracy, as well as shifting alliances between royalist-conservative, liberal-progressive, and military-authoritarian elements of Thailand's ruling class. This was the era of 'factional constitutionalism' – 'the most outstanding feature' of which was 'the drafting of a new constitution to match and protect each major shift in factional dominance' (see Wilson 1962: 262). In the aftermath of the revolution, the state's security apparatus rapidly accumulated enough power to permit its men to run the country, directly or indirectly, for all but a brief democratic interlude after World War II. What the military lacked was the internal cohesiveness and the reliable basis of legitimacy required to establish a durable regime. The two weaknesses were very much related, for the absence of a widely accepted standard of legitimacy – itself the result of a vacuum left by the betrayal of the ideals articulated in 1932 – imposed few constraints on the ability of political actors constantly to shift alliances in an effort to turn the tables on their rivals. This state of affairs was brought to an end in the late 1950s after the military, under the leadership of Field Marshal Sarit Thanarat, formed an alliance with conservative royalists, based on an official national ideology that identified the nation with the monarchy. Its effectiveness in providing more solid foundations for the new regime's legitimacy was a function of the resources expended for its propagation as well as the repression of alternative visions, the emphasis placed on effective government performance, and the distribution of rents to constituencies such as the urban bourgeoisie.

The mechanisms of institutional reproduction triggered by Sarit's conservative 'revolution' were sufficiently strong for the palace and the military – in concert with their allies in the state and civil society – to maintain a pre-eminent position in the political life of the country, retaining the means and the authority to subvert any regime whenever their power, status, or resources came under attack. The ensuing period of relative stability, however, lasted a mere decade. As is often the case, what had once been the sources of the military regime's strength would eventually assist in its undoing. On the one hand, the military's reliance on the support of the palace and the metropolitan business community, which had been key to the regime's stability, came with two dynamics of potential change: 1) the possibility that these groups might exploit their role in the ruling coalition to expand their powers at the military's expense; and 2) the possibility that the new standard of legitimacy set by Sarit – the endorsement of King Bhumibol – would allow those excluded from the ruling circle to challenge the military by competing for the monarchy's favour. On the other hand, the tendency of asymmetries of power and legitimacy to expand over time was counteracted by social transformations set in motion by Sarit's own developmental policies, which had aimed to secure the acquiescence of ordinary people, now denied a political role of any kind. Such transformations led to the growing effectiveness of mass mobilization behind more or less explicit counter-hegemonic projects, often adorned in royal symbolism in order to deter repression and drive a wedge between the military and the monarchy.

At various points in the sequence leading up to the coup of 22 May 2014, different combinations of intra-elite divisions and pressures from below led to the country's partial or full democratization (in 1968, 1973, 1978, 1992, and 2011). Each movement in the direction of greater democracy, however, was eventually met with a conservative reaction by which the palace, the military, and the bureaucracy sought to restore or salvage their prerogatives against the onslaught of elected politicians and/or the intensifying mobilization of civil society, which characterized the periods comprised between 1969–71, 1973–76, 1978–91, 1992–2006, and 2011–14. Whenever possible, the reaction manifested itself in an attempt by the 'invisible hand', as it is known in Thailand (*mue thi mong mai hen*), to bend elected institutions to the will of the royalist establishment. Whenever necessary, civilian governments were removed in military coups. At least prior to the latest incident, every royalist coup staged since the 1970s against an elected Prime Minister and/or an elected parliament has formed part of an attempt to restore key aspects of a variously remote *status quo ante* – in 1971 to before 1968, in 1976 to before 1973, in 1991 to before 1988, and in 2006 to before 1997. In all these instances, the attempted restoration featured the violent suppression of mass-based oppositions, with hundreds of people gunned down in the streets of Bangkok in 1973, 1976, 1992, and 2010. Whether the crackdowns proved 'successful' (as in 1976 and 2010) or 'unsuccessful' (as in 1973 and 1992), the failure of the restoration eventually gave way to an adaptation, complete with a return to electoral democracy. Designed to preserve the royalist order's power and legitimacy, in the face of either constituted or latent oppositions, in time each adaptation ended up empowering elites and other social constituencies that would later challenge the status quo, leading in turn to another coup, another massacre, and another adaptation.

The result has been a cyclical process that has seen Thailand go through several forms of electoral democracy, pseudo-democracy, and dictatorship. The process could be described as 'path dependent' not because it involved the amplification of previous outcomes – regime instability aside – but rather because each success scored by the forces of electoralism and majoritarianism has prompted those opposed to muster greater political strength, and vice versa, leading to the cycling of alternative regime types (see Page 2006: 13; Bennett and Elman 2006: 258). Partly as a result of rising income levels, however, over successive iterations of the cycle, spells of non-democratic rule have grown shorter, while electoral democracy has grown more resilient. Despite all appearances to the contrary, then, Thailand may yet be on the verge of shaking off its volatile and largely non-democratic past, converging to the kind of (path-independent) stable equilibrium Przeworski (2009) expects electoral democracy to represent in the presence of relatively high levels of income. Indeed, the severity of Thailand's ongoing political crisis is perhaps above all explained by the extent to which the losers of previous political struggles have succeeded in challenging the power and legitimacy of the royalist order, disrupting each of the mechanisms of institutional reproduction that had previously sustained the influence of unelected institutions over the country's political system. Based on Thailand's recent history, the restoration that the ruling military junta seems intent on prosecuting in 2014 is destined for certain failure – as all previous attempts dating back to 1971. Alas, the same history suggests that a great many people may have to die before royalists reverse course.

Plan of the book

The remainder of this book examines Thailand's contemporary political development, up to the present day, through a form of comparative historical analysis known as 'process tracing', a strategy of inquiry the methodological literature deems ideal for the development of middle-range theories seeking to make sense of historical processes characterized by complex causation and path dependence (see George and Bennett 2005: 209–13). Goldstone (2003: 47–8) defines it as follows:

> Process tracing consists of analyzing a case into a sequence (or several concatenating sequences) of events and showing how those events are plausibly linked given the interests and situations faced by groups and individual actors. It does not assume that actions always bring their intended consequences, only that actions are understandable in terms of the knowledge, intent, and circumstances that prevailed at the time decisions were made. Process tracing involves making deductions about how events are linked over time, drawing on general principles of economics, sociology, psychology, and political science regarding human behaviour.

While the account proceeds, for the most part, in chronological order – and aims for the kind of narrative flow that might render the book accessible to a wider audience – it seeks not just to tell a story, but to provide an 'analytical causal explanation couched in explicit theoretical forms' (George and Bennett 2005: 211).

Beginning with the revolution that overthrew the absolute monarchy on 24 June 1932, the account identifies the causal processes set in motion at 'critical junctures' by 'figuring out which aspects of the initial conditions observed, in combination with which simple principles', such as the mechanisms of institutional reproduction and change described earlier, 'would have combined to generate the observed sequence of events' (see Goldstone 1991: 59). If 'critical junctures', however, are generally defined as periods of significant uncertainty and contingency, circumstances in which anything goes are rare, as variously constraining historical legacies are always embodied in 'initial conditions' that render different developmental courses more or less practicable. For this reason, the comparative historical analysis begins in Chapter 2 with an examination of the state-building process that marked the beginning of Siam/Thailand's 'National Revolution', highlighting the territorial and national oppositions that developed with the rise of a bounded, centralized kingdom as well as the measures taken in defence of the new absolutist state – above all, the articulation of the official ideology that forms the basis of Thailand's contemporary 'royal nationalism'. While the decision to settle on any given starting point is always somewhat arbitrary, the literature suggests that the problem of 'infinite regress' be averted through the identification of 'critical antecedents', defined as 'factors or conditions preceding a critical juncture that combine with causal forces during a critical juncture' (see Slater and Simmons 2010: 889). The events of this period fit the definition of 'critical antecedents', because they not only set the stage for the removal of the absolute monarchy, but also shaped the historical context, the choice set, and the competitive environment (i.e., the 'initial conditions') the Promoters faced in the wake of their seizure of power.

Chapter 3 credits the actions of the People's Party on 24 June 1932 for opening the first major 'critical juncture' in the political development of modern Siam/Thailand, examining the interplay of structural and contingent factors that subsequently steered the country onto the path to military rule. After noting the significance of this period to Thailand's history of regime instability, the analysis rejects the widely held belief that the Promoters' failure to carry out a democratic revolution was inevitable, given the prevailing circumstances or the nature of their operation. While conceding that initial conditions militated against the emergence of a stable constitutional regime, the chapter identifies the main reason for the revolution's failure in the People's Party attempt to seek compromises with royalists. The royalist counter-revolution subsequently set in motion a series of events that led, by the onset of World War II, to the emergence of Field Marshal Plaek Phibun Songkhram as the leader of an increasingly authoritarian regime.

Chapter 4 provides an account of the instability that marked the period bookended by Phibun's first rise as Prime Minister in 1938 and his eventual exit from the scene in 1957. It analyses the deficit of legitimacy that plagued the first Phibun administration and the actions taken to address such vulnerabilities, including the rediscovery and adaptation of elements of King Vajiravudh's 'official nationalism'. The chapter characterizes the brief period following Phibun's fall in 1944 as another critical juncture, in which Thailand had a realistic chance of consolidating a democratic regime. After the country's fledgling democracy collapsed in 1947, as a consequence of the three-cornered factional competition between conservative royalists, liberal progressives, and the military, the continuing fluidity of coalitional alignments also prevented the consolidation of any of the regime forms with which the country experimented during Phibun's second stint as Prime Minister (1948–57). The instability paved the way for the rise to power of Field Marshal Sarit Thanarat in 1957 and the concoction of a new rationale for military rule, founded on the wholesale rejection of the ideals that had inspired the 1932 revolution.

Chapter 5 explains how the dictatorship of Field Marshal Sarit changed the course of history in Thailand. It argues that while the formation of a new alliance between monarchy, military, and bureaucracy – with the capitalist bourgeoisie in a supporting role – was not conducive to the emergence of a durable authoritarian regime, the mechanisms of institutional reproduction triggered in this period rendered Thailand's ruling class sufficiently entrenched to defend its extra-constitutional prerogatives long after challenges from below began to materialize upon the country's entry into the era of mass politics. The chapter examines the ideological, institutional, and policy innovations pursued during Sarit's conservative 'revolution'. It analyses the transformation of Thailand's political regime after Sarit's death, especially as it pertains to the monarchy's increasingly prominent political role. It explains the mass protests of 1973, which brought down the country's military regime, as resulting from a combination of socio-economic transformations and internal divisions within the regime. And it describes the conservative reaction to the challenges mounted during the democratic period against the cultural hegemony of Thailand's official nationalism, culminating in the student massacre of 1976 and the establishment of one among the most repressive regimes in the country's history.

Chapter 6 begins with a discussion of the 'semi-democracy' that emerged in Thailand in the late 1970s, emphasizing how and why the adaptations pursued to the workings of 'Thai-style democracy' and the national ideology of Thainess – though successful in forestalling challenges to the monarchy's power and prestige – failed to secure the new regime's stability beyond General Prem Tinsulanond's tenure as Prime Minister (1980–8). This time, the system's destabilization was brought about by the ability of elected politicians to exploit opportunities presented by the new institutional arrangements and eventually shake off the tutelage of the military and the bureaucracy. A failed attempt to restore Thailand to the days of 'Premocracy', bracketed by General Suchinda Kraprayoon's military coup in February 1991 and a new massacre of pro-democracy demonstrators in May 1992, eventually gave way to a new adaptation, inaugurating Thailand's longest spell of electoral democracy to date. The chapter explains how the network monarchy's continuing efforts to weaken elected governments and prevent the aggregation of political forces capable of challenging its extra-constitutional authority, combined with the devastating effects of the 1997 Asian Crisis and the unintended consequences of the 1997 constitution, set the stage for Thaksin Shinawatra's rise to power.

Chapter 7 traces the rise of Thaksin Shinawatra, his subsequent downfall, and the resulting political crisis, up to the general elections of 3 July 2011. The analysis fleshes out the argument summarized in this introductory chapter, explaining the re-emergence of conflicts left unsettled by the country's National Revolution as the combined result of long-term cultural change, socio-economic transformations, conscious strategic decisions, and contingencies arising from the struggle for power waged by Thaksin's political machine against the network monarchy. Special focus is placed on the process by which Thaksin and his allies have mobilized support by activating latent social cleavages, including those originating in the country's process of state and nation building, in the years following the 2006 military coup. The chapter concludes with a discussion of the existential threat that the counterhegemonic vision articulated by the Red Shirt movement, centred in part on the fulfilment of promises broken in the wake of the 1932 revolution, has come to present to the country's royalist order.

Chapter 8 summarizes the book's findings and highlights its contributions to the literature on Thailand's political instability, comparing the explanation developed in this study with its principal rivals. It also ventures some tentative generalizations aiming to inform the general literature on regime instability. A final section is reserved for a discussion of events that have taken place after the 2011 elections, up to the military coup of 22 May 2014 and its immediate aftermath. While underscoring the high degree of uncertainty surrounding when and how Thailand's political crisis will eventually arrive at a definitive resolution, the conclusion expresses a measure of confidence in the country's future democratic prospects.

2 The birth of 'Thainess'

The reign of King Chulalongkorn (r. 1868–1910), the Chakri Dynasty's fifth, transformed the Kingdom of Siam into a modern absolutist state. By then, Siamese monarchs had long claimed ownership of all land and all life within their domains. Whether by necessity or by choice, however, they had rarely lived up to the exalted titles of 'Lords of the Land' (*Phra Chao Phaendin*) and 'Lords of Life' (*Chao Chiwit*). In the capital, kings had often been constrained by powerful princes and noblemen. Outside the capital, the rulers of outlying territories and tributary states typically enjoyed a great deal of latitude to govern their own affairs. Upon Chulalongkorn's ascension to the throne, Siam lacked each of the characteristics of a modern state. Its organization was extraordinarily complex, but the Siamese state apparatus functioned as a hierarchy of patron–client relations designed to facilitate the control and mobilization of manpower (see Akin 1969: 93), not as a rationalized, differentiated, professional bureaucracy. Various ministries and departments exercised overlapping authority over most important government functions. Clearly demarcated external boundaries did not exist, owing to the court's longstanding disinterest in asserting its rule uniformly within the confines of a 'bounded' territory (see Thongchai 2004 [1994]: 74–80). Monopoly over 'legitimate' forms of both violence and theft had never been fully asserted – not just in distant tributary states, where local rulers had accepted, and often sought, the suzerainty of more than one regional power, but also in the provinces, where officials with overlapping jurisdictions were free to collect fees from the population for private purposes or gain, at least so long as their patrimonial rule did not become so oppressive as to result in the excessive flight of manpower.

It has been pointed out that this style of administration did not result from the weakness of Siamese kings, as much as it reflected outlooks and priorities quite unlike those that define modern Westphalian polities (see Englehart 2001: 13–15). Chulalongkorn's motives for transforming the Siamese administration were varied. The advance of British and French colonial empires, from all directions, provided the impetus to mark territory and place peripheral areas under the direct rule of Bangkok, so as to strengthen claims over territories and populations whose ambiguous status (through Westphalian lenses) the Europeans had learned to exploit to their advantage (see Thongchai 2004 [1994]: 93). Meanwhile, if Siam's integration into a new trading regime, imposed by Western powers in the mid nineteenth century, placed a premium on the establishment of a state with greater control over the land and its resources (see Kullada 2004: 37), the social changes these developments had engendered (see Englehart 2001: 91–2), as well as the greater supply of labour resulting from population growth and Chinese migration (see Akin 1969: 143–4), presented King Chulalongkorn with challenges he chose to tackle by appropriating European models of statecraft and administration. While Chulalongkorn's reforms are better described as conservative than progressive, their goal being the maximization of the monarchy's power (see Anderson 1978: 218) and perhaps even the state's 'ritual purification' (see Streckfuss 2011: 77–9), the result was nonetheless to revolutionize, from above, Siam's administration.

Still a minor and recovering from a bout of malaria that had just killed his father, King Mongkut (r. 1851–68), Chulalongkorn's reign had started under circumstances prefiguring a weak king, much less one as transformative. Aside from having been placed under the tutelage of powerful conservative princes, the young King had to contend with noble families who had asserted a dominant role in the country's administration. Despite officially ending the regency of Somdet Chao Phraya Si Suriyawong, Chulalongkorn's coming of age and second coronation in 1873 did not alter the balance of power inside the court. The King promulgated a number of reforms to palace protocol and governance, but was forced to relent after facing stiff opposition. In the end, Chulalongkorn simply outlived his rivals. As the men who surrounded him died off in succession, the King replaced them with younger, like-minded officials, taking full charge of his own court (see Kullada 2004: 38–65).

The reform process gathered steam accordingly. King Chulalongkorn reorganized major government ministries, enforcing a degree of functional separation in the administration of tax collection, military affairs, and justice, assigned to respective departments. Steps were taken to organize a standing army and a national educational system. Royal Commissioners were dispatched to remote provinces and tributary states to tighten Bangkok's control, and in time supplant local rulers as the seat of real power. Forced to give up claims to all territories east of the Mekong River in 1893, the King and his officials recommitted themselves to centralization, administrative reforms, and improvements in the country's defence, communications, and infrastructure. In the mid 1890s, a new system of provincial administration, *Thesaphiban*, formalized Bangkok's control over the provinces, to be overseen by a growing contingent of salaried officials organized along colonial lines. In the ensuing decade, major initiatives standardized school curricula as well as religious hierarchy, doctrine, and teachings, now more closely aligned with the priorities of the state. The system of justice was rationalized by drafting a new criminal code and by instituting a modern court system structured hierarchically. Meanwhile, advances in mapping and treaties with colonial powers gave Siam precise borders corresponding with Thailand's current surface area. By Chulalongkorn's death in 1910, Siam had been transformed into a bounded absolutist state.

Siam's process of state building has been celebrated not only for its speed, but also for its relative peacefulness. The resistance of local rulers and notables was neutralized through a mixture of co-optation and manipulation. Pockets of popular resistance were crushed with little mercy or regard for the underlying grievances, but the repression did not lead to prolonged insurgencies and sustained bloodletting. Still, one cannot exchange the absence of violence on a large scale for the absence of conflict, for Chulalongkorn's reforms also gave rise to social cleavages that would come intermittently to define political struggles in Siam/Thailand for over a century. The manner in which centralization proceeded planted the seeds of regionalism in places such as the country's Northeast (Isan). Within Siam's expanding ruling class, moreover, debates over the country's form of government, the role of the monarchy, and the content of Siam's national identity began almost as soon as the reforms started gaining momentum. Siam/Thailand's 'official nationalism' came to be crafted as a response to both the territorial and national oppositions that emerged as the country developed into a modern state.

King Chulalongkorn could be said to have carried out the first major stage of the process of 'National Revolution', one entailing the 'growth of national bureaucracies', the development of greater state capacity, the widening in 'the scope of government activities', and the assertion of central control over peripheries (see Lipset and Rokkan 1967: 13). As in Europe, the early stages of the Siamese state-building process gave rise to 'territorial cleavages', defined as 'strictly local oppositions to encroachments of the aspiring or the dominant national elites and their bureaucracies' by which 'peripheral regions, linguistic minorities, and culturally threatened populations' resist 'the pressures of the centralizing, standardizing, and "rationalizing" machinery of the nation-state' (see Lipset and Rokkan 1967: 10–13). State formation also engendered oppositions *among* national elites, whose differences over the new state's organization came to centre on the same issues that had divided their Western counterparts – issues of sovereignty, citizenship, constitutionalism, and democracy. The state's subsequent effort to develop and propagate an official nationalist ideology opened another crucial stage of Siam's National Revolution – an attempt on the part of centralizing authorities to achieve national integration by promoting the emergence of a single national identity, as well as by enforcing a measure of cultural and linguistic standardization throughout the national territory.

This chapter examines both the *territorial* and *national* oppositions that emerged as a consequence of reforms introduced in the Fifth and Sixth Reigns, as well as the efforts made to neutralize challenges to absolutist rule through the production and dissemination of a state-sanctioned nationalist ideology. While successfully laying the foundations for Thailand's 'royal nationalism', and engineering the rise of a new sense of nationhood, the measures taken in defence of the absolutist state crystallized the oppositions the state had sought to confront, resulting in the formation of the very cleavages around which Thailand's ongoing political crisis revolves. In more immediate terms, the events at the turn of the twentieth century not only set the stage for the coup d'état that overthrew the absolute monarchy on 24 June 1932, but also help explain the political landscape the Promoters confronted in the wake of their seizure of power. An analysis of these developments, therefore, serves to identify 'critical antecedents' (see Slater and Simmons 2010) – pre-existing conditions causally relevant to the choices made at the 'critical juncture' inaugurated by the absolute monarchy's removal.

Territorial oppositions

On the eve of the destruction of its capital of Ayutthaya, carried out by the Burmese in 1767, the 400-year-old Kingdom of Siam 'controlled' less than half of Thailand's current surface area (see Grabowsky 1995a: 4). The Kingdom was limited to the Chao Phraya River basin, the coastal region corresponding to Thailand's eastern seaboard, the southwestern corner of the Khorat Plateau around the town of Nakhon Ratchasima, and a portion of the Malay Peninsula reaching south to the frontier town of Songkhla. To the north, Ayutthaya was flanked by principalities centred in Chiang Mai, Lampang, Lamphun, Phrae, and Nan. These statelets had been frequently at war with both Siam and Burma, and had most recently been placed under Burmese suzerainty. Beyond Nakhon Ratchasima, much of Thailand's modern-day Northeast had for centuries been in the sphere of influence of the Lao kingdom of Lan Xang and, following its disintegration in 1707, its successors in Luang Prabang, Viang Chan (Vientiane), and Champasak.[1] To the east of Siam lay the Kingdom of Cambodia, much weakened since its heyday centuries earlier, and by the fall of Ayutthaya, a vassal of Annam (see Vella 1957: 95). To the south, the Malay sultanates of Kedah and Patani had drifted in and out of Siamese suzerainty for two centuries, without ever becoming integrated into its administration (see Worawit 1995: 197–8).

The sacking of Ayutthaya was followed by a period of disintegration. Siam's tributaries declared their independence; the major towns of Phitsanulok, Nakhon Ratchasima, and Nakhon Si Thammarat also broke away for a time. The Kingdom was rapidly reconstituted under the leadership of King Taksin the Great, crowned in 1768 in the new capital of Thonburi, and his main general, Chao Phraya Chakri – the latter went on to succeed Taksin on the throne in 1782, becoming the first King (King Buddha Yodfa Chulaloke, or King Rama I, r. 1782–1809) of the reigning Chakri Dynasty, with Bangkok as his capital. In short order, Siam not only recovered Ayutthaya's old domains, but also placed the northern principalities, Cambodia,[2] and the three Lao kingdoms under its suzerainty. In the South, Siam expanded its influence over the Malay sultanates of Patani, Kedah, Terengganu, and Kelantan; Perak was briefly brought into its sphere of influence in 1809 (see Wenk 1968).

In the decades thereafter, Siam's expansion was the cause of considerable turmoil in its dependencies to the South and Northeast. Forced to acknowledge the independence of Perak and Selangor in a treaty with the British in 1826, it was with some difficulty that King Nangklao (Rama III, r. 1824–51) quelled rebellions in Kedah and Patani, the latter now divided into seven small principalities, before 'pacifying' the region in the 1840s (see Vella 1957: 71–7). Worse, in an attempt to counter growing Siamese presence in the Khorat Plateau, the King of Viang Chan, Chao Anuwong, assisted by his son, the ruler of Champasak, attacked Siam in 1826, marching all the way to the town of Saraburi. The Siamese counter-attack led to the razing of Vientiane and a brutal campaign to depopulate the east bank of the Mekong, forcing the re-settlement of

[1] Keyes (1967: 8–9) points out that Vientiane's control did not extend far beyond the western bank of the Mekong River, though the sparsely populated Khorat Plateau was becoming increasingly 'Lao' as a consequence of migrations resulting from the political turmoil that areas east of the Mekong experienced in the eighteenth century (see also Grabowsky 1995b: 110–14). In 1760, statelets with a largely Khmer population (*Huamueang Khamen Pa Dong*, or 'Forest Khmer Domains') in the present-day lower Northeast along the Cambodian border were formally integrated into the administration of the Kingdom, but their full inclusion only took place in the Thonburi/Bangkok period (see Keyes 1967: 67, fn. 2).

[2] Siem Reap and Battambang were brought under direct Siamese control in 1794.

its inhabitants across the river. The entirety of the Khorat Plateau, as well as territories that had belonged to Viang Chan and Champasak, was integrated into Siam, such that by the time the French arrived in the region in the late nineteenth century Luang Prabang stood as the only independent kingdom in present-day Laos, albeit as a vassal of Siam.

The system of administration that survived into the Fifth Reign of the Bangkok era was based on territorial units – the *mueang* – whose features are not fully rendered by the term's standard translations as 'city' or 'province' (see Englehart 2001: 57–9). Much like the Kingdom itself, the *mueang* was defined by its centre as opposed to its borders, which were often not marked with any precision. Given the abundance of land and the scarcity of labour, moreover, power and prestige generally flowed from the control of people, as opposed to territory (but see Reynolds 1987: 163). There existed four classes of major *mueang* (*huamueang*), reporting to ministries (*krom*) in Bangkok whose prerogatives were subdivided on the basis of functional and territorial criteria. Fourth-class *huamueang*, administered by acting governors or magistrates (*Phu Rang*), were those closest to Bangkok. The *huamueang* located farther away, with the exception of the Northeast, were classified as first, second, or third class, depending on their size and importance, with varying responsibilities for overseeing smaller *mueang* and sometimes neighbouring tributary states (*prathetsarat*).[3] In principle, the *mueang*'s governors (*Chao Mueang*) and other main officials were appointed by Bangkok, but in practice the court based its decisions on assessments of local relations of power. In some places, that meant that succession was for all intents and purposes hereditary. Local officials, who received no regular salary, were responsible for administration, law enforcement, justice, and taxation, from which they derived much of their income (see Tej 1977: 20–4).

Beyond the formal distinctions, substantive differences between the administration of tributary states and *huamueang* of various classes were not especially clear-cut. While they could not conduct their own foreign policy, major *mueang* were often allowed to exercise levels of autonomy comparable to those enjoyed by tributaries. The poverty of communications certainly played a role, but it has been argued that autonomy reflected primarily a choice on the part of Bangkok (see Englehart 2001: 13–14). Indeed, there exists plenty of evidence to suggest that

[3] The classification into first, second, third, and fourth class did not apply to northeastern *huamueang*, aside from Nakhon Ratchasima (see Vickery 1970). With the exception of Nakhon Ratchasima, northeastern domains were allowed to preserve a different system of administration based on Lao political traditions (see Toem 2003 [1970]: 289–99).

Bangkok could assert its will over *huamueang* near and far, as well as its tributary states, when it wanted or needed. As Englehart (2001: 77) points out, the most serious constraints on royal power were those set by members of the King's own court, far more so than the local nobility in the provinces.

The structure of traditional Siamese society was, up to the reign of King Chulalongkorn, formalized by a system known as *sakdina* ('power over rice fields'), which assigned individuals an official rank, measured by a numerical value, on the Kingdom's social and political hierarchy. At the bottom of the hierarchy were slaves, who may have formed as much as one-third of the population. More numerous were freeman commoners (*phrai*), most of whom either registered with a master (*nai*), and provided him with 3 months' unpaid labour each year (*phrai som*), or registered in the King's service (*phrai luang*).[4] *Phrai luang* were attached to various government departments or officials, and typically subjected to heavier *corvée* requirements. At any rate, while opportunities for upward mobility from *phrai* to noble (*khunnang*) status were in practice extremely limited (see Akin 1969: 97–124), in principle there existed no hereditary landed nobility independent of the state. In the provinces, powerful *nai* received official titles and appointments to government posts, which came with the right to the services of an additional number of *phrai luang* attached to the government. In the capital, likewise, with the exception of the immediate relatives of kings (the *chao*, or 'princely' class), one's *sakdina* rank, noble status, and attendant privileges were (at least theoretically) a function of conferred title and position in the state's administration. Titles and appointments were not inherited, and could at any time be rescinded by the King.

The reforms to Siam's territorial administration went hand-in-hand with those made to the central government. Fast though it was by almost any standard, the process did not unfold according to a well-defined plan, aside from the King's widely publicized determination to expand his own power (see Chulalongkorn 1989 [1887]). As Chulalongkorn's initial attempts to reform the central government in the 1870s met with resistance within his court, the King took to stationing semi-permanent Royal Commissioners (*Khaluang*) to the outlying *huamueang* and tributaries, often backed by some military force, followed over time by the establishment of the offices of the Permanent Commissioner (*Khaluang Pracham Huamueang*) and High Commissioner (*Khaluang Yai*) in different localities. While these appointments ostensibly served the purpose of supervising the defence of Siam's frontier, the commissioners in practice

[4] There existed several varieties of *phrai* beyond this basic distinction (see Anchali 2003).

used their power to initiate reforms at the expense of the local nobility. In the absence of precise guidelines from Bangkok, the commissioners were encouraged to proceed at their own discretion (see Tej 1977: 64).

The assertion of King Chulalongkorn's full control over the central government in the mid 1880s provided the opportunity to overhaul the administration at both the national and the territorial levels. Steps were taken to reorganize key ministries and enforce greater functional differentiation in their activities. Significantly, this included the centralization of revenue collection, whose previous dispersion had provided noble families with access to resources they had used to further their own power at the King's expense, and the establishment of a centralized, hierarchical system of justice, which replaced the unwieldy array of courts previously operated by various government departments. While these reforms took time to be fully implemented, by the early 1890s the court was in a position to begin tightening central control over the provinces as well. The task fell upon Prince Damrong Rajanubhab, chosen to lead the *Krom Mahatthai*, newly repurposed as a true Ministry of the Interior, while some of the King's most capable half-brothers were appointed High Commissioners and dispatched to delicate outlying territories.

Prince Damrong's tenure coincided with the emergence of a fully bounded kingdom, albeit one that excluded some of the territory over which the Siamese court had initially planned to consolidate its rule. By 1909, treaties with the British and the French, which Siam agreed to under duress, fixed the kingdom's borders at their current positions. In a series of agreements with the British, Siam had previously given up claims to the tributaries of northern principalities in Burma's Shan State, and then to some of its own tributaries on the Malay Peninsula (Perlis, Kedah, Terengganu, and Kelantan). The British had in turn acknowledged Siamese sovereignty over Satun and the 'Seven Malay States' that had once formed the Sultanate of Patani. Siam had been forced by the French to renounce claims to two of its tributaries – the Kingdoms of Luang Prabang and Cambodia – together with the entire east bank of the Mekong, as well as cede territories west of the Mekong around Champasak and opposite Luang Prabang. Finally, Siam relinquished territories in western Cambodia in exchange for the end of the occupations of Trat and Chanthaburi.

In the territory that was left, Prince Damrong pursued the cause of centralizing the administration with dynamism and zeal. The *huamueang* system was replaced with a system of administration known as *Thesaphiban*. Upon being appointed Minister of the Interior, Damrong began to divide the country in a number of clearly demarcated *monthon* (or circles), which served as the main administrative unit in the localities. In the first decade of the twentieth century, *monthon* were established for all the outlying territories and tributaries that had gradually been brought under Siamese control. Local rulers were often allowed to retain their titles, but eventually none of their power or financial autonomy. By the end of Chulalongkorn's reign in 1910, the task of centralizing the state approached completion. Each *monthon* was governed by a Superintendent Commissioner (*Khaluang Thesaphiban*), flanked by officials appointed by the capital to oversee such activities as the collection of revenue, law enforcement, military conscription, education, public works, and justice. A similar re-organization took place at lower administrative levels, although the process was hampered by the penury of funds and a lack of qualified personnel. Despite the uneven nature of its implementation, the reforms made Siam into a modern, centralized state.

The relative peacefulness of the state-building process has been attributed to a variety of factors. Perhaps most important was the degree to which King Chulalongkorn had been able to put together a central government distinguished by rare unity of purpose. Other factors, however, more specifically pertain to the circumstances of tributaries and outlying territories, and the manner in which central authorities managed to exploit the situation to secure the quiescence of local rulers. In the northern tributaries, Bangkok's task was favoured by the local authorities' mismanagement of economic relations with (and growing indebtedness to) European powers (see Rujaya and Wyatt 1995: 73). While keen to avoid humiliating local rulers, moreover, the central government effectively deprived them of the means by which to put up serious resistance, gradually reducing: 1) the finances at their disposal – first through the rationalization of the system of tax farming (see Hong 1984: 116–23), then through the centralization of revenue collection (see Tej 1977: 115–18); 2) their ability to exercise their powers of patronage, concentrating powers of appointment into the hands of the central government and its local representatives (see Tej 1977: 118–21); and 3) their control of manpower, gradually phasing out the *corvée* system until it was eventually abolished in 1905 (see Tej 1977: 116). Aside from providing local rulers with stipends generous enough to live comfortable lives, the government encouraged the petty local nobility to join the provincial administration, even at the cost of slowing down the system's full implementation (see Tej 1977: 184–95).

Yet the process could only be described as 'peaceful' in relative terms, for hundreds of people gave their lives to resist Siamese expansion in a series of uprisings in which a number of Siamese officials were themselves killed. These rebellions involved a varying cast of characters, drawn from different sections of provincial society. The conspiracy in the Seven Malay States, which was foiled in late 1901 and early 1902, appears to have involved only the local sultans, who agreed to resist Siamese power and unsuccessfully pleaded with the British to intervene. As the central government moved in to neutralize the opposition, resulting in the arrest of the Sultans of Tani (Pattani) and Ra-ngae, as well as the son of the Sultan of Raman, no news of what was taking place seems to have filtered down to the local population (see Tej 2008: 81). A more mixed case is the rebellion that broke out in the northern tributary state of Phrae in July 1902, an episode known as the Shan Rebellion (*Kabot Ngiao Mueang Phrae*). Staged by ethnic Shan marauders, the rebellion seems to have received the encouragement and assistance of the local nobility including the Prince of Phrae, who escaped to Luang Prabang after Siamese troops restored order. A subsequent investigation uncovered some evidence pointing to the Prince of Lampang as a co-conspirator (see Tej 2008: 30).[5]

For the most part, however, the protagonists of these rebellions were others: petty local nobles and ordinary people. With regard to the former, opposition was rooted in the loss of power, perhaps especially the erosion in their ability to dispense patronage that resulted from the gradual abolition of the status of *phrai*. Ironically, this too was an important factor behind the opposition of ordinary people: the replacement of a system based on a measure of reciprocity with a more impersonal system less sensitive to the people's circumstances and needs (see Tanabe 1984: 87–8). In this sense, these rebellions are comparable to those that broke out elsewhere in Southeast Asia as a result of the development of colonial states distinguished by greater extractive capacity, increased pressure to stabilize their revenue, and lesser concern for their subjects' ability to meet the demands imposed on them (see Scott 1976). Whether the demands made by the typical *nai* of his *phrai* were, on the whole, greater or smaller than those advanced by the central government, the *nai*'s interest in maintaining a large and stable following of *phrai* – as well as perhaps his world view and his more limited capacity for coercion – had more or less obligated him to make demands his followers could meet, and to adjust these demands to his followers' circumstances. The fact that, in Siam, the process of state building and the penetration of capitalism were slower and less traumatic than they were elsewhere in the region may have rendered the uprisings less violent and widespread (see Chatthip 1984: 130), but did not prevent rebellions from breaking out altogether.

[5] The Shan rebels, however, had been successfully repelled from Lampang after seizing the town of Phrae. Tej (2008: 34) points out that the rulers of other tributary states were similarly aggrieved, but the presence of large contingents of Siamese troops in Lamphun and Chiang Mai successfully discouraged overt opposition. As for Nan, Tej (2008: 34) argues that the principality had not yet been affected as much by the reforms.

The popular rebellions in Siam's northern and northeastern peripheries were triggered by similar factors, most often related to the local people's outrage at the actions of representatives of the Siamese state. The first major rebellion broke out on the outskirts of the city of Chiang Mai in 1889, before the introduction of Prince Damrong's reforms. The Phya Phap rebellion was provoked by the callousness with which some tax farmers had gone about collecting taxes from the local population. While the rebels had planned to attack the city of Chiang Mai and chase out Siamese officials, the local government aided Siamese troops in quelling the disturbances (see Tanabe 1984: 90–102). In Phrae, too, the behaviour of Bangkok's representatives figured prominently in the widespread popular support enjoyed by the Shan rebels in 1902. Local people refused to assist fleeing central government officials, turning them in to the rebels who summarily executed them. No local official was singled out for similar treatment (see Tej 2008: 30).

By far the best-known popular uprisings against the centralization of the Siamese state are the 'Holy Men Rebellions' (*Kabot Phu Mi Bun*) that flared up in the country's Northeast. Compared with the episodes of resistance described earlier, the Holy Men Rebellions developed over a longer period of time, attracted a significant popular following, and achieved a level of territorial diffusion unseen in other regions. Indeed, incidents were reported in some two dozen locations throughout the Khorat Plateau (see Tej 2008: 22) as well as French-controlled Laos (see Gay 2002). Millenarian ideas of universal purification and liberation, to be brought about by the followers of 'men with merit' (*phu mi bun*) or 'men with extraordinary powers' (*phu wiset*) after a cataclysmic event of some kind, have had currency for centuries in the region (see Keyes 1977; Wilson 1997). But while the cultural character and historical roots of this phenomenon are beyond doubt, as are the non-political origins of at least some of these movements (see Gay 2002: 295), it is perhaps too limiting to describe the events of 1902 as 'less a function of political change than a persistent feature of the traditional political culture' (Englehart 2001: 48), because there is no indication that any of the episodes up to that point had ever come close to approximating the scale and territorial diffusion of the 1901–2 movements (see Tej 2008: 13). Nor were these rebellions purely 'reactionary', as Ramsay (1979) describes the disturbances in the northern towns of Chiang Mai and Phrae. For while the rebels borrowed heavily from historically rooted cultural repertoires, in an effort to appeal to peasant consciousness (see Chatthip 1984: 123) and establish their legitimacy (see Tanabe 1984: 88), the 'restorative' motives of some of the participants were combined with a decidedly more 'transformative', anti-state ideology (Chatthip 1984: 124–5). It could also be said, following Anderson (1978), that insofar as the central government's intent was 'centralization', not 'modernization', the rebels resented less the onset of 'modernity' than the impositions of state power.

As elsewhere, the popular support enjoyed by the rebels had to do with the increasingly rigid demands that the state made of ordinary people (see Keyes 1977: 294). At the same time, the fact that popular involvement was far greater and more diffused was likely a function of the Holy Men's success in 'unifying peasant consciousness' through appeals to ritual, religion, and ethnic history, and in combining these appeals with an egalitarian ideology that promised righteousness, peace, and absence of exploitation in a transformed society miraculously endowed with material abundance (see Chatthip 1984: 123–7). The importance of ritual was not exclusive to the northeastern rebellions, as demonstrated by the Phaya Phap revolt in Chiang Mai (see Tanabe 1984: 94–102). Ethnic identity, moreover, had been successfully mobilized against Siamese centralization in both Chiang Mai and Phrae, where the Shans reportedly feared Siamese discrimination (Tej 2008: 35). What seems to have set the northeastern rebellions apart was the fact that these aspects of the Holy Men's ideology were integrated into a more complete package, which combined appeals to a pre-nationalist Lao ethnic identity,[6] based on collective historical memories of massacre and forced relocation, with a vision of the future equipped with both a socio-economic and political dimension – an egalitarian utopia set in purified communities re-oriented towards the city of Vientiane, newly risen from the ashes of Siamese destruction.

Unlike the uprisings in Chiang Mai and Phrae, which were promptly crushed by Siamese troops, the Holy Men Rebellions were given a chance to fester over months. By 1902, the disturbances had grown into a matter of some concern in the Siamese court. While the popular support enjoyed by the rebels was characteristically dismissed by Siamese officials as a function of the stupidity and credulousness of the local population (see Tej 2008: 13–14),[7] it is with some alarm that their correspondence speaks of the revolts as the talk of the town in every corner of the region (see

[6] Lao nationalism was notoriously slow to develop. Moreover, the fact that the French had sought to foster a Lao national consciousness defined largely in opposition to the Thai/Siamese discouraged appeals based on an idea of the Lao nation including the majority of those living in Northeast Thailand (see Ivarsson 2008: 162–3).

[7] Thai authorities have consistently described dissent in these terms, up to the Red Shirt protests of 2010. Curiously, the same attitudes were common even before the Bangkok period. Each of the major *phrai* uprisings that took place in the Kingdom of Ayutthaya (see Charnvit 2010) are described in official chronicles through dismissive language that highlights the leaders' trickery and exploitation of gullible followers. Official descriptions of the *phrai* rebellions of 1581, 1694, and 1698 can be found in Cushman's (2000: 82–3, 322, 326–7, 333, 341–4, 358–61) synoptic translation of the *Royal Chronicles of Ayutthaya*.

Keyes 1977: 297). In addition to the scale of the rebellions, the Siamese state is said to have felt most threatened by their ideology, particularly in light of the implicit challenge that the self-styled messiahs posed to the authority of the King as the most meritorious person in the realm (see Englehart 2001: 49). Most of the rebellions, moreover, had initially taken the form of peaceful resistance and non-compliance to some of the demands of the state (see Chatthip 1984: 117–18), but episodes of violence were reported in instances when the rebels came into contact with Siamese officials. Siamese troops eventually sprang into action in 1902, suppressing one of the rebellions in Khukhan (Sisaket) before attacking a group of rebels who had burned down the town of Khemmarat, in the vicinity of Ubon Ratchathani. Lacking in discipline and sophisticated weaponry, the rebels were routed and suffered hundreds of casualties.

The efficiency with which its troops had quelled the rebellions gave the central government little comfort, because the Siamese authorities recognized the danger that future disturbances might present to the country's territorial integrity. Bangkok had the means to co-opt the local nobility, but the loyalty of local populations could only be secured by making provincial populations in the Northeast and elsewhere feel that they legitimately owed it to the state. Aside from a further build-up in the state's coercive apparatus, therefore, the 1902 uprisings catalysed efforts to conceive an ideology capable of binding peripheral populations to the Siamese state, the need for which had been highlighted by members of the court even before the state launched its reforms to the provincial administration. While, on the whole, remarkably successful in giving rise to a new sense of national identity, official nationalism never eliminated, and in some ways reinforced, the territorial cleavages that had emerged in response to the founding of royal absolutism.

National oppositions

The emergence of territorial oppositions in response to the growth of national bureaucracies, the centralization of governmental authority, and the projection of the central government's power over the periphery is something to be expected in comparative perspective. So is the development of oppositions at the national level – conflicts over the organization of the state, the priorities it should pursue, and who should control it. In much of Western Europe, where absolutist states had been built over hundreds of years, the diffusion of nationalist ideologies beginning in the late eighteenth century not only rearranged the continent's political boundaries but also fuelled conflicts over popular sovereignty, citizenship, secularism, and democracy, which in turn transformed the internal organization of the new 'nation-states'. Siam's telescoped state-building process gave rise to many of the same conflicts in the late nineteenth century.

King Chulalongkorn was confronted with requests to establish a constitutional monarchy just as he started building an absolutist state. In 1885, eleven members of the Siamese royal elite stationed in Europe, led by Prince Prisdang, responded to the King's solicitation for advice on how to deal with colonial powers, submitting a short treatise that recommended sweeping reforms designed to keep the Europeans at bay (see Prisdang 1989 [1885]; for a summation, see Murashima 1988: 83–4). The treatise correctly identified the possibility that the Europeans might 'take pity' (*songsan*) on Siam, however contrived the sentiment, as the most serious threat to the country's self-government. Somewhat more facile was the authors' conclusion that the threat could be defused by reforming the country's political institutions on the European or Japanese model, making Siam appear more worthy of its independence as 'a country owned by its people' (*mueang khong ratsadon*).

The proposed reforms included the promulgation of a constitution, the reorganization of the executive, the institution of a salaried bureaucracy operating according to more rational and meritocratic standards, the establishment of the principle of equality under the law as well as something like equality of opportunity (*tong hai manut mi khwam suk samoe kan*; literally, 'human beings should be made to have happiness in equal measures'), the adoption of a Western legal system, and the promotion of freedoms of expression, press, and assembly (see Prisdang 1989 [1885]: 49–50). Aside from convincing the Europeans to accord Siam the same rights and status enjoyed by other 'civilized' (*siwilai*) countries, the implementation of these reforms would signal to the Siamese people that 'there will be no more oppression and injustice' (*kan kot khi lae ayuttitham tang tang mai mi ik to pai laeo*), thereby promoting their love for the nation, their eagerness to contribute to the country's prosperity, and their willingness to make sacrifices in its defence (see Prisdang 1989 [1885]: 51).

It has been argued that the signatories to the appeal were motivated by private interests – namely, the desire to see power shift from the King to leading officials in the bureaucracy (see Kullada 2004: 104–8). At the same time, while the recommendations were framed as an effort to affirm the proponents' gratitude to the King and determination to defend Siam's external sovereignty (*ekkarat*), the document contains one of the earliest uses of the word *chat* ('birth', or 'lineage') to designate a 'nation' qua imagined political community (see Murashima 1988: 82–4).

In this sense, the significance of the appeal lies in the identification of the 'nation', and the national interest, not with the preservation or expansion of royal authority, but rather with ideas of constitutionalism, popular sovereignty, equality under the law, and social justice. This marked the beginning of a debate, by all accounts still ongoing, for the soul of the incipient nation-state – the earliest bifurcation of a nascent nationalist ideology into more 'populist' and 'royalist' strands.

By the time the question was put directly to the King, similar ideas had been spreading through the ranks of the state's expanding bureaucratic apparatus. Their appeal having previously been limited to a few Western-educated noblemen, it was the 'bureaucratic bourgeoisie' created by the King's administrative and educational reforms that proved especially receptive to popular nationalist ideas (see Kullada 2004: 117–25). These mid-ranking officials had been recruited from among commoners, many of them of *phrai* extraction, into the state's revamped civilian administration, the military, the judiciary, and educational institutions (see Nakharin 1992: 52). Their concerns were private and public, their motivations both instrumental and ideological. On the one hand, the coexistence of a salaried bureaucracy with a system of patronage designed to preserve the privilege of the old nobility stifled the opportunities for career advancement available to those whose connections and family background lagged behind their educational attainment. Dissatisfaction only deepened as the supply of capable officials grew, making competition more intense, and upward mobility correspondingly more difficult (see Kullada 2004: 124; Nakharin 1992: 53–7). On the other hand, the exposure that these officials had received to Western liberal ideas provided ideological content to their grievances, their discontent with arbitrary royal power and privilege, and their growing identification with an idea of 'the nation' dissociated from the person of the King.

The mid-ranking officials soon came to pose a serious insurrectionary threat to the regime. In 1912, shortly after Chulalongkorn's death, junior officers in the military dominated the group of conspirators involved in a thwarted rebellion (*Kabot Ro. So. 130*, or R.S. 130). Once again, while the conspiracy was based primarily on concerns over the career prospects of the 'bureaucratic bourgeoisie', recruitment efforts emphasized themes that echoed liberal, popular nationalist ideas (see Kullada 2004: 154–78; see Nattapoll 2011). The recruitment lecture whose text was seized by the authorities condemned the King's placement above the law for allowing 'all kinds of evils' (*kan chua rai yang nueng yang dai*) (see Leng 2007 [1912]: 84). The text called for equality under the law and for doing away with a system in which 'the King has elevated his own to the highest class, as deities (*thewada*), and relegated the people to the most wretched class, as though they were animals' (Leng 2007 [1912]: 89). The rebels also called for a constitution and a representative assembly, without offering specifics about their structure and content.

Among commoners not employed in the bureaucracy, too, the late reign of King Chulalongkorn saw a 'political awakening' (see Warangkana 2003) of sorts. The growing criticism of the status quo was made possible by the diffusion of technology that rendered the printing press available to enterprising members of a small but relatively well-educated urban intelligentsia (see Reynolds 2006: 56–9). This led, towards the end of the nineteenth century, to a proliferation of newspapers and books commenting on the issues of the day, at times offering radical proposals to reform the Siamese polity. The ongoing process of state building fuelled the discussion and criticism, particularly given the growing sense among the urban intelligentsia that the reforms did not go far enough to guarantee Siam's status as an independent, civilized nation. Initially captivated by King Chulalongkorn's reformist pronouncements, new voices among the commoner class – people of *phrai* extraction and descendants of assimilated Chinese immigrants – now clamoured for 'real civilization' (*khwam siwilai yang thae ching*) (see Nakharin 1992: 17).

Some of the more virulent criticism of the government came from foreigners and the Siamese people in their employ, who were shielded by the extra-territorial provisions of treaties Siam had signed with European powers in the mid nineteenth century (see Nakharin 1992: 8). This was the case, for instance, of the magazine *Chotmaihet Sayamsamai*, published by American missionary Dr Samuel J. Smith in the early to mid 1880s. *Sayamsamai* became one of the earliest representatives of the media 'crusading' against economic exploitation, the privilege of the nobility, and inequality in wealth, taxation, and educational opportunities, and discussing the well-being of the nation in terms of the treatment it offered to ordinary people (see Kullada 2004: 108–10). Much of the criticism, however, came from Siamese subjects who took considerable personal risk to speak out against the perceived injustice and backwardness of Siamese society. This included writers and publishers as well as a group of independent lawyers who took to filing Royal Petitions (*Dika*) on behalf of ordinary people who had suffered wrongs of various kinds. These petitions, which began to rise sharply in the Fifth Reign (see Warangkana 2003: 111), are cited by Nakharin (1992: 119) as evidence of the fact that ordinary people were more than spectators in the process of change that led to the overthrow of the absolute monarchy.

While the audience for the public criticism of the government remained limited to a few thousand educated people in Bangkok, some of it proved highly influential, commanding not only the attention of the authorities, but at times also a response by the King himself. Among the earliest purveyors of popular nationalist ideas, K.S.R. Kulap Kritsananon and Thianwan (T.W.S. Wannapho) are often discussed together as the most prominent essayists, columnists, and publishers of the day (see Chai-anan 1981). While both advocated the government's responsibility to educate and develop the people, their lives and works exhibit interesting contrasts. K.S.R. Kulap was a polygamist, fathering eighteen children from twelve wives, a relentless self-promoter, and known to play fast and loose with both sources and facts, something that landed him repeatedly in legal trouble (see Reynolds 2006: 59–73). Perhaps in keeping with his more traditional outlook, K.S.R. Kulap spoke of politics in generalities – such as the need to have just, responsive, and responsible leadership – and stopped short of laying out a vision for the country's future. He was more pointed in his criticism of the nobility's conspicuous consumption of foreign goods from what Reynolds (2006: 74) describes as a 'cultural nationalist' perspective, expressing 'dismay at the lack of confidence in Siamese ways'.

Thianwan was an iconoclast in his own right, flaunting his sophistication by sporting Western-style footwear, clothing, and facial hair. He emerged undaunted from a 17-year stint in prison (1882–98), earned for his work as a lawyer in the service of ordinary people, to put forth in the pages of his self-published newspapers a radical agenda for the civilization of Siam along European lines (see Thianwan 1989 [1904–5], 1989 [1905], and 1989 [1907]; other texts are described in Copeland 1993: 26–8). His proposals included reforms to the country's institutional architecture – the adoption of a constitution, an elected legislature, a professional bureaucracy, and a modern military – as well as improvements to its physical infrastructure, particularly with regard to transport and communications. Thianwan argued for the abandonment of traditional practices such as slavery and polygamy, and against the state's reliance on revenue from gambling and opium consumption. He was an advocate for the empowerment of women and the provision of government services to the poor, the sick, and orphaned children. Thianwan's writings emphasized the need to enact a wholesale cultural transformation of Siam, aimed at changing the attitudes of both ordinary people and state officials. In the former, Thianwan bemoaned the lack of curiosity and knowledge, as well as the complete absence of legal-rational reasoning. In the latter, he condemned the sycophancy, the indifference to the well-being of the people, and the absence of standards of competence and merit in the awarding of ranks. In response, Thianwan called for unity between the various classes, the establishment of free universities financed by taxing the wealthy, and a transparent government that did not deceive the people as if they were 'the enemy'.

Critics of K.S.R. Kulap and Thianwan were quick to seize upon their shortcomings and stylistic eccentricities. K.S.R. Kulap was rebuked publicly by King Chulalongkorn, as well as some of the country's more powerful princes, for his tendency to fabricate and plagiarize material in his historical studies and biographies of powerful men (see Reynolds 2006: 68–76). King Chulalongkorn (1989 [1903]: 127–8) also berated those such as Thianwan who idealized European society and history, pointing out that the European ideal they held up as a model for Siam did not really match the reality in Europe. On this score the King was quite right, for Thianwan's writings had little room for the contradictions, hypocrisies, and injustices of the Western societies he admired.[8] In 1905, Chulalongkorn's son and successor, Crown Prince Vajiravudh, mocked both K.S.R. Kulap and Thianwan in an account of a meeting of a fictional Siamese parliament. The main characters are based on the two writers themselves, cast as representatives whose gasbaggery causes a ruckus on the floor of the assembly (see Vajiravudh 1989 [1905]). Even so, the fact that two Kings felt compelled to respond attests to the challenge presented by K.S.R. Kulap and Thianwan's ideas, which were dangerous inasmuch as they identified the old ruling class as the problem. Thianwan's proposals in particular pointed to the nobility's rule as the greatest threat to Siam's independence and prosperity, while putting forth a vision of the nation conceived as the kind of 'deep, horizontal comradeship' typical of popular nationalisms (Anderson 1991 [1983]: 15). Having framed the reforms as necessary to foster 'love of the nation' (*khwam rak chat*), Thianwan defined 'the nation' in terms of its people, not its rulers, setting the development and empowerment of ordinary men and women as the standards by which the well-being of the nation, as well as the government's legitimacy, should ultimately be measured.

Having only just gained the upper hand over more conservative factions of the nobility, King Chulalongkorn responded to the request for a constitution put to him in 1885 by arguing that limitations to his authority would compromise the enactment of reforms necessary to protect the country's independence. In the ensuing years, the King moved away from reasoning exclusively on grounds of expediency, sketching out a more ideological defence of his personal power in an effort to cement the loyalty of the bureaucracy. In a series of pronouncements, Chulalongkorn elaborated on his opposition to liberal reforms by contrasting (and greatly overstating) European and Siamese conceptions of kingship, as well as by

[8] As Thongchai (2000a: 538) has put it, in the eyes of many, and 'regardless of truth, "Europe" appeared as a trope for *siwilai*, modernity, and progress'.

asserting the incompatibility of 'European' institutions, such as a parliament and political parties, with Siamese traditions (see Chulalongkorn 1989 [1903]: 121–2).

The King, however, had himself opened the door for proposals of this kind. Aside from his well-known admiration of many things Western (see Thongchai 2000a: 539), earlier in his reign King Chulalongkorn, the erstwhile leader of 'Young Siam', had dressed up the ambition to strengthen his power in the need for the country to become civilized along European models (for instance, see Kullada 2004: 68). The King and his closest collaborators, of course, also spoke of the importance of distinguishing 'good' from 'bad' European imports (see Kullada 2004: 97) and of the wisdom exhibited by Siamese leaders who had been able to 'pick and choose' from among variously beneficial Western innovations (see Peleggi 2007: 10). Even still, proponents of constitutionalism and liberal reforms were not swayed by arguments they had reason to interpret as a betrayal of the King's own reformist agenda. Among some of the 'younger and most ambitious officials', by the second half of his reign, Chulalongkorn had come to 'represent all that was old-fashioned and detrimental to progress' (Kullada 2004: 104).

Nation as reaction

Peoples speaking tonal, monosyllabic 'Tai' languages migrated from southern China into the Southeast Asian mainland between the seventh and twelfth centuries. The migrations reshaped the ethnic, linguistic, and cultural make-up of the region, primarily through the displacement and assimilation of the Mon-Khmer civilization (see Coedès 1966: 102). Today, 'Tai' peoples (Thai, Lao, and Shan) are numerically, culturally, and politically predominant in two countries, Thailand and Laos, and constitute significant minorities in Myanmar and Vietnam. The word generally transliterated as *tai* (ไท), misleadingly for the purposes of pronunciation, has been in use in the area corresponding with present-day Thailand even before major Tai kingdoms were formed in the region in the thirteenth century. It later morphed into the (homophonous) word ไทย(*thai*), possibly as a result of Ayutthaya-era translations of fourteenth-century Sukhothai inscriptions written in the Thai-Pali script (see Jit 1976: 599–600; see also Turton 2000: 11). The expression *mueang tai,* whose variant *Mueang Thai* still serves as an informal moniker for 'Thailand', appears to have been in use since the Kingdom of Sukhothai to describe Tai political domains (see Jit 1976: 590).

Rather than an entire population, the word *tai* initially described a segment of society that had achieved a certain social and civilizational status. As Jit (1976: 558) explained, the word was originally used to describe 'social(ized) people' (*khon thang sangkhom*), distinguished from people living in something of a state of nature (*khon thang thammachat*). Later, the word *tai* acquired the meaning of 'free people' (*serichon*) (see Jit 1976: 589–90; see also Coedès 1968: 197), and thereby described literate persons who were not in conditions of slavery or servitude, practised Theravada Buddhism, spoke Central Thai, and lived in an organized polity under written legal codes (see Renard 2006: 302). As such, the *tai* were contrasted with *kha* (low tone) and *kha* (falling tone): the former, 'illiterate forest people [who] had oral codes, mostly were animists, and lived in wooden structures beyond the pale of what the Tai considered civilization' (Renard 2006: 295; see also Turton 2000); the latter, people in conditions of slavery (*that*) or semi-servitude (*phrai*). Stipulating its authenticity, the Sukhothai-era Ramkhamhaeng Inscription (dated 1292) contains the expression '*phrai fa kha tai*' (literally, '*phrai* of the sky, servant of the *tai*') to describe the general population.[9] Jit (1976: 590) noted that, while the word '*tai*' could also refer to 'clan' (*phao*), in this context it meant 'free men', who were not *phrai* or slaves, without distinction of ancestry or race.

Up to the nineteenth century, the word *thai* appears to have been largely a marker of elite identity, designating people who had achieved a certain social status, lived a civilized lifestyle, practised a similar culture, and embraced a certain value system. Until then the word does not seem to have strongly implied common descent, for, while it did not apply to the inhabitants of northern tributary states or the Khorat Plateau, commonly referred to as *lao*, foreigners (Persians, Chinese, or descendants of prisoners of war from elsewhere in the region) and local minorities could be considered *thai* if they attained noble status and embraced the values and customs of the royal elite (see Renard 2006: 303). The situation started to change in the Third and Fourth Reigns of the Bangkok era (see Saichol 2008a), when official documentation began to describe 'the *thai*' as a *chat-phasa*, or an ethno-linguistic group – *phasa* meaning 'language', and the word *chat* now designating a 'group of people who by birth shared a common language and cultural traits' (Murashima 1988: 82) – alongside other ethno-linguistic groups such as the Malay, Cham, Lao, Mon, and Khmer. Although nineteenth-century Siam was by all accounts recognized as being more ethnically diverse than Thailand is today (see Streckfuss 2012), the state did not have a particularly marked ethnic character, and little effort was made to enforce cultural and ethnic homogeneity among the country's population. Unassimilated Chinese immigrants lived by different rules, while tribal peoples suffered a great

[9] The expression *phrai fa kha phaendin* is still in use to describe 'commoners' or 'subjects'.

deal of discrimination. Other minorities, however, received much the same treatment as everyone else (see Englehart 2001: 50–3).

The word *chat* gradually came to describe a 'national political community' in the late nineteenth century (Murashima 1988: 82), but it took some time before the expression *chat thai* was fully embraced to describe the 'Thai nation', even as *Mueang Thai* and *Prathet Thai* were used interchangeably with *Sayam* (Siam) to refer to the country. The expression *chat thai* is not featured in many of the writings cited earlier, where the word *chat* often appears on its own or in conjunction with *banmueang* (as in *chat banmueang*) – a word for country, state, or nation. As he informed the King in 1899, Prince Damrong himself initially worried that the expression *chat thai* would cause ethnic minorities to feel excluded, given the recent use of the word *chat* to describe characteristics acquired at birth, and the government's inability to accomplish, in the short run, the goal of turning minorities 'into Thai' (see Saichol 2008c).

King Vajiravudh is rightfully credited for crafting Thailand's 'official nationalism'. The work, however, had started during the reign of his father, King Chulalongkorn – partly in response to external threats, and partly as a reaction to the territorial and national oppositions that had emerged in the process of building an absolutist state. The nation conceived by the state ideology that took shape in the second half of King Chulalongkorn's reign stands in direct contrast to the manner in which Siam's early popular nationalists had begun to imagine it. Its priority was to buttress the legitimacy of the King as the wielder of absolute power, which was increasingly questioned by the bureaucracy and the commoner upper-middle class, and eventually to identify the nation with the King.

Almost as soon as he was asked to adopt a constitutional monarchy, King Chulalongkorn (1989 [1887]: 98–9; see also Murashima 1988: 85–6) asserted that Siamese kings, unlike their European counterparts, had never been faced with popular demands to limit their absolute authority, something he attributed to their righteous, enlightened rule. Later, Chulalongkorn (1989 [1903]: 131) argued publicly that 'people in *Mueang Thai*' had never been divided in their opinions – divisions that institutions such as a parliament, political parties, and a free press would certainly inflame – but had rather always practised 'unity in one and the same opinion: the King's opinion'. Chulalongkorn's incipient state nationalism emphasized the King's role as the embodiment and guarantor of the country's cultural traditions. Building on previous pronouncements that had sought to strike a balance between the embracement of modernity and the preservation of Siamese customs (see, for instance, Wyatt 1969: 198), the King used his 1903 treatise on 'unity' to chastise those who resisted all forms of change as well as those who had shown themselves too eager to embrace Western values and institutions wholesale. Instead, Chulalongkorn (1989 [1903]: 131) urged everyone to get behind the 'middle path' he was intent on pursuing, which combined an openness to adopt necessary reforms with a determination to preserve Siamese customs.

Chief among these traditions was Buddhism, which the King invoked as an aspect of Siam's identity that required protection from the diffusion of Western ideas and practices. Buddhism was made into one of the main sources of legitimacy for the new absolutist state. Chulalongkorn praised Buddhism as a 'religion of the common people' (*sasana khong ratsadon*) for inspiring kings to govern righteously, without oppression or concern for their own wealth (see Saichol 2008b). As Chulalongkorn, however, presented himself as the embodiment of Siamese Buddhism, his government took steps to reshape it based on the needs of the absolutist state. Undertaken in the name of preserving tradition, the 1902 Sangha Act reorganized the Buddhist clergy along the same lines as the state, taking as a model the Thammayut sect founded by King Mongkut (see Keyes 1987: 57). While the *Sangha* had been highly decentralized in both its organization and doctrine, the reform imposed a centralized hierarchy that maximized the King's control over appointments (see Tambiah 1976: 233–41) and standardized religious training, teachings, texts, and practices to match the ideology of the court (see Keyes 1987: 58–9). Meanwhile, Chulalongkorn greatly expanded his ritual role, in an attempt to entrench the King's position as the symbolic centre of Siamese Buddhism (see Saichol 2008b). The emphasis on religion served a clear political purpose: so long as it is exercised in accordance with principles and traditions that form the nation's heart and soul, absolute power is not only tolerable, but also desirable. Buddhism was also of considerable use to justify the hierarchies of superior and inferior men that threatened to unravel as a result of the abolition of slavery, the demise of the *phrai* system, and the recruitment of commoners into the bureaucracy. The issue was especially sensitive because commoners – particularly those who had acquired education, wealth, and status, sometimes referred to as *phrai kradumphi* ('bourgeois *phrai*') – had begun to agitate against aristocratic privilege more aggressively and articulately than at any point in the past.

The challenge before conservative royalists was to find new sources of legitimacy for 'traditional' hierarchies and replace the institutions that had previously enforced them with something that had sufficient appeal to stem the tide of the emerging popular nationalism. The official nationalism conceived in the Fifth and Sixth Reigns sought to instil in commoners the notion that being Thai required everyone to accept their station in life (see Nakharin 1992: 17) and perform the 'duties' (*nathi*) attendant to their position without challenging inequalities of power, status, and wealth. King Chulalongkorn himself argued that 'social order' required 'big people' (*phu yai*) to treat 'small people' (*phu noi*) with generosity, while *phu noi* should show deference to *phu yai* (see Saichol 2008a). Buddhist superstitions of karma and merit offered familiar rationalizations that could be drawn upon to present these hierarchies as both natural and beneficial; at a time of institutional and cultural change, these ideas were recognized as essential to the new system's legitimacy (see Englehart 2001: 103). Equally seminal was King Chulalongkorn's (1989 [1903]: 134) argument that the extraordinary times called for everyone to 'unite' behind him in defence of the nation, proffered just as the modern legislation sanctioning criticism of the King was being drafted with the help of European advisors (see Streckfuss 2011: 87–91).

The late Fifth Reign was not only a formative period with regard to the new nation's content, but its expanse and limits as well, which were adjusted to coincide with its emerging 'geo-body' (see Thongchai 2004 [1994]). The importance of classifying provincial populations and ethnic minorities as part of the same *chat*, for reasons of both internal and external security, was recognized early on. Even in the late 1880s, King Chulalongkorn argued that various ethno-linguistic groups (*chat-phasa*) 'like the Thai, Lao, and Phuan' were all 'members of the same *chat*' (cited in Saichol 2008a). Not long thereafter, Prince Damrong (cited in Streckfuss 1993: 142) explained his reforms to the provincial administration by noting the need 'to make all the people Thai, not Lao, nor Malay at all'. A first step was the renaming of territorial divisions at the turn of the twentieth century, in favour of a nomenclature that de-emphasized their separate political and ethnic character (see Tej 1977: 146). As noted, however, Damrong was sceptical of the possibility of turning peripheral populations 'into Thai' in the short run. Confronted with territorial and ethnic forms of resistance to the centralization of state power, King Chulalongkorn (cited in Tej 1977: 154) himself expressed some sympathy for the desire of self-rule evidenced in rebellions in the South, North, and Northeast, noting that 'we have perverted the administration of the Lao provinces and the Seven Malay Provinces from its true state'. The King went so far as to say that the 'deviousness' of Siam's administration in peripheral territories compared unfavourably with British colonial rule: 'We, on the other hand, treat the provinces as our own, which is not true, for the Malays and Lao consider that the provinces belong to them'.

Ultimately, the confluence of international and domestic pressures injected into the King and his collaborators the resolve not only to bring provincial populations under the authority of the Siamese central government, but also to remake most of them into 'Thai', embracing this ethnic/racial term for the nation as a whole. The choice is said to have been influenced by the prevailing European discourse on race and ethnicity generally, and specifically by the French government's strategy of pressing its 'legal' claims over Siam's Northeast on the grounds that Lao and Khmer peoples suffered oppression at the hands of the Thai (see Streckfuss 1993: 132–8). At the same time, the revolts in the North and Northeast disrupted social order, something that had long served as a pretext for colonial expansion, at one point leading Siamese troops to violate provisions of the 1893 Franco-Siamese Treaty by entering, without permission, an area within 25 km of the border with French Laos. The fact that the revolts had taken on a marked ethnic character was of special concern to Siamese authorities, judging from the results of investigations conducted in the aftermath of the rebellions, and the measures taken on that basis (see Battye 1974: 412–19).

The course of action followed by the King's government in the country's North and Northeast had at least two prongs. On the one hand, *chat thai* was redefined more inclusively, emphasizing the new meaning of *chat* as nation – 'a community of people who shared a cultural commonality defined by being the subject of the same monarch' (Thongchai 2004 [1994]: 134–5) – in an attempt to make the nation's confines coincide as much as possible with the country's territorial boundaries. The people of northern and northeastern Siam were now said to have been 'Thai' all along – as Prince Damrong (1955 [1935]: 68) pointed out three decades later, King Chulalongkorn's government was merely the first to recognize that people who lived in former dependencies in the North and Northeast 'really were Thai' (*thi ching pen chon 'chat thai'*). In practice, this required ceasing to recognize these ethnic minorities as 'separate peoples', such that these groups would effectively 'disappear from within the boundaries of the kingdom' (Streckfuss 1993: 142).

On the other hand, the emergence of a single national consciousness required more than a few strokes of the pen, but rather, for the first time, the enforcement of a degree of cultural homogeneity. Alternative identities had to be suppressed, refashioned into regional identities, or at any rate prevented from morphing into separate national identities. The episodes of territorial resistance in the early 1900s, in this sense, may have given the King reason to reconsider the reforms' tempo and style, but not their overall goals. In the aftermath of those incidents, the political, financial, and judicial administration of most peripheries and former tributaries was definitively brought under central control (see Tej 1977: 155–63), so as to reduce the independence of local authorities and minimize the distinctiveness of local legal systems and administrative styles. The revolts also provided the impetus for the creation of a conscript army, first established by the Conscription Edict of 1905 as a 'cudgel against hooligans' and an 'instrument of political centralization' (Battye 1974: 429).

The expansion of provincial education went hand-in-hand with the reforms to the Buddhist monkhood, as part of the 'general integration of the provinces into the life of the Thai nation' (Wyatt 1969: 246). Under the leadership of Prince Wachirayan (who later became Supreme Patriarch) and Prince Damrong, thousands of new schools had been founded in the provinces between 1898 and 1901, making use of Buddhist monasteries the government aimed to bring under its control (see Wyatt 1969: 238). Beginning in 1902, reforms to both the Buddhist *Sangha* and the Ministry of Public Instruction, coupled with changes in school curricula and the deployment of Education Commissioners to newly centralized territories, laid the foundations for universal education. It is around this time that education began to be seen, as has been the case ever since, as a matter of national security (see Wyatt 1969: 329–30). Monasteries/schools brought under the aegis of the central government were transformed into agencies of national integration, charged with establishing Central Thai as the national language and with propagating values the court wanted to instil into its subjects. Whereas, moreover, great variation had previously characterized religious practices in the provinces, the assertion of state control over the religious hierarchy, and the resulting (unprecedented) emphasis on royal-sanctioned orthodoxy (see Englehart 2001: 48), aimed squarely at the annihilation of northern and northeastern variants of Buddhism, which were 'intimately linked with regional and political autonomy', and their replacement with an official version that better served the 'interests of standardization and homogenization' (Tambiah 1976: 239–40).

The emerging definition of what it meant to be 'Thai', as it took shape in the first decade of the twentieth century, exhibits elements of both continuity and change with the term's historical usage. The term no longer designated a social class, and was extended – first as the name of an ethno-linguistic group, then as a marker of national identity – to categories of people, like (former) slaves and *phrai*, to whom the term had once not applied. If Bangkok's project of cultural standardization, moreover, was self-consciously undertaken with the goal of turning ethno-linguistic minorities 'into Thai', one of the earliest measures taken towards that goal was simply to redefine those groups as such, with retroactive effect.

These groups were now said to have 'always been' part of the 'Thai nation', claimed to have been in existence for over a millennium despite its recent invention and ongoing construction. Their history was rewritten and infused with a teleological character – a progression towards the unity of all under the leadership of Siam's kings (see Thongchai 2004 [1994]: 145–50), presented at once as their natural state and their ultimate destiny. At the same time, even as it reclassified new categories of people as Thai, Siam's incipient official nationalism preserved some of the term's original meaning when it came to defining the nation's internal structure and expanse, and in sketching out just what 'being Thai' entailed. If people could now be considered Thai regardless of class and regional origin, being Thai required not only the adoption of state Buddhism and the values and world view of the court, but also the acceptance of one's position on hierarchies of both 'class and status' and 'ethno-geography' (see Thongchai 2000b: 41), which the absolutist state had defined as the essence of the new Thai nation.

Thailand's nascent official nationalism, in other words, may have redefined people belonging to various social classes and ethno-linguistic groups as equally Thai, but from its inception it recognized some Thais as more equal than others. On the one hand, as King Chulalongkorn pointed out, real Thais perform duties that come with their social status, and keep unity 'in one and the same opinion: the King's opinion'. By implication, then, those who break rank or question social hierarchies can be accused of being 'not really Thai', as they are to this very day. On the other hand, whereas the word Thai came to describe the entire nation, it was not altogether abandoned as the label for an ethnicity thought of as racially and culturally superior to others. As Streckfuss (1993: 143) has written, 'the merger of nationality and race' made the Thai 'at once a race (the great Thai race with "lesser" subdivisions of Lao, Shan, etc.) and a subdivision within that race', thereby 'preserving the privileged position of the Thai vis-à-vis the Lao, Shan, and other "ethnic" groups'.

The 'civilization' of ethnic minorities and 'yokels' (*chao ban nok*; see Thongchai 2000b) – some of whom, in the words of then Crown Prince Vajiravudh (cited in Renard 2006: 311–12), had to be 'tamed' or 'domesticated' (*chuang*) as one would an animal – justified Bangkok's subsequent treatment of its peripheries as colonies, in much the same way the European variant of this discourse provided an excuse for empire. The expression 'internal colonialism' has been used to designate several aspects of territorial rule: the Siamese state's implementation of administrative models fashioned after those of European colonial powers such as British Burma (see Englehart 2001: 99; Anderson 1978); the systematic extraction of wealth from the provinces, in the form of both taxes and profits, for reinvestment in Bangkok (see Chatthip 1999: 51–9); and, finally, an enduring attitude of 'paternalism' and 'disdain' for provincial subjects (see Morell and Chai-anan 1981: 43). The discourse of superior and inferior groups, moreover, still legitimizes what has been called Thailand's 'ethnocracy' (see Von Feigenblatt 2009), a society in which the members of subaltern ethnicities can choose to either accept (central) Thai values and culture, or alternatively face discrimination, political marginalization, and, in some cases (as in those of some hill tribes), even the withholding of legal nationality (see Renard 2006: 317–18).

Official nationalism

The skeletal official nationalism that took shape during the reign of King Chulalongkorn was fleshed out and articulated more fully under his son and successor, King Vajiravudh. A talented writer and playwright, Vajiravudh did much of the work himself, contributing ideas, texts, and symbols that remain central to Thailand's state-sanctioned national ideology. Often criticized for his profligacy, his self-indulgence, his favouritism, and his general disinterest in crucial aspects of the country's administration (see Vella 1978: 169–70), King Vajiravudh dedicated himself to midwifing the birth of a nation united behind the leadership of its monarch. His ideas exhibit a strong measure of continuity with those sketched out in the previous reign. Only Vajiravudh's aggressive tone and militaristic rhetoric were entirely novel.

As elsewhere, the task involving some of the heaviest lifting was the identification of the new nation with the person of the King and the institution of the monarchy, thereby reconciling nationalist ideas with pre-nationalist social hierarchies. Vajiravudh's defence of royal absolutism was based on reasoning that has been referred to as 'Hobbesian' (see Kullada 2004: 138; Vella 1978: 60) on account of both its framing and conclusions. In a series of speeches given in June and July 1911, Vajiravudh (1914 [1911]: 45–9) argued that human beings, like other animal species, associate with one another to boost their strength and better protect their lives. In times of external danger or internal discord, commitment to unity bears no fruit as long as all have licence to say or do as they please. The task of 'speaking for the whole group' must instead be delegated to a single person, who exercises his or her power on behalf of the people as a whole and rules for the happiness and prosperity of all.

In abstract terms, therefore, the people are 'sovereign', but should be understood to have delegated their sovereignty, irrevocably, to a single Leviathan wielding absolute powers.

While it is possible that King Vajiravudh had received at least an introduction to the philosophy of Thomas Hobbes during his time at Oxford and Sandhurst, his defence of royal absolutism drew upon more home-grown ideas of Buddhism and kingship (see Barmé 1993: 28). The need for absolute and decisive authority, above all, was grounded in society's protection from the kind of anarchy into which it would degenerate if everyone were to be given the right to pursue selfish interests and desires. This suspicion has deep roots in Buddhist 'mythological tradition', as does the 'social contract theory of kingship' that was invoked to explain the manner in which power is delegated to the king by 'the people', for their own benefit (see, for instance, Tambiah 1976: 483). These ideas had been enlisted in the legitimation of the absolute monarchy since at least the 1880s (see Murashima 1988: 86–7).[10] At the same time, Buddhist ideas associating leadership with merit and righteousness allowed King Vajiravudh to sidestep the thorny question of just how a Leviathan might be removed, should he fail to perform according to his mandate, because a Buddhist Leviathan is by definition the kingdom's most meritorious person – once his merit is exhausted, karma will inevitably bring about his downfall (see Tambiah 1976: 486–7).

Throughout his reign, King Vajiravudh sought as much as possible to identify Buddhism with the state, the monarch, and the military. In that effort, he often benefited from the assistance of his uncle, Prince Wachirayan, whose authoritativeness and prestige as Supreme Patriarch were called upon repeatedly to provide religious sanction to the King's ideas and initiatives. The King's concern for the preservation of religion, however, seems to have stemmed almost entirely from his preoccupation with order and conformity. Only once in the lengthy discussion of the importance of religion that appears in his 1911 speeches does the King even discuss a specific aspect of Buddhist religious doctrine, and then only to rebut the contention that Buddhism would be incompatible with militarism (see Vajiravudh (1914 [1911]: 68–9). This seems to have been a particularly sensitive issue for King Vajiravudh, judging from the

[10] Nattapoll (2013: 13–15, 81–2) notes that the modern variant of the myth that kings in Thailand ascend to the throne by the consent of the 'political community' was articulated by King Mongkut. Originally, the idea served the attempt made by Mongkut and his son, Chulalongkorn, to transfer powers held by noble families to the King. Beginning in the late Fifth Reign, conversely, conservative royalists have invoked the professed direct linkage between the people and the King to argue against subjecting the King's powers to constitutional limitations.

harsh treatment and humiliation later inflicted on a high-ranking monk who had declared the military profession to be a sin (see Vella 1978: 223–4).

Indeed, Vajiravudh's reliance on Buddhist ideas was highly selective, excluding most notably those aspects of karmic theory that justify challenges to constituted authority (see, for instance, Keyes 1977: 287). Vajiravudh (1914 [1911]: 50) instead equated any such challenge with a threat to the nation and the life of its people, providing intellectual foundations for the modern claim that even the most innocuous slights against the monarchy constitute crimes against 'national security'. Comparing the King to a ship's captain, Vajiravudh presented those who would dare question his authority, and thereby prevent him from properly discharging his functions, as a threat to the survival of everyone aboard the ship. Insulting or violating the King was said to amount to threatening the well-being of the nation he represented, insofar as it undermined the leader's ability to deal with the nation's problems. Consequently, King Vajiravudh (1914 [1911]: 51–2) reasoned that it was the duty of every person to fight the King's enemies, both foreign and domestic, as they would anyone who threatened their own lives. Even in instances when people had suffered oppression and injustice, Vajiravudh (1914 [1911]: 59) reiterated that challenging the status quo was no way to seek redress. All members of the nation, like the passengers of a ship that is taking in water, should join hands to suppress agitators, regardless of whether they might have cause to sympathize with their grievances.

King Vajiravudh (1914 [1911]: 44) defined 'preserving the Thainess of the nation' (*raksa khwam pen thai haeng chat*) as the responsibility of all, duty-bound to 'love the King, love the nation, love the religion' and protect all three from the (mostly unnamed) enemies aiming to destroy them. The survival of the nation would hinge on the unity of the Thai people, their commitment to loving the nation more than themselves, and their willingness to discharge 'duties' (*nathi*) that varied with their position on the country's social hierarchy. The King explained his organic theory of society by explicitly comparing the nation to a human body whose organs perform different but interrelated functions, such that the failure of one organ to work properly affects the health and functioning of others, triggering a chain reaction that ultimately threatens the entire body. To preserve the organism's integrity and vigour, therefore, the nation should be presided over by a single leader who assigns powers and duties to 'big men' (*phu yai*), delegating to them the responsibility to 'command' (*bangkhap bancha*) others and keep discipline. As for the 'little people' (*phu noi*) placed under the *phu yai*'s command and control, their service to the nation was to be measured exclusively in terms of their submission, compliance, and readiness to sacrifice their own lives to do as they were told by their 'superiors' (*phu pen nai neua ton*) (Vajiravhudh 1914 [1911]: 77–8). On that basis, Vajiravudh (1914 [1911]: 77–8) classified those who shirk or dissent, those who 'think only of themselves', and those who 'believe themselves to be better than their superiors' as enemies of the group's harmony (*prong dong*) and therefore deserving of stern punishment (Vajiravudh 1914 [1911]: 81).

Conceiving of the people only in terms of their duties, King Vajiravudh abhorred constitutionalism and democracy, and wrote copiously of his disapproval for Asian revolutions inspired by those ideals. Given Siam's history and circumstances, the nation would cease to exist, he claimed, should false 'patriots' and blind imitators of the West manage to bring democracy to the country (see Vella 1978: 71). The demands for individual autonomy, in particular, were dismissed as a way by which a person 'merely sought a rationalization for doing as he pleased, claiming the Western right to personal freedom as an excuse for his lack of discipline or respect, his entire devotion to self, and his basic immorality' (Vella 1978: 180). Having defined 'the Thai' as 'a people that would not submit to be anyone's servant' (Vajiravudh 1914 [1911]: 4), the King described constitutional government as the fastest way to consign the nation to servitude – equating, as autocrats often do, (individual) freedom with (collective) slavery.

While King Vajiravudh spoke of 'Thainess' to provide ideological content to the new national identity – such that subjects who did not love the King, had no respect for Buddhism, or failed to put the interests of the nation before their own could not be considered 'true Thai' – the King's ideas were also highly influential in setting the nation's racial, ethnic, and cultural boundaries. Often cited is Vajiravudh's (1914 [1911]: 56–7) take on the evolution of the word *chat*, whose meaning he stretched to signify 'a group of people who live together', and on the expression *chat thai*, said to designate those 'born into the group that calls itself Thai'. The requirement of birth was, as ever, flexible: a Westerner (*farang*) could never be Thai, but a Chinese immigrant could, and indeed should, become one. Individuals and groups not considered Thai by birth, however, could join *chat thai* only if, aside from embracing the King's ideology, they adopted Central Thai as their language and the state-approved variety of Buddhism as their religion.

Among the groups placed beyond the Thai nation's ethno-cultural boundaries, King Vajiravudh is well known for his antipathy towards the Chinese. It has long been pointed out that the large number of Chinese immigrants who came to Southeast Asia in the nineteenth century found it easier to integrate into Thai society (see Sidel 2008) – where, by 1910, they accounted for just under 10 per cent of the population, concentrated in Bangkok and other urban centres (see Charnvit 2000: 61) – than they did elsewhere in the region, such that 'anyone who used a Thai name, spoke the language, and behaved as a Thai was accepted as a Thai regardless of ancestry' (Skinner 1960: 89). In keeping with that tradition, King Vajiravudh's rhetorical attacks on the Chinese did not translate into especially repressive or discriminatory policies. Chinese immigrants, however, served as the foil against which the King highlighted the virtues and proper behaviour expected of a real Thai (see, for instance, Kasian 2009: 267). Vajiravudh seized upon the tendency of more recent Chinese migrants to preserve Chinese customs – instead of assimilating into Thai society as their predecessors had done (see Vella 1978: 186–90) – to complain that the Chinese increasingly refused, or 'did not submit' (*mai yom*), to be Thai. Lower rates of intermarriage and the continuing growth of a community now more inclined to cling to a separate ethnic identity fuelled a more generalized suspicion that Chinese migrants were not sufficiently loyal to the nation and were susceptible to the appeal of 'un-Thai' ideas such as republicanism and Chinese nationalism. Chinese workers' strikes in the early 1910s and the foiled plot of 1912, in which officials of partial Chinese descent played a leading role, crystallized the King's perception of this minority as a threat to the 'organic unity' of the nation (see Charnvit 2000: 62).

Far more gracious and nuanced was the verbal treatment reserved for Malay Muslims, whose position was a great deal more ambiguous. On the one hand, the King professed his tolerance of Islam and sought to present himself as the protector and patron of the Malay minority, presumably in exchange for the group's loyalty to the throne. On the other hand, the King stopped short of including Malay Muslims in *chat thai*. Although some Siamese officials harboured some hope that Malay Muslims would eventually come to identify as Thai, for the time being their language, customs, and religion, however tolerated, placed them 'irrevocably outside the boundaries of Siam's national citizenry' (Loos 2002: 81). The emphasis placed on state Buddhism by Siam's official ideology, in particular, caused the Deep South, unique among other regions, to be 'rejected as foreign and structurally barred from complete integration of the state through the institutionalization [. . .] of its differences' (Loos 2002: 95). In much the same way, the ethno-cultural boundaries of Thainess also continued to exclude tribal groups who did not speak Central Thai and practised animism. On account of their purported savagery, such groups were never even accorded the same respect and tolerance. As Tambiah (1976: 446) points out, it would later become the policy of the state, based on its ethno-nationalist ideology, to regard minorities considered 'politically and culturally inferior' as peoples 'to be nationalized or domesticated or, if they resist, simply eliminated'.

The Sixth Reign's official nationalism was disseminated through more than the words contained in King Vajiravudh's prolific output of speeches, essays, and plays. Indeed, the King dedicated much of his time and artistic talents to developing innovative ways in which to instil in his subjects the national consciousness he had helped devise for them. Thailand's national flag, the titles now used for its kings, some of its national holidays, and the requirement that people adopt surnames were products of this period, often resulting from the King's personal initiative. Siam's eventual participation in World War I and the various public initiatives launched by Vajiravudh to highlight the country's martial traditions and ascendant military might were also designed to increase national pride and bind the people to the monarchy.

Vajiravudh's reign is probably best remembered for two initiatives undertaken for the purpose of imparting the King's nationalist ideology to the Siamese public. The first was the creation, within months of his succession, of the Wild Tiger Corps (*Kong Suea Pa*), a paramilitary organization whose ranks swelled to thousands of members drawn primarily from the civilian bureaucracy. As Kullada (2004: 148–53) explains it, the Wild Tigers were above all a way for the King to establish a direct relationship with middle bureaucrats, whom Vajiravudh deemed not sufficiently loyal to the monarchy and dangerously susceptible to foreign ideas. The second major initiative, one whose legacy was ultimately more profound, was the promulgation of the 1921 Primary Education Act, which mandated compulsory education for children throughout the kingdom. King Vajiravudh did not live long enough to benefit personally from the Act, which took many years to implement beyond his death in 1925. Like most of King Vajiravudh's ideas, however, the system of national education – self-consciously designed to 'educate his nation to its nationhood' (Vella 1978: 160) – would later prove central to the authorities' efforts to enforce the universal acceptance and internalization of the state-sanctioned version of what it meant to be Thai.

In public, King Vajiravudh (cited in Vella 1978: 66) blustered that critics of the monarchy were 'not one in a million', comprised mostly of 'buffoons' and 'sinful destroyers'. The King, however, knew better than to believe his own rhetoric. As influential as they were in the long run, in the short term Vajiravudh's ideas and initiatives had little effect on shoring up the loyalty of the country's officialdom. The thwarted rebellion of 1912, in particular, could not be dismissed as a youthful indiscretion, or the act of a handful of 'buffoons'. Aside from the fact that the conspiracy might have involved as many as 800 officials, King

Vajiravudh was specifically informed that many more knew about the plot and had done nothing about it (see Kullada 2004: 156). The public revulsion for the King's profligacy and the self-indulgence of members of the royal family only made things worse. By the end of the Sixth Reign, the boom of popular newspapers catering to an upper-middle-class readership led to the popularization of verbal and visual content that routinely portrayed royals and noblemen as a corrupt, debauched, parasitic elite (see Copeland 1993; Barmé 2002). To little avail were King Vajiravudh's frequent contributions to public debates. Nor was the court's attempt to buy itself favourable coverage of much value (see Nakharin 1992: 98), swamped as it was by demands for reform rooted in aspirations of a far different nature. The absolutist regime's reluctance to repress public dissent,[11] much like the mercy that King Vajiravudh had shown for the conspirators of R.S. 130, was at odds with the King's own public philosophy, which highlighted the necessity to mete out swift and decisive punishment against any dissident who threatened the nation's unity. Deep insecurities of both a personal and political nature rendered King Vajiravudh's bark far worse than his bite.

Parameters of national identity

By the end of the Sixth Reign, the nationalist ideology that legitimized Siam's newly built absolutist state had set the official parameters of Thai national identity, at least with regard to the dimensions that Fearon (1999) considers relevant for the purposes of 'identity politics' and 'identity conflict'. The new Thai nation, that is, was delimited by *membership rules* based on ethno-cultural traits, to the exclusion of minorities who did not practise state Buddhism, did not speak Central Thai, and did not embrace 'civilized' customs as prescribed by the court. The still evolving ideology of 'Thainess', moreover, provided *content* to Thai national identity – most important on this count was its identification of King and nation, as well as its hierarchical conception of society buttressed by selectively chosen traditional beliefs about the Buddhist cosmos. Finally, ethno-cultural and ideological traits provided the bases upon which different in-groups and out-groups – 'Others Within' and 'Others Without', to borrow Thongchai's (2000b) phrasing – were reserved varying *moral valuations* and *political treatment* (see Chapter 1, p. 23).

[11] The state did occasionally crack down, but the effectiveness of repression was hampered by some of the publishers' skilful use of legal loopholes and fear within the King's court about incurring even more criticism, both at home and abroad. Indeed, the limited attempts made to silence critics antagonized the press even further (see Copeland 1993: 72–9).

The belief in natural and beneficial social hierarchies justified conferring upon men of high status (*phu yai*), higher moral valuation and privileged treatment, at least so long as their political attitudes matched the absolutist state's ideology. Similarly, the moral valuation and political treatment of ethnic minorities – both inside and outside the boundaries of the Thai nation – were to vary with their level of 'civilization', often defined on the basis of their cultural similarity to the Central Thai and their perceived allegiance to the state. Outside *chat thai*, the consideration and tolerance extended to Malay Muslims far exceeded that enjoyed by 'savages' such as the members of animistic hill tribes. Within *chat thai*, the lowest moral valuation was reserved for 'backward' northeasteners. Beginning in the Fifth Reign, the state had pursued a policy of reclassifying the population of Siam's North and Northeast as Thai, while flattening aspects of their culture that might have prevented them from identifying as such. What differences did remain formed the basis upon which northeasterners are still treated as inferiors, and thereby deserving of a more marginal role in the country's administration. As Rujaya and Wyatt (1995: 79–80) have claimed, by the 1930s it may have been, in some ways, 'better to be a northern "Thai" than to be just a "Thai"', given the respect accorded to northerners for their perceived physical beauty, culture, and history. The same was never true of northeasterners, who have long been stereotyped as ugly, lazy, gullible, ignorant, stupid, and, perhaps as a result, a great deal more wavering in their loyalty to the nation.

Much has been made (see Sulak 2002: 36) of the contrast between King Vajiravudh's nationalism with the version articulated by Prince Damrong Rajanubhab in the late 1920s and early 1930s. Damrong, in particular, is credited for putting forth a less threatening, more enlightened definition of 'Thainess', one that highlighted 'love of freedom and independence', 'dislike of violence', and propensity for 'assimilation, or compromise' (see Damrong 1927: 9). The difference, however, was more about tone than substance. Like his nephew, Damrong (1927: 28) defined as the foundational element of real 'Thai-style government' the authority of the King over the land, and the people's service to the state to help preserve the nation. Much of his work, moreover, was dedicated to providing ideological legitimacy to the hierarchical structure of Thai society (see Saichol 2003). Damrong was also adamant that Siam's traditional, paternalistic style of government rendered a constitution superfluous, because the people already enjoyed 'freedom' and 'justice' under the rule of kings 'of the people' and 'for the people'. As for membership of the Thai nation, Damrong eventually returned to his original belief that, moving forward, 'all ethnic groups' (*khon tang chat tang phasa*) should be dissolved, such that they would ultimately consider themselves Thai. In the interim, Damrong set out systematically to redefine the cultural and artistic contributions made by ethnic minorities as part of a single, anachronistic 'Thai' heritage (see Saichol 2008c and 2008d).

Ironically, Siam's official nationalism was helpless to achieve the one goal for which it had been originally designed: to protect the absolute monarchy. By the 1930s, most of the large peripheral populations inside the kingdom reportedly identified themselves as Thai and did not perceive their regional or ethnic identities as incompatible with an overarching Thai national identity, perhaps given the absence of alternative 'nations' with which to identify (see Keyes 1977: 300). Official nationalism, however, did nothing to attenuate the dissatisfaction of the 'bureaucratic bourgeoisie' or the small but influential class of urban intellectuals and professionals. These constituencies, which by and large espoused a different form of nationalism, provided the personnel and popular support that powered the removal of the absolute monarchy in 1932. In a strange twist, it would be thanks to some of the monarchy's sworn enemies that the ideas produced in the defence of absolutism came to provide the foundations upon which Thailand's state-sanctioned nationalism still rests. Once the 1932 revolution lost its democratic momentum, the search for new sources of legitimacy induced the country's military rulers to appropriate elements of King Vajiravudh's official ideology, paving the way for the articulation of the royal nationalism that would later serve as the basis for the dictatorship of Field Marshal Sarit Thanarat.

Since that time, Thailand's official nationalism has effectively moulded the individual and collective identities of tens of millions of people, facilitated the national integration of most large populations brought under Bangkok's rule in the Fifth Reign, and helped beat back challenges to the social and political order favoured by individuals, groups, and institutions situated at the top of the hierarchy it was designed to legitimize. To a considerable extent, however, Thai politics has continued to revolve around the cleavages that emerged in this period, reflecting to date unresolved conflicts over the nation's membership rules, the content of Thainess, and the political role afforded to constituencies defined on the basis of class, ethno-linguistic traits, and regional origin. Although at times latent or dormant, these cleavages were activated and mobilized repeatedly over the past eight decades. At the national level, demands for democracy and political inclusion advanced by subaltern groups have presented a constant challenge to established socio-political hierarchies, exemplified most potently by the demonstrations that have brought hundreds of thousands of people to the streets since the 1970s. With the partial exception of Malay Muslims, moreover, territorial forms of opposition never aimed to establish separate nation-states, but were at times fuelled by visions of the Thai nation at odds with the hierarchical, ethno-cultural, Bangkok-centric view that was conceived, propagated, and enforced by the state. The political crisis the country has been mired in since 2006 combines the national and territorial conflicts originating in Thailand's unfinished process of National Revolution, featuring quite prominently demands for full citizenship and equality under the law advanced by constituencies long consigned to a marginal political role – be it on account of their ideas, class, or regional provenance.

3 Revolution forsworn

As the sun rose on the clear morning of 24 June 1932, the city of Bangkok went about its business as if nothing had happened. No disruption was reported to commercial activity, communications, or public services as unsuspecting residents crowded the city's streets, markets, and temples. Only the sight of military personnel and vehicles blockading access roads to the Ananta Samakhom Throne Hall suggested that something unusual was taking place. Most of the 102 members of the People's Party (*Khana Ratsadon*) – comprised of fifty-two mid-ranking military officers (thirty-four from the Army and eighteen from the Navy), and fifty civil servants – were assembled there, together with some of the old regime's top officials, who had been arrested at dawn and escorted to the revolutionary headquarters. It was the early hours of the afternoon before news spread that the People's Party had seized power from King Prajadhipok, as fliers containing the revolutionaries' blistering communiqué – the First Announcement of the People's Party – began to circulate around the city. The operation had been executed cleanly, by trickery and stealth. 'Apparently by force of persuasion' (Sivaram 1981 [1936]: 22), the senior officials held hostage at the Throne Hall agreed to instruct public employees to heed the orders issued by the provisional government of Colonel Phraya Phahon Phonphayuhasena.

Still to be worked out was the role that King Prajadhipok would play in the transition, as the Promoters awaited a response to the blunt telegram they had sent to the country's erstwhile absolute monarch, who was then sojourning at his palace in the seaside resort town of Hua Hin, some 200 km southwest of the capital. Just as the residents of Bangkok learned of the seizure of power, grounded in the cronyism, incompetence, and venality of the King's government, news of the coup reached King Prajadhipok and Queen Rambhai Bharni on the golf course. The King is reported to have taken the news with aplomb, urging the young Queen to finish her round while he met with his advisors. Shortly thereafter, Prajadhipok rejected the possibility of putting up a fight to reclaim his absolute powers and accepted the rebels' demands. The next day, Their

Majesties returned to Bangkok by special train. Once there, King Prajadhipok issued a Royal Proclamation declaring the seizure of power to have been 'lawful' and agreed to promulgate a temporary constitution that made Siam a 'constitutional monarchy'. The newly appointed Assembly of the People's Representatives (*Sapha Phu Thaen Ratsadon*) met on 28 June, electing Phraya Manopakorn Nititada ('Mano') the country's first-ever Prime Minister.

As easy as it was for the Promoters to seize power on 24 June 1932, realizing the vision set forth in their 'First Announcement' proved a different matter altogether, as Siam's transition to democracy soon yielded to a gradual descent into military dictatorship. What is worse, many of the People's Party's stated objectives remain unfulfilled to this day. Perhaps most crucially, if the revolution had foremost been inspired by the ambition to place the King 'under the law of the land' (*yu tai kotmai thammanun kan pokkhrong phaendin*), recent events demonstrate that the monarchy still stands above the constitution, to say nothing of the efficacy with which 'good people' regularly invoke the monarchy's protection to exempt themselves from the law. Largely as a result of the royalist revival ushered in by the failure of the 1932 revolution, the goal of building a democratic state that guarantees all Thai nationals equal exercise of their rights of citizenship is not only far from full realization, but also remains short of universal acceptance in a programmatic sense. Indeed, the 'First Announcement' is in many ways a more radical document now than it was then.

The manner in which Thailand marked the 80-year anniversary of the end of the absolute monarchy, on 24 June 2012, is a testament to the significance of the events of 1932 to the country's current predicament. As usual, no ceremony was organized by the state in observance of a date that was celebrated as National Day between 1939 and 1960. In the time since, royalists have done what they could to rewrite history and credit the country's embracement of 'democracy' to the benevolence of its monarchs, claiming among other things that the adoption of a constitution took place thanks to, or at any rate consistent with the wishes of, King Prajadhipok. Still, royalists have no reason to commemorate an event that temporarily saw the monarchy stripped of most of its prestige, power, and property – when Field Marshal Sarit Thanarat decreed that National Day be observed, not on 24 June but on King Bhumibol's birthday on 5 December, the measure had punctuated the royalist triumph over the personalities and ideas that once powered the People's Party. In 2012, however, the anniversary did not come and go unnoticed, as 35,000 'Red Shirts' marked the occasion with a demonstration at the Democracy Monument in Bangkok. Having long since presented the movement as the true inheritor of the legacy of the People's Party, the Red Shirts came together to denounce the fact that, 80 years on, Thailand remained no real democracy – and, perhaps more importantly, to reaffirm their commitment to finish the job. From the rally stage, the United Front for Democracy against Dictatorship (UDD) leader Nattawut Saikuea traced the movement's roots all the way back to episodes that preceded the fall of the absolute monarchy, such as the foiled plot of 1912 and the reform proposals that Prince Prisdang and others submitted to the King in 1885. Nattawut delivered his speech in a red T-shirt emblazoned with the word *phrai*, another symbol the UDD had drawn from that era alluding to the unfinished nature of the struggle for individual equality.

This chapter reflects on the import of the People's Party's seizure of power. Rejecting the notion that the Promoters' failure was inevitable, given the prevailing circumstances or the nature of operation they conducted, the account offered in these pages examines the interplay of structural and contingent factors that steered the country down one of the several developmental courses realistically open in the wake of the 24 June coup. For the purposes of explanation, 24 June 1932 could be said to have marked the opening of the first major 'critical juncture' in the political development of modern Siam – a crucial formative period in which the regime instability Thailand has experienced ever since is rooted. Aside from the changes that the coup wrought on both the formal and informal structure of the Siamese polity, the abolishment of the absolute monarchy was significant insofar as, having scrambled established institutional arrangements, it inaugurated a period of institutional flux, uncertainty, and factional competition in which key constituencies vied for power on a far more equal footing than they had before. This situation, therefore, fits both the major characteristics of a 'critical juncture' – an unusually high degree of uncertainty and openness to a range of alternative outcomes and 'a *substantially* heightened probability that agents' choices will affect the outcome of interest' (see Capoccia and Keleman 2007: 348). Following Capoccia and Keleman (2007: 354–5), the analysis of the critical juncture roughly comprised between the coup on 24 June 1932 and King Prajadhipok's abdication on 2 March 1935 consists of an attempt to 'reconstruct, in a systematic and rigorous fashion, each step of the decision-making process, identify which decisions were most influential and what options were available and viable to the actors who took them, and clarify both their impact and their connection to other important decisions'.

Coup or revolution?

Perhaps a good place to start, in characterizing the events of 24 June 1932, is the age-old debate about whether the People's Party carried out a 'coup d'état' (*kan ratthaprahan*) or a 'revolution' (*kan patiwat* or *kan aphiwat*). The general literature does not always draw a clear distinction. Tanter and Midlarsky (1967: 265) once proposed a typology of 'revolution' where three of the four types are varieties of 'coup d'état'. A sharper distinction was drawn by Hannah Arendt, who objected to 'calling every coup d'état a revolution' (Arendt 1990 [1963]: 34). Only in instances when 'the pathos of novelty is present and where novelty is connected with the idea of freedom', she wrote, 'are we entitled to speak of revolution'. In the same passage, Arendt implies that the 'pathos of novelty' might be inferred from the magnitude of the change that follows a seizure of power, the extent of popular participation, and the degree of 'unquiet' it causes for 'the people at large' (Arendt 1990 [1963]: 34–5). It is based on a similar reasoning that one of the best-known popular histories of Thailand concludes: 'The military coup that toppled the absolute monarchy on 24 June 1932 can in no sense of the word be accurately described as a revolution' (Wyatt 2003: 234).

The People's Party was not the vanguard of a 'popular revolution'. With prominent exceptions, moreover, the Promoters had little intention to carry out what Skocpol (1979) refers to as a 'social revolution', one that would have engineered a radical realignment in the country's class structure. Certainly, the Promoters *did* appeal to class disparities and grievances. Perhaps above all, the use of the term *ratsadon* for 'the people' – as Charnvit (2000: 14) puts it, people with 'rights and a (legitimate) role in government' – signalled that the coup had been staged on behalf of ordinary men and women, for the term *ratsadon*, unlike *phonla mueang*, had previously referred only to subaltern classes. In addition, the 'First Announcement of the People's Party' – perhaps not surprisingly, given that the document's author was Pridi Banomyong (aka, Luang Pradit Manutham),[1] the leader of the Promoters' civilian faction – placed the economic exploitation practised by the 'bloodsucking' nobility front and centre, and argued that 'the King's government had treated the people as slaves [. . .] and as animals'. The denial of educational opportunities was described as the primary means by which the nobility had sought to deny ordinary people any knowledge of the 'evils' perpetrated on them. The Announcement promised to 'seize the money which those of royal

[1] In those days, commoners serving as mid- to high-level government officials were generally known by their royally bestowed honorific names (*ratchathinnam*) prefixed by ranks of minor nobility (*bandasak*), which sanctioned their acquired status as *khunnang* and hence their entry into the nobility – in order of importance, *somdet chao phraya*, *chao phraya*, *phraya*, *phra*, *luang*, *khun*, *muen*, and *phan*. The practice was abolished in 1942, but most of the historical personalities from this era are generally referred to by their honorific names and titles. Pridi Banomyong is one exception.

blood amass from farming on the backs of the people' and to reinvest the proceeds to boost the well-being of the country as a whole, thereby guaranteeing everyone 'freedom from being the *phrai*, servants, and slaves of the royal class' (*mi seriphap phon chak kan pen phrai pen kha pen that phuak chao*). Its concluding sentence is downright messianic, promising 'the things that everyone desires' and heralding the advent of *Sri Ariya*, a utopian golden age associated with the coming of the second Buddha.

The egalitarian paradise never came, however, because no serious attempt was made to rearrange the class structure of Siamese society. Pridi remained committed to his vision of social as well as political transformation, as did his followers among members of parliament and the urban intelligentsia. But most of the Promoters did not share, or were not especially invested in, Pridi's ambitions. The economic policies pursued by the new regime exhibited a strong measure of continuity with those of the absolutist regime. Pridi himself was purged from the government in April 1933, after attempting to push a radical economic plan through the Assembly. Within days of the coup, moreover, the Promoters publicly downplayed even the *political* significance of their actions. On 28 June 1932, a day after the King affixed his signature on the new temporary constitution, newspapers reported that the People's Party objected to the term 'revolution' – what they had done was merely to establish a 'Government by and for the people with the King's consent' (*Bangkok Times Weekly Mail*, 28 June 1932). For very different reasons, by then both the Promoters and the King described the transition to constitutional monarchy as having taken place in accordance with the wishes of both, presenting the coup not as a revolutionary act, but the result of a misunderstanding caused by each side's ignorance of the other's intentions.

Indeed, as he told Queen Rambhai upon learning of developments in Bangkok, King Prajadhipok had anticipated the possibility of a coup and had long considered measures to forestall it, including granting a constitution. Two documents attest to the King's examination of alternatives to the absolute monarchy – a skeletal draft submitted in 1926 by Francis B. Sayre, in response to the King's request for advice on necessary reforms, and an outline completed by two officials in the Ministry of Foreign Affairs, Raymond B. Stevens and Phraya Siwisan Waja, in March 1932.[2] It is clear, however, that the documents were not inspired by the ideals of individual equality and freedom in which the People's Party would later justify its seizure of power. The twelve articles of the 1926 draft envisioned the appointment of a Prime Minister, to whom much of the day-to-day administration would be delegated, but no provision

[2] Both documents are reprinted in full in Batson (1974a: 34–6, 86–9).

was made for an elected legislature, while the King retained all legislative, executive, and judicial powers. Whereas, moreover, the outline submitted to the King in March 1932 proposed that the legislature be structured in a manner similar to the one the People's Party would later devise, it also suggested that the King alone should have the authority to hire and fire the Prime Minister. Absent from both drafts are mentions of any rights reserved for the country's population.

The failure to enact either of the proposed constitutions is generally attributed to the opposition of 'the princes', some of them undoubtedly quite illustrious and powerful, who advised King Prajadhipok. But while there are good reasons to believe that Prajadhipok may have needed to secure the support of 'the princes' – perhaps especially the five men who served on his Supreme Council – before enacting reforms of this import, it is not difficult to see why their arguments might have resonated with the King. In 1926, Prince Damrong Rajanubhab objected in writing that the promulgation of a constitution could raise questions about the King's competence and commitment to govern the country. Presciently, Damrong (1974 [1926]: 37–41) warned of a potential situation where, in the event of a conflict between the King and a popular Prime Minister, the King might find himself on the wrong side of public opinion. In March 1932, the outline prepared by the King's advisors was accompanied by notes written by Stevens and Siwisan, counselling *against* the implementation of their own proposals. Phraya Siwisan (1974 [1932]: 90–3) speculated that the reforms might have signalled weakness to aspiring usurpers.

The reason why King Prajadhipok was likely sensitive to the risks that introducing a more or less 'democratic' constitution carried for the institution of the monarchy and his own image as a competent, committed steward of the nation's interests is that, if nothing else, the King had consistently exhibited a high degree of self-awareness about those very issues. Until shortly before King Vajiravudh's death, Prajadhipok was a long shot to succeed him – a 'dark horse', in his own words. On multiple occasions, moreover, King Prajadhipok had revealed, with disarming sincerity, his discomfort with the volume of work with which he had been tasked, as well as a marked sense of insecurity about his own ability to perform duties of such complexity and importance. The frank admission of his unpreparedness to tackle the effects of the global economic depression (see Batson 1984: 205) is often cited as evidence of his unease about the enormity of the responsibilities that had been placed on his shoulders.

Indeed, King Prajadhipok had not considered the possibility of introducing a constitution out of any desire to bestow 'democracy' upon the Siamese people, and his own writings confessed to a great deal of scepticism about its viability. It was in the aforementioned exchange with Francis B. Sayre, in 1926, that the King offered 'an emphatic NO' to the question of whether the country was 'ready to have some sort of representative Government' (Prajadhipok 1974 [1926]: 18). A year later, in a memorandum titled 'Democracy in Siam', Prajadhipok (1974 [1927]: 48) questioned the suitability of 'parliamentary government' to 'the racial qualities of the Siamese'. All along, King Prajadhipok's interest in a constitution was motivated by concerns that had little to do with the rights and freedoms the Siamese people should or should not enjoy. First, Prajadhipok was worried about the possibility that a 'bad king' might be on the throne in a situation where the only available remedy would be, as he put it, 'to chop off his head' (see Prajadhipok 1974 [1927]: 50). He was therefore committed to finding ways to institute checks on the king's powers and reform the laws of succession. Second, Prajadhipok sought ways to defuse the potential for the monarchy to succumb to a rebellion, which seemed imminent to him in light of the widely shared disgust that King Vajiravudh's reign had brought on the royal family, as well as the demands for representative democracy, however illogical or misguided, pressed by key social constituencies. Convinced that 'the prestige of Kingship in this country can hardly be lower' and that 'it would be a wild goose chase to try and get back any of the old glory' (Prajadhipok 1974 [1926]: 18), the King thought it preferable to implement, gradually, reforms that might otherwise come more abruptly, through revolution, at the cost of compromising the survival of the monarchy and the prosperity of Siam. At the same time, Prajadhipok did not want to do anything that might hasten the monarchy's downfall, hence his sensitivity to the opposition of Prince Damrong, Phraya Siwisan, and others.

It is impossible to tell whether, had the 24 June coup not taken place, King Prajadhipok would eventually have granted a constitution. It is safe to say, however, that the King had not departed from his predecessors' position that constitutions and elected legislatures were unnecessary or unworkable, given the country's backwardness and culture, for he clearly believed that to have been the case. Moreover, there is no indication that King Prajadhipok questioned any of the key tenets of the 'official nationalism' devised by his father and his brother. To the extent that the King was willing to consider relaxing some of its provisions, and examine alternatives to absolutism, he had done so out of a well-founded suspicion that refusing to do so no longer served the interests of the monarchy. King Prajadhipok (1974 [1927]: 48–9) thought, that is, that the government had to entertain alternatives because, while 'the majority of the people do not think *rationally*, but think only sentimentally', those who preyed on their credulity could make trouble for the monarchy if they did not get what they wanted. Nothing in King Prajadhipok's words and behaviour before 1932 suggests any level of convergence, in ideology or practical aims, between the monarchy and the People's Party. If anything, the King's actions are symptomatic of the intensification in the battle of ideas between different conceptions of the nation, not a sign of the conflict's abatement.

If what makes a 'revolution' are the 'pathos of novelty' and its 'connection to freedom', the People's Party could be said to have initially embodied a great deal of both. The 'First Announcement of the People's Party' expressed grievances and aspirations that the 'bureaucratic bourgeoisie', as well as the small but influential group of urban professionals and intellectuals, had developed over decades. Its condemnation of the *ancien régime* echoed criticism of the nobility that had appeared in print beginning in the 1880s and 1890s. Similarly, the statement that the country belonged to the people, the treatment of 'the people' as citizens with natural rights, and the commitment to equality, economic opportunity, and education affirmed values that had been put forth, in one form or another, since about the same time, and had bloomed in the 1920s into a 'movement for popular sovereignty' whose vanguard of essayists, columnists, and cartoonists was enthusiastically supported by much of the reading public in Bangkok (see Copeland 1993: Chs. 6–7). These themes were central to the efforts that members of the People's Party had made, since the organization's founding in 1927, to recruit and motivate adherents among young Siamese men studying in Europe. Not only did Pridi Banomyong acknowledge, later in life, the intellectual debt he owed to men like K.S.R. Kulap and Thianwan (see Pridi 2000 [1972]: 132); in the wake of the coup, both Pridi and Phraya Phahon also explicitly described the People's Party's actions as the continuation of the struggle launched with the thwarted plot of 1912 (see Charnvit 2000: 26).

In this sense, although the operation of 24 June 1932 took place without the involvement or the knowledge of anyone outside the mid-level state officials who belonged to the People's Party, the Promoters' *coup de main* was the culmination of a broader process of social and cultural change in which ordinary people and parts of the commoner upper-middle class had played a far more significant role – the latter inspiring the ideas of popular sovereignty, equal citizenship, and constitutionalism in which the Promoters grounded their recruitment efforts and earliest pronouncements. After the coup, the pages of Siamese newspapers brimmed with a sense of anticipation for what the 'New Siam' might bring. Within days, the government was swamped with petitions it had encouraged ordinary people to file to seek redress for their grievances, to the point of soon having to announce it did not have the capacity to handle the volume of submissions (see *Bangkok Times Weekly Mail*, 3 August 1932). At any rate, for a country like Siam, the mere fact that commoners were now in charge of the government, and royalty placed 'under' a constitution that vested sovereign power in the people, in and of itself marked an epochal transformation in the terms by which different constituencies were asked to relate to their government. Once again, it matters little that the Promoters, within hours of the coup, made the strategic choice to downplay the significance of their actions, or that they suppressed the existing copies of the 'First Announcement'. These choices, and others like them, account for the fact that the coup's 'revolutionary' potential went largely unfulfilled. But the cautious, compromising posture adopted by the Promoters after they had seized power did little to change, *ex post*, the significance of what had already taken place, or the 'pathos of novelty' and the desire for freedom that had inspired, in the years leading up to the coup, a growing number of commoners to challenge their 'natural' superiors.

In what is perhaps the most widely read Thai-language study of the 24 June coup, Nakharin (1992: 8) argues that the People's Party's seizure of power was a milestone in the country's transformation into a 'nation-state' (*rat prachachat*). The process was driven, in order of their importance and the intensity of their participation, by middle bureaucrats (*kha ratchakan radap klang*), parts of the urban (upper-)middle class (*khon chon chan klang nai khet mueang luang*), and ordinary people (*ratsadon*). Standing in the way was the noble class (*chao nai*), who by and large shared King Chulalongkorn's and King Vajiravudh's belief in 'natural inequalities' (*khwam mai thao thiam kan yu laeo doi thammachat*) (Nakharin 1992: 38), as well as the conservative officials who staffed both the top and the bottom rungs of the bureaucracy. Nakharin ascribes different motives to the groups that spearheaded the change: the new nationalism of middle bureaucrats, and their desire to create a 'national bureaucracy' operating according to meritocratic standards; the desire for rights, freedom, and democracy of the urban middle class; and, finally, the dissatisfaction of ordinary people with the intrusions of the state. Consistent with this reasoning, Nakharin (1992: 81) argues that the process that led the People's Party to seize power in 1932 was 'genuinely novel' (*baeb mai yang thae ching*). Up to as recently as three decades earlier, there had existed no rationale in Siam for doing anything of the sort.

The Promoters' dilemma

The basic dilemma the Promoters were presented with upon seizing power was whether, in Schattschneider's (1988 [1960]) words, to 'privatize' or 'socialize' their fight against the royalist establishment. 'Privatizing' the conflict – limiting it, that is, to the elite level – had the benefit of making the fight more manageable and less unpredictable, but had the drawback of giving the *ancien régime* the opportunity to fight on its own turf. 'Socializing' the conflict presented greater risks as well as greater potential rewards. On the one hand, the mobilization of a broader and more varied set of constituencies beyond the military and civilian bureaucracy offered the Promoters a chance to score a more decisive victory over the competition and establish more solid foundations for the constitutional regime. On the other hand, as Schattschneider (1988 [1960]: 3) pointed out, the 'contagion' of conflict threatens to weaken the control exercised by its original participants – an unsettling prospect for a group, like the People's Party, deeply insecure about its popular appeal beyond a small class of urban intellectuals and professionals.

Anderson (1978: 225) has argued that the 1932 coup failed to result in a 'decisive break' with royal absolutism because it had not been fuelled by the kind of 'social radicalism and indeed mass nationalism' responsible for bringing down European absolute monarchies. Rather, the coup had been staged by 'absolutism's own engine, the functionalized bureaucracy', which was 'incapable by itself of breaking with the perspectives and traditions of absolutism' (Anderson 1978: 225–6). Anderson (1978: 225) emphasizes the 'depth and duration of absolutism' to explain why Siam did not experience, as much of Europe had, 'massive popular revolutions generated in reaction to the transforming policies of entrenched absolutism'. Having taken only a few decades to complete a state-building process that had stretched over centuries in many European countries, Siam's absolutist regime had not lasted long enough, or penetrated deep enough into society, to generate mass oppositions. In turn, the absence of a mass movement to which they could turn for support could be said to have placed a crucial constraint on the options available to the Promoters in the wake of their seizure of power.

Perhaps even more stringent constraints were imposed by the *timing* of the coup, especially given the *sequencing* of two processes central to the political development of modern nations – the National Revolution and the Industrial Revolution (see Lipset and Rokkan 1967: 13–23). In much of Western Europe, the nineteenth-century struggle between liberals and conservatives over issues of sovereignty, citizenship, and constitutionalism had intersected with the emergence of market economies and the beginning of the industrial age. Increased levels of urbanization, social mobility, literacy, and media consumption, in turn, had made it possible for liberals, whom Caramani (2004: 199) describes as 'the motor of the National Revolution', to mobilize popular support. In a subsequent stage, towards the end of the nineteenth century, the rise of working-class movements pressing for full political inclusion ensured that there would be no turning back. Those who had previously fought to restore royal prerogatives, defend aristocratic or clerical privileges, and uphold traditional social hierarchies challenged by the diffusion of popular nationalist ideas could only avoid being swept away by devising their own appeals to the masses. By the time universal male suffrage was granted in the aftermath of World War I, conservatives had largely given up on advocating for a return to the *ancien régime,* having been forced to accept the core principles upon which constitutional monarchies, or even republics, were founded (see Caramani 2004: 199–212). With the resulting 'massification' of politics, a threat far more serious to the survival and stability of Europe's liberal-democratic regimes was presented by the rise of 'anti-system' mass movements on both the left and the right.

Siam's process of National Revolution was set in motion well before the emergence of a working-class movement, or for that matter any form of mass mobilization. As Nakharin (1992: 119) has pointed out, ordinary people were not simple spectators in the absolute monarchy's demise. But it is telling that the main vehicle by which their grievances had been articulated were Royal Petitions filed on behalf of individuals, as opposed to forms of collective action and organization. While such grievances often had to do with Siam's transition to a market economy, moreover, both the scope and the depth of such changes had been extremely uneven across Siam's national territory. The penetration of markets had been deepest in the Central Region, where landlessness, tenancy rates, and rural indebtedness had already become major problems. At the same time, the exploitative manner in which capital accumulation proceeded forestalled actual economic development, and failed to promote the rise of a 'new mode of production' that could spur technological innovation, the rise of a rural middle class, or the transformation of peasants into industrial workers (see Chatthip 1999: 57–8) – conditions that had been conducive to mass mobilization elsewhere. In the North and the South, meanwhile, early capitalist activity had been centred primarily on teak and tin mining, respectively. In the North, these businesses were often run by foreigners; in the South, they employed mostly immigrant Chinese labour. Until the 1920s, when improvements in communications led to the diffusion of commercial farming, the economic and social life of most northern and southern communities had undergone little change, and it was not until decades later that such regions saw peasants and workers organize. Change occurred even later and more slowly in the Northeast (see Chatthip 1999: 60–72). Throughout much of the country, episodes of popular resistance remained small in scale and localized in scope. The state's countermeasures had for the most part succeeded in pre-empting even the sort of inchoate rebellions that had broken out in the provinces in the early 1900s (see Somchai 2006: 32).

While Anderson (1978: 225–6) spends too few words on the subject to make it clear whether he himself deems the People's Party's failure to break 'with the perspectives and traditions of absolutism' to have flowed inevitably from the fact that the coup had been staged by men drawn from 'the engine' of the absolutist state, the available evidence does not support a deterministic interpretation of this argument. Lack of mass popular support, to be sure, loomed large in the calculus made by the Promoters, particularly in their initial choice to seek accommodations with the *ancien régime*, rather than attempt to dismantle the system altogether. To make matters worse, the fact that Siam's small industrial/commercial bourgeoisie was dominated by ethnic Chinese, whom the Promoters distrusted, deprived the People's Party of a potentially crucial ally, while the ethnic divisions within Bangkok's working class rendered its officials nervous about the potential that their mobilization might empower Chinese labour (see Skinner 1957: 219). Each of these factors, once again, may have discouraged the People's Party from broadening their fight against the royalist establishment, and induced its leaders to opt for managing the conflict instead. By no means, however, did such conditions render inevitable the failure of the democratic revolution some of its members planned to complete.

The choice set faced by the Promoters included alternatives that some of their leaders were very much intent on pursuing, perhaps above all the option of building mass popular support in a more deliberate fashion. The initial course taken by the Promoters, in fact, consisted of a two-pronged strategy that combined short-term compromises with the absolutist establishment with longer-term efforts designed to establish mass organizations that could help support the government and assist in the transition to representative democracy. The fact that those efforts were later abandoned, and that the People's Party eventually boxed itself into relying exclusively on the bureaucratic apparatus, cannot be attributed entirely to its members' cultural outlook. Although some of the most powerful Promoters, perhaps especially those in the senior military clique, undoubtedly held conservative attitudes and political views, plenty among them had little regard for 'the perspectives and traditions of absolutism'. Rather, factors of both a structural and contingent nature were responsible for making the short-term goals shared by most of the Promoters incompatible with the long-term ambitions of Pridi and others. In short, the initial accommodations made for conservative royalists set in motion a chain of events that led to the failure of the long-range efforts by which some of them had hoped to shepherd the country through a successful democratic transition.

If the coup had gone off without a hitch, the success of the revolution was compromised by a series of decisions taken immediately after the seizure of power, by which the Promoters created an opening for the old order's predictable attempt to reassert its authority. Several measures were taken in those days against the revolutionists' better judgement. The People's Party suppressed its 'First Announcement', which had also featured the threat to establish a republic, and apologised to the King for the offensive language it contained.[3] Moreover, although the constitution written by Pridi Banomyong had originally been intended to serve as a 'permanent' constitution, the People's Party agreed to King Prajadhipok's demand that the document be promulgated as a provisional charter. The content of the permanent constitution introduced on 10 December 1932 – designed by a nine-member committee on which Pridi served as the People's Party's lone representative – reflected several concessions made to the King. While the increased prerogatives that the December constitution vested in the King were neither very extensive nor very incisive (see Thawatt 1972: 120–1), the result was nonetheless to dilute the Promoters' own power (see Riggs 1966: 161).

In retrospect rather incredibly, the Promoters initially chose to 'withdraw' and hence forego the opportunity to build on their initial advantage. Citing their youth and inexperience, they allowed senior members of the old royalist establishment to hold key government posts (see Landon 1939: 32–3; see also Sivaram 1981 [1936]: 39–40). Only about forty members in the seventy-seat Assembly were appointed from the ranks of the People's Party. Phraya Mano, a former Supreme Court justice and not a member of the People's Party, was made Chief Executive, after consultations in which the Promoters had considered appointing none other than Prince Boworadet. Also, whereas the temporary constitution provided for a dual executive – a fourteen-member 'People's Committee' (numbering eleven Promoters) appointed eight ministers, none of whom had participated in the coup – the permanent constitution instituted a single executive body, the State Council (*Khana Ratthamontri*, or Council of Ministers). Significantly, while the Promoters retained a one-vote majority in the twenty-member executive, no members of the People's Party initially held ministerial portfolios. Worse yet, given the

[3] The apology was formalized in a self-abasing letter that the Promoters submitted to the King months later (reproduced in Thak 1978: 11).

Promoters' own lack of cohesion, the cabinet's new structure and composition made it easier for Mano to push through measures designed to roll back the revolution (see Riggs 1966: 161). Shortly before his death, Pridi Banomyong (2000 [1982]: 169) reflected on the People's Party's failure to 'sustain victory' and 'avoid counter–revolution', identifying the Promoters' most fateful lapse in their decision to invite 'old bureaucrats' to join the government.

Its initial bluster notwithstanding, the People's Party gave the old regime every opportunity to erode the initial gains of the revolution. None of the property the princes had been accused of embezzling was seized. Equally important, the deference with which the King was treated, as well as the efforts made to persuade the public that the King agreed with the objectives of the revolution, unduly boosted the *ancien régime*'s democratic credentials, giving royalists an opportunity to dress up their opposition to the People's Party in their commitment to the democratic system of government the King had 'willed', if only vicariously, into existence. Once again, it is important to recognize that this was not the only option available. The royalist project of cultural hegemony being still in its infancy, the coup had been largely shrugged off in the provinces, where the King of Siam remained a distant figure to which the population had developed little emotional attachment.[4] In Bangkok, where life had gone on without disruption, the coup was met with indifference, when not enthusiasm (see Batson 1984: 237–9). As King Prajadhipok knew all too well, the 'educated classes' in the capital had long turned on the monarchy. By taking senior princes into custody, then, the People's Party had neutralized the only realistic source of opposition to the coup. Indeed, although King Prajadhipok is widely credited for the avoidance of bloodshed, members of his own entourage expressed serious doubts over whether both fight and flight were viable alternatives, once the coup had taken place (see Stowe 1991: 18).

Different explanations have been provided over the years for the magnanimity exhibited by the Promoters. Some attributed it to their 'good intentions' (Landon 1939: 33). Pridi blamed it on their lack of practical expertise, poor planning for the coup's aftermath, and the wishful thinking that clouded their assessment of the old regime's willingness to cooperate (see Pridi 2000 [1982]: 169). An internal report by the British

[4] As recently as the mid 1950s, a study conducted by an American anthropologist in a northern village chosen for its 'representativeness' reported that 61 per cent of respondents did not know the meaning of 'monarchy', despite the fact that the sample was limited to residents with the highest levels of educational attainment and exposure to the outside world. Only half could even identify the King by name (see Kingshill 1991: 243–5).

Foreign Office claimed at the time that the Promoters abandoned the idea of doing away with the monarchy after Prince Dewawongse persuaded them that European powers would have likely intervened, had the new government failed to guarantee a sufficient measure of continuity (Barmé 1993: 67–8). Internal differences of both a personal and ideological nature may also account for the absence of a broad consensus on more sweeping reforms. What is clear is that the concern paramount in the minds of the Promoters, whatever their ultimate intentions, was the smoothness of the operation, for the sake of which their leaders were willing to sacrifice some of the revolution's transformative potential. The People's Party, and later the country as a whole, would pay a steep price for the Promoters' miscalculation.

Counter-revolution

The constitution promulgated on 10 December 1932 inaugurated a system of tutelage that mapped out a three-stage transition to full representative democracy. In the first phase, set to last until elections could be organized, the unicameral Assembly would be composed of seventy members who had been appointed in the wake of the 24 June coup. In the second phase, the Assembly would be made up of an equal number of elected 'first-category' members and 'second-category' members formally appointed by the King through a selection process dominated by the State Council. In the third phase, to begin after 10 years, the entire Assembly would be elected by the people. In principle, the constitution also guaranteed the country's citizens a host of liberal freedoms – speech, assembly, and association. If the first few months after the coup had witnessed a great deal of political debate and activity, however, the government retained a variety of means, both legal and extra-legal, to restrict individual rights. Phraya Mano's administration routinely put pressure on the print media, ordering the closure or (more commonly) the suspension of news outlets the government accused of inciting unrest. While, moreover, political parties were not explicitly banned, the government reserved the right to withhold or deny the registration of political associations.

The campaign to roll back the revolution began in earnest after the 24 June coup, through an attempt to undermine the legitimacy of the Promoters and weaken the public's trust in the ability of the new government to protect Siam from upheaval. Publicly, the royalist opposition relied on newspapers like *Thai Mai* and the Siam Free Press' *Bangkok Daily Mail*, *Krung Thep Daily Mail*, and *Seriphap* to attack the government. Luang Wichit Wathakan, for one, wrote a number of columns and pamphlets that not only criticized the government's performance but also raised the possibility that the People's Party would reserve for the monarchy and Buddhism the same treatment that the Romanovs and the Russian Orthodox Church had received from the Bolsheviks (see Barmé 1993: 76–8). The papers of the Siam Free Press, part-owned by King Prajadhipok's father-in-law Prince Sawat, similarly took to drawing parallels between the new government and the Soviet regime, arguing that the Promoters planned to move the country in the direction of communism. Just as key royalists raised the spectre of communism in books, columns, and interviews, others commissioned incidents and disturbances designed to make the threat appear real and imminent. Conservative figures close to the King were involved in covert efforts to create disorder and disseminate communist literature. Concurrently, a series of strikes by Chinese workers and rickshaw drivers broke out in the first few months after the People's Party came to power (see Skinner 1957: 219), contributing to an atmosphere of increased confusion and fear (see Thompson 1967 [1941]: 67). The powerful princes Boriphat and Purachatra were later accused of having bankrolled the disturbances with donations amounting to several hundred thousand baht (see Nattapoll 2010: 155–61; Barmé 1993: 72, 96).

Aside from portraying the People's Party as a group of dangerous radicals, the purpose of the royalist campaign was to expose the government's inability to keep the peace through constitutional means, and hence goad the Promoters into betraying democratic principles in an attempt to prove their mettle. In this endeavour, the royalists were quite successful. Having already clamped down on the virulent criticism of the monarchy that much of the print media had unleashed in the weeks after the coup, the government responded to intensifying social upheaval by getting tough on the press and Chinese labour. In addition, the government's concerns about political instability and softening public support induced the People's Party to lean more heavily on the King. Their conspicuous request for forgiveness and the accommodations pursued by the December constitution were likely related to the Promoters' self-consciousness about their deficit of legitimacy.

King Prajadhipok scored another major victory shortly after the permanent constitution was enacted. In early January 1933, a group of conservatives led by Luang Wichit Wathakan submitted registration papers for a new political group, the 'National Party' (*Khana Chat*). The boilerplate description provided for its mission and organization made no mention of electoral competition (see *Bangkok Times Weekly Mail*, 9 January 1933), but it was clear that this group was intended to provide an alternative to the People's Party. By then, some of the Promoters still aspired to make the People's Party into a mass organization. In late August 1932, the party's spin-off group – the People's Association, or Association of the People's Party (*Samakhom Khana Ratsadon*) – boasted that its membership had risen to 10,000 and announced that branches would soon be opened in the provinces (see *Bangkok Times Weekly Mail*, 30 August 1932). Thereafter, newspapers reported a flurry of activity by the new organization – meetings, fund raising, recruitment, merit-making ceremonies, the adoption of new internal regulations, and even an incipient effort at establishing a measure of symbolic content. At the same time, a number of high-level dignitaries from the People's Party attended a ceremony for the country's first trade union, the Tramwaymen's Association, whose activities were now explicitly aimed at supporting the government (Bangkok Times Weekly Mail, 25 October 1932).

Whereas the People's Association had, up to that point, remained ambiguous about its electoral objectives, the appearance of the National Party forced the Promoters to show their hand. While some publications close to the People's Party criticized the attempt to register a royalist party (see Murashima 1991: 16), both Pridi and Luang Wichit later confirmed details of a conversation in which the two men agreed that the National Party should be registered; Pridi, moreover, reported that the Promoters held a meeting, in the presence of Phraya Mano, when it was decided to approve the National Party's registration. Pridi claimed to have instructed People's Party officials to prepare for an electoral campaign immediately thereafter (see Assembly of the People's Representatives 1935: 203–4, 285).

Phraya Mano's about-face may well have been facilitated by the attitudes of some of the Promoters and their supporters in the media (see Murashima 1991: 18), but the decision was made at the urging of King Prajadhipok. In a letter written to the Prime Minister on 31 January 1933, the King expressed 'great nervousness' (*khwam witok pen an mak*) over the plan to register a political party (see Prajadhipok 1935 [1933]: 176–8). In Prajadhipok's view, party competition posed a threat to cause violence and unrest, given the Siamese people's lack of preparedness; political parties should be allowed to form only once the people had demonstrated proper understanding of 'government, morality, and constitutionalism'. The King also noted that, to avoid the appearance of double standards, the denial of the National Party's registration should be accompanied by the disbandment of the People's Association. The Prime Minister, of course, had his own reasons to go along with the King's recommendations. Having long since fallen out with several of the Promoters, Pridi chiefly among them, Mano saw in the disbandment of the People's Association an effective way to both reduce their power and assure greater personal control over the legislature. Having no interest in furthering the revolution, Mano relied on King Prajadhipok to buttress his personal power and diminish the influence of the Promoters. After securing the King's support, Mano denied the registration of the National Party and approached Luang Wichit, promising that the People's Party would also be disbanded.[5] The People's Association voluntarily dissolved in April 1933, after a series of crippling regulations had forbidden state employees from taking part in its activities (see *Bangkok Times Weekly Mail*, 22 April 1933).

It is impossible to say what would have happened if the National Party had been allowed to compete against the People's Association in legislative elections. At the very least, however, this constituted a missed opportunity for the country's nascent democracy. At the time, Pridi and Luang Wichit were not only young but were also genuinely towering figures on account of their knowledge, intellect, and charisma. After the elections of October/November 1933, when both served as 'second-category' members of the Assembly, the two men frequently dominated parliamentary debates – both elected and appointed legislators were generally keen to defer to their positions and legal interpretations. In addition, the two were the country's most thoughtful and articulate advocates of competing ideologies and conceptions of the nation. Once again, whether or not Pridi and Luang Wichit could have played the same role that Thomas Jefferson and Alexander Hamilton played in the emergence of a two-party system in the United States (see Aldrich 1995) is hard to tell. At the same time, electoral competition between the People's Association and the National Party offered the best chance for Siam to develop, early on, the kind of institutions that might have helped build a functioning democracy.

For King Prajadhipok, this outcome had both short- and long-term benefits. In the long term, strong, organized political parties with an independent base of support in the electorate – even those, like the National Party, with an avowedly royalist platform – could have morphed into one of the throne's competitors for political power. Whether or not this consideration even crossed Prajadhipok's mind, however, the short-term benefits of getting the People's Association disbanded were attractive enough to induce the King to lobby for the denial of the National Party's registration. Not only did the dissolution of the People's Association deprive ambitious Promoters whom the palace detested and feared, above

[5] Luang Wichit claimed to have responded that this was neither his problem nor his intention (see Assembly of the People's Representatives 1935: 204). Thompson (1967 [1941]: 71), however, argued at the time that 'it was generally accepted that such an eclipse of the People's Party was precisely what the sponsors of the Nationalist Party [sic] were aiming at'.

all Pridi, of an organizational vehicle to political power – the destruction of the People's Party also aggravated some of the personal conflicts that had been brewing in the ranks of the government (and the Promoters themselves), offering the King an opportunity to recover some of the prestige and clout he had been forced to relinquish on 24 June.

Divisions between the Promoters are reported to have first emerged just days after the coup, when Phraya Song Suradet – one of the leaders of the People's Party's senior Army faction and mastermind of the operation – angrily rebuked Pridi over some of the language employed in the draft constitution submitted to the King. The strategy that Phraya Mano seems to have adopted, with King Prajadhipok's backing, was to enlist Phraya Song to deepen the rift between Pridi's supporters and the senior military faction, then essentially purge both and neutralize the People's Party junior military clique in a series of reshuffles.

Mano's stratagem fell only a few days short of completing a successful counter-revolution. After an audience with the King, Pridi was invited to submit an economic plan aimed at realizing the 'six principles' of the revolution. Perhaps buoyed by the sympathetic response received from a government-appointed investigative committee (see Landon 1939: 303–23), which rejected the plan only after failing to come to unanimous agreement on the majority opinion that it should be implemented, Pridi circulated his 'Yellow Book' among supporters in the Assembly, who demanded that the government allow a parliamentary debate on the subject. By the time the executive rejected the plan – Mano having secured the support of the non-Promoters in his cabinet as well as the Promoters less supportive of Pridi – the atmosphere in the Assembly had turned incandescent. The government alleged that Pridi's 'radical' faction, said to control thirty seats, had begun carrying pistols in the Assembly. In turn, the thirty members of what Mano referred to as the 'middle party' stayed away out of fear for their safety, leaving the ten or so supporters of the government powerless to prevent the Assembly from approving the economic plan, or indeed any measure the 'radicals' may have wanted. Mano claimed that, as a result, the choice before the country was to either accept communism or resort to extra-constitutional means to forestall its advent (see *Bangkok Times Weekly Mail*, 13 April 1933). In a lengthy commentary (reproduced in Thak 1978: 193–234) replete with references to the Soviet Union, meanwhile, King Prajadhipok personally rubbished Pridi's economic plan as a communist scheme.

On 1 April 1933, after securing the King's signature on the unlawful decree, Mano staged a self-coup. The Assembly was prorogued until new elections could be held, its legislative powers transferred back to the King. Pridi and four of his supporters were forced out of the State Council, while Pridi himself was sent abroad to 'continue his studies'. A new and exceedingly broad 'Act Concerning Communism' imposed stiff jail terms on those advocating 'any communist doctrine', while an amendment to the Civil and Commercial Act gave the state more expansive powers to deny or lift the registration of associations deemed 'likely to endanger the public peace' (see *Bangkok Times Weekly Mail*, 3 April 1933). Newspapers that criticized the prorogation of the Assembly or defended Pridi's economic plan were suspended or closed, while Mano (cited in Sivaram 1981 [1936]: 62) openly warned journalists that they would be 'drastically dealt with' if they failed to 'support the Government's policy of excluding communism from Siam'. The King's Secretary (cited in Stowe 1991: 50) described the self-coup as 'merely a strike at the snake's tail'.

Having purged Pridi, Phraya Mano moved swiftly – indeed, perhaps too swiftly for his own good. Suddenly, on 10 June, the four leaders of the People's Party's senior military clique – Phraya Phahon, Phraya Song, Phraya Ritthi Akhane, and Phra Prasat Pitthiyayuth – submitted their resignations, effective 24 June 1933. This turn of events should have given Mano some pause, but the Premier instead pressed ahead and reshuffled the ranks of the military. Two conservatives were nominated to fill the posts of Commander-in-Chief of the Army and Director of Military Operations, respectively held by Phraya Phahon and Phraya Song. Sensing that the replacement of the senior-most military leaders of the Promoters with staunch royalists foreshadowed the end of the revolution, junior Promoters in the Army and Navy, led by Colonel Luang Phibun Songkhram and Naval Commander Luang Supha Chalasai, resolved to take power by force, before it was too late. After securing Phraya Phahon's cooperation, the junior Promoters struck on 20 June 1933. Much like the previous year, the seizure of Bangkok was clean and bloodless.

Upon taking the office of Prime Minister, which he would occupy until September 1938, Phraya Phahon initially recommitted himself to some of the stated objectives of the revolution (see *Bangkok Times Weekly Mail*, 21 June 1933). Taking no chances of another hostile takeover, however, Phahon retained his position as Commander-in-Chief of the Army. The State Council and other key posts in the country's administration were reserved for Promoters, while those who had aided Mano's counter-revolution were retired. The Assembly was reconvened almost immediately, the constitutional provisions suspended by Mano quickly restored. Shortly thereafter, Pridi was invited to return to Siam – to clear his name and take the lead in the country's economic reform, provided he dropped the idea of nationalizing land and industry (see *Bangkok Times Weekly Mail*, 1 September 1933).

Phraya Phahon has been praised for the moderate, 'revengeless' approach he took to dealing with Mano and King Prajadhipok, as well as subsequent challenges that would soon be mounted by disgruntled royalists. Perhaps concerned about the fact that his signature had appeared on the Royal Decree that suspended the constitution back in April, Phahon nudged the Assembly to approve the legality of legislation passed in the last two and a half months of Mano's administration. Requests that Phraya Mano be prosecuted and the King impeached for suspending the constitution were denied, while a defamation suit against the King – submitted by supporters of Pridi in the Tramwaymen's Association – was met with criminal charges for the petitioner, Thawat Rithidet. In the vain pursuit of stability, the Promoters had set a precedent for effectively legalizing suspensions of the constitutional order blessed by the King.

King Prajadhipok, however, would still have none of it. In an open letter to the reconvened Assembly, he hastened to remind 'all members' of 'the importance I attached to the Constitution when I gave it to them' (cited in *Bangkok Times Weekly Mail*, 6 July 1933). Shortly thereafter, royalist publications resumed peddling rumours of impending communist takeover. Despite expressing admiration for Phraya Phahon in public, moreover, King Prajadhipok undertook a campaign to discredit the new government with foreign powers. In a letter to foreign advisors attached to the government, the King described Phraya Phahon as someone 'not blessed with brains' and argued for the necessity of keeping the Promoters in check by invoking 'the bogey' of foreign intervention. 'One must use that bogey to the last', the King wrote, 'even if there is no chance of foreign intervention taking place'. Prajadhipok then explained his motivations for staying away from Bangkok: 'With the King at large and free to lead a revolt they have to be more cautious' (cited in Barmé 1993: 82–3, 99).

The royalist rebellion King Prajadhipok foreshadowed in his private correspondence broke out in the middle of October, as the country's first legislative elections were in full swing throughout the country. Prince Boworadet, aided by troops from Nakhon Ratchasima, Ayutthaya, Nakhon Sawan, and Petchaburi, took control of Don Muang Airport, laid siege to Bangkok, and issued an ultimatum for the government to resign. The government pushed back hard against the rebels. In 2 weeks of heavy fighting, Phibun's troops first chased Boworadet's troops out of Don Muang and Bang Sue, then crushed the insurgents around their northeastern stronghold in Pak Chong. By the end of October, the revolt was quelled.

The King's role in the Boworadet Rebellion remains controversial. Some, Prajadhipok included, have pointed out that Prince Boworadet had a difficult relationship with the King and other royals. Prajadhipok's critics at the time pointed to the composition of the rebels' ranks and the royalist credentials of Boworadet's lieutenants. The King's ambiguous behaviour during the revolt also raised suspicions. At the height of the violence, as Phraya Phahon requested his return to Bangkok, the King made a precipitous escape to Songkhla, while other members of the royal family crossed the border into British Malaya. Shortly thereafter, His Majesty's Private Secretary issued a bland statement expressing regret over 'the suffering caused by the civil war' and announced a donation of THB 10,000 to the Red Cross Society (see *Bangkok Times Weekly Mail*, 17 October 1933). According to a Special Court convened by the Phibun government years later, however, King Prajadhipok had provided Prince Boworadet with a sum twenty times as large to finance the rebellion (Barmé 1993: 101). While there is good reason to be sceptical of the findings released by the Special Court in 1939, accounts offered by the King's own associates support the notion that Prajadhipok was deeply involved in the rebellion's planning, financing, and execution (see Nattapoll 2010: 158–60; see also Nattapoll 2013: 22–33, 145–9).

Within months of the rebellion, the Promoters had definitively crushed the counter-revolution, if only at the cost of betraying some of the revolution's own principles. While the government eventually exhibited a measure of restraint in dealing with those convicted of an active role in the rebellion, hundreds of officials were arrested or dismissed from government service over their (at times merely suspected) involvement in the rebellion. Royalist newspapers were closed down as the government tightened the screws on dissent. A draconian 'Act to Protect the Constitution', moreover, criminalized public expressions of disrespect for the constitution or the constitutional regime, an all-purpose definition that placed few limits on the government's authority to silence its critics. King Prajadhipok left the country in early 1934, officially for medical reasons, never again to return to Siam. Roughly a year later, on 2 March 1935, at the conclusion of long and contentious negotiations with the government, Prajadhipok abdicated in favour of his nephew, the 9-year-old prince Ananda Mahidol.

By the time King Prajadhipok sailed to England, he had long regarded the threat of abdication as his 'strongest weapon' in dealing with the government – a weapon he claimed in August 1933 to have 'used several times already' (see Barmé 1993: 83). What seems to have prompted the King to consider acting on his threats, however, were two decisions the Assembly took during the extraordinary session held in August and September 1934. In both instances, the Assembly had enacted, without change, legislation that the King had chosen not to sign, as per his constitutional prerogative: the Inheritance Tax Act, which had failed to include an exception for Crown Property, and an amendment to the

Code of Criminal Procedure, which had stripped the King of the power to approve death sentences. Aside from seeing his objections dismissed so readily by the Assembly, the King was troubled by the tone of the parliamentary debate, in which legislators had accused him of refusing to accept the principle of equality under the law on the subject of taxation (see *Bangkok Times Weekly Mail*, 6 August 1934) and of encroaching on the legislature's authority on the subject of criminal procedure (see *Bangkok Times Weekly Mail*, 29 September 1934).

It is around this time that King Prajadhipok took to making specific demands as a condition for staying on the throne. In late September 1934, two Royal Notes were sent to the government through an intermediary. In the first Royal Note (see Prajadhipok 1935 [26 September 1934]: 133–5), the King professed his dismay over three matters the government would have to address to avert his abdication: 1) the dismissal of Mom Chao Suphasawat (the Queen's brother) and other government officials suspected of involvement in the Boworadet Rebellion; 2) the government's planned elimination of the Palace Guard; and 3) the prospect that the Ministry of the Royal Household might be scrapped or reformed. In the second Royal Note (see Prajadhipok 1935 [26 September 1934]: 136–52) presented to the government on the same occasion, King Prajadhipok elaborated on his objection to the Inheritance Tax Act, voicing disappointment over the insinuation that his opposition was more self-interested than principled. After making a somewhat convoluted case about the difficulty of assessing tax on Crown Property and the damage that the status of the monarchy would suffer from submission to this form of taxation, Prajadhipok promised the government that, without exception, he would no longer sign any legislation that damaged the King 'directly or indirectly'. The King made four additional demands the government would have to meet to prevent his abdication: 1) cease casting aspersions on the King; 2) 'strictly repress' anyone who criticised the monarchy or the Chakri Dynasty; 3) reaffirm its loyalty to the throne; and 4) reassure those who suspected the government of having socialist leanings and reconcile with those involved in the Boworadet Rebellion by reducing their jail terms and restoring their pensions.

Frustrated with the government's response, King Prajadhipok issued the strongest statement yet about his intention to abdicate in a memorandum to the Royal Secretary in Bangkok (see Prajadhipok 1935 [27 October 1934]: 9–14). A few days later, the government announced that a delegation would travel to England to meet with the King, in an attempt to come to a workable agreement under the constitution. Given the tenor of earlier communications, the government's envoys might have been taken by surprise when, in their first meeting with King Prajadhipok, they were treated to a lecture on representative democracy (see

Direk 1935 [12 December 1934]: 24–30). The delegation's account of the meeting mirrors the contents of the third and final Royal Note the King submitted a week later (see Prajadhipok 1935 [20 December 1934]: 99–113), which features a series of eight demands designed to reform Siam into a 'real democracy'.

Much of the third Royal Note was taken up by the King's views on the issue of 'second-category' members of parliament, whose continued existence was blamed for many of the country's problems. While judging the role of second-category members of parliament a 'violation of the principles and doctrines of a real democracy', the King hastened to make clear that he still believed appointed legislators were needed in the transitional period – his objections, that is, were only to the manner in which they had been selected. After discussing a few, equally undemocratic alternatives to the selection procedures in place, King Prajadhipok turned to another topic, demanding that the government amend Section 39 of the constitution and strengthen his veto powers. In the event of a royal veto, the King suggested that the government consider holding a referendum, dissolving the Assembly, or requiring a supermajority to override it. A further set of demands took direct aim at the restrictions the government had placed on political rights. On this point, King Prajadhipok warned the government that this would be its last chance to grant full freedom of expression as well as freedom of assembly and association, including the possibility to organize political parties. Similar concerns were reiterated in the King's request that the government repeal the Act to Protect the Constitution.

The government's response was polite but firm. In his memorandum to the King, the Prime Minister (see Phahon 1935: 115–28) noted that the government had already taken steps to accommodate most of the demands contained in the Royal Notes received in late September – the exception being to interrupt judicial proceedings that were already before the courts. As for the additional demands, the Prime Minister stated his openness to the idea that dismissed government officials should see their pension restored, as well as the possibility of commuting the sentences of convicted rebels, if only at the end of the Special Court's proceedings. Phraya Phahon, however, rejected the King's demands on the issues of second-category members of parliament, royal vetoes, freedom of speech/association, and the repeal of the Act to Protect the Constitution. In subsequent meetings in London, King Prajadhipok declared the negotiations closed (see Direk 1935 [20 January 1934]: 52–6) and accused the government of having sent the delegation only as 'propaganda' (see Direk 1935 [24 January 1934]: 60–4). The King requested that the Assembly be given a chance to consider his demands before he was to render a final decision on his future. A few days later, on 31 January 1935, the legislature entered secret deliberations, rushing to consider the matter in a single sitting at the government's request. By 11 p.m., the Assembly had unanimously endorsed the rejection of King Prajadhipok's demands, effectively closing the book on the Seventh Reign.

March to authoritarianism

Some two and a half months before his abdication, King Prajadhipok (1935 [20 December 1934]: 105) had issued a stern warning to Phraya Phahon's government. 'There are those who still believe in the absolute monarchy because of its long history', he wrote, 'but nobody will stand for the absolute rule of the *khana*.' In truth, the People's Party never came close to exercising 'absolute rule'. Nonetheless, the King had correctly diagnosed in its lack of legitimacy the new regime's Achilles' heel – something that Prajadhipok himself had done much to aggravate and expose. All indications are that government officials were well aware of the problems posed by their lack of legitimacy and were quite nervous about the regime's reliance on performance for legitimation. Their defensiveness on this subject was on full display in speeches that leading Promoters gave on the occasion of the 2-year anniversary of the People's Party's seizure of power. In response to criticism that the government had not done enough to improve the economic situation, Phibun used his radio broadcast to blast the monarchy, arguing that the constitutional regime had produced in 2 years 'more benefits than the governments of the former century and half' – a reference to the fact that the dynasty was exactly 150 years old at the time the absolutist regime was toppled in 1932. Aside from blaming 'the negligence displayed in the last one hundred and fifty years' for the depths of the economic problems the country faced, Phibun chastised royalists for preventing the government from fully dedicating itself to addressing these challenges (see *Bangkok Times Weekly Mail*, 30 June 1934). More measured in his tone, Pridi replied to those 'who are given to criticize the government by saying that it has done nothing more than promulgating laws' with the cliché that 'Rome was not built in a day'. He went on to offer a discussion of improvements made, mostly through legislation, in the administration, the protection of internal order, the economy, the government's financial position, and education (see *Bangkok Times Weekly Mail*, 6–7 July 1934).

By then, the Promoters had been attempting to entrench the constitution as the source of the new regime's legitimacy, unveiling a series of initiatives designed to instil reverence for the constitution and identify the government with its protection. An Association of the Constitution Party (*Samakhom Khana Ratthathammanun*), led by Pridi, was established in December 1933 and began opening branches throughout the country, often placed under the control of local government officials (see Murashima 1991: 27). A year later, Phraya Phahon's Constitution Day address explained that 'Constitution' had been added to 'the principles of Nation, Religion, King' to mark the fact that the people now had a role in the country's administration, without distinction of class or birth. The Prime Minister feigned 'delight' at the realization that 'the people of Siam' now held the constitution to be 'sacred' and predicted that its prestige 'will keep the Kingdom one and indivisible'. On the same occasion, Pridi waxed mystical again by speaking of the constitution as 'the highest form of *dharma*', such that 'those who adhere to the constitution find that they have derived contentment of heart' (*Bangkok Times Weekly Mail*, 15 December 1934).

The government's own actions, however, undermined the ongoing efforts to turn the constitution into a reliable source of legitimacy. On the one hand, for reasons of pure convenience, the government remained determined to whitewash King Prajadhipok's and Phraya Mano's suspension of the constitution in 1933, and eventually defeated a legislative effort to strike down all laws promulgated after the Assembly had been illegally prorogued (see *Bangkok Times Weekly Mail*, 25 January 1935). That its unlawful suspension could be swept under the rug in the name of expediency belied the notion that the constitution was in any way 'sacred'. On the other hand, the more authoritarian measures taken by the government in the name of protecting the constitution, and the routine attempt to portray its opponents as enemies of the constitution, cheapened the document as a mere instrument of politics. In fact, insofar as 'protecting the constitution' came to be seen as an excuse for betraying their own principles, the Promoters drew little benefit from their efforts to play up the 'sacredness' of the document. In the long run worse still, the People's Party's insistence on arrogating the role of sole protectors of the constitution and sole legitimate representatives of 'the people' effectively prevented Siam's constitutional regime from establishing a basis of legitimacy independent of the government that happened to be in power at the time. Barmé (1993: 113) also makes the crucial point that the government's attempt to sacralize the constitution through rituals and slogans inherited from the absolutist regime 'had compromised its stated democratic ideals by having the constitution absorbed into a conservative, elite discourse'.

The defeat of the royalist counter-revolution presented Phraya Phahon's government with a window of opportunity to place the process of democratization back on track. In December 1933, the first partially elected Assembly was sworn in, officially opening the second phase of the planned democratic transition. The Assembly was composed of seventy-eight appointed 'second-category' members and an equal number of 'first-category' members selected on a provincial basis by sub-district (*tambon*) representatives elected by the people. While Phraya Phahon's tenure coincided with the emergence of a vigorous opposition in the Assembly, however, the Promoters missed the opportunity to revive the country's democratization. Aside from the government's continued reliance on censorship, most consequential was its failure to encourage broader participation, which rendered the new regime vulnerable to attempts to subvert it from the inside.

During its first 4-year term, as well as the subsequent legislatures that came into office after elections in 1937 and 1938, the Assembly repeatedly took up the issue of legalizing political parties, a cause spearheaded by a number of its elected members (for an overview, see Murashima 1991: 35–42). The matter was the subject of frequent parliamentary debates, interpellations, and efforts to introduce legislation, while some of the most vocal representatives made repeated attempts to register actual party organizations. The government stonewalled and obstructed each of these efforts, reverting to the position that had once been King Prajadhipok's: namely, that the country was not ready for party competition, because the public did not yet properly understand democracy. The direct elections of 'first-category' members held in 1937 and 1938, therefore, consisted entirely of races between unaffiliated candidates.

Murashima (1991: 52) attributes the government's posture to the People's Party's cliquish nature and authoritarian designs. In his view, the Promoters' repeated statements of their intent to 'further democracy' were a mere stratagem to consolidate authoritarian rule without alienating elected members of parliament, on whose support the government depended for its veneer of democratic legitimacy. The eventual extension of the interim constitutional provisions that the government was able to secure in 1940, prolonging the period of 'tutelary democracy' by another 10 years, is cited as evidence that the People's Party had only intended to use weak representative institutions as a smokescreen. Murashima (1991: 52) goes on to suggest that, while the government had invoked the spectre of the absolute monarchy's return as justification for denying the registration of political parties, and for curtailing rights more generally, the fight was really about an authoritarian regime intent on quashing the royalist opposition's democratic aspirations – in his own words, 'the old elite was carrying on a fight against the clique government of the People's Party and demanding the democratization of Thailand's [sic] political system and the creation of a multiparty system that would truly speak for and benefit the people'.

This interpretation is crude in its formulation and mistaken in its substance. For one thing, although it is certainly the case that the danger posed by royalists was later exaggerated by Phibun to eliminate his political enemies, the threats that royalists continued to pose to the constitutional regime (and key figures thereof) were not imaginary. King Prajadhipok and his allies, having already exploited the Promoters' initial conciliatory stance to try to destroy the People's Party, were later implicated in repeated attempts on Phibun's life, plots to murder Phahon and Pridi, and various conspiracies to overthrow the government. Again, this is not just supported by the findings of Phibun's kangaroo courts, but the admission of the former King's own henchmen (see Nattapoll 2010: 160–1). The Promoters, to be sure, bear a large share of the responsibility for the failure of Siam's democratic revolution. But that in no way warrants Murashima's (1991: 52) claim that royalists were fighting for 'the implementation of a full-blown British style of democracy'. As attested in the voluminous correspondence that King Prajadhipok exchanged with the government in the run-up to his abdication, being relegated to the same position as the British monarch was in fact one of his main frustrations – at one point, the King specifically complained that the government had made him 'take on the same status as the King of England', something he was not prepared to accept (see Prajadhipok 1935 [27 October 1934]: 9–14).

Up to the transmission of the Royal Note dated 20 December 1934, King Prajadhipok had never been on record as supporting 'a real democracy'.[6] Aside from the fact that all previous requests made of the government had dealt exclusively with the monarchy's prestige, wealth, and power – to say nothing of the departure his last set of demands marked from positions articulated in writings spanning the reign's entire duration – even in his late conversion to democracy the King's own words evidenced a clear distaste for 'constitutional monarchy', more so than an abhorrence of 'dictatorship'. While, in particular, one could sympathize with the King's discomfort with a position requiring him 'to take responsibility [for legislation] without having any power' (*rap phit chop doi mai mi amnat loei*), for better or worse, that is precisely what a constitutional

[6] Murashima (1991: 14) cites a speech that King Prajadhipok gave in November 1932 as evidence that, 'since the revolution, the king had become a supporter of democracy and a multi-party political system'. Given that its contents directly contradict statements made by the King in private correspondence before and after the fact, it is rather more plausible that the speech was an exercise in public posturing, of a piece with Prajadhipok's effort to fashion himself as the architect of Siam's democracy.

monarch is expected to do. As for King Prajadhipok's allies, conclusive proof of their utter disinterest in representative democracy came some time later, at the end of World War II, when royalists actually had a chance to implement a British-style parliamentary system under one of the country's most democratic constitutions. What they did instead was enter into an alliance with Phibun and support the restoration of military rule in exchange for Pridi's banishment, the repression (and murder) of Pridi's liberal-progressive followers, and a vastly expanded set of royal prerogatives.

The Promoters' failure to allow the registration of political parties – and, more broadly, the failure to live by their own stated ideals – was not part of a grand plan to establish a one-party dictatorship, but the result of two contingencies produced by the initial struggle against royalist forces. First, even the most democratically inclined among the Promoters proved willing to support undemocratic measures, however temporarily, out of fear of seeing the revolution rolled back. Pridi himself is widely credited for drafting the Act to Protect the Constitution, while his tenure as Minister of the Interior coincided with the use of odious police methods to harass and intimidate the royalist opposition. Still in power but shaken by the counter-revolution, the People's Party could be said to have more generally resolved to manage the conflict instead of broadening it, opting to tighten its control over civil society instead of taking a chance on its mobilization (see Chai-anan 2002: 55). Second, the counter-revolution led to the strengthening, within the People's Party, of the personalities and factions least interested in the establishment of a democratic regime. Indeed, even more devastating to Siam/Thailand's prospects of democratization than the success royalists had in baiting the new government into betraying its principles was the effect that the counter-revolution had on the balance of power within the People's Party – namely, the growing dominance asserted by Phibun's more authoritarian faction, based primarily in the junior military clique, over the more liberal wing led by Pridi, composed for the most part of civilian Promoters.

The rise of Phibun and his clique is rooted in the events of 1933, when junior Promoters in the Army and Navy took the lead in removing Mano from office; Phibun's profile was raised further after he led the counteroffensive against Prince Boworadet's rebels. These incidents marked a shift in the relations of power within the military: aside from the removal of military officers directly associated with the absolutist regime and the royalist rebellion, the junior Promoters who had been sidelined under Mano's tenure gained the upper hand over the People's Party's more conservative senior military clique, led by Phraya Song Suradet, which had been tainted by its role in the Assembly's prorogation and the suspension of key provisions of the constitution. At the same time, the Navy's decision to declare its neutrality during the Boworadet Rebellion tipped the scales within the military in favour of the Army, especially with regard to budgetary priorities. Meanwhile, Pridi's temporary exile, under a cloud of suspicion for alleged communist sympathies, had left the more progressive Promoters exposed to accusations of secretly plotting to establish a communist regime.

Phibun's dominance did not follow immediately from these events. Phraya Song continued to have his supporters among senior military commanders who controlled troops and artillery, while Pridi's return saw him restored to positions of power and prestige. The relative longevity of Phraya Phahon's tenure in office was a reflection of the divisions within the People's Party; Phahon had no independent power base of his own, but he was the only figure with the temperament and stature required to hold the various factions together. The events of 1933, however, did give Phibun an edge over his rivals, which he skilfully built upon to gradually assert his dominance. While Phraya Phahon was nominally in charge of the Army, his responsibilities as Prime Minister meant that the Army's actual leadership was left in the hands of Phibun. Broadly speaking, Phibun exploited his position in two ways. First, he undertook a gradual effort to take control of the organization. While the process was not completed until 1939, when Phibun used the pretext of a rebellion to purge the Army of Phraya Song's supporters, by the 1938 elections he had succeeded in placing his men in most key positions. Second, Phibun used his post as Minister of Defence to exact from the government vast increases in the military's budget, which almost doubled between 1933 and 1938 (see Landon 1939: 54), at the expense of priorities advocated by other cabinet members. Not only did the outsized budgets give rise to a much strengthened military; Phibun also won control over defence allocations in 1936, and therefore near-complete authority to apportion the funds for purposes of patronage, after stripping the Assembly of the right to specify in advance how the money was to be spent (see Stowe 1991: 89).

Several government reshuffles gave the executive an increasingly pronounced military character (see Thompson 1967 [1941]: 91). Military men, moreover, were frequently appointed as second-category members of the Assembly or given posts in the civilian administration, state enterprises, and local government (see Thompson 1967 [1941]: 89; Stowe 1991: 101–2). Phibun also used his powers of patronage to expand his support in the Navy and the civilian bureaucracy, undercutting the power base of potential rivals, and expanded his influence over King Ananda's Regency Council through his friendship with the Senior Regent, Prince Athit Thip-apha. Phibun's ascendance was evidenced by his appointment as Acting Prime Minister during Phraya Phahon's extended sick leaves, as well as his ability to intimidate the Assembly into whitewashing a corruption scandal that implicated many of his associates in the sale of royal land (see Stowe 1991: 96–7). When Siam held regularly scheduled elections in November 1937, Phibun was still not strong enough to take power, leading to Phahon's reappointment. Phibun, however, became Prime Minister following early elections held only a year later, and went on to hold the office until 1944.

Pridi (2000 [1973]: 242) would later claim that Phibun had come into office as a 'democrat', attributing his authoritarian turn to the influence of 'some people', like Luang Wichit Wathakan, 'whose vision was inherited from the age of slavery'. While it is true that the slide into authoritarianism was gradual, and was not completed before the end of 1941, Pridi's account ignores the fact that, by 1938, the writing had been on the wall for some time. On different occasions during Phraya Phahon's premiership, Phibun had raised eyebrows with public statements that prefigured his intentions. In 1934, he claimed that the military was more important to the country's prosperity and survival than both its dynastic and representative institutions (see Stowe 1991: 84). In 1936, he openly called for dictatorship, claiming that the licentious creed of democracy would lead the country to disaster (see *Bangkok Times Weekly Mail*, 16 June 1936).[7] Phibun, moreover, had dabbled in Luang Wichit's aggressive brand of nationalism long before he became Prime Minister and had experimented with initiatives to militarize society as early as 1935, when he founded the youth movement/militia Yuwachon (see Landon 1939: 56–67). That he would exhibit dictatorial ambitions upon coming to power, then, was no surprise to anyone. Indeed, the support that Phibun enjoyed beyond the circle of officials under his patronage was rooted precisely in the promise he held as a strong leader vaguely in the mould of Hitler and Mussolini (see Crosby 1945: 89; Charnvit 2008: 189).

As it turns out, Pridi himself was the main obstacle left in Phibun's way. As Stowe (1991: 93) has put it, by 1936 'the impression of Pridi as a wild revolutionary was fading as he was coming to be regarded as one of the more moderate and stabilizing influences in the cabinet as well as a staunch upholder of democratic values in the face of Phibun's evident dictatorial ambitions'. Although still the subject of rumour and innuendo, Pridi remained a force to be reckoned with, especially given his energetic performance as Minister of the Interior (1933–5) and Minister of Foreign Affairs (1936–7). Pridi, moreover, enjoyed a degree of support among educated people in the capital, not to mention that he retained

7 He reversed himself a few weeks later, when he expressed support for 'true freedom' and democracy (see *Bangkok Times Weekly Mail*, 25 June 1936).

a considerable personal following among the elected members of the Assembly who had emerged as the main check on Phraya Phahon's government – forcing the Prime Minister's resignations on three occasions over five years. A legislator at the centre of all major initiatives aiming to register political parties, Ubon Ratchathani's Thong-in Phuriphat, was among Pridi's main allies in the legislature (see Keyes 1967: 26), as were the progressive members of parliament most determined to further the country's democratization. Unlike Murashima (1991), these men had seen through King Prajadhipok's late conversion to democracy; in the secret deliberations held by the Assembly to consider his demands, 1 month before his abdication, elected representatives excoriated the King over his repeated attempts to overstep the bounds of his constitutional authority (see Assembly of the People's Representatives 1935: 230–347).

One could speculate that the selectiveness of Pridi's memory stemmed from the fact that he had been very publicly supportive of Phibun during the first 3 years of his government. Privately, however, the relationship had been straining, both as a result of specific policies Phibun had pursued upon coming to power – the royalist purge in 1939, the embracement of irredentism in 1940, and the dealings with the Japanese in 1941 – as well as the obvious attempt made by Phibun to gradually curb Pridi's own power. Indeed, while different interpretations have been offered for the role that Pridi played early on in support of Phibun's rule,[8] it is misleading to say that there was any such thing as a 'Phibun/Pridi-led faction' (Murashima 1991: 44). There were in fact two different factions, which did make common cause against the royalist opposition, but were otherwise very much in competition with one another over matters of both interest and vision.

Pridi and his followers were not immediately excluded from the government upon Phibun's rise to Prime Minister in 1938. On the contrary,

[8] Writers like Kobkua (1995), for instance, present Pridi as jointly responsible for some of the excesses of Phibun's government – including the 1939 purge of royalists, which is described as fitting both men's desire to eliminate their political rivals. Among other things, Kobkua (1995: 16) points to the unanimity with which the cabinet reached its decision to deny the men sentenced to death any leniency. Two key facts, however, are glossed over in this account. The first is that Pridi resigned from the Ministry of Finance in the wake of the executions, in January 1940; Phibun rejected his resignation. The second is that Pridi and his supporters by then understood the risks of going against Phibun's wishes. The risks were especially acute in light of the allegations that had been levelled years earlier against Pridi; hence the reticence to oppose Phibun in both the cabinet and the Assembly (see Stowe 1991: 135). Much the same could be said with regard to the irredentist campaign, which, while very popular in the Assembly (even among some of his own supporters), Pridi had opposed. Pridi, in this sense, may be faulted for not taking a stronger public stand against Phibun's policies, but it is a stretch to argue that he was equally responsible for their implementation.

Pridi was appointed Minister of Finance and was given a mandate to reform the country's financial administration. Simultaneously, however, Phibun manoeuvred Pridi out of a position in which he could serve as a serious challenger. The Prime Minister concentrated power into his own hands – aside from taking the position of Commander-in-Chief of the Army, he took over the Ministries of the Interior, Defence, and Foreign Affairs. With his principal rivals, he took a carrot and stick approach. On the one hand, he appointed a number of 'liberals' among Pridi's supporters to the cabinet, seeking to bind them more closely to himself. On the other hand, he made an example of the soldiers, noblemen, publishers, and members of parliament caught up in the dragnet of the phantom Song Suradet rebellion, effectively cowing the press and the Assembly into submission. As Crosby (1945: 88) described it, progressive legislators and ministers 'were given clearly to understand that, politically, it was as much as their lives were worth to oppose the Prime Minister upon any issue on which he had set his heart'. Pridi's role became increasingly marginal, until he was dropped from the cabinet and kicked upstairs to the Regency Council in the aftermath of the Japanese invasion in December 1941.

Original sin

The terse statement with which King Prajadhipok abdicated his throne is by far the best-known and most widely read political document from the early years of the country's post-absolutist history. The statement reads in part:

> I feel that the government and its party employ methods of administration incompatible with individual freedoms and the principles of justice. I am unable to agree to any person or any party carrying on such a government in my name.
>
> I am willing to surrender the powers I formerly exercised to the people as a whole, but I am not willing to turn them over to any individual or any group to use in an autocratic manner without heeding the voice of the people.

Having couched the decision to abdicate in the rhetoric of freedom and democracy, King Prajadhipok's statement has been central to the decades-old quest by royalists to credit the country's shift towards constitutionalism and 'democracy' to the House of Chakri. In the mythology propounded by the state since at least the 1970s, Prajadhipok is immortalized as the King who gave the Thai people democracy and stood up for his democratic principles when those to whom he had 'willingly' entrusted the country's administration took advantage of the opportunity to seize power for themselves.

The Promoters helped lay the foundations for what would become the 'legend' of King Prajadhipok (see Ferrara 2012; for its historical genesis, see Somsak 2001: 20–30; Prajak 2013 [2005]: 415–43). Aside from ascribing to the King a crucial (if entirely fictional) role in the transition to constitutional monarchy, thereby allowing King Prajadhipok to claim to have bestowed democracy upon the Siamese people himself, the actions taken by the Promoters before and, especially, *after* King Prajadhipok's abdication are often interpreted as vindication for both the sincerity of the King's commitment to democracy as well as his assessment of the Promoters as incipient autocrats. By the onset of World War II, the country had completed its reversal into *de facto* military dictatorship and had seen the emergence of a virulent form of nationalism that emphasized social conformity and 'state identity' over constitutionalism (see Chai-anan 2002: 58). Thailand's new self-styled 'leader' (*phu nam*), for his part, made no bones about his admiration for the fascist regimes of Italy, Germany, and Japan (see Reynolds 2004a).

In the end, the People's Party did not just fail to carry out a democratic revolution – objectively an arduous undertaking in that time and place. Through their own actions, the Promoters in fact made it more difficult for *future* constitutional, democratic regimes to take hold. By the late 1930s, just as the Promoters appeared to have vanquished the royalist opposition, the ideas of constitutionalism and democracy that had swept them into power were well on their way to being emptied out of their meaning. What is worse, the People's Party's failure to mobilize mass support through popular nationalist appeals was compounded by Phibun's subsequent revitalization of the official nationalism that had been formulated in defence of royal absolutism. This improbable turn of events not only created the opening that royalists would later exploit in their resurgence after World War II, but also offered just the rationale for presenting the subsequent revival of the monarchy's political role as central to establishing a superior form of 'democracy' – one entirely devoid of the characteristics of an actual democracy, but nonetheless purportedly more ideally suited to the country's unique circumstances, traditions, and national identity. Eighty years on and counting, Thailand still bears the burden of the Promoters' failure, the ancestral sin of its inveterately half-fledged democracy.

4 The age of betrayal

The rise of Colonel Luang Phibun Songkhram illustrates what is perhaps the simplest and most intuitive causal mechanism driven by 'increasing returns' – the idea that 'power begets power'. After the coup of 20 June 1933, Phibun emerged from a highly fluid situation with an edge over potential competitors. He then skilfully used what power accrued from the initial advantage he enjoyed over his rivals to concentrate more and more power into his own hands. Upon becoming Prime Minister in December 1938, Phibun acted quickly to consolidate his position. Within 2 months, the police had arrested dozens of people involved in an alleged conspiracy to overthrow the government and, it was alleged, restore the absolute monarchy. Among them were not only Phraya Song Suradet's allies in the military, but also prominent royalists including senior members of the royal family. Eighteen of the fifty-one people tried before the Special Court were executed by the end of 1939, while twenty-five others were sentenced to life in prison, together with an additional three whose death sentences had been commuted. The purge had an immediate chilling effect on both the press and the Assembly, whose members now realized that opposing Phibun meant inviting charges of sedition. From that point on, whenever the Assembly took up issues where Phibun's position had been clearly spelled out, it became common for the most outspoken representatives to voice their objections in the debate phase, only to then join the majority vote in favour of the government's position.

Aside from neutralizing, purging, and intimidating his enemies, Phibun lavished perquisites and glory on the constituency from which he drew his power – the military. Members of Phibun's military clique were given cabinet seats and resources in abundance. On a more symbolic level, Phibun sought to make the military the central institution in the life of the country. The grand celebrations organized by the government on 24 June 1939 – the first time the date was observed as National Day – were choreographed to cast the military as the guarantor of the constitutional regime and its institutions. While the event was made to coincide with the opening of a new session of parliament and the laying of the first stone for the planned Democracy Monument, the proceedings were dominated by displays of military might. Over time, however, even the military would find itself increasingly overshadowed by Phibun's cult of personality, which extolled his virtues as a cross between a modern strongman and a Buddhist *dhammaraja*, presenting the Prime Minister as the principal agent of the country's progress and chief defender of its proud traditions.

Phibun was the beneficiary of 'increasing returns to power' – as Thelen (2004: 289) describes the concept, 'situations in which victors at one stage impose institutional solutions that reflect and entrench their interests, thus biasing outcomes in the next round'. It would be too simplistic, however, to claim that the new equilibrium was so entrenched that only the 'exogenous shock' brought about by World War II could break Phibun's dominance. It is certainly the case that Phibun's removal from office in 1944 was precipitated by the reversal of fortunes in the Japanese war effort, and the emboldening of the resistance led by Pridi Banomyong. At the same time, the instability of Phibun's rule had deeper roots in the failure to provide his personal authority with a more solid basis of legitimacy. Even as Phibun's *power* was increasing, his *authority* had continued to lag some distance behind. Aided by the unpopularity of the Japanese occupation, Phibun's enemies succeeded in exploiting his regime's structural weaknesses, aggravated by the unintended consequences of measures that Phibun had taken to fix or mask such flaws. If 1942 was the high-water mark of Phibun's power and popularity, it was not long thereafter that the tide began to turn.

The ease with which Phibun had been able to turn himself into a *de facto* military dictator was owed to the constitutional regime's lack of legitimacy and popular support, which placed few costs on his departure from the ideals of the revolution. Recognizing the dubious value of the constitution as a source of legitimacy, Phibun relied on his chief ideologue, Luang Wichit Wathakan, to provide his personal rule with new ideological foundations. Ironically, it is to King Vajiravudh's 'official nationalism' that Phibun and Wichit turned for inspiration. But if the government's propaganda effort, which availed itself of a nascent broadcast media, awakened an unprecedented sense of national community and patriotic zeal among the (urban) population, Phibun's own cult of personality was much less successful in establishing Phibun as the embodiment of the nation, and more generally in forging a lasting emotional bond between the people and their self-appointed 'leader'. In turn, continued dependency on patronage for the support of the bureaucratic apparatus left Phibun vulnerable, particularly once the resources at his disposal began to dry up.

This chapter provides an account of the regime instability that Siam/Thailand exhibited until Phibun's eventual departure from the scene in 1957. Phibun's first fall in 1944, orchestrated by an alliance of royalists and liberals, could be said to have opened another 'critical juncture', in which the country had a realistic chance of consolidating a democratic regime. The three-cornered factional fight that broke out in the aftermath of World War II between royalists, liberals, and the military, however, not only resulted in the collapse of the country's fledgling democracy, but also ushered in fragile and shifting new alignments, whose frequent undoing prevented the consolidation of *any* of the regime forms with which the country experimented during that time. The cycle of instability was only put to an end by the coups staged by Field Marshal Sarit Thanarat in 1957 and 1958, which reconciled royalists and the military in an alliance founded on the wholesale rejection of the liberal ideals that had inspired the 1932 revolution, providing a new rationale for military rule in the protection of the monarchy and a reactionary idea of the nation. The state-sanctioned nationalist ideology that took shape thereafter owed much to Phibun's rediscovery and re-elaboration of King Vajiravudh's official nationalism.

The roots of instability

Perhaps more than anyone else's, it is the work of Luang Wichit Wathakan that accounts for the continuity in the conceptions of 'Thai-ness' articulated under the absolute monarchy, under Phibun, and under Sarit/Bhumibol. Together with the writings of Prince Damrong, Luang Wichit's historical works, penned before and after 1932, have shaped the official version of the country's history. As a cabinet member and Director of the Fine Arts Department in the late 1930s and early 1940s, Luang Wichit was responsible for crafting the ideology with which Phibun had sought to legitimize his rule. He subsequently proved quite eager to tweak key tenets of that ideology to provide new intellectual foundations for the palace–military alliance that supported the regime of Field Marshal Sarit, whom he served as a key advisor until his death in 1962. For better or for worse, Luang Wichit's ideas remain central to Thailand's state-enforced national identity.

Aside from being somewhat overly dramatic, Pridi Banomyong's characterization of Luang Wichit as a man whose world view was 'inherited from the age of slavery' is not entirely accurate. For while Wichit was steeped in the ideas articulated in defence of the absolute monarchy, he was also influenced by the modern ideology of European fascism. The new official nationalism crafted in support of Phibun's regime combined elements of the two. From fascism, Wichit borrowed not only an authoritarian, militaristic approach to national identity – taking themes that had already figured in King Vajiravudh's ideas to more extreme levels – but also a decisively more 'statist' and more 'populist' idea of the nation, one that placed far greater emphasis on the role of the masses in supporting the state, and in turn conceived of the state as much more than its dynastic institutions. Indeed, just as Mussolini – a republican early on in his career – ultimately concluded that fascism was not incompatible with monarchism, the reason why Luang Wichit found it relatively easy to switch between royalist and anti-royalist positions is that the role of monarchy was not central, either way, to the nation as he had conceived it.

Luang Wichit's work had echoed King Vajiravudh's ideas even before Phibun became the Prime Minister. Works of history written since the mid 1920s had sought to present the Thai nation (*chat thai*) as a timeless construct defined largely in racial terms. Wichit not only sought to provide a comparative account of the history of the Thai nation alongside the world's other 'great races', but also imbued such history with a fantastic narrative that emphasized the nation's centuries-old struggle for independence and sovereignty over a territory that matched its purported expanse (see, for instance, Barmé 1993: 49–50). Historical plays authored in the mid 1930s resembled Vajiravudh's for their anachronistic style and emphasis on themes such as the Thai people's fighting spirit, their willingness to sacrifice for the nation, and their unity behind (invariably pre-Chakri) great leaders (see Charnvit 2008: 213–19). Although himself a descendant of assimilated Chinese, moreover, Luang Wichit doubled down on King Vajiravudh's disparagement of his co-ethnics. In a famous speech given in July 1938, he argued that the Chinese were in fact 'worse than the Jews' and intimated that measures should be taken to deal with the problem they posed, just as the Nazis were doing at the time.

Key tenets of King Vajiravudh's official nationalism served Phibun's purposes well. Perhaps most seductive was Vajiravudh's identification of the nation with a single leader, behind whose rule every member of society was required to unite for the good of the nation as a whole. Casting himself as just such a leader, however, presented some challenges for Phibun. First, Vajiravudh's ideas had not been particularly effective in bolstering the absolute monarchy's position, as the 1932 revolution itself underscored. Second, whereas Vajiravudh was able to ground his claims in traditional conceptions of Buddhist kingship, Phibun himself was no king, but a commoner of decidedly humble origins. Finally, there was the issue of the constitutional regime, which could not have been abandoned completely given the emphasis that the People's Party had placed on its accomplishments and defence.

Elements of the model set by European fascist regimes, founded in part on the glorification of the power and will of their leaders, were appropriated in the effort to overcome these challenges (for instance, see Reynolds 2004a). Following on their example, Phibun and Wichit resolved to appeal to the masses – particularly those groups that had previously been most supportive of the ideas of constitutionalism and democracy. Phibun's ambition to use the state to enforce social conformity among the masses and maximize the nation's cohesiveness behind a leader presented as its sole true conscience and embodiment was without precedent in the history of Siam. Phibun and Wichit also did not neglect to provide, as Mussolini had done, the modern leadership cult with 'cultural' foundations, presenting the Prime Minister as a modern-day Sukhothai king charged with defending the country's traditions. Phibun, in particular, took to emphasizing Buddhism as central to 'the prosperity, strength, and well-being of the nation' (Kobkua 1995: 130), taking on the role of the faith's main patron (see Handley 2006: 61–2) and once again restructuring the religious hierarchy to match the structure of the new regime (see Tambiah 1976: 241–52). As for democracy, the concept now stood for little more than a system of government dominated by the military behind the fig leaf of a constitution and a weak legislature.

Phibun's cult of personality took shape gradually, and only assumed cartoonish proportions in the last 3 years of his first tenure as Prime Minister. But the work of casting Phibun in the role of the nation's supreme leader, giving him functions once reserved for kings, had started almost immediately. On 24 June 1939, the government issued the first of twelve proclamations it called *Ratthaniyom*, an expression generally translated as 'State Conventions' or 'Cultural Mandates'. On that occasion, Phibun and Wichit explained that the point of the proclamations was to teach the population proper etiquette, such that 'the Thai people be made truly Thai' (see Barmé 1993: 144–7). Significantly, Wichit argued that, whereas Siamese kings had previously given their opinions in *Ratchaniyom*, *Ratthaniyom* were expressions of 'public opinion'. While he explained how this could possibly be the case by claiming that the Prime Minister was the expression of the Assembly, which was in turn (partly) elected by the people, the implication was that the will of the leader by definition embodied the will of the nation – a concept that King Vajiravudh had previously sought to convey in presenting himself as a national monarch. Phibun himself claimed that the leader (*phu nam*) deserved to be followed because of the 'good deeds he has performed' and the need to show the world that 'we, the whole nation, can act as one person' (cited in Kobkua 1995: 83). Even the metaphor Luang Wichit invoked to illustrate the point harked back to Vajiravudh. Wichit equated Phibun to the captain of a ship to whom, for the good of the entire nation, every citizen owed unquestioned loyalty and obedience (see Barmé 1993: 146). The difference is that this time the ship was actually going somewhere, to an island of happiness surrounded by treacherous seas, as opposed to merely staying afloat – perhaps a sign of the more ambitious, messianic nature of state nationalism's latest iteration.

While the State Conventions issued between 1939 and 1941 revived many of the themes that had appeared in King Vajiravudh's speeches and writings, their content and the manner of their enforcement reveal just how much farther Phibun and Wichit were willing to go, as Kobkua (1995: 103) has put it, to 'transform' the collective 'mind of the society' and exact conformity in the actual practice of the state's version of Thainess. Phibun was not the first to believe social conformity to be a good thing, or to conceive of citizenship primarily in terms of duties, as opposed to rights. Phibun, however, actually expected the people to do as they were told, on penalty of social ostracism, imprisonment, or monetary fine.

The first State Convention, issued on the new National Day in 1939, provided that the country be known as *Prathet Thai* domestically and Thailand internationally. Months later, the National Assembly approved an amendment to the constitution giving the name change the force of law. Far from being a formality or mere acknowledgement of local usages, the abandonment of Siam marked important departures from previous understandings of the nation. First, while King Vajiravudh's definition of who should be considered (and consider him/herself) Thai excluded prominent ethnic minorities such as Malay Muslims, who could nonetheless be citizens of 'Siam', Wichit and Phibun were intent on denying all minorities living within the country's borders a separate identity of any kind. The position was reaffirmed in the third State Convention, which instructed the people that no distinction should be drawn between 'Northern Thai', 'Isan Thai', 'Southern Thai', and 'Muslim Thai', and that everyone should simply be known as *chao thai*. The Convention did not even acknowledge the possibility that such peoples might identify as Lao, Shan, or Malay – words the government sought to expunge from both the official and unofficial lexicon (see Barmé 1993: 151). Second, while the attempt made in the Fifth and Sixth Reigns to de-emphasize terms for 'Lao' and 'Shan' was essentially a defensive measure taken in the hope that members of those communities already inside the country would eventually come to identify as Thai, Luang Wichit was the main purveyor of the notion that Bangkok should take it upon itself to unify all the 'Thai' peoples by reclaiming all 'Thai' lands from neighbouring countries.

Just how expansive Luang Wichit believed the Thai nation to be was demonstrated in a radio broadcast in May 1939, in which he explained the rationale for changing the country's name (see *Bangkok Times Weekly Mail*, 29 May 1939). Wichit made the case that the Thai nation comprised not just the 13 million people living in Siam at the time, but up to 20 million living in various Chinese provinces, some 4 million living under French and British rule – not including the Khmer, said to now be almost 100 per cent Thai – as well as an additional 26 million scattered about the region. Luang Wichit claimed that each of these 63 million people already identified as Thai. Adopting 'Land of the Thai' as the moniker for the country would therefore signal to the 'Thai' living outside its borders that the country represented the foundation for a 'Great(er) Thai Kingdom'. In keeping with the racialist thought of King Vajiravudh, however, such peoples were not to be included in the new polity as equals. Elsewhere, Wichit made the point that among the 'Thai brothers' on the 'Golden Peninsula', the Thai-Siam would play the role of 'elder brothers', while the Khmer (and presumably others) would be relegated to the status of 'younger brothers' (cited in Barmé 1993: 125).

While the irredentist fervour that inflamed the country between 1939 and 1941 was perhaps the most useful device by which the government aroused a sense of national pride and public support, on this count Phibun found himself outmanoeuvred by those, like Luang Wichit, who wanted the rhetoric backed up by action. Irredentist ambitions, particularly at the expense of French Indochina, achieved great popularity with the general (middle-class) public, the press, the military, and the Assembly. As the news articles, radio broadcasts, and street demonstrations calling for war intensified – particularly in the wake of France's fall to the Nazis – Phibun was reportedly led to fear that inaction might result in his removal at the hands of more hardline officers (see Stowe 1991: 150–1). After unsuccessful attempts were made to press the issue through diplomatic channels, Phibun fully embraced the irredentist cause in a radio broadcast in October 1940, when he announced preparations for war and referred to the people of Laos and Cambodia as 'our Thai brethren' (see *Bangkok Times Weekly Mail*, 21 October 1940). Hostilities along the border with French Indochina broke out soon thereafter; they came to an end months later, when the Japanese imposed a settlement that gave Thailand parts of western Cambodia and territories in French Laos west of the Mekong River, opposite Luang Prabang and Pakse. As it became clear that Thailand would earn from the negotiations only a slice of its touted 'lost territories', the government banned irredentist demonstrations, arguing that they had now exceeded 'appropriate limits' (*Bangkok Times Weekly Mail*, 3 February 1941).

The State Conventions also sought to define what made a good citizen. Aside from instilling respect for national symbols such as the flag, the national anthem, and the royal anthem, State Conventions prescribed that it was the duty of all to protect the nation and consider the national interest before taking actions of any kind. After listing some activities construed as betrayals of the nation, State Convention No. 2 (3 July 1939) explicitly made it the duty of every individual to actively intervene to stop any such conduct – Luang Wichit was reportedly in favour of the idea that the people should enforce this command through public lynchings (see Stowe 1991: 124). It bears noting that the national interest citizens were asked to uphold was not open to individual interpretation. As Phibun made clear in a speech given on 31 March 1940 (see *Bangkok Times Weekly Mail*, 2 April 1940), the government reserved the right to define who and what was responsible for 'damaging the nation'. This idea had also figured in King Vajiravudh's speeches, but Phibun added teeth. While Vajiravudh had shown a degree of tolerance and mercy for those he thought were damaging the nation, Phibun's statement that the 'noisy work' of building the nation required that dissidents be removed from its premises, as one would with children crying during a religious sermon, was no idle threat. The eighteen men who had faced Phibun's firing squad months earlier had experienced first-hand just what the Prime Minister meant.

Most far-reaching, and ultimately most unpopular (see Charnvit 2008: 219), was the attempt made through the State Conventions to regulate the Thai people's private lives. Citizens were not just encouraged to eat Thai foods, wear Thai clothes, and buy Thai products (State Convention No. 5, 1 November 1939), or warned that only by having a real profession could they earn society's respect (State Convention No. 7, 21 March 1940), or urged to learn how to read, write, and speak proper Thai (State Convention No. 9, 24 June 1940). The *Ratthaniyom* went to extraordinary lengths to prescribe dress attire (State Convention No. 10, 15 January 1941), regulate daily activities including meals, sleep, leisure, and bathing (State Convention No. 11, 8 September 1941), and advise everyone to protect children, older people, and people with disabilities (State Convention No. 12, 28 January 1942). Meanwhile, the government's propaganda machine – perhaps above all the inane radio dialogues between fictional characters Man Chuchat and Khong Rakthai (for a selection from 1941–2, see Thak 1978: 260–316) – harped on endlessly about the need for people to 'follow the state', especially in matters of dress and personal behaviour, identifying obedience as a sign of 'civilization'.[1]

In and of itself, the idea that citizens should be led by the state to embrace 'civilized' or 'cultured' customs – be they indigenous or foreign – was nothing new. Nationalists of both the 'popular' and 'official' variety had put forth proposals along these lines since the days of Thianwan and Chulalongkorn. What was new about Phibun's approach was not only the amount of energy and resources the government put into the effort to 'encourage' certain practices, but also the attempt to give them the force of law. While State Conventions were not binding, the 1940 National Culture Act (reprinted in Thak 1978: 255–6) provided an enforcement mechanism, contemplating fines for those who failed to practise proper customs, conduct, and the 'promotion of Thai nationalism'. A subsequent 'Royal Decree Prescribing Customs for the Thai People' (reprinted in Thak 1978: 257–8) added yet more detail to the proper behaviour and attire required or permitted in different circumstances. An Employment Act passed in September 1941, meanwhile, made it compulsory for able-bodied men of legal age (under 55) to be gainfully employed (see *Bangkok Times Weekly Mail*, 12 and 17 September 1941). Most odiously, the government imposed the requirement that all Thais must embrace Buddhism; those who refused to convert were subjected to discrimination in official employment (see Kobkua 1995: 130).

Perhaps the most distinctive aspect of the official nationalist ideology that took shape under Phibun, compared with the more royalist versions that preceded it and followed it, was its emphasis on egalitarian as opposed to hierarchical conceptions of the nation. Under Phibun's leadership, the idea of individual equality articulated by the People's Party in 1932 became a defining feature of the 'new political culture' (*watthanatham thang kan mueang mai*) the government sought to foster through its policies (see Charnvit 2008: 195). Among other things, Phibun set out to abolish officially recognized inequalities and banned some of the symbols of traditional social hierarchies, including titles of minor nobility and the ornate language *rachasap* used to address members of the royal family. The attempt to dismantle the hold that the Chinese community exercised on the economy (see Charnvit 2008: 225–34) was also justified, in part, on the basis of egalitarian ideals.

Not unlike King Vajiravudh before him, Phibun would benefit from the ideas crafted in support of his rule far less than his successors. In

[1] The first names of the fictional characters make up the word for 'security' (*mankhong*). Their last names mean 'uphold the nation' (*chu chat*) and 'love Thai(land)' (*rak thai*).

the short term, to be sure, Phibun's popularity received a boost from the nationalist propaganda his government churned out. While the success of the effort was limited to constituencies the government could reach on a sustained basis, primarily through its radio broadcasts (see Charnvit 2008: 212), at least in the capital city the administration's aggressive, chauvinistic rhetoric resonated with the public – in fact, so much so as to leave Phibun somewhat vulnerable to being outflanked on his right. But although this period was crucial insofar as it was the first in which a sense of national identity came to be deeply felt by a broad cross-section of the Thai public, and insofar as the content of that national identity had enduring features that form the basis of Thailand's official nationalism as it exists today, all that did not suffice to make Phibun's nationalism the basis of a stable regime – not during his first term as Prime Minister (1938–44), and certainly not after he came back from the wilderness in 1947.

Phibun's attempt to build what Chai-anan (2002: 51) has called 'a more modern variant of absolutism' did not encounter a great deal of public opposition, at least initially. For a time, the opposition to Phibun's government – whether in the press, civil society, or the Assembly – had been successfully intimidated, co-opted, or swept up in the irredentist propaganda. Still, the fact that Thailand under Phibun remained 'suspended between royalist absolutism and popular nationalism' did leave the regime, as Anderson (1978: 226) puts it, without any 'real foundation of or criteria for internal or external legitimation'. On the one hand, claims that grounded the regime's legitimacy in the idea of popular sovereignty grew increasingly threadbare as Phibun's government became more authoritarian. On the other hand, the continued promotion of egalitarian ideals – eschewing organic, hierarchical conceptions of society – undermined Phibun's self-appointed status as the nation's 'leader', depriving the regime of a rationale for why, as Mussolini (2001 [1932]: 86) proposed, the will of an entire people finds its truest expression in 'the conscience and will of a few, if not, indeed, of One'.

In that context, Phibun's decision to turn up the volume on his leadership cult – something that has been described as 'an ill-fated move to replace the monarchy as the central official symbol' (Barmé 1993: 170) – was of little to no avail. Once again, it was not entirely the case that the country was either so habituated or emotionally attached to the monarchy that it could not tolerate its replacement with an alternative object of national veneration – although royalists certainly resented Phibun for trying. Nor was it entirely the case that, having stripped the monarchy of its power, seized much of its property, and humiliated the institution by touting the Special Court's scandalous findings, Phibun could not convince the public to accept the replacement of one form of spiritualized personal authority with another – although liberals might have seen it that way. The problem was rather that Phibun had proven largely incapable of building a durable base of support outside the bureaucracy. Meanwhile, if the members of Phibun's clique *inside* the bureaucracy had every incentive to keep him in power so long as their personal association with 'the leader' boosted their status, power, and wealth, they had been given no reason to do so beyond the benefits the Prime Minister could provide to reward their compliance, or conversely the costs he could impose on disloyalty. Ultimately, even the generals would conclude that the monarchy's revival, accompanied by the rediscovery of ideas conceiving of the nation in hierarchical as opposed to egalitarian terms, provided more solid foundations for military rule.

Occupation and resistance

The political career of Field Marshal Plaek Phibun Songkhram reached a turning point on the afternoon of 8 December 1941. Earlier that day, as the Japanese attacked Pearl Harbor, warships had dropped tens of thousands of Japanese troops in various locations along Thailand's gulf coast, from which they proceeded to execute the country's invasion. Late in the evening of 7 December, Japanese diplomats had given the government a few hours' advance notice, but in Phibun's absence no decision was made on whether to cooperate or put up a fight. By the time the Prime Minister reached Bangkok at dawn the next day, what window of opportunity might have existed to implement the contingency plans devised months earlier had all but closed.

While the government could hardly have been expected to make a different choice under the circumstances, its decision to grant Japan the requested 'transit rights' – which the Japanese took as a green light to place the country under occupation – generated a great deal of consternation among the general public and political elites. Almost immediately, the ceasefire activated both the liberal and royalist opposition to Phibun's rule, which had been dormant since the Prime Minister made an example of Phraya Song's alleged co-conspirators. As Pridi Banomyong tells the story, when he returned home from the cabinet meeting on the evening of 8 December, friends and supporters were already awaiting him there (see Pridi 2000 [1981]: 197). Together, they resolved to build an underground resistance movement. Abroad, meanwhile, royalists also sprang into action. The head of the Thai legation in Washington, M.R. Seni Pramoj, condemned the government's capitulation and pledged his cooperation with the Allies' war effort (see Reynolds 2004b: 9–14).

In the United Kingdom, where Thai diplomats did not defy Bangkok's orders, the more liberal students were joined by close members of King Prajadhipok's family (the former King had died 6 months earlier) in making similar representations to the British authorities.

The Prime Minister took immediate steps to exploit the occupation to his own advantage. While the cabinet had rejected the possibility of entering into a political and military alliance with the Japanese, Phibun soon began negotiating Thailand's active participation in the war on the side of the Axis powers. After moving pro-Western politicians into positions where they were expected to prove less of an impediment to good relations with the Japanese, as well as his own designs, the Prime Minister secretly pledged his assistance to the invasion of Burma, then proceeded to sign a treaty sanctioning Thailand's alliance with Japan. By the end of January 1942, Thailand had declared war on both the United States and the United Kingdom.

Whether Thailand *chose* to join the war on the side of the Japanese, or was forced to do so, has been debated ever since. Even the Allied powers viewed the matter differently – the United Kingdom took Thailand's enemy status seriously, while the United States clearly did not. Ultimately, Phibun could be said to have made a conscious decision, albeit under circumstances that were decidedly not of his choosing. It was above all what took place on 8 December 1941 that induced Phibun to go all in. The success of the Japanese attack on Pearl Harbor – and conversely the unpreparedness shown by the United States and the United Kingdom – convinced Phibun that, if Japan was going to win the war, jumping on the victor's bandwagon early was in Thailand's national interest as well as his own. The Japanese sweetened the deal by promising to cede to Thailand much of northern Malaya and Burma's Shan State. Aside from the potential that further territorial expansion held to boost Phibun's own strength and popularity, the prospect allowed the alliance with the Japanese to sail through the Assembly. After occupying the whole of Southeast Asia by mid 1942, Japan kept its promise. The eastern Shan State and the Malay regions of Perlis, Kedah, Terengganu, and Kelantan were ceded to Thailand a year later.

On the strength of Japanese backing, a more cohesive cabinet, and rapturous propaganda extolling the great successes that Thailand's Northern Army had achieved in the Shan State, Phibun's cult of personality reached new heights. As Thai citizens were ordered to display Phibun's picture in their homes, government slogans identified the nation's security and survival with the people's unity in 'believing' and 'obeying' the leader. Immediately after the war, Phibun (1978 [1945]: 349) claimed in a letter to newspapers that these slogans were not an instrument of 'dictatorship', but a way to unify the nation behind him in preparation for fighting *against* the Japanese. Whatever the reason, the symbolism glorifying Phibun's personal authority took the place that had previously been reserved for the monarchy, such that when Phibun proposed that a new capital be built in the northern town of Phetchabun some suspected he had dynastic aspirations of his own. Perhaps swept up in his own propaganda, Phibun also pursued his fixation with the Thai people's personal behaviour and attire in a series of eccentric decrees. The chewing of betel was prohibited, and betel trees were ordered to be cut down nationwide. New regulations mandated that men and women wear hats in public, on the conceit that 'Hats Lead a Nation to Power'. Unmarried men were hit with a new tax designed to boost population growth, while married men were instructed to kiss their wives upon leaving home for work. Perhaps strangest of all, given that the country was in the middle of a war, public officials were ordered to attend mandatory practices of traditional dance every Wednesday afternoon.

As the tide of war turned in 1943, Phibun's popularity and power began to decline. Aside from the numbers of people killed or injured in the air raids, the intensification of Allied bombings on Bangkok and its surroundings led to increasingly frequent and long-lasting disruptions in public services, piling serious public health problems on top of the inconvenience experienced by the city's population. Meanwhile, the Japanese occupation had reduced Thailand's economy to a shambles. The disruption in trade that followed the Japanese invasion caused Thailand's revenues to collapse as well as severe shortages in petrol and manufactured goods, including medicine. Just as the Allied powers, moreover, proceeded to freeze Thailand's reserves abroad, the necessity to print massive amounts of money to finance the Japanese war effort led to galloping inflation and an exponential increase in the cost of living. Through it all, the growing detachment from reality exhibited in the Prime Minister's decrees only added to the public's disillusionment. Crucially, the combination of external conditions and internal policy blunders also caused a gradual breakdown in Phibun's executive authority, particularly as the bureaucracy took to ignoring, defying, or dragging its feet on orders to speed up the construction of roads and other infrastructure. Aside from the penury of funds, the fact that construction was carried out by conscript labour that often went unpaid and forced workers to toil in malaria-infested areas, with little in the way of adequate medical care, rendered the situation increasingly unmanageable for the various ministries responsible, while angering members of parliament whose constituencies supplied much of the workforce (see Charnvit 2008: 383–91).

As Phibun's support grew more tenuous, his opposition was correspondingly emboldened. During 1942, the resistance movement at home and abroad – collectively referred to as *Seri Thai* (Free Thai) – had been able to accomplish little. Outside the country, a hundred or so Thai students had been training with Allied forces, but internal rivalries of both a personal and ideological nature, as well as the different designs the United States, the United Kingdom, and China had on Thailand, prevented *Seri Thai* from making efficient use of its limited human resources (see Stowe 1991: 258–77). Initially, moreover, *Seri Thai* abroad was very much in the dark about the existence of a domestic resistance movement. Throughout the first 18 months, all that Pridi could do from his position on the Regency Council was attempt to make contact with Allied forces abroad. Several delegations were sent for that purpose, at great personal risk for those who undertook the missions, to the Kuomintang's capital of Chungking. Equally daring were the Thai students whom Allied forces dropped behind enemy lines by parachute or flying boat beginning in 1943 – operations in which most were injured, many were killed, and none escaped capture – as well as those who volunteered for gruelling treks to infiltrate Thailand via Yunnan.

After many attempts, by mid to late 1943, Pridi's domestic resistance was in almost daily contact with Allied forces in the region. This allowed for much better coordination in the bombing campaign against military targets inside Thailand, which became more effective and precise, and in the efforts made by the Allies to drop military officers, weapons, and medical supplies to help *Seri Thai* develop an effective guerrilla force. Indispensable to the resistance's growing effectiveness was the cooperation of an unlikely figure – Deputy Prime Minister and Police Director-General Adun Detcharat. Once one of Phibun's closest friends and protégés, Adun had initially turned a blind eye to *Seri Thai*'s activities. By mid 1943, his intelligence apparatus kept the resistance informed about the movements of Japanese troops, while his men aided in the recovery and transport of the supplies and personnel smuggled by air into the country. Officially in police custody, the Thai students who had been captured after being dropped inside the country were also allowed to maintain radio communications with the Allies.

The decline of Phibun's power and popularity, coupled with the Japanese's growing mistrust in his leadership, also gave Pridi a chance to pursue more institutional remedies. In August 1943, Pridi was placed under investigation after the Senior Regent, Prince Athit Thip-apha, referred to Phibun the contents of a conversation in which Pridi appears to have quipped that Thailand should be so lucky as to have figures like King Vittorio Emanuele III and Marshal Pietro Badoglio, who had recently removed Mussolini from his post and placed him under arrest. While Pridi was able to reassure investigators by claiming he had been joking, he had set out to do something similar months earlier. Whether or not it was the product of a strategy laid out in advance, for this purpose Pridi engineered what theorists of institutional change have called 'conversion'. He repurposed the institutions of the National Assembly and the monarchy – which had become marginal under Phibun – and carved out a space for both to once again play an important political role.

Mahoney and Thelen (2010: 16) have identified 'conversion' as a type of gradual institutional change involving 'the changed enactment of existing rules due to their strategic redeployment'. The strategic redeployment of institutions is one of the alternatives that those who are penalized by the way existing rules are structured and enforced can use in an attempt to gain the upper hand over those who benefit from the status quo. Conversion, however, is a strategy that is only available under certain circumstances: weak veto possibilities by those who wish to preserve the status quo and a high degree of discretion in the enforcement of the existing rules. Both conditions were present in Thailand at the time. On the one hand, Phibun's veto power had weakened as his popularity declined. On the other hand, a wide gap had opened during the first few years of Phibun's rule between powers that the constitution vested in the Assembly and its actual political role. With regard to the monarchy, moreover, the language in the constitution was ambiguous enough to leave room for interpreting certain powers reserved for the King in a formal sense as real powers that could be exercised independently of the government. Ironically, it was Pridi, the man royalists most hated, who pioneered the revival of the monarchy's power.

The earliest manifestation of Pridi's 'strategic redeployment' of the monarchy was an episode that took place when Phibun suddenly announced his resignation as Prime Minister in February 1943. After unsuccessfully attempting to clarify his intentions, Pridi and Prince Athit – at the time the only two members of the Regency Council – approved the resignation. When Phibun angrily withdrew it and forced the Propaganda Bureau to retract its public announcement, Pridi's supporters in the Navy moved a gunboat up the Chao Phraya River to his palace as a message to the Prime Minister. Days later, Pridi refused to attend a meeting to which Phibun had summoned him to demand an explanation for the Regents' conduct, on the grounds that representatives of the King could not be ordered around by the Prime Minister. The same happened only a month later, when the Regency Council rejected emergency legislation that had been approved by the Assembly, declaring it unconstitutional. In both instances, Phibun backed down.

Similar manoeuvres were taking place in the Assembly. In June 1943, Pridi orchestrated the election of Thawi Bunyaket and Khuang Aphaiwong – both had resigned from the cabinet and joined *Seri Thai* following the incident described earlier – as Speaker and Deputy Speaker of the Assembly. In that case, Phibun was able to thwart their appointment, but not before suffering considerable public embarrassment. Over the following year, Pridi and his allies among elected representatives from the Northeast – chiefly among them the 'Four Isan Tigers' (*Si Suea Isan*) Thong-in Phuriphat, Tiang Sirikhan, Chamlong Daoruang, and Thawin Udon (see Charnvit 2008: 347) – worked to exploit Phibun's growing unpopularity in an effort to restore the legislature as a meaningful check on the government. Tensions came to a head in mid July 1944, when the Assembly took advantage of the absence of around half of the serving members of parliament to defeat bills that would have authorized funding for the construction of the new capital in Phetchabun and a Buddhist city in Saraburi. Ironically, Charnvit (2008: 393) points out that Phibun might never have lost these votes, had a large number of appointed, 'second-category' members of parliament not been tied up working on his boondoggles up-country.[2]

Expecting to be reappointed, Phibun was persuaded to resign. Much to his surprise, however, Pridi pressured the National Assembly to select Khuang Aphaiwong as Prime Minister. At that point, Phibun leaned on his close friend and ally, Prince Athit, to intimidate Khuang into withdrawing and, when that failed, withhold his signature on the decree approving Khuang's appointment. As Prince Athit bought time, Phibun called a meeting of the cabinet but was rebuffed by some of its members, who claimed he no longer had the authority to do so. Caught between not wanting to incur Phibun's wrath and not wanting to cast his entire lot with Phibun, Prince Athit resigned his post, leaving Pridi as sole Regent. On that day, Khuang's appointment as Prime Minister became effective.

While Pridi had successfully engineered *Seri Thai*'s formal takeover of the government, Phibun remained popular in the Army. Considering that the country was still under martial law, moreover, Phibun continued to wield enormous power as Supreme Commander of the Armed Forces. Having retreated to an Army stronghold in Lopburi, he issued decrees undermining the authority of the government, and rallied his supporters in preparation for a possible coup. On 24 August 1944, however, the government issued an order by which it declared Phibun's role as Supreme Commander (*Phu Banchakan Thahan Sung Sut*) unconstitutional,

[2] For a discussion of competing interpretations of these events, see Batson (1974b: 104–7).

arguing that the constitution vested the position of Supreme Commander in the King, and announced that henceforth the armed forces would be led by the new office of Commander-in-Chief (*Mae Thap Yai*), assigned to former Prime Minister Phahon Phonphayuhasena. Given Phahon's stature and popularity, senior Army officers responded when summoned to a meeting by the new Commander-in-Chief, while commanders with responsibility for troops stationed in Bangkok and Thonburi agreed to the request that they only execute orders from him. Faced with defeat, Phibun temporarily retired to his country home outside Bangkok.

Quite aside from Phahon's gravitas, it was self-preservation that induced Phibun's closest associates not to stage a coup on his behalf. Adun, who had earned a fearsome reputation by carrying out Phibun's purges in the late 1930s, warned that anyone who tried to stage a coup would be dealt with harshly. The Navy's conspicuous protection of the government and the Regent also gave Phibun's supporters some doubts about a coup's chances of success (see Charnvit 2008: 398). At any rate, while the government had secured a commitment by the Japanese not to intervene in the leadership transition, it is likely that the Japanese would have disarmed Thailand's military had serious fighting broken out between the Army and Navy. Finally, like everyone else, Phibun's commanders were aware of the warning issued by the Allies that anyone who supported the collaborationist leader would face war crimes charges, such that staging a coup for Phibun could have brought upon its protagonists a great deal of unwanted attention after the war. By then, after all, Phibun's clique included ambitious men who would play a major role in Thai politics for many years to come – men like Phin Chunhavan, Sarit Thanarat, Phao Siyanond, and Thanom Kittikachorn. As the events of the subsequent decade would show, these men had few qualms about stabbing Phibun in the back whenever they thought it convenient.

Another chance for democracy

The period between 1944 and 1957 was one of considerable instability, rooted in the shifting nature of political coalitions. Throughout this time, the absence of a precise standard of legitimacy, as well as the Promoters' previous failure to instil in the population a strong attachment to the constitutional regime and its institutions, allowed political elites to switch back and forth between supporting different political regimes that, regardless of their true nature, were invariably described as forms of 'democracy' superior to those they replaced. Phibun's ouster at the hands of the domestic wing of *Seri Thai* brought a new coalition into power, founded on an alliance between the more liberal and progressive elements that dominated *Seri Thai* domestically and the conservative royalists who played a leading role in the resistance abroad.[3] The alliance was sanctioned by the issuance of a royal pardon, granted by Pridi in his capacity as Regent, which freed political prisoners jailed by the Special Court in 1939. Aside from the shared aversion to Phibun and his military clique, the imperative to manage the end of the Japanese occupation and its aftermath, and see to it that Thailand would not be burdened by excessively onerous peace terms, was the glue that initially kept the alliance together. Its eventual collapse proved a setback from which Thailand has yet fully to recover.

Khuang Aphaiwong's administration, inaugurated on 1 August 1944, remained in office until the Japanese were defeated a year later. During that time, *Seri Thai* had grown increasingly bold in its anti-Japanese activities, so much so that it appears as though a showdown with occupying forces was only averted by the atomic bombs that exploded in the skies over Hiroshima and Nagasaki. After rescinding the declaration of war against the United States and the United Kingdom, Khuang stepped aside. The interim government of Thawi Bunyaket, in office for a mere 17 days, reached a tentative agreement on the principles governing the terms of peace, welcomed thousands of British troops who came to disarm the Japanese, and decreed that the country once again be known as Siam. Upon his return in mid September, the Assembly selected Seni Pramoj to serve as Prime Minister – both as a gesture of goodwill towards royalists and as a means to place the government's leadership in the hands of a politician who had played no role in the Japanese occupation.

Seni Pramoj's brief tenure as Prime Minister (September 1945 to January 1946) coincided with the beginning of a new transition to representative democracy. Aside from lifting restrictions to freedom of expression and freedom of the press, the government organized elections for a new set of 'first-category' members of parliament on 6 January 1946 and allowed the registration of political parties. An entirely new constitution, promulgated in May 1946, included provisions designed to reduce the bureaucracy's stranglehold over the country's political institutions, banning civil servants from holding political office. While among Thailand's most democratic, the constitution made several concessions to royalists, reserving a new set of emergency powers for the King and lifting the prohibition against the participation of the nobility in the country's political life. The constitution also abolished the position of appointed 'second-category' members of parliament and set up a bicameral National

[3] Nattapoll (2009: 36–7) usefully points out that royalists at the time were divided on many issues, perhaps including who should be King.

Assembly with an elected upper house. Controversially, however, the initial composition of the House of Elders (*Phruetsapha*) was to be decided by the legislature in place at the time, which meant in practice that many 'second-category' members helped select themselves to the upper house. The provision was widely interpreted as a means for Pridi to stack the National Assembly with supporters, although he hardly needed to do so given his supporters' electoral strength. The country's transition to electoral democracy was completed on 5 August 1946, when a by-election was held to fill the House seats previously held by appointees.

The Japanese defeat marked the opening of another 'critical juncture' in Thailand's process of political development – a brief period in which structural constraints that had previously impeded meaningful change were temporarily loosened. At this juncture, despite adverse initial conditions such as the continuing absence of mass support and the opposition of bureaucratic forces, democratic institutions did have a fighting chance to establish some permanency. The leaders of *Seri Thai* enjoyed a great deal of popularity for 'saving the country's honour', while the prominence of institutions such as the National Assembly and the monarchy had been revived under Pridi's leadership at the expense of the military. Siamese citizens generally did not regard Phibun as the Allies did and largely disapproved of his arrest on charges of war crimes (the judiciary later rescinded the charges upon finding the retroactive application of war crimes legislation unconstitutional). Still, the Allied presence helped keep the military on the sidelines, providing the new coalition with a window of opportunity to consolidate a democratic regime. As in the wake of the People's Party's seizure of power, this outcome was never especially likely or easily accomplished. By the same token, it would be much too convenient to say that the effort was doomed from the start. As in all 'critical junctures', the aftermath of World War II in Siam was defined by the presence of a heightened potential for change, as opposed to its actual realization. Ultimately, that particular dog did not bark, but for reasons other than it was constitutionally incapable of doing so. Echoes of the dog that did bark still reverberate today, because the brief period of democratic development between 1945 and 1947 set a precedent that would be repeated several times over in the six decades thereafter.

As ever, the reason why conservative royalists turned against the nascent democratic regime is that they disagreed with the choices made by the people in democratic elections. The (non-partisan) elections of ninety-six 'first-category' members of parliament, held in January 1946, gave pro-Pridi legislators an edge over royalists, who briefly organized themselves in the Progress Party (*Phak Kao Na*) of the brothers Kukrit and Seni Pramoj. Just 48 days into its term, Khuang Aphaiwong's new administration stepped aside, replaced with a government headed by Pridi. When by-elections were held in August 1946, pro-Pridi political parties won roughly three-quarters of the available eighty-two seats. The royalist Democrat Party, founded in April 1946 with Khuang as its leader, received a mere 15 per cent of the seats, concentrated in Bangkok and its vicinities (see *Bangkok Post*, 9 August 1946).

While it is certainly the case that these political parties were personalized and elite-based, as opposed to anything resembling mass organizations, the measure of party aggregation that took place in this period represented a great deal of progress for the country's democratic development. Specifically, the parties were an expression of what Lipset and Rokkan (1967: 13) described as 'functional cleavages', formed through the merger of conflicts between the centre and the periphery on the one hand, and among national elites on the other – oppositions that had first developed in the context of the formation of Siam's absolutist state. This was the culmination of a process set in motion by Siam's first legislative elections in 1933, in the aftermath of which many 'first-category' members of parliament had begun to gravitate towards Pridi.

By 1946, Pridi was the head of an electoral/parliamentary coalition that included two main groupings – defined in part by the personal and categorical differences of their leaders, and in part by overlapping ideological and territorial cleavages. His more populist, progressive supporters in *Phak Sahachip* (Cooperative Party), led by the 'Four Isan Tigers', were strongest in northern, northeastern, and southern constituencies. These regions were the most impoverished and neglected by the state, so it was no coincidence that members of *Sahachip* leaned towards more leftist positions, because their constituencies were those with the most to gain from more democracy, more state involvement in the economy, and more redistributive fiscal policies (for a similar argument, see Kobkua 1995: 213–14). The more moderate, liberal wing of Pridi's coalition, meanwhile, coalesced in the Constitutional Front (*Naeo Ratthathammanun*), led by more establishment figures such as Direk Chaiyanam and Rear Admiral Thamrong Nawasawat. The party, which dominated races in the Central Region and the Lower North, was popular with the middle bureaucrats who supported Pridi (see Charnvit 2008: 440–1). Meanwhile, the right-wing opposition to Pridi had coalesced in the Democrat Party (*Phak Prachathipat*), which brought together conservative Promoters such as Khuang Aphaiwong, staunch royalists such as the brothers Pramoj, and some of the country's major owners of property and land, whose interests and cultural outlook aligned to favour more conservative policies and a more hierarchical conception of Thai society – ideas which, as the 1946 by-election results showed, did not have a great deal of resonance with provincial voters and politicians.

Had the social and political forces organized in these three groups managed to maintain, despite their differences, a fundamental consensus on the rules of the game, the alignment that emerged after World War II might have served as the basis for the emergence of a workable democratic system of government, notwithstanding the military's opposition. Even Phibun, in announcing plans to return to an active political role in March 1947, felt compelled to form his own political party – *Thammathipat* – and to describe how he intended to stage his comeback by outlining an electoral strategy (see *Bangkok Post*, 22 March 1947). The military, of course, retained the means to overthrow the government, but that is true of just about any country that has a military force.[4] Had the basic consensus actually held, the military would have been denied the cover of legitimacy to seize power through extra-constitutional means.

Unfortunately, the Democrat Party's congenital defect, which remains its most salient trait today, is that its leaders and backers have a difficult time living by election results they do not like. Seni Pramoj's claim that the Democrats would only win elections when 'the people truly understand politics' (see *Bangkok Post*, 29 January 1947), is reminiscent of statements that the leaders of the Democrat Party insist on making today. The party has held on to these views despite the fact that its popularity has not improved as a consequence of the modernization Thailand has undergone over the past five decades. An additional source of concern for royalists, beyond the existing state of play, was that the future did not promise anything better. The mobilization of workers in strikes and demonstrations that attracted tens of thousands of participants in 1947 (for an overview, see *Bangkok Post*, 31 December 1947), in particular, impressed upon many that mass participation would spell disaster for the already outmatched conservatives (see Kobkua 1995: 193).

The effort mounted by the Democrats to rid themselves of Pridi was not confined to the halls of parliament. Their best opportunity came when King Ananda Mahidol was found dead in his bed in Bangkok's Grand Palace on the morning of 9 June 1946, with a single bullet through his forehead, just months after he had returned from Switzerland. Perhaps most plausible is that Ananda had been killed accidentally by his

[4] Before the end of the war, some British officials recommended the 'disbandment of the Siamese Fighting Services, or at least their reduction to such dimensions that they will be no more than adequate for the maintenance of internal peace and order' (Crosby 1945: 152). For various reasons (see Darling 1965: 41–3; see also Tarling 1978), Allied powers passed on this chance to place the country's political development on an entirely new course.

younger brother and successor, Bhumibol Adulyadej, with whom he shared a passion for gunplay.[5] Whether to shield the new King from embarrassing revelations, or out of genuine incompetence, Pridi's government provided unconvincing public explanations for the incident (see Kruger 1964: 103–13), which royalists exploited to peddle allegations that King Ananda had been murdered on Pridi's orders. As a Democrat Party member of parliament yelled 'Pridi killed the King' in a crowded Bangkok cinema, Prince Dhani Nivat and the brothers Kukrit and Seni Pramoj took to slandering the Prime Minister with foreign diplomats and the public, financing the dissemination of baseless conspiracy theories against Pridi and his supporters (see Nattapoll 2009: 42–50; Handley 2006: 80–1).

Having failed to stem the accusations of regicide by censoring the press, Pridi resigned as Prime Minister after the August 1946 by-elections, despite his overwhelming victory at the polls. His successor, Thamrong Nawasawat, did not fare any better. Aside from the ongoing criticism justified by the weak state of the economy and the lack of a definitive explanation for King Ananda's death, the opposition seized on the government's many self-inflicted wounds, above all corruption scandals in which cabinet members and legislators were caught embezzling state funds and profiteering from the government's economic programmes (see *Bangkok Post*, 31 December 1947; see Praphon, 31 December 1947). The bungling of negotiations over the territorial dispute with France was also a major source of embarrassment (see Kobkua 1996). As Democrats coupled their accusations of anti-monarchist subversion with charges of corruption, the Thamrong government went through several reshuffles and sustained a series of high-profile defections. Throughout 1947, newspapers were abuzz with speculation over who would be chosen to replace Thamrong upon his departure, invariably described as imminent.

Apparently, Thamrong had finally resolved to step aside on 10 November 1947, but was denied a chance to do so of his own accord because a military coup removed him from his post on the night of 8 November. While the coup's figurehead was Phibun, by most accounts Phibun was not involved in the planning of the operation (see Fineman 1997: 38). Rather, the coup was the work of men who had been mostly educated within Thailand, had not taken part in the revolution 15 years earlier, and had never held any political office. These officers were not animated by the desire to restore Phibun to his old position, but resented the military's

[5] The accidental fratricide thesis has been argued most recently in Marshall (2012), on the basis of a comprehensive review of the evidence. Conservative intellectual Sulak Sivaraksa is also a long-time proponent of this thesis (see Schiller, 3 August 2011).

marginalization in the years since Phibun's ouster (see Nattapoll 2009: 35). Most prominent in the 'Coup Group' (*Khana Ratthaprahan*) that dominated the political scene for a decade thereafter were Lieutenant-General Phin Chunhavan and Colonels Phao Siyanond, Sarit Thanarat, and Kat Katsongkhram. Phibun's appointment as Commander-in-Chief of the Armed Forces was designed to unify the military, parts of which remained loyal to the government. Western powers initially withheld their recognition of the new regime, but their stance towards Phibun and the military had softened as the developing world gradually turned into a battlefield in the war against communism. The United States and the United Kingdom were willing to accept *de facto* military rule as long as royalists were reserved a leading role in the government.[6]

For their part, conservative-royalist politicians and members of the royal family were happy to cooperate, provided that the operation returned them to power and eliminated Pridi from the scene. Indeed, a secret alliance between conservative royalists and Phibun sympathizers had been in existence for that very purpose for several months (see Nattapoll 2009: 51–9). In the hours after the coup, the British Ambassador (cited in Kobkua 1995: 23) reported back to London that the coup had been carried out by 'a right-wing movement supported by the royal family'. In the absence of King Bhumibol, the stamp of approval was affixed by the Regent, Prince Rangsit, who promptly signed the temporary constitution presented to him by the Coup Group. Prince Rangsit had spent 5 of the previous 8 years in prison, having been sentenced to death by Phibun's Special Court in 1939 – much like the other diehard royalists whom Phibun had jailed in 1939, he had no gratitude for the man who had rescued the monarchy from oblivion, returned his freedom, and restored his titles. As for King Bhumibol, it was only days before he would endorse from afar the first of many coups staged during his long reign. Consistent with the wishes of both royalists and Western powers, Khuang Aphaiwong was asked to form a government.

The repression of pro-Pridi forces began in earnest. Pridi himself made an adventurous escape to Singapore, just moments before armed men stormed his residence, later described as 'riddled with machine gun fire' (*Bangkok Post*, 31 December 1947; see also Kruger 1964: 114–21). The Coup Group had explicitly justified its seizure of power by accusing Pridi of regicide as well as plotting a 'republican revolution' scheduled for the night of 30 November 1947. On the pretext of gathering evidence

6 As Fineman (1997: 41) puts it, 'compared with the rustic, northeastern politicians prominent in Pridi's cabinets, the bilingual cosmopolitans of Khuang's government held great appeal for Westerners'.

of both plots, soldiers raided the homes of leading supporters of Pridi, sometimes turning up large caches of weapons left over from the war. With their leaders in exile, in prison, or in hiding, the parties that had previously dominated the legislature barely contested the sham elections held in January 1948, winning only five out of a total of a hundred lower-house seats. The deck having been stacked in its favour, the Democrat Party won an absolute majority in the House – for the first and only time in its history – allowing Khuang to remain in office.

By the end of 1947, the coup was already understood to have marked a major turning point. The *Bangkok Post* described the coup as a counter-revolutionary measure 'motivated by reactionary forces who had never accepted the revolutionary overthrow of 24 June 1932' (*Bangkok Post*, 31 December 1947). But if Khuang had stacked his government with conservative-royalists, including several officials who had served in King Prajadhipok's government before 1932, this was only part of the story. For while the leaders of the Coup Group had little time for the ideals of the 1932 revolution, they had no intention to allow 'reactionary forces' to exercise powers beyond what was strictly necessary for them to consolidate their own position. The temporary alliance with conservative-royalists was only motivated by the desire to provide the coup with some legitimacy domestically and internationally, as opposed to any convergence in either ideals or long-term plans.

More secure in its position, in April 1948, the Coup Group did not hesitate to force Khuang to resign and impose Phibun's return as Prime Minister. Democrats in the National Assembly, who had voiced no objection to the coup 6 months earlier, were now up in arms, complaining of the betrayal of democratic principles (see *Bangkok Post*, 21 April 1948). Having taken the government from the Democrats, however, the Coup Group still found it expedient to secure the quiescence of conservative-royalists. In one such gesture, the government went ahead with the planned election of a Constituent Assembly, tasked with drafting a new 'permanent' constitution. The constitution eventually promulgated in 1949 cut back somewhat on the sweeping powers the 1947 interim charter had granted the King to select the Prime Minister, appoint members of the upper house, veto legislation, and take over the government during national emergencies, with little interference from elected officials. Nonetheless, it formalized the monarchy's return to political prominence, through provisions that conferred upon the monarchy considerable power over, and almost complete autonomy from, all three branches of government (see Kobkua 2003: 50–4). The Coup Group was known to strongly disapprove of the draft constitution, but stopped short of preventing its promulgation. True to form, the thirty legislators who voted against the constitution's passage were described as 'representatives of the northeastern provinces and Muslims from the South' (*Bangkok Post*, 28 January 1949).

Another matter on which royalists were happy to work with the Coup Group was the elimination of Pridi's supporters from the political scene – indeed, from the face of the earth if possible. In late September 1948, three men were put on trial for the death of King Ananda – the royal pages Chit Singhaseni and But Pathamasarin, and the King's former Private Secretary Chaliao Pathumrot – for allegedly aiding Lieutenant Wacharachai Chaisitthiwet in carrying out the murder on Pridi's orders. After emerging from hiding, moreover, the leaders of former pro-Pridi parties in the National Assembly were arrested on accusations of planning the secession of the Northeast as well as their suspected involvement in an anti-government conspiracy (*Kabot Senathikan*) foiled in late September 1948. Some were rearrested after Pridi, former *Seri Thai* elements, and portions of the Navy staged an unsuccessful coup in late February 1949, known as the Grand Palace Rebellion (*Kabot Wang Luang*). Only days following Pridi's failed comeback, Thongpleo Chonlaphum and three of the 'Four Isan Tigers', Thong-in Phuriphat, Thawin Udon, and Chamlong Daoruang – all of them former cabinet members under Pridi and Thamrong – were murdered in police custody, in an episode known as the 'Kilo 11' incident. The fourth 'Isan Tiger', Tiang Sirikhan, was arrested in mid March 1949 and put on trial for treason.

None of the royalists, like Seni Pramoj, who now based their claim to power on the need to heed 'public opinion' (see *Bangkok Post*, 5 February 1948), found cause to complain about the character assassination (and physical elimination) of the politicians who had crushed the Democrats in free elections less than 3 years earlier. Having praised the 1947 coup as reflecting 'the will of the people', Seni (cited in Nattapoll 2013: 174–6) now maintained that the 'majority' in a true democracy was not necessarily the largest part numerically, but the part with the greatest 'knowledge and loyalty to the nation'. Indeed, while its leaders often clashed with the government in parliament and in the press, conservative royalists initially did not organize an especially spirited opposition to the Coup Group and its nominees. As late as mid 1950, Democrat Party stalwarts publicly compared Phibun's government favourably with Thamrong's (see *Bangkok Post*, 2 June 1950); earlier that year, Seni had called on his party to withdraw a motion for a general debate in parliament on the grounds that the economic situation had improved under Phibun (see *Bangkok Post*, 12 January 1950). Meanwhile, Khuang Aphaiwong deflected questions on how his foreign policy would differ from Phibun's by noting that the issue was moot. The Democrats, he stated, would not form a government for the foreseeable future because the party had no 'guns' and lacked the military support necessary to run the country (see *Bangkok Post*, 14 January 1950).

Upon coming back to power, Phibun mounted a concerted effort to build a legislative majority at the expense of the Democrats. Aside from enlisting independents and smaller parties in his coalition, Phibun used the election of twenty-one additional seats in June 1949, as well as the defection of some Democrat Party members of parliament, to reduce the government's dependency on the passive support of his principal rivals in the legislature. By late June 1949, it was reported that 75 out of a total of 121 members of the House of Representatives supported Phibun as Prime Minister (see *Bangkok Post*, 22 June 1949). Six months later, the Democrat Party's contingent had been cut down to thirty-nine seats, a number that was reduced further when a fourth pro-government party was formed in the Assembly (see *Bangkok Post*, 23 January 1950). As its numbers dwindled, the parliamentary opposition intensified, joined by the surviving members of Pridi's old coalition.

The 'Radio Coup' staged on 29 November 1951 was apparently carried out over Phibun's objections, although the Prime Minister was allowed to continue in office. The Coup Group acted just days before King Bhumibol's final return from Switzerland and 3 months ahead of scheduled general elections that had seemed destined to produce a highly fragmented lower house. In its radio broadcast on the evening of 29 November, the Coup Group announced the abrogation of the 1949 constitution and the reinstatement of the 1932 charter. Political parties were disbanded and the National Assembly replaced by an appointed legislative body. Aside from doing away with the royally appointed Senate and other royal prerogatives sanctioned in the 1949 constitution, the new rules paved the way for the Coup Group's leaders to join the cabinet without resigning their military posts. In the years since the 1947 coup, after all, the government's prosecution of staunchly anti-communist policies had earned the full support of the United States, removing the main obstacle that had initially induced members of the Coup Group to remain ensconced behind the scenes. This time, Khuang and Seni refused the coup-makers any cooperation, stating their intention to boycott upcoming elections (see *Bangkok Post*, 29 December 1951). Four years earlier, a principled stand of this kind might have proven critical in denying the Coup Group the legitimacy it desperately needed. By now, it made little difference either way.

Road to restoration

Phibun's second spell as Prime Minister, while longer than the first by almost 4 years, was far less ambitious. With the introduction of the 1949 constitution, the country reverted back to 'Thailand', but none of the social engineering efforts Phibun had energetically pursued, and which post-war governments had quickly undone, were ever revived. Phibun's anti-communism, to be sure, was grounded in rhetoric that stressed Thai national values and culture. What was missing was the clear idea of the nation in whose image Phibun and his collaborators had previously sought to remake Thai society, as the Prime Minister opted for a decidedly more pragmatic course (see Kobkua 1995: 137). At the same time, Phibun no longer had much of a choice on the matter. With no power base of his own, his job as Prime Minister hinged on the Coup Group leaders' willingness to tolerate him – and their unwillingness to tolerate one another – in that position.

Just how disposable Phibun was to the Coup Group was demonstrated during the 'Manhattan Rebellion' staged by Pridi's supporters in the Navy in late June 1951 – perhaps the bloodiest attempted coup of the past century (see Charnvit 2008: 475). The rebels had kidnapped Phibun at gunpoint, in the hope of using his physical safety as a bargaining chip. In response, the Coup Group authorized airstrikes and artillery fire against the flagship Sri Ayutthaya, where Phibun was held hostage. The Prime Minister narrowly escaped from the sinking ship with his life, and no doubt emerged from the murky waters of the Chao Phraya River with a clear idea of just how readily the leaders of the Coup Group were willing to sacrifice him to protect their own power.

Things were complicated further by the coup of 29 November 1951. In the five and a half years that followed, whatever power Phibun was able to wield hinged on his capacity to exploit the bitter divisions that had emerged between the Coup Group's two main factions – Sarit Thanarat's 'Sisao Thewet' and the 'Soi Ratchakhru' group of Army Commander-in-Chief Field Marshal Phin Chunhavan and his son-in-law, Police Director-General Phao Siyanond. Aside from engaging in the wholesale plunder of the state's coffers, both cliques ran protection rackets that extorted money from both legal and illegal businesses. Phao's clique drew much of its income from opium trafficking; Sarit's from state enterprises such as the Lottery Bureau. Ironically, the removal of a democratically elected government in 1947, which conservative royalists had supported in the name of good governance, legality, and order, had been followed by the establishment of a regime a great deal more corrupt, repressive, and lawless. At any rate, while Phibun was virtually powerless to check the greed and violence of Phao and Sarit, he was more successful, for a time, in balancing between one and the other. Although he was much closer to Phao than he was to Sarit, Phibun did not hesitate to side with the latter whenever Phao threatened to prevail. The infusion of American funds had allowed Phao to build a police force whose firepower rivalled the Army's, while profits from illegal businesses helped him establish a formidable political machine. Phao eventually resolved to eliminate Sarit upon the latter's appointment to Commander-in-Chief of the Army in 1954, but was thwarted by the Prime Minister (see Kobkua 1995: 209–10). Aides later noted that Phibun's mistrust of Phao, which led him to pass on the opportunity to deal decisively with Sarit, was eventually his downfall (see Somsak 2001: 32).

While the failure of the Manhattan Rebellion forced Phibun to abandon ambitions to build a power base in the Navy, which was eviscerated in the wake of the incident, the Radio Coup presented a different opportunity to do so, having wiped the slate clean of organized oppositions. The introduction of an amended version of the 1932 constitution in 1952, moreover, offered Phibun a chance to build an electoral and legislative base in a context that made it virtually impossible for oppositional forces to challenge the government. While political parties were still banned, Phao established a new caucus of legislators in the wake of the election of 'first-category' members of parliament in February 1952. The 'Legislative Studies Committee', as it was known at the time, quickly displaced the National Assembly as the real seat of legislative power because its meetings at the Manangkasila Villa made all relevant decisions about the passage and amendment of legislation. The group, which included some 100 members of parliament (about two-thirds of the total), was held together not only by the fact that it provided the only way for legislators to exercise any power, but also by Phao's skilful use of material inducements and his hard-nosed enforcement of discipline within its ranks. Newspapers reported that the group kept its members 'loyal through social services for them and their families, including housing, educational facilities for their children, medical aid and assistance in cremation expenses' (*Bangkok Post*, 30 October 1952). In mid 1953, the group announced the adoption of a stringent set of rules that punished public statements and voting behaviour deviating from the official line (see *Bangkok Post*, 8 July 1953).

The opposition was correspondingly stripped of any influence. Some legislators made valiant efforts to oppose the government and introduce legislation to democratize the system at the national and local levels. Their helplessness, however, was obvious. In January 1953, opposition members admitted to the press that they would have a better chance to shape legislation if they, too, joined the 'Phibun forever party' (see *Bangkok Post*, 13 January 1953). To their credit, many never did, and remained fearless in their opposition at considerable risk for their lives and their freedom. For their part, Phao's 'knights' (*asawin*) continued to terrorize progressive politicians long after the 'Kilo 11' incident. The only surviving member of the four pro-Pridi 'Isan Tigers', Tiang Sirikhan, was murdered in police custody in late 1952; the life-less body of another member of parliament critical of Phao, Phon Malithong (Samut Sakhon), ended at the bottom of the Chao Phraya River less than 2 years later (see Thak 2007 [1979]: 60–2). Meanwhile, some 200 leftist politicians, writers, thinkers, and students were arrested in December 1952 and accused of plotting against the government – the incident is known as the 'Peace Rebellion' (*Kabot Santiphap*). Anti-communist legislation introduced in 1954 subsequently gave the government expansive powers to arrest members of parliament, especially those who insisted on publicly identifying as 'socialist'.

As Deputy Minister of Defence, then General Sarit explored the possibility of joining the fray by exploiting the vacuum left by the exile of Pridi, the elimination of leading politicians from the Northeast, and the desperation of opposition members of parliament. In late August 1952, after meeting with northeastern legislators, Sarit announced plans to set up his own legislative group, which was expected to recruit the entirety of the Isan delegation (some forty-three members) and much of the opposition (another twenty-eight members, not counting the fifteen opposition legislators from the Northeast) (see *Bangkok Post*, 1 September 1952). Boasting northeastern origins himself, Sarit professed his understanding of the region's problems and issued a policy agenda to develop the region (see *Bangkok Post*, 26 September 1952). Ultimately, however, Sarit relented, possibly concluding that it would have been difficult to match the power of Phao's Legislative Studies Committee, and that it was premature to mount an open challenge against his main rival.

It was in an attempt to extricate himself from Phao and Sarit that Phibun moved aggressively to democratize the system in the mid 1950s. Upon his return from a trip to the United States and the United Kingdom in June 1955, he legalized political parties, lifted restrictions to freedom of expression, assembly, and the press, and made cabinet members available to answer questions from the media in press conferences. Contemporaneous accounts suggest that Phibun was impressed with the degree of independence that leaders like Winston Churchill and Dwight Eisenhower exercised thanks to their electoral popularity (see Wilson and Phillips 1958: 115). It was also reported at the time that Phibun enjoyed the spectacle of ministers getting 'debagged' by the press, and hoped to benefit from the media's interest in Phao's illegal dealings (see Pickerell and Moore 1957: 93–4). Phibun must have understood the risks presented by the reforms, undertaken over the objections of both Phao and Sarit. The liberalization of speech exposed him to public criticism as much as anyone else, particularly because he could not have expected not to be held responsible for the actions of men formally under his authority. Aside from providing a platform for attacks against the government, the resulting 'Hyde Park' movement took quite radical/socialist overtones, giving a voice to the dissatisfaction over Thailand's close relationship with the United States and a host of other hot-button issues such as King Ananda's death and Pridi's exile (see Ockey 2002). The press, now subject to looser restrictions, served as an amplifier for even the most incendiary speeches, providing regular coverage of the frequently raucous proceedings at Sanam Luang.

Based on recent experience, which had seen him struggle to manage an alliance of six government parties prior to the 1951 Radio Coup, Phibun could also have predicted that the legalization of political parties would have weakened his legislative coalition. Aside from allowing opposition parties to reconstitute, the measure offered pro-government politicians an opportunity to establish separate electoral vehicles and, therefore, exercise greater bargaining leverage in the apportionment of ministerial portfolios. Predictably, the long campaign for the February 1957 elections witnessed a proliferation of parties on both the government's and the opposition's side. So long as Phao's grip on the legislature was loosened, however, Phibun seemed content with the fact that his government party, *Seri Manangkasila*, would now provide him with a less cohesive majority than the Legislative Studies Committee once did. Indeed, at times Phibun seemed willing to risk the break-up of *Seri Manangkasila* if he could not bring the party in line with his positions.

One such incident took place when the party rejected a package of electoral reforms that would have liberalized the right to stand for election by lowering age requirements, by lifting restrictions on Thai citizens with alien (i.e., Chinese) fathers, by abolishing educational qualifications, and by mandating government officials to resign their posts prior to running for office. When Phibun threatened to resign over the party's decision, presumably to be replaced by Sarit, Phao stepped in physically to coerce its members, driving some of them to tears (see *Bangkok Post*, 21 January 1956). Phibun did not appear shaken when over thirty members of parliament walked out of the party's meeting, expressing intentions to form a new party. On the contrary, he doubled down by announcing that members of *Seri Manangkasila* – who had enjoyed perks including the use of a jeep and an allowance of THB 2,000 per month – would henceforth be stripped of their monthly allowance, which was financed by the state under a programme meant to counter communist psychological warfare operations (see *Bangkok Post*, 24 January 1956). The threat does not seem to have been followed through, perhaps because the very next day the proposals earned unanimous support within the party (see *Bangkok Post*, 25 January 1956). Phibun was determined to make the party his own, or ensure it would be no one else's.

In the effort to build his own electoral machine, Phibun also sought to benefit from the growing mobilization of workers, manifested in the increasing frequency of strikes and demonstrations as well as the proliferation of initiatives to register independent trade unions. Again, Pridi's exile and the intimidation of leftist politicians had created opportunities for Phibun to co-opt progressives inside and outside parliament. In June 1956, Phibun introduced labour legislation that guaranteed workers the right to strike, reduced the work week to 48 hours, mandated overtime pay, and sanctioned the right to receive paid sick leave and vacation days (see *Bangkok Post*, 18 June 1956). The Labour Act was watered down considerably in advance of its passage – by some government supporters' own admission, in recognition of the fact that *Seri Manangkasila* needed the votes of labour as well as the money of capitalists (see *Bangkok Post*, 21 August 1956) – but the legislation's entry into force was accompanied by further pro-labour ministerial decrees and regulations (see *Bangkok Post*, 13 December 1956). In advance of the elections, activists with avowed pro-Pridi sympathies and/or socialist leanings were actively recruited in *Seri Manangkasila*. While rejecting the appropriateness of communism to Thai culture, Phibun now described himself in favour of a 'mild version of socialism' (see *Bangkok Post*, 5 February 1957).

As Phibun struggled to assert himself over his rivals in the Coup Group, he was also forced to contend with the continuing challenge presented by conservative-royalists. Despite their exclusion from parliament and the setback suffered in the Radio Coup, royalists continued to enjoy benefits that accrued from their post-war reorganization, and the restoration of the monarchy's control over Crown Property and palace affairs,[7] as well as the campaign carried out between 1946 and 1951 to bolster the popularity of young King Bhumibol. In the King's absence from the country, senior princes and palace officials had taken advantage of the temporary expansion of the monarchy's power, as well as its new-found

[7] Before agreeing to the promulgation of a new constitution in 1952, Bhumibol insisted that the text be amended, thereby preserving the control that the King had regained over Crown Property, the Royal Household, the Royal Guard, and the Privy Council after the 1947 coup (see Kobkua 2003: 141; see also Nattapoll 2010: 167).

financial liquidity and independence, to revive royal ceremonies, rituals, and festivities, thereby reasserting the monarchy's role as a source of charity and patronage (see Handley 2006: 94–9, 106–10). King Bhumibol's permanent return to Thailand in late 1951 coincided with the beginning of a new attempt to elevate the monarchy's symbolic power, moral authority, and popular appeal, an effort whose success was facilitated by the charm and charisma of King Bhumibol and Queen Sirikit. In response, the Prime Minister banned royal tours to the provinces in 1955 and countered with efforts to elevate his own standing through the promotion/patronage of Buddhism and the appropriation of historical symbolism with which he sought to portray himself as the 'father of the nation' (see Handley 2006: 119–30). Phibun's decision to stake out ground on the left side of the ideological spectrum, seeking to capitalize on the appeal of more progressive ideas with politicians and labour activists, was also in all likelihood related to the desire to offer an alternative to the Democrat Party's staunch royalism, its strong pro-Western stance, its conservative economic platform, and its open support for large landowners in the effort to repeal legislation meant to check the excessive concentration of agricultural land.

Aside from failing to give Phibun the intended advantage over his rivals, the abortive democratic reforms rapidly led to the collapse of the Coup Group's 10-year hold on power. As it turns out, the Prime Minister had underestimated the educated public's dissatisfaction with the government, as well as Sarit's growing popularity 'with the press, the students, the disenchanted public, and certain politicians' (see Thak 2007 [1979]: 73). At the same time, Phao's diminished standing deprived Phibun of an effective ally with whom to counter Sarit's rise, increasingly supported by the palace. It should be noted that the alliance of Sarit and the palace was one of convenience – it was only later that Sarit and Bhumibol formed a strong personal and ideological bond. Prior to 1957, Sarit had given few indications of any deeply held convictions. Indeed, it was Phao who had initially enjoyed King Bhumibol's 'goodwill' (see Kobkua 1995: 204); his efforts to curry favour with the palace had most recently included, in February 1955, hastening the execution of the three innocent men convicted over King Ananda's death (see Handley 2006: 125; Somsak 2005).

While Sarit had previously shied away from openly challenging Phao's political machine, the events that took place after the elections of 26 February 1957 presented opportunities to weaken his rivals' hold on power. The election had given *Seri Manangkasila* a narrow majority of elected representatives and therefore a comfortable majority overall. At the same time, the irregularities that marred the elections – and at least the suspicion that fraud on a much larger scale had occurred – led to student demonstrations and a firestorm of criticism in the press. Almost by accident, Sarit was given a chance to test the waters and could only have been pleased with the results. After speaking sympathetically to student protesters, he received an enthusiastic response from the press as well as members of parliament on both sides of the aisle. Phibun dealt with the scandal by seeking to keep his enemies as close as possible. After declaring a State of Emergency that placed in Sarit's hands the responsibility for defending the kingdom's security against a contrived plot involving unnamed foreign agents, Phibun formed a cabinet that featured Phao as Minister of Interior, Sarit as Minister of Defence, and Phin as Minister of Agriculture. Lieutenant-General Thanom Kittikachorn and Major-General Praphat Charusathien, both of them Sarit's men, were made Deputy Ministers of Defence and the Interior, respectively.

The Prime Minister's efforts did nothing to silence the criticism, mostly directed at Phao, for allegedly rigging the elections. Senior princes, Democrat Party politicians, and royalist opinion leaders, meanwhile, signed on to the effort to remove Phibun in a military coup as early as April 1957 (see Nattapoll 2010: 170–1). The brothers Pramoj took a leading role in discrediting Phibun with the public – while Seni spearheaded a legal challenge aiming to invalidate the elections, Kukrit led the charge in the press. Worse still for Phibun, the government party was increasingly rife with dissension. Some of it was ideological, motivated by the dissatisfaction over the Prime Minister's left turn. Some of it was self-interested, because Phibun was accused of having favoured outsiders over long-time loyalists in his efforts to broaden the coalition. All of it, however, was rooted in Phao and Phibun's declining authority.

On the strength of the expressions of support he received from politicians on every side of the political spectrum, Sarit made his intentions clear. In April 1957, he revived efforts to build a base among northeastern members of parliament – many of them socialists – and pledged his support for a host of initiatives to develop the region (see *Bangkok Post*, 13 April 1957). Shortly thereafter, Sarit's supporters in the Assembly formed a new political party, *Phak Sahaphum*. As royalists in parliament and the press undermined the electoral basis of Phibun's legitimacy, King Bhumibol himself took a series of actions designed to signal his displeasure with the Prime Minister (see Handley 2006: 137), whom he had come to consider a competitor for 'spiritual hegemony' (see Handley 2006: 126–31; see also Kobkua 1995: 85–6). Faced with the increasingly obvious nature of the challenge, Phibun moved to counter Sarit's influence and even sent emissaries to China to re-establish relations with Pridi (see Somsak 2001: 31–5). The success of the countermeasures, however, was compromised by Phibun's mishandling of new corruption scandals and a devastating drought in the Northeast (see Thak 2007 [1979]: 75–7). Increasingly isolated, Phibun lashed out against the opposition, whom he accused of plotting his removal in a military coup, and fell back on his alliance with Phao. His opponents seized on the opportunity to accuse Phao and Phibun of conspiring to overthrow the monarchy. On the same day in July 1957, members of both the Democrat Party and *Sahaphum* publicly raised questions about the Prime Minister's commitment to the monarchy (see *Bangkok Post*, 7 July 1957). A month later, during a general debate in parliament, the same parties made their accusations explicit, highlighting the strident criticism of the aristocracy featured in newspapers controlled by Phao. Phao was also accused of having disparaged the King personally, among other things by informing members of *Seri Manangkasila* that Bhumibol had made large financial contributions to the Democrat Party (see Thak 2007 [1979]: 78).

The time to act had come. On 20 August 1957, Sarit and his protégés Thanom, Praphat, and Air Marshal Chalermkiat Watthanangkun resigned from the government; in a show of support, some forty-six appointed members of parliament resigned their membership of *Seri Manangkasila*. While the move had been prompted by Phibun's attempt to cut off Sarit's access to money, by banning government officials from sitting on the boards of public and private enterprises (see Kobkua 1995: 29), the royalist press cheered Sarit's 'principled' stance (see Thak 2007 [1979]: 79). Not long thereafter, Sarit and his supporters in the Army issued an ultimatum, demanding that Phibun resign and relieve Phao of his duties. The next day, on 16 September 1957, Phibun pleaded with the King for support, but was told in no uncertain terms to resign. The military seized power a few hours later, forcing Phibun and Phao to leave the country for good. King Bhumibol gave the coup immediate legal sanction and publicly praised its intentions. His collaborators reassured foreign diplomats that the coup had been 'just what the royalists wanted' (see Kobkua 1995: 30).

Coup de grâce

The age of instability bookended by the beginning and the end of Phibun's time as the country's Prime Minister remains of great significance to Thailand's political development. While the volatility in the prevailing coalitional alignments prevented the consolidation of any of the several regime forms with which the country experimented during this period, any study of the 'historical construction' of the present cannot fail to note just how profoundly the events of this era have contributed to shaping the country's political development, and hence how crucial they are to the conflict Thailand experiences today. Phibun's 20 years at the helm may have failed to set Thailand's political regime on any particular developmental course. Its significance, rather, lies in the developmental paths it foreclosed, for decades to come.

Field Marshal Sarit's twin seizures of power on 16 September 1957 and 20 October 1958 dealt the *coup de grâce* not only for the leaders of the People's Party, but also for the ideals in which the Promoters had grounded the removal of the absolute monarchy – ideas of popular sovereignty, equal citizenship, constitutionalism, and democracy. The military and the civilian bureaucracy, which had served as the engine of the 1932 revolution, were now in the hands of men with a far more conservative and parochial world view. The monarchy, which had experienced an improbable resurgence, was in a position to reassert its role as the central institution in the political, social, and economic life of the country. By this time, the palace was in some ways more reactionary, and no doubt far more confident and ambitious, than it had been during much of the Sixth and Seventh Reigns. The educated public, whose dissatisfaction had greased the skids of the absolute monarchy's collapse, was now less committed to the popular nationalist ideals that had been systematically betrayed, snubbed, and muddled in the quarter-century since the revolution. Just as the mobilization of peasants and workers had started gathering steam in the late 1940s and early 1950s, moreover, the movement had not only been deprived of a national leadership by the exile of Pridi and the murder of the country's most prominent progressive politicians; the revival of conservative-royalist ideas, combined with the state's anti-communist rhetoric, also provided new rationales to deny them rights and representation. Sarit, too, would call his lawless military dictatorship a 'democracy'.

If Thailand's National Revolution had lost much of its momentum under the People's Party, and had ground to a halt under the Coup Group, the process was rolled back by several decades under the palace–military coalition forged by King Bhumibol and Field Marshal Sarit. Not only would it take almost 30 years for Thailand to develop a regime as democratic as the one that governed the country after World War II; even then, the weakness of liberal and progressive forces, combined with the prominence of the monarchy, the conservativeness of the bureaucratic apparatus, the ambivalence of the middle-class public, and the continued hold of an ideology legitimizing hierarchies of superior and inferior citizens would also render the democratic regime that students and workers willed into existence incapable of overcoming the legacies of the royalist coups of 1947, 1957, and 1958. Indeed, the rise to power of Field Marshal Sarit could be said to have marked the opening of an era – the era of 'Thai-style democracy' – that has only now just reached its long-awaited epilogue.

5 The good dictatorship

The coup d'état staged by Field Marshal Sarit Thanarat on 16 September 1957 reconciled two institutions that had been mostly at odds over the previous quarter-century. The Army remained the dominant institution in the country's government – a position it had earned in the mid 1930s, temporarily lost in 1944, regained in 1947, and subsequently defended from challenges mounted by the Navy, the Police, and the National Assembly. For King Bhumibol, the coup ended what Kobkua (2003: 154), without irony, refers to as a 'political ordeal' – the indignity of being forced to operate within the confines of a constitution and play second fiddle to commoners who did not acknowledge the monarchy's claims to extra-constitutional powers. King Bhumibol's new-found freedom from the strictures of constitutionalism was evident from the start. In seizing power, Sarit had not bothered abrogating the 1952 constitution, yet Bhumibol had no reservation about sanctioning Phibun's illegal replacement and the disbandment of the Assembly. In the Royal Command appointing Sarit as the 'Military Defender of the Capital' (*Phu Raksa Phra Nakhon Fai Thahan*), Bhumibol blamed the coup on Phibun's failure to maintain 'tranquillity and order' and claimed that 'the people' had 'lost trust in the government' (see Bhumibol, 16 September 1957). Apparently, the King went so far as to help in the drafting of the junta's statements (see Kobkua 2003: 155).

Beyond the determination to entrench both institutions in their rightful position, squarely above the law, Sarit appears to have had no plan for the coup's aftermath. Indeed, it may be ventured that the 1957 coup marked the opening of the last major 'critical juncture' in Thailand's political development, owing not only to the relaxation of constraints on major change that resulted from the ultimate defeat and exile of People's Party politicians, as well as the rivals that Sarit faced inside the security apparatus, but also to a high degree of uncertainty about where the country would be headed next. Initially, Sarit's 'Military Group' (*Fai Thahan*) seemed content with preserving a version of the old system, minus Phibun and Phao. After appointing a caretaker civilian government led by Pote Sarasin, the junta held elections in December 1957. The elections produced a National Assembly split three ways between the Democrat Party, *Sahaphum*, and independents, most of whom had previously been members of *Seri Manangkasila*. Given Pote's refusal to continue in office and Sarit's illness, which required him to seek treatment abroad, Thanom Kittikachorn was chosen as Prime Minister. Thanom, however, faced many of the same problems as his predecessors. Members of *Sahaphum* resented the attempt made by Sarit to broaden his legislative base by forming a new party. The press and the Assembly failed to fall in line. Voters, too, did not cooperate to the extent expected, because the new government party – *Chatsangkhomniyom* (National-Socialist) – underperformed in the March 1958 by-elections. Even the ailing Sarit, to his great annoyance, was not spared from criticism.

It did not take long for the Field Marshal to tire of the niceties of constitutional government. As the *Cremation Volume* put together by the Council of Ministers to celebrate his life describes it, Sarit found himself deeply dissatisfied over the fact that 'there still existed a parliament, political parties, a free press system that could criticize the government', and 'labour unions that could go on strike whenever they were unhappy with their employers'. In spite of its best efforts, the government could not 'do its work properly' under these circumstances (cited in Thak 2007 [1979]: 95). After sneaking back into Thailand, Sarit staged a self-coup on 20 October 1958, doing away with the constitution, the elected legislature, political parties, and indeed all forms of legal opposition and dissent. This *autogolpe* by Sarit famously ushered in an era of 'despotic paternalism', a time during which the government's heavy-handedness was only matched by the prodigious thievery of its leader. In place of the 1952 constitution, Sarit introduced a bare-bones temporary charter in early 1959. Most infamous among its twenty articles was the seventeenth, known as M-17, which gave the Prime Minister the power to 'issue any order or take any action', with force of law, against anyone deemed to have disturbed the kingdom's peace or threatened its security. In essence, M-17 amounted to a legal licence to arrest and execute, without trial, anyone the government wanted removed from the political field of battle. Meanwhile, freedoms of speech and association were rescinded and most political activities repressed, while the recurrent election of legislative representatives was scrapped in favour of a style of 'representation' by which the fatherly leader would visit his 'children' around the country, listen to their concerns, and suitably interpret their demands.

As Sarit dismantled the vestiges of the 1932 revolution, he endeavoured to provide the new regime with more solid foundations of legitimacy. Perhaps most importantly, the Field Marshal saw in the restoration of the monarchy's prestige a source of legitimacy far more potent than the pretence of constitutionalism and elections – one that would afford him the opportunity to dress up harsh dictatorial measures in a paternalistic attire. With the backing of the United States government, which identified in King Bhumibol's cult of personality an antidote to the spread of communism, Sarit began the process of exalting the monarchy. Meanwhile, the egalitarian ideals championed by some in the People's Party were superseded by the government's unabashed attempt to perpetuate existing inequalities. The most powerful domestic capitalists were nurtured by the state, protected from competition, and granted a privileged position on the country's revamped social hierarchies. Entire sectors of Thailand's economy were auctioned off to foreign and domestic corporations in exchange for billions, paid on the condition that the generals make life difficult for smaller, local competitors and repress any labour movement that might seek better pay and work conditions for Thai workers (see Akira 1996: 179–80). The government now insisted that the rural population be content to eke out a simple existence up-country, the refusal of many to embrace their station in life portending the 'deterioration' of Thai society (Thak 2007 [1979]: 105–6, 122).

The iron-fisted rule of Sarit Thanarat came to an end in early December 1963, when the Field Marshal succumbed to cirrhosis of the liver. Despite having lasted a mere 5 years, it is widely acknowledged that this period dramatically changed the course of history in Thailand. It was during this time that the alliance of monarchy, military, and capitalist class was forged, and that King Bhumibol began to earn the adoration, power, and riches that have held the coalition together, if somewhat precariously, through the vicissitudes of the past five and a half decades. Indeed, whereas the preceding period was marked by the failure to produce stable coalitions, the alliance formed by Sarit proved far more durable. The alliance has not always been as close as it was in those days, nor has it ever been cohesive enough to give rise to the kind of strong authoritarian regimes that emerged elsewhere in the region (see Slater 2010). The divergence in the interests of the palace, the military, and old money, in turn, encouraged predictable challenges from below, reflected in growing demands for political inclusion. Still, Thailand's ruling coalition proved sufficiently entrenched to neutralize, absorb, repress, or adapt to most such challenges, all the while maintaining its extra-constitutional prerogatives, its predominant position on the country's social hierarchy, and its effective control of much of the state apparatus. The coalition's various components may never have found the wherewithal to invest their slice of the patrimonial pie in the establishment of a true 'authoritarian

Leviathan', but never lacked the motivation and unity of purpose to obstruct or subvert the development of democratic institutions, to say nothing of the brutality they have been willing to unleash when circumstances warranted.

While the alliance put together under Sarit did not show much interest in building strong political institutions, it was far more effective in asserting its cultural hegemony, centred on a state ideology that combined elements of the absolute monarchy's official nationalism with the preoccupation with social conformity of the first Phibun government, as well as ideas of kingship and society put forth more recently by royalist intellectuals. The resulting ideology of 'Thainess' has been sufficiently flexible to accommodate the transformations that 'Thai-style democracy' has undergone since that time, mostly as a result of strategic adaptations undertaken in response to changing conditions on the ground. Nonetheless, the royal nationalism that found its synthesis under Sarit not only acquired, in the eyes of millions of Thais, the kind of natural and self-evident quality that effectively turned it into the cultural norm it had been said to embody in the first place, but also continues to inhibit open debate about the content of Thailand's national identity, placing those who question the country's hierarchy of power, status, and merit beyond the pale of true 'Thainess'.

'Thai-style democracy'

The announcements issued by the Revolutionary Council (*Khana Patiwat*) on the evening of 20 October 1958 declared that the junta had seized power 'in the name of the Thai people' (*nai nam khong puangchon chao thai*) – a message complemented by the admonition that 'the people' do as they were told (see Revolutionary Council 1958a: 3). The Revolutionary Council also issued two statements explaining why the coup had been staged, ostensibly with the support of the outgoing government as well as 'the majority of those who worry about the survival of the country' (see Revolutionary Council 1958b: 5). In a lengthy pronouncement interspersed with orders of a more practical nature, the junta attributed the coup to the actions of communists, said to have infiltrated Thailand's political, social, and economic institutions in an 'attempt to assert their influence over the spirit of the Thai people' (*phayayam sang itthiphon nuea chitchai khong prachachon chao thai*). While no evidence appears in the statement of any such activities, beyond vague references to communist literature and 'many clever forms of propaganda and other schemes' (*chai withi kotsana chuan chuea lae phaenkan thi chalat lai yang*), the threat was described as serious enough to 'leave the government with no time and space' to act (see Revolutionary Council 1958c: 11). Field Marshal Sarit had therefore taken it upon himself to initiate a 'revolution'.

The statement goes on to demonstrate just what Sarit meant by 'revolution'. After acknowledging the fact that the Thai people had fought for basic rights and freedoms, the junta explained that 'some individuals' had taken advantage of the protections afforded by the constitution to destroy the unity of the nation. Not only was the constitution described as powerless to prevent 'the ultimate disintegration of the country' (*khwam taek salai khong prathet chat nai thi sut*); also, the problem could not be rectified by a mere change in government, or reforms of a more incremental nature. The only available course of action was a 'revolution' meant to provide the government with more adequate instruments to confront the nation's enemies (see Revolutionary Council 1958c: 12). On the first anniversary of the coup, Sarit (1964 [1959]: 56) expressed satisfaction over the fact that the government now had the right instruments of 'revolutionary power' (*amnat patiwat*) – above all, Article 17 of the 1959 constitution. In the mid 1960s, in its own commemoration of Sarit's life, the Royal Thai Army (1964: 121) told much the same story, arguing that it was only by lifting the legal constraints on the government that the nation could be saved from destruction. Among the rules said to have prevented the government from protecting the nation was the Anti-Communism Act of 1954 – which, as the Royal Thai Army (1964: 120) lamented, forced the authorities to release suspects against whom they could produce no evidence.

Official accounts of the 1958 coup (Revolutionary Council, 1958a, 1958b, 1958c), although exceedingly vague about the nature of the threat, paint Thailand as a nation on the verge of extinction. The reality was an entirely different matter. By 1958, communism had made significant inroads among many of Thailand's neighbours. Labour unrest, although trifling by Western standards, had reached an intensity with which the Thai public may have been unfamiliar (see Morell and Chai-anan 1981: 184). Nonetheless, communists in Thailand were still a negligible force – one that was no match for a state with the means available to the Thai government through American patronage. Even after Sarit's death, communist fighters only numbered in the hundreds (see Handley 2006: 182–3). While communists later did manage to build a measure of support among provincial populations, fuelling the insurgency's intensification in the late 1960s and 1970s, they did so largely as a consequence of the regime's own policies.

Indeed, what had prompted Sarit to stage his 'revolution' was not the threat of communism, but rather the desire to do away with the limited version of democracy that operated under the 1952 constitution. No longer hampered by rules of due process, Sarit's government arrested hundreds of intellectuals, politicians, and activists. The press was dealt with harshly, because Sarit (1964 [1959]: 57) would later explain that many newspapers only served as mouthpieces for communists and 'evil-thinking people' (*phu khit rai*), such that their closure was the only way to safeguard the unity of the nation. Sarit's government also dedicated itself to the enforcement of social order and conformity, using a heavy hand to deal with arsonists, hooligans, drug dealers, prostitutes, rickshaw drivers, and anyone else he found cause to brand an enemy of the nation or a threat to its 'orderliness' (*khwam riaproi*). The repression of non-conformists also extended to the Buddhist clergy, reorganized through measures that centralized its structure, maximized the government's control over appointments and doctrine, and purged monks who resisted the subservience of Buddhism to the political agenda of the authoritarian state (see Tambiah 1976: 252–61). Under the 1959 constitution, finally, a royally appointed legislature was assigned the task of writing a permanent charter – something that took almost a decade to complete – and, in the meantime, of rubber-stamping the government's policies.

Aside from smashing all oppositions, Sarit paid special attention to boosting the legitimacy of his rule, to be achieved through ideological innovation and energetic government performance in the pursuit of priorities such as national integration and development. The hope was that the people of Thailand would support the revolutionary regime not just out of fear of the imaginary menace against which Sarit offered them protection, but out of a sincere belief in the regime's effectiveness, moral goodness, and cultural appropriateness. In more abstract terms, Sarit sought to entrench the 'revolutionary' regime by relying on mechanisms of institutional reproduction harnessing the self-reinforcing properties of power and legitimation (see Mahoney 2000: 521–5; Thelen 1999: 392–9).

As Thak (2007 [1979]: 92) has put it, the 'revolution' Sarit sought to carry out aimed to replace the hybrid system of government inherited from the 1932 coup with something putatively more 'Thai'. The instability the country had experienced and the grave threats it was said to confront were blamed by Sarit and his associates on the adoption of Western ideas and institutions, which the Revolutionary Council aimed to replace with a 'Thai' version of democracy. The so-called 'Thai-style democracy' (*prachathippatai baeb thai*) that took shape thereafter replaced the concern for individual rights and freedoms with a preoccupation for stability and security, requiring in turn the suppression of free speech, political competition, and legislative representation; the elimination of 'Western' procedures of selection and accountability; and the establishment of a political system dominated by an unchecked executive wielding absolute powers. Undergirding this new system of government was the revival of hierarchical, organic conceptions of the nation. Indeed, ordinary people were to be denied a political role altogether, because Thailand's prosperity and harmony could only be achieved if everyone knew their place, remained unified behind the government's leadership, and refrained from pressing any demand for political inclusion, economic opportunity, or social change (see Thak (2007 [1979]: 100–5).

As in the time of King Chulalongkorn and King Vajiravudh, the organic, hierarchical conception of society revived under Sarit was anchored in Buddhist ideas of karma and merit. The revival of social hierarchies as central to Thainess and 'Thai-style democracy', however, presented something of a challenge. To the extent that Thai Buddhism had historically been 'positively related to a conception of an ideal political order', its 'cornerstone' had never been a coarse and frequently intoxicated military general, but 'a righteous monarch who would promote a prosperous society and religion' (Tambiah 1976: 431). Even as Sarit went about presenting himself as the 'father of the nation', supposedly on the *pho khun* model of King Ramkhamhaeng of Sukhothai, the restoration of the monarchy as the pinnacle of Thailand's state-sanctioned social hierarchies was therefore central to his 'revolutionary' agenda. The expansion of King Bhumibol's ceremonial and ritual role, the accentuation of the King's position as the head of Buddhism and the armed forces, the encouragement of royal tours to the provinces and foreign countries, and the resurrection of practices (such as prostration and *rachasap*) that elevated the King above humanity (see Handley 2006: 143–52; Thak 2007 [1979]: 204–8) provided the military regime with more solid symbolic foundations. What is more, Bhumibol's image as a sophisticated, righteous, and benevolent monarch partially masked, at home and abroad, the regime's corruption and brutality.

While it does not appear that King Bhumibol was as directly involved in the 1958 coup as he had been in the previous year's operation, the King is described as not having minded 'one bit' the rollback of the 1932 revolution (see Kobkua 2003: 158). Indeed, it is very likely the case, as Kobkua suggests, that Bhumibol shared with Sarit the conviction that 'the security of the nation' took precedence over 'the democratic form of government' (Kobkua 2003: 158). Nonetheless, the monarchy had both ideological and instrumental reasons to support Sarit's rule, beyond the national security threats overhyped by the Revolutionary Council to earn the public's support for its actions. On the one hand, palace officials like Prince Dhani Nivat (see Dhani 1946), as well as royalist intellectuals like Phraya Anuman Rajathon (see Anuman 1954), Kukrit Pramoj (see Saichol 2006), and many others (see Nattapoll 2013: Ch. 4), had revived the notion that Thailand never needed a constitution – not as long as it was ruled according to the dharma by kings who were effectively 'elected', as had supposedly been the case in Thailand before the influx of Western ideas. On the other hand, the monarchy had much to gain from Sarit's 'revolution', which elevated the institution to a position of power it had not enjoyed since 1932.

The 1959 constitution addressed the issue of sovereignty through phrasing consistent with previous documents dating back to the first permanent constitution of 1932, stating: 'Sovereign power comes from Thai people' (*amnat athippatai ma chak puangchon chao thai*).[1] In practice, however, Hewison and Kengkij (2010: 186) are correct in their assessment that Sarit 'effectively made the King sovereign, in place of the previous notion that the people were sovereign'. The conception of sovereignty articulated under Sarit had much in common with King Vajiravudh's. Whereas the King and his government were said to embody the popular will and 'represent the aspirations of the nation', sovereignty was delegated to them irrevocably by the people, who took no part in the 'exercise of legislative, executive, and judicial power' (see Thak 2007 [1979]: 103), and were granted no means by which they could withdraw the authority exercised on their behalf. Whereas, moreover, the permanent constitution of 1932 had followed the recognition that 'sovereign power comes from the Siamese people' with a statement that 'the King, as head of state, only exercises said power according to the provisions of this constitution' (*phramahakasat phu pen pramuk song chai amnat nan tae doi bot banyat haeng ratthathammanun ni*), the new charter featured no such restriction. The King could once again 'do no wrong' and was elevated above the law, as were in practice the generals who administered the country in his name. What were demanded of the people submission and obedience, possibly on penalty of Thailand's newly legalized forms of extra-judicial arrest and execution.

Buddhism and the monarchy served not only as 'collective identity symbols of the nation' (Tambiah 1976: 473), but also as the vehicles through which the regime's nationalism and its ideology of national development were carried into the provinces. Regionalism, particularly in the Northeast, was a persistent problem – as a contemporaneous account described it, the kingdom's 'most serious divisive force' (Wilson 1962: 215). The problem, if anything, was compounded by the fact that, since

[1] The provisional charter of 1932 had used far more direct language (Article 1): 'Supreme power belongs to all the people' (*amnat sung sut khong prathet nan pen khong ratsadon thang lai*).

1932, regional cleavages had found their expression at the national level in a way that reinforced national oppositions over both the form of government and the policies it should pursue, adding a territorial dimension to the struggle for greater democracy and social justice (see Keyes 1967: 36–49). The dismantlement of legislative institutions and the persecution of northeastern members of parliament had complicated matters further. For the reality of continuing neglect, underdevelopment, discrimination, and official abuse, combined with a rising awareness of regional disparities and social inequalities, not only weakened the regime's legitimacy but also compromised the extent to which local populations could be made to feel part of the national community. With the state's increasing physical presence in the periphery, for purposes of both security and development, scarce national integration threatened to turn into active opposition, particularly as the state's activities 'inadvertently politicized many of the peasants and awakened their awareness of their place in the Thai social order' (Thak 2007 [1979]: 172). The problem was not exclusively a northeastern one, especially given the government's decision to side with large landowners in repealing legal protections for peasants and farmers in other regions.

Quite sensitive to the regionalist challenge (see Keyes 1967: 51), Sarit sought to further national integration through more than just repression. On the one hand, the government propagated its official ideology through the national education system, the teachings of the Buddhist monkhood, and the promotion of the monarchy, much of it funded by the United States Information Service (USIS) (see Handley 2006: 149). On the other hand, the regime's emphasis on national development – again, much of it carried out with American funds – sought to cement the loyalties of local populations. Both Sarit and Bhumibol undertook highly publicized tours to the provinces in an attempt to underscore the sincerity of the authorities' concern for the welfare of provincial subjects. Still, the effort to raise standards of living in the provinces was not inconsistent with the government's determination to preserve the existing social structure: local people were urged to be content with their lot, renounce ambitions to political or economic empowerment, and offer the state their unquestioned loyalty (see Thak 2007 [1979]: 153).

Just as the vast majority of the population was asked to embrace their inferior position in Thailand's social order, Sarit and Bhumibol were hard at work to impress upon urban elites that their privilege, too, was permanent as long as the regime enjoyed their support. At least since the late 1930s, wealthy families had shared their largesse with big men in the military and civilian bureaucracy, appointing them to lucrative positions on their companies' boards of directors and funnelling money to public and privately owned firms controlled by generals. Beginning with the 1947 coup, the practice was extended to all sectors of the economy, as the Coup Group's 'bureaucratic capitalists' cashed in on the business community's dependency on access to political patronage (see Akira 1996: 137–8, 170–2). Aside from leading to fast-paced economic growth and a vast expansion in both the industrial and financial sectors, Sarit's new development agenda favoured the increased concentration of capital in the hands of a few (Sino-Thai) family-owned conglomerates, which benefited not only from the continuing association with the military but also the dismantlement of labour protections, land controls, and representative institutions, increases in foreign direct investment and government expenditures, and reduced competition from both state enterprises and private firms.

While Sarit's policies gave these families a vested economic interest in the regime's preservation, the monarchy was deployed to solidify the alliance by legitimizing the commoner elite's superior position on the nation's social hierarchy, all the while rendering its status dependent upon the continuing prestige of the royal institution. King Bhumibol personally undertook activities aimed at strengthening the loyalty of the bourgeoisie. On the one hand, the King performed functions and rituals designed to 'consolidate a complex of alliances between political, royal and business families' (Thak 2007 [1979]: 214). On the other hand, the King developed links with the commoner elite and upper-middle class by granting audiences, officiating at ceremonies, dispensing new titles and decorations, and perhaps above all by accepting donations for the various philanthropic activities in which the royal family was engaged at the time, thereby offering donors a chance to accumulate merit and status through their association with the monarchy (for more detail, see Handley 2006: 149–50, 174; Thak 2007 [1979]: 214–18).

Already the country's most powerful institution at the time Sarit launched his revolution, the military parlayed its new alliance with royalists and capitalists into a decade of regime stability, effectively triggering mechanisms of institutional reproduction founded on the aforementioned dynamics of *power* and *legitimation*. With regard to the former, if the expansiveness of the new coalition had allowed the imposition of rules, such as the 1959 constitution, that granted the regime unchecked, despotic powers, the application of such powers – whether to dispatch organized oppositions, intimidate potential challengers, or promote economic development – further solidified the government's effective hold on power. With regard to the latter, the regime's association with the monarchy gave it a new basis of legitimacy that worked in tandem with repression and patronage to favour its reproduction. If, in particular, the repression removed any real competition or resistance to the government's official ideology, the regime's resulting capacity to secure the voluntary compliance of key segments of the population – persuaded of both the effectiveness and cultural appropriateness of 'Thai-style democracy' – allowed it to minimize its recourse to physical coercion, providing the space for Sarit to supplement his despotism with the benevolent 'paternalism' that further boosted the regime's legitimacy and moral authority.

Thak's (2007 [1979]) seminal work on Sarit's 'despotic paternalism' offers a comprehensive treatment of both the 'paternalistic' and 'despotic' features of the regime. Thak, however, arguably fails to apply the required degree of scepticism to the regime's official line, taking at face value the notion that Sarit's aim was to establish a more traditionally 'Thai' system of government. In fact, while Sarit may have benefited from the appropriation of traditional symbols and pseudo-historical claims to legitimacy, 'Thai-style democracy' was less the contemporary adaptation of an 'unwritten constitution' dating back to the thirteenth-century Kingdom of Sukhothai than it was a synthesis of the official nationalism articulated under the absolute monarchy – based on the nationalist historiography pioneered by the likes of Prince Damrong – with the statism and obsession with social conformity that had characterized the nationalist ideology crafted during Phibun's first tenure as Prime Minister.

It is no coincidence that the man Sarit called upon to plan his 'revolution' was none other than Luang Wichit Wathakan (see Thak 2007 [1979]: 115–19), who had first spoken of a 'human revolution' (*manut patiwat*) as a means to revert to 'true' Thai characteristics in the late 1930s. Not only had Luang Wichit long shown himself 'adept at using the past, or rather his peculiar conception of the past, to justify or affirm contemporary realities' (Barmé 1993: 160); two decades earlier, before recycling the idea in support of Sarit, Luang Wichit had also sought to present Phibun as the true inheritor of the Sukhothai tradition. Among other things, it was Luang Wichit who had repurposed King Vajiravudh's official nationalism in the service of Phibun, adding a new twist – namely, the idea that the state should shape the private and public behaviour of the population and, conversely, the notion that the only 'legitimate, "real" Thai were those members of the populace who acted in full accordance with the behavioural criteria propagated by the state' (Barmé 1993: 150).

Once again, the version of 'Thainess' espoused by Sarit and his supporters did draw upon genuine traditions, particularly through its emphasis on the central role of the monarchy and on Buddhist ideas of *dhammic* rule, political order, and hierarchies of merit/status (see Tambiah 1976: 487–9). At the same time, not only was the state's appropriation of such traditions based on a reading of history inseparable from the nationalist ideology that inspired it; also, the rediscovery and propagation of such traditions, and, conversely, the suppression of ideas with an equally good claim to 'traditional' status,[2] in fact served a far less traditional purpose: legitimizing the rule of a venal military regime, of which Thailand had little history, that wielded absolute powers of the kind no ruler in Thailand had enjoyed prior to the late nineteenth century, in the pursuit of goals, such as 'national development' and 'national integration', no government had even considered prior to the Fifth Reign, through means of propaganda and repression that had only become available in the previous few decades. The Thai state's new-found preoccupation with enforcing 'unity' through education and mass media, and its tendency to brand those who failed to conform as 'un-Thai', mentally defective, or otherwise lacking in any legitimacy to participate in the political life of the country, had nothing to do with the establishment of a traditionally 'Thai' style of government. It had everything to do with a modern agenda of cultural and political hegemony, prosecuted in part by retrofitting an ostensibly 'timeless' national culture to match a configuration of power it could then be claimed to have brought into being.

A few 'good' men

The volume produced by the Royal Thai Army to commemorate the life of Field Marshal Sarit begins its account of the 1958 coup by arguing that 'the Thai nation', in existence 'for almost a thousand years', only managed to maintain its sovereignty and independence thanks to the work of 'good people' (*khon di*) who led it each time it was confronted with danger (see Royal Thai Army 1964: 118). The *khon di* discourse has since supported the contention that a government's legitimacy is rooted, not in its electoral mandate but in the 'goodness' of its leaders, the assessment of which is reserved for the King and other royalists who derive from their proximity to the monarchy the authority to speak for 'the people'.

On the day Sarit died, King Bhumibol and Queen Sirikit sent a hand-signed note of condolences to the late Prime Minister's wife Wichitra (see Royal Thai Army 1964: 254), praising the departed as a statesman who discharged his duties 'without ever thinking of himself at all' (*doi mai nuek thueng ton eng loei*). Little could have been farther from the truth. The Field Marshal, it was discovered not long thereafter, had amassed a

[2] For example, see Jackson (2002), Keyes (1977: 287), McCargo (2004: 155–6), and Tambiah (1976: 445).

personal fortune approaching USD 140 million (see Thak 2007 [1979]: 224) thanks to the systematic misappropriation of government funds and profits reaped from legal and illegal businesses in which he had been involved for over a decade. King Bhumibol had long known what Sarit had been up to (see Kobkua 2003: 155), but could hardly have been expected to acknowledge it publicly, given their close relationship. Royalists generally rationalize the palace's active support of Sarit as dictated by the King's commitment to the national interest, suitably defined as whatever made the monarchy more popular and powerful (for instance, see Kobkua 2003: 158–9). By that standard, Sarit's 'revolution' had been a godsend.

The Field Marshal's death was not followed by immediate changes in the formal structure of government. Still, the 1960s witnessed a gradual shift in the balance of power in favour of the King, who went from being an object of national veneration and pride to asserting himself as the most important player on Thailand's political scene. Now in his late thirties, Bhumibol was in a position to convert the symbolic capital that accrued from his personal popularity, the monarchy's revival, and the anti-communist propaganda overseen by the United States into real political power. The task was facilitated by the fact that Sarit's successors, Field Marshal Thanom Kittikachorn (as Prime Minister) and Field Marshal Praphat Charusathien (as Interior Minister, Deputy Prime Minister, and Commander-in-Chief of the Army), although almost equally crooked, had none of Sarit's stature and charisma. While firmly in control of the state's administrative/repressive apparatus, neither could credibly claim to have inherited the roles of 'father-lord' (*pho khun*) and embodiment of the nation's will.

King Bhumibol stepped into that vacuum, repurposing the institution of the monarchy in response to opportunities provided by the increasingly perceptible slippage between the theory and practice of 'Thai-style government'. The King made use of the central role he had been assigned in the legitimation of the new regime, exploiting the ambiguities of the existing institutional arrangements and the weakened stature of its military leaders. As he did so, Thailand's regime, although formally unchanged, increasingly resembled the local adaptation of a model of Platonic guardianship – a three-tiered hierarchy in which a few 'good men' with superior karmic merit and access to the dharma, the King foremost among them, were responsible for assuring harmony in society by conquering, with the aid of their auxiliaries in the armed forces, the base desires of the ignorant many.

The doctrine of 'Thai-style government' and the nationalist ideology that legitimized it underwent some adjustments as the King took on a more active political role. Perhaps more than any other thinker, it was Kukrit Pramoj who had set the intellectual foundations for Sarit's adoption of a 'royal nationalism' that emphasized the King as the heart of a nation defined by its hierarchical structure (see Saichol 2005: 115). On par with Luang Wichit, moreover, Kukrit had played a role in defining the image of the ideal 'Thai-style leader' (*phu nam baep thai*) wielding unchecked, absolute powers for the benefit of the entire nation, as had supposedly been the case at some point in, if not throughout, 'Thai' history. Beginning in the early to mid 1950s, Kukrit's writings idealized the absolute monarchy as an 'excellent golden age' (*samai thong kham an di loet*), a time when the country was secure, peaceful, and prosperous thanks to a system of government 'without politics', in which enlightened monarchs could rule without concerning themselves with petty political squabbles. Like many other royalists (see Nattapoll 2013: 170–96), Kukrit not only argued that the government of 'commoners' (*samanchon*) established in 1932 perverted the true essence of 'Thainess', but also claimed that the absolute monarchy was more 'democratic' – in substantive, if not procedural terms – than the regimes of the constitutional era. The answer to the uncertainty and instability of the intervening period was said to be the return to a version of Thainess that placed the King at its centre and allowed 'good people' to run the country without interference (see Saichol 2005: 115–30).

Partly in response to leftist critiques of Thai society, Kukrit also offered a spirited defence of the traditional system of feudal hierarchies (*sakdina*). Not only was the complex stratification of society defended as preferable to the social disorder and moral decline brought about by the diffusion of egalitarian ideals; traditional hierarchies were also praised as a source of morality and harmony, as the reciprocity mandated by Buddhist precepts rendered the system free of exploitation. When the members of all classes 'knew their place, low and high' (*ru thi tam thi sung*), inequalities were accepted without problems. Nor did the *sakdina* hierarchy impede social mobility. During the absolute monarchy, people were said to have succeeded or failed depending only on their abilities and karma (*khon thuk khon cha yu nai thana yangrai ko laeo tae khwam samat rue 'kam' khong ton*). The idea of karma served a similar purpose as Plato's 'Noble Lie', for while it guaranteed that everyone deserved the position they currently occupied, and that only 'good men' would rise to the top of the hierarchy, it also made it possible for slaves and *phrai* to live a dignified existence through the benevolence of their superiors (see Saichol 2005: 141–50, 239–42, 329). Monarchy and hierarchy, of course, were very much related in Kukrit's thought, because the sanctification of the monarchy was central to the legitimacy of 'natural' inequalities of goodness and power (see Saichol 2005: 335).

With Luang Wichit, Kukrit popularized the notion that 'Thai-style government' required the concentration of all power in the hands of a paternalistic 'Thai-style leader', like Sarit, who sacrificed himself to provide the nation with justice and prosperity while guaranteeing that the various parts of the social organism worked in harmony. To such a leader, the people owed 'political quiescence' (*khwam ngiap thang kan mueang*). Sarit's dismantlement of democratic institutions received a full-throated endorsement from Kukrit, as a means to undo the contamination of 'Thainess' with the 'otherness' (*khwam pen uen*) blamed for the divisiveness of the post-1932 period (see Saichol 2005: 147–53). At any rate, the people were not ready to play an active role in the country's government, because their ignorance made them unaware of their true needs and hence easily misled by evil politicians (see Saichol 2005: 258). Ordinary people could only be allowed to participate once they understood that real democracy is about electing 'good people'. In the meantime, absolute military rule remained the best way to ensure that *khon di* would remain in charge of the government. By definition, 'Thai-style government' guaranteed that there would be no abuse of power. The only check and balance Thailand ever needed was the presence of an inviolate monarch, under whose reign no injustice would ever be allowed to take place.[3]

The corruption scandal that broke shortly after Sarit's death exposed this notion as a fantasy. In response, Kukrit blamed those who disclosed evidence of the Field Marshal's corruption for destroying the people's confidence in 'Thai-style government' and its institutions (see Saichol 2005: 367–8). Still, Kukrit's active support of Thanom's regime fizzled as it became evident that Sarit's successor was altogether too weak to rein in the corruption of those around him, take charge of the nation's problems, or command the respect, support, and fear Sarit once did. Aside from becoming increasingly critical of the government, Kukrit provided fresh ideological foundations for the ever more prominent and politically active role of the monarchy, casting King Bhumibol in the role of 'Thai-style leader'. The King was not just presented as the father of the people and the guarantor of the unity and 'goodness' of the nation, but a leader who worked to solve real problems and develop the country, as well as a 'pure force' who, without a political agenda, actively ensured

[3] Unlike some of his contemporaries, Kukrit did not stigmatize the Brahmanical *devaraja* (god-king) cult of the Ayutthaya era as a foreign import that polluted the practice of righteous Buddhist kingship (*dhammaraja*) attributed to Sukhothai. Rather, he proposed that modern kings should combine both traditions (see Saichol 2005: 265–7). This idea provided the basis for the revival of practices, such as prostration, that King Bhumibol's predecessors had abolished in an effort to increase the monarchy's proximity to its subjects.

that the government did not abuse its powers or shirk its responsibilities (see Saichol 2005: 378).

As Saichol (2005: 441) puts it, Kukrit was the chief purveyor of an ideology that made the King once again synonymous with the nation. If military leaders like Phibun and Sarit had previously been cast as the expression of the nation's will, while the monarchy played a variously significant but largely symbolic role, the notion of Thainess and 'Thai-style government' articulated in the mid to late 1960s reserved for King Bhumibol the role of speaking for the nation. Ever since, military generals have had to renounce any claim to being anything more than the King's auxiliaries – their extra-constitutional role justified purely on the basis of protecting the monarchy and the nation with which the monarchy is identified, sometimes against the irrational exuberance of those who disregard their 'Thai' obligation to 'know their place'. It would henceforth be the King – the only person in the realm with access to the true dharma, much as Plato had justified the power of 'philosopher guardians' based on their exclusive grasp of 'the idea of the good' – who would act as the ultimate arbiter of a government's fitness to serve. On this point, the extant academic hagiographies of King Bhumibol (see Kobkua 2003: 165; Nakharin 2006: 90) concur with more critical works on the subject (see Handley 2006: 177; Morell and Chai-anan 1981: 68): by the late 1960s and early 1970s, His Majesty was once again the kingdom's most powerful political figure.

While the centrality of each institution to the other's survival and power always required that differences between the military and the monarchy eventually be reconciled or swept under the rug, such differences have nonetheless emerged regularly in the time since Sarit's death. The pressure that King Bhumibol placed on Thanom and Praphat to introduce a new permanent constitution in 1968 and organize multiparty elections in 1969 was the first major incident of this kind – one this study has credited for triggering the first iteration of a cyclical sequence that accounts for the regime instability the country has experienced in the era of 'Thai-style democracy'. Given the King's well-publicized distaste for 'Western' constitutionalism, his short-lived democratic turn in the late 1960s has been subject to varying interpretations. Perhaps most plausible is the notion that, while King Bhumibol's public stance in support of a constitution did not reflect any 'conversion' on his part (see Handley 2006: 199; Morell and Chai-anan 1981: 69), more pragmatic considerations led him to believe that Thailand needed to soften its authoritarian image at home and abroad (see Handley 2006: 194–5). Handley (2006: 195, 205–6) also argues that any benefit the King might have drawn from his advocacy of the system's partial democratization did not reflect a self-conscious attempt to elevate his own power and standing at the expense of the military. This was rather an unintended consequence of his actions, which Bhumibol would attempt to undo upon realizing he had contributed to the regime's destabilization, emboldening its opponents to unleash a wave of criticism against Thanom, Praphat, and their cronies.

Be that as it may, the introduction of the 1968 constitution represented a major victory for the King, whose will had prevailed over the reluctance of Thanom and Praphat. The constitution's content was better still, for its lengthy preamble offered a rewrite of recent history that placed the monarchy at the centre of the country's 'democracy', arguing that Thailand had first become a 'Democracy with the King as Head of State' (*prachathippatai doi mi phramahakasat pen pramuk*) when King Prajadhipok promulgated the country's first permanent constitution in December 1932. The qualifier 'with the King as Head of State', which had previously featured only in the royalist constitution of 1949 (see Nattapoll 2013: 46), served as a new way to describe a form of 'democracy' with the King as sovereign (see Hewison and Kengkij 2010: 182; see also Chalermkiat 1990: 137–8). Since 1932, the preamble stated, this particular version of democracy had 'developed sequentially' (*dai wiwatthanakan ma doi lamdap*), in a way that required many changes to the constitution so as to keep it 'current' (*mo som kae kan samai*). The constitution, in other words, presented military coups as instruments of democratic development.

The constitution's provisions did not present much of a threat to the status quo. Unlike the obscenity it replaced, the new charter did guarantee a host of political and civil rights; despite the fact that each such right was described as 'perfect' or 'complete' (*boribun*), the language describing acceptable limitations was so broad as to permit the state to draw the line wherever it was most convenient. Indeed, the revised anti-communist legislation introduced the subsequent year made encouraging others to 'lose faith in religion or the traditions and customs of the Thai race' into a criminal act of a communistic nature (see Streckfuss 2011: 237–8). In addition, while the constitution established an elected lower house, the royally appointed Senate was granted control over the selection of the Prime Minister; given that confidence votes were to take place in joint sittings, any government commanding Senate support only needed some 15 per cent of the elected members of the House to win a confidence vote with an absolute majority of both houses (the Senate was three-fourths the size of the House). The Senate was also empowered to delay the passage of most legislation by as much as 1 year.

Its built-in safeguards notwithstanding, the limited democracy installed by the 1968 constitution was short-lived. The elections of

February 1969 had actually yielded positive results for the government. The party formed to support Thanom as Prime Minister – *PhakSaha Prachathai* (rendered in English as the United Thai People's Party, UTPP) – leveraged its control of the state bureaucracy to win 75 of 219 seats; after the election, *Saha Prachathai* was joined by 50 of the 72 candidates elected to the House as independents, giving the party a comfortable majority. Perhaps most encouraging to the regime was the extent to which it had made inroads in the Northeast. While most of the candidates affiliated with parties other than the Democrats and *Saha Prachathai* still came from northeastern constituencies, voters in Isan, as a contemporaneous account put it, 'rejected the neutralist-socialist parties that had heretofore dominated the region and, instead, chose UTPP and independent candidates supporting the government' (Neher 1970: 253).

Kukrit Pramoj had reasons to be bitter for being passed over for the Prime Minister's job, in the aftermath of which his verbal attacks against the government intensified (see Saichol 2005: 369). At the same time, Kukrit did not fail to express his sadness over something far worse than military dictatorship: the involvement of elected politicians in the country's administration. Ignoring the massive corruption in which the country's unelected leaders had engaged since 1958, Kukrit bemoaned the expected return to 'the unruly corrupt days' of the Phibun era, lamenting the fact that the country was poised to give up 'one great freedom' Sarit had bestowed upon the Thai people: 'the freedom from politics' (cited in Neher 1970: 257). In reality, the problems were others. On the one hand, there was plenty of politics in the ruling circle, particularly as the designation of Thanom's son (and Praphat's son-in-law) Colonel Narong Kittikachorn as the strongmen's successor generated a great deal of resentment in the military (see Thak 2007 [1979]: 229). Meanwhile, the King's public criticism of the government had emboldened others in the press and civil society to do likewise (see Handley 2006: 204–5). On the other hand, many among the much-maligned politicians elected to parliament actually took their constitutional responsibilities seriously. In practice, that meant that the House of Representatives, while never coming close to threatening the government's position, was not quite the rubber-stamp to which the 'Three Tyrants' (*sam thorarat*; Thanom, Praphat, and Narong), as they would soon be known, thought themselves entitled.

The self-coup staged by Thanom and Praphat in November 1971 was framed as a repeat of Sarit's *autogolpe* 13 years earlier – indeed, as Thak (2007 [1979]: 228) put it, a 'replay of Sarit's 1957 and 1958 coups all at once'. The new junta recycled the name Revolutionary Council

(*Khana Patiwat*) and issued a series of statements reminiscent of its earlier incarnation. As ever, the coup was justified by the presence of grave threats to the monarchy and the nation, said to be impossible to defeat through means other than absolute dictatorial powers. Thanom, moreover, inaugurated a new practice of making conspicuous usage of royal images and symbols as he announced to the Thai people that their rights and freedoms were being terminated for their own protection (see Thak 2007 [1979]: 229). Having come to regret or second-guess the public push made for a constitution 3 years earlier, the King refrained from making statements that could be interpreted as condemnation. Meanwhile, three members of the abolished parliament, who petitioned the courts to declare the coup-makers' actions illegal, were jailed on charges of treason for up to a decade (see Streckfuss 2011: 129–34). Such was the price of questioning the authority of 'good men' to lead the nation, unencumbered by rules written for the rabble.

Enter the masses

The alliance between the military, the palace, and major capitalists put together by Sarit in the late 1950s had not found it especially difficult to consolidate power and manage conflict. Part of this had to do with the weakness of the opposition, which had been deprived of its leading personalities through exile, arrest, and murder. By then, moreover, most of the country's population was not appreciably more involved in politics than it had been at the time of the 1932 coup. Writing in the midst of Sarit's conservative revolution, Wilson (1962: 57–8) noted 'a clear distinction', based primarily on the level of education, 'between those who are involved in politics and those who are not'. Those involved – the educated classes in the capital city – were said to pose no threat to the status quo, given their vested interest in the preservation of 'traditional notions of social hierarchy'. Even university students, whose protests had contributed to Phibun's downfall in 1957, were easily brought in line by Sarit (see Prajak 2013 [2005]: 35). For the most part, the students remained apathetic about the Field Marshal's death in 1963 (see Morell and Chai-anan 1981: 137–9); among those who were active on campus, progressives were still far from dominant (see Reynolds 1987: 30–6).

As for the peasantry, estimated at 'more than 80 per cent of the population', Wilson (1962: 57–8) identified 'its inarticulate acquiescence to the central government and indifference to national politics' as fundamental to the stability of the country's social and political structure. More controversially, the peasantry's 'political inaction' was attributed to 'a tolerable economic situation which provides a stable subsistence without encouraging any great hope for quick improvement'. Others have pointed out that the rural population was not quite as free of grievances (Bowie 1997: 61). Even still, while much of the country had experienced significant economic change since the signing of the Bowring Treaty of 1855, the increased economic insecurity produced by the commercialization of the agricultural sector and explosive population growth had not been accompanied by the emergence of a strong political consciousness,[4] perhaps because economic change had failed to trigger much in the way of actual development or modernization (see Ingram 1971: 216–17). The repression of the Sarit era also effectively silenced the small working-class movement that had emerged after World War II (see Morell and Chai-anan 1981: 186).

As noted, one of the reasons why the end of the absolute monarchy did not settle Thailand's National Revolution is that the process did not intersect, as it did in Western Europe, with the 'massification' of politics brought about by the Industrial Revolution. An economic transformation of comparable import did take place in Thailand beginning in the late 1950s. Once again, however, the sequencing of Thailand's National and Industrial Revolutions – that is, the occurrence of the latter at a time when the alliance of the monarchy and the military was deeply entrenched – helps explain the contradictory effects exerted by the subsequent political awakening of new constituencies.

As Anderson (1977: 15–18) described it, the economic boom of the 1960s, fuelled by the American war in Vietnam, resulted in the dramatic growth of the service economy and vast increases in the secondary and tertiary student populations, multiplying the size of the petty middle class and the urban bourgeoisie several times over. At the same time, increased landlordism in the provinces pushed young men to join the ranks of the working class and the underemployed in Bangkok. These developments not only rearranged Thailand's social structure, giving rise to new classes whose aspirations were not matched by the limited political role reserved for them under military rule, but also generated new rivalries and resentments, both within and across classes. The potential for upheaval increased as the bureaucracy approached saturation, foreclosing traditional routes to social advancement for new graduates, and especially when the economy slowed as a result of American disengagement.

While Sarit's 1958 coup was followed by a decade of rare stability in the formal structure of Thailand's political regime, by the mid to

[4] Thailand's population had grown from 12.5 million in 1932 to 20 million in the early 1950s. By the early to mid 1970s, it approached 40 million (see Saneh 2001: 8).

late 1960s, what had once been the sources of the military regime's strength had turned into potential vulnerabilities. On the one hand, the socio-economic transformations engineered by the regime's developmental policies resulted in the increased politicization of some of the social constituencies such policies had been designed to persuade to stay in their place. Workers and peasants remained largely inactive, but their growing political awareness, combined with continuing repression, economic slowdown, inflation, wage stagnation, and inequality, as well as the increased land tenure problems related to rural indebtedness and the scarcity of land, made these groups increasingly available for mass mobilization (see Saneh 2001: 7–11; Morell and Chai-anan 1981: 186–7, 207–13). In the time since Sarit's death, moreover, the student population had grown more active and politicized (see Prajak 2013 [2005]: 38–112). While it had largely refrained from mobilizing in frontal opposition to the regime, the period of relatively open politics between 1968 and 1971 had seen the emergence of the student movement as the 'most powerful extra-bureaucratic force in the country' (Morell and Chai-anan 1981: 144). Perhaps most important of all was the role of the expanded middle class, caught between the desire to play a greater political role and the fear of losing its newly acquired social status and improved standards of living.

On the other hand, the regime's identification with the monarchy, followed by the precipitous rise in the King's power and prestige at the expense of the country's military rulers, undermined the cohesiveness of the ruling coalition. Bhumibol may not have acted with the intention to undermine Thanom and Praphat. Still, his push for a semi-democratic constitution in 1968 was evidence of a clear divergence of interests between the monarchy and the military. This divergence was likely aggravated by the government's growing unpopularity with urban constituencies that increasingly looked to the King for leadership and guidance, and to whom Bhumibol likely felt the need to listen, in the spirit of the invented tradition of *ratchaprachasamasai* – 'the mutuality of king and people' (see Connors 2008: 148–51) – that would be popularized by Kukrit Pramoj a few years later. By the late 1960s, the very factors that had previously guaranteed the regime's power and legitimacy – its despotic rule, its economic performance, its expanded coalition, and its royal nationalism – had combined to undermine its stability.

The 1968 constitution was an attempt to defuse foreign pressures and domestic dissatisfaction with the regime by enacting what Przeworski (1991) has called a 'controlled opening of the political space', rendered possible by the fact that the King's will could now prevail over the wishes of hardline elements in the military. Somewhat predictably, however, the

1968 constitution actually led to intensifying criticism of the government and pressures for further reforms. Worried by the increased assertiveness exhibited by elected politicians, the press, and budding civil society organizations – to say nothing of the intensification in the communist insurgency in the provinces – the military and the monarchy temporarily closed ranks in support of the 1971 coup, by which they sought to restore a form of dictatorship as 'narrow' as the one imposed by Sarit in 1958. Whether oppositional forces were truly caught by surprise by the 1971 self-coup (see Thak 2007 [1979]: 230) or consciously chose to bide their time (see Morell and Chai-anan 1981: 145), their initial reaction was muted. As the generals imposed the repressive measures designed to restore the *status quo ante*, however, the opposition actually grew more confident in its ability to take on the regime. Crucially, the opposition understood that cracks had opened up in the ruling coalition, both between the monarchy and the military and inside the military itself. The mistaken belief that King Bhumibol supported Thailand's democratization, in particular, was critical to the growing confidence exhibited by the opposition, above all the students, in their ability to challenge the Three Tyrants.

It took about a year for the students to muster the strength, but, when they did, Thailand's first genuine mass movement took shape rapidly, fuelled by the continuing deterioration in the country's economic situation. The first major campaign launched by the National Student Centre of Thailand (NSCT) was a boycott of Japanese goods, complete with a well-attended march staged in November 1972, in defiance of martial law. A little over a month later, after the promulgation of a new interim constitution modelled on Sarit's 1959 charter, the students forced the government to withdraw an order designed to bring the judiciary under tighter regime control. Another major success for the student movement came in June 1973, when a demonstration 50,000 strong earned the reinstatement of nine Ramkhamhaeng University students and the Rector's resignation. The nine had been expelled for publishing in their magazine a satirical statement making light of two recent events: the extension of Thanom's active military post and the scandal sparked a month earlier by the crash of a military helicopter transporting a party of Narong's associates back from an illegal hunting trip at the Thung Yai Wildlife Sanctuary.

On the eve of the massive demonstrations of October 1973, Thailand was something of a tinderbox. A series of social transformations had cumulated over the previous decade, building up pressures on the regime that now approached, partly as a result of the government's own actions, a 'threshold' or a critical level (see Pierson 2004: 83–7), such that relatively minor events could trigger an explosive disruption. Aside from the students' mobilization, 1973 had also seen intensifying labour unrest (see Morell and Chai-anan 1981: 188). The government, increasingly powerless to solve the country's economic problems, had galvanized its opposition by committing a series of missteps and by signalling weakness in repeatedly reversing itself. The mixed signals coming from King Bhumibol, who showed sympathy for the students as he sought to distance himself from the junta, were interpreted as evidence of support, particularly given that associates of the King no less illustrious than Kukrit Pramoj had taken to calling for the government's resignation (see Saichol 2005: 423).

It was, however, Field Marshal Praphat Charusathien who detonated the explosion of anti-government sentiment. On Praphat's orders, eleven student leaders were arrested on 6 October 1973 while publicly campaigning for a 'real' constitution. Two more activists were arrested on similar charges over the next 48 hours. The government brushed off demands for their release, while Praphat publicly accused the student movement of sedition and communism. By then, the regime expected to be able to repress any protest that might result, but it miscalculated the willingness of members of other social constituencies, including slum dwellers, workers, and the middle class, as well as young people attending secondary and vocational schools, to support the university students. After the leadership of the movement resolved on 9 October to protest day and night until the government agreed to promulgate a new constitution within 2 months, the demonstration on the Thammasat University campus swelled to 50,000 on 11 October and 100,000 on 12 October. Faced with demands for the unconditional release of the thirteen activists, backed up by threats of 'decisive measures' (*matrakan nai khan det khat*) (see Charnvit 2001: 189), the government offered bail but was turned down by the students. By the time their representatives went to inform King Bhumibol of the situation on the evening of 12 October, the crowd of protesters had grown to 200,000.

At the expiry of the ultimatum set for midday on 13 October, a crowd half a million strong streamed from Thammasat University to the Democracy Monument. The potential for a confrontation seemed to be averted that afternoon, when the King brokered a deal between the students and the military regime, which committed to free the thirteen activists and introduce a new constitution within a year. Still, thousands refused to disperse – a determination possibly hardened when the regime announced on radio that the movement harboured terrorists bent on fomenting chaos. At around midnight, the crowd was on the move again, marching to the Chitralada Palace 'to seek the protection of royal *barami*' (*phuea nang ao phra barami pen thi phueng*) (see Charnvit 2001: 195). What happened after palace representative Vasit Dejkunjorn called on the demonstrators to disperse before dawn on 14 October remains the subject of some controversy (see Somsak 2001: 72–83). What is certain is that as the students, surrounded by police, found most of the exit routes blocked, violent clashes broke out. In the hours following the incident, the Army was sent in to crack down on the demonstrators. Security forces shot their automatic weapons into the crowds in street fights all along Ratchadamnoen Avenue. Colonel Narong is said to have personally joined in, firing on protesters from a helicopter. Enraged by the repression, which claimed the lives of at least seventy-seven people, students destroyed property, attacked police stations, and set ablaze symbols of the regime like the buildings housing the Lottery Bureau and the Public Relations Department (see Klima 2002: 62–5).

At 7.15 p.m. on 14 October, just over an hour after Thanom resigned his post as Prime Minister, the King appeared on television to decry the violence and announce the formation of a new government, led by Privy Councillor Sanya Thammasak. The effort to remove the Three Tyrants, however, was complicated by the fact that Thanom, like Phibun three decades earlier, remained the Supreme Commander of the Armed Forces and used the position to urge soldiers to repress those determined to destroy 'democracy', as well as the armed 'communist terrorists' (*phu ko kan rai khommiunit*) in their midst (see Charnvit 2001: 201–2). Clashes continued until the evening of 15 October, when the palace and the newly appointed Commander-in-Chief of the Army, General Krit Siwara, with the support of both the Navy and the Air Force, finally forced Thanom, Praphat, and Narong to resign all positions and leave the country. It was only then that the situation finally began to return to normal. At great expense of life and property, the students appeared to have won.

The biggest winner, however, was arguably King Bhumibol. The King had not wanted the situation to end as it did, with the ouster of the military regime. He had allowed the country's democratization only once it became clear that resisting change in those volatile circumstances could have done irreparable harm to the prestige of the military as well as the monarchy. It remains an open question whether the pressure that forced the Three Tyrants to leave the country could have been mustered a day or two earlier, as the King and his associates sought to broker deals that offered demonstrators only as little as necessary for them to disperse, or whether the violence of 14–15 October was actually required to aggravate the rifts inside the armed forces that rendered the departure of Thanom, Praphat, and Narong even possible. Whatever the underlying truth of the matter, King Bhumibol's public intervention and well-publicized role behind the scenes were an unqualified triumph for the monarchy. While the King was subsequently given the credit for taking down the increasingly unpopular military dictatorship almost single-handedly, the central role played by the palace in the situation's resolution underscored the institution's real power, elevating further its popularity and prestige.

While the palace's propaganda machine made sure to highlight the King's actions as those of a modern-day Ramkhamhaeng, ready to answer his children's call to resolve a dispute in the interest of justice, many of his subjects had wanted to believe that all along. The student movement had sought Bhumibol's blessing and guidance in their fight against the military regime. For at least some in the leadership, the choice may have been strategic – a way to broaden the movement's appeal, drive a wedge between the monarchy and the Three Tyrants, and inoculate the protesters from the charges of communism and anti-monarchism that would inevitably be levelled against them as an excuse for repression (see Charnvit 2001: 197–8). Throughout the crisis and its aftermath, however, even the leadership of the movement appears to have been subject to a great deal of wishful thinking and confirmation bias – they wanted the King to be on their side and hence discounted words and behaviour suggesting that the 'royal institution' never did shift 'its support away from the military to the people' (Morell and Chai-anan 1981: 69).

Perhaps not surprisingly, given that even the Communist Party of Thailand (CPT) shied away from attacking the monarchy, the leadership of the 1973 student movement was careful to sidestep the issue of the monarchy's power and constitutional status almost entirely. The declaration issued on 6 October 1973 by the student activists arrested by Praphat (reprinted in Thamrongsak 2007: 159–60), for instance, did open by saying that 'Thailand belongs to all the Thai people' (*Prathet Thai pen khong chao thai thuk khon*) and described peace, freedom, and justice as natural rights that 'belong to every member of the Thai citizenry in equal measures' (*pen khong prachachon chao thai thuk khon doi thao thiam kan*). The movement, however, did not complement claims for popular sovereignty and equal citizenship with any criticism of the role that the monarchy had played in sanctioning military coups, in propping up corrupt military dictatorships, or in legitimizing hierarchical conceptions of the Thai nation.

The students, in fact, were far from immune to the influence of Thailand's royal nationalism. Their critique of the military government's subservience to foreign interests, for instance, was framed in the same anachronistic historical narrative that had been devised in support of the old absolutist state, which emphasised the Thai nation's centuries-old quest for sovereignty and independence (see Prajak 2013 [2005]:

293–307; 412–15). At least some within the movement, moreover, had embraced the myth of a 'democratic monarchy' and blamed the country's military dictatorship not on the royalist coups of 1947, 1957, and 1958, but on the actions of the People's Party in the 1930s (see Prajak 2013 [2005]: 395–444). Indeed, another declaration issued by activists calling for a constitution on 6 October 1973 (reprinted in Thamrongsak 2007: 161–2) highlighted portions of King Prajadhipok's abdication statement that credited the monarchy with the transition to constitutional rule. It was as a result of the students' appropriation of royalist thought and historiography that, as Handley (2006: 209) has written, the struggle came largely to centre on 'competing claims of loyalty to nation, religion, king'. What is more, the students' actions implicitly upheld the established notion that, while the King theoretically exercises sovereignty on behalf of the people, 'political legitimacy [in Thailand] emanates down from the monarchy', as opposed to 'up from the people' (Morell and Chai-anan 1981: 25). Even in democracy's supposed heyday, official nationalism seemed to have emerged triumphant.

Still, King Bhumibol and his associates could not have failed to notice the potential challenges that the rise of a mass movement for 'democracy' presented for the role of the monarchy. While the palace took much of the credit for resolving the situation, the fact remained that the students had thrice disregarded the King's exhortations to disperse. At the end of the day, it had been the students who forced Bhumibol's hand, pushing him to resolve the situation on their terms. For all the conspicuous shows of fealty made by the young demonstrators, moreover, the presence of more radical elements among them was no secret. The threat became all the more manifest as censorship was lifted, 'overnight', in the wake of the Three Tyrants' departure, resulting in the proliferation of literature that previously had been (or would have been) kept out of circulation (see Anderson 1977: 22). While some of this literature did reflect objectives that went beyond 'an attempt to install an American or Western-style, bourgeois-capitalist constitutional regime' (Flood 1975: 63), the greatest threat to the country's royalist order was not presented by the calls for socialist revolution. Rather more troubling, given its potential to capture the imagination of a far greater cross-section of Thai society, was the popular nationalism that had begun to take root among parts of the student movement in the run-up to 14 October. As Anderson (1977: 23) pointed out, the popularity of works that challenged 'the historical centrality and nationalist legitimacy of the monarchy', exploring the 'Thai past in categories that implicitly denied or marginalized the traditional royalist-nationalist mythology', prefigured 'a Copernican shift of perspective on the core element of conservative Thai ideology'.

'Right kill left'

The toppling of the Three Tyrants brought the era of indefinite military rule to a close. Henceforth, the military would no longer be able to run the country, for any meaningful period of time, without at least the pretence of acknowledging the public's right to a basic set of political and civil liberties. The 'real' democracy ushered in by the massive demonstrations of 1973 proved less durable. As ever, for conservatives in the palace, the military, and civil society, the issue with the liberal-democratic regime was less its inability to solve problems inherited from years of dictatorship than the possibility it might subordinate the royalist establishment to the constitutional order, opening up the system to greater and more inclusive forms of mass participation.

The government appointed by the King to see the country through the transition presided over the introduction of a new constitution in 1974. While the constitution was more liberal than previous charters dating back to 1946, the royally appointed legislature had spent months tinkering with the draft to water down its provisions. Still, the governments in office between 1973 and 1976 struggled to manage the multiplicity of social demands that emerged from the rapid 'contagion' of conflict. Despite the movement's fragmentation, students continued to press their demands for greater democracy and social justice in hundreds of demonstrations. Much to the chagrin of the security establishment, the students also worked to expose human rights abuses committed by the armed forces in counter-insurgency operations, including the systematic, gruesome killings of some 3,000 villagers (the 'Red Drum Massacre') carried out between 1972 and 1975 in the southern province of Phatthalung (see Haberkorn 2013). Buoyed by the triumph of people power, workers stepped up their struggle for better pay, work conditions, and welfare benefits (see Morell and Chai-anan 1981: 187–96), while peasant groups started demonstrating throughout the country to demand guaranteed paddy rice prices, the enforcement of rent controls, land reallocations, and legal protections from exploitation (see Morell and Chai-anan 1981: 213–25; see also Haberkorn 2011: Ch. 2). Prime Minister Sanya Thammasak was proactive in his attempt to address some of the concerns put forth by workers and farmers. But if the volume of requests for government intervention quickly exceeded what any government could do in the short term, the radical content of some of the demands went well beyond what Sanya and his backers were willing to give.

Sanya's successors had to contend with an additional challenge. While the general elections held in January 1975 were among the most competitive in the country's history, the twenty-two parties that won seats in the House of Representatives were little more than electoral vehicles for politicians with a strong local base. Even the largest parties – the Democrat Party, Social Justice, and *Chat Thai* – were dominated by personalities whose parliamentary cliques piled intra-party factionalism on top of the legislature's extreme levels of inter-party fragmentation. After Seni Pramoj failed to earn the confidence of the House, Social Action Party leader Kukrit Pramoj was tasked to piece together a coalition government. Having realized his dream of becoming Prime Minister, however, Kukrit no longer had the option of becoming the kind of decisive 'Thai-style leader' he had once fancied himself. The painstaking process of accommodating such a bewildering array of parties, as well as the factions within them, eventually resulted in the formation of a sixteen-party coalition.

If previous efforts made to democratize the country had faced initial conditions that militated against the emergence of a stable democratic regime, the situation was possibly even more problematic in the mid 1970s. King Bhumibol and the increasingly militant Queen Sirikit, now at the height of their popularity, had clearly stated their preference for military rule, at least under the circumstances (for instance, see Handley 2006: 230). The military remained strong despite the ouster of Thanom and Praphat – or perhaps because of it, in that Krit Siwara made sure to remind the public that he had personally forced the Three Tyrants to leave the country, refusing to stand idly by as demonstrators were gunned down in the streets (see Klima 2002: 65). As conservatives in the appointed legislature were busy rewriting the draft constitution, delaying its passage, Krit consolidated his power behind the scenes, substituting his own men for Thanom and Praphat's protégés. In an attempt to establish a foothold in parliament, Krit bankrolled the campaigns of dozens of candidates running in the 1975 elections.

Whereas the period since Sarit's death had been marked by a gradual divergence in the interests of the palace and the military, the two institutions found a measure of renewed common purpose, wasting no time limiting the damage that might result from the country's democratization. The fact that, as of the mid 1970s, every country in former French Indochina had fallen to communist insurgencies only added to the growing siege mentality of conservative royalists. By 1973, the CPT's own ranks had grown to several thousand fighters, while communists were known to have infiltrated the student movement's radical wing. In the months and years thereafter, the palace and the military responded to the country's democratization by funding, training, indoctrinating, and promoting groups whose violent actions had the effect of reminding the country of just how badly it still needed the protection of its self-appointed guardians, even at the cost of sacrificing some of its hard-fought freedoms. The target constituency for this campaign was the urban middle class, whose support for the student-led demonstrations of 1973 had caused the crackdown of 14 October to backfire on the Three Tyrants.

The shifting posture of the Thai middle class resulted from a combination of factors. Its insecurities were heightened by the further deterioration in the country's economic situation, particularly as Thailand began to feel the effects of the global oil crisis, and the upheaval generated by the explosion of political participation (see Anderson 1977: 18). The leadership of the student movement, too, bears responsibility for alienating middle-class support, as its radical turn after 1973 placed the movement increasingly outside the mainstream of Thai society (see Morell and Chai-anan 1981: 172–6). At the same time, if these developments made the students into a target for middle-class displeasure or resentment, it was the hysteria whipped up by royalists over imaginary threats to the nation's existence that turned student leaders – as well as the leaders of trade unions, farmer organizations, and moderate leftist political parties – into legitimate targets for murder and mob violence.

The King made arguably the most significant contribution, peppering his speeches with references to 'dangers from all sides, from within and from without' (see Bhumibol 1979 [4 December 1975]: 36), conspiracies to 'obliterate our country from the world map' (see Bhumibol 1979 [4 December 1975]: 24), and the potential for political conflicts to spiral into a 'total free for all' (see Bhumibol 1979 [4 December 1974]: 10). The song 'We Fight' (*Rao Su*) composed by the King at the end of 1975 (see Somsak 2001: 115–48) spoke of those who 'want to destroy' (*yak tham lai*) the country and 'threats of annihilation' (*khu kha lang khot*) against which the Thai people should prepare to fight to the death. Meanwhile, prominent monks with close ties to the palace, such as the infamous Kittiwuttho Bhikkhu, provided not just a religious rationale for political assassinations, suggesting that the 'bestial types' who would seek to destroy the nation, the religion, or the monarchy 'are not complete persons', but spoke openly of the merit and happiness that would accrue to the country if tens of thousands of students and communists were to be murdered, as per the duty of real Thais (see Handley 2006: 232). Radio stations controlled by the Army added fuel to the fire, broadcasting hateful right-wing songs and rabid speeches that incited violence against leftists, students, and other 'scum'. Even the urbane Kukrit Pramoj (cited in Saichol 2005: 546–7), from the height of his position as Prime Minister, proposed that those who threatened the sovereignty of the kingdom be 'punished violently, without mercy' (*long thot phu phit yang run raeng prat chak khwam prani*).

The rest of the work was done by three organizations mobilized by officials in the Internal Security Operations Command (ISOC) and the Border Patrol Police (BPP). The Village Scouts (*Luk Suea Chao Ban*), founded in 1971, expanded into a national mass movement in 1973 and 1974, thanks to ISOC's stewardship and the royal family's patronage. The King made no secret of his involvement and support. Bhumibol wrote the organization's code of conduct, bestowed the kerchief and insignia awarded to initiates, encouraged public donations to the movement, and frequently spoke at Village Scout rallies and oath-swearing ceremonies. But if, in Handley's (2006: 223) words, the Village Scouts became Bhumibol's 'private army', the King did not disdain to participate in some of the activities of another group, the Red Gaurs (*Krathing Daeng*), recruited mostly from mercenaries and thugs who specialized in attacking student demonstrations and breaking strikes. Some of the King's associates, such as the aforementioned Kittiwuttho Bhikkhu and jurist Thanin Kraivichien, were involved in a third group, *Nawaphon*, described by its leaders as the 'ideological right' (see Prajak 2006: 17).

The violence unleashed by these groups started in 1974 with the murder of a Ramkhamhaeng University student leader. In the ensuing years, royalist vigilantes embarked on a sustained campaign of bombings and assassinations. The violence claimed the lives of some fifteen students, at least forty-six provincial activists associated with the Farmers' Federation of Thailand (FFT), and leftist politicians, as well as dozens of their supporters. Another target of the violence was the liberal-democratic regime established in 1973. Aside from openly protesting against some of the progressive reforms spearheaded by Kukrit Pramoj's elected government, as well as the government's insistence on US troops leaving Thailand by March 1976, extreme right-wing groups sought to undermine the administration indirectly, by disrupting the public order it was already struggling to maintain. A constant refrain in Thailand's official ideology had been that freedom equalled anarchy and chaos. Now that the Thai people had won their freedom, royalists made sure that anarchy and chaos would not be far behind.

Previous work on the subject has emphasized the sociological significance of the rise of extreme right-wing groups in the mid 1970s, described as a 'product of the great boom and its anxious aftermath' (Anderson 1977: 20; see also Bowie 1997; Prajak 2006). For the purposes of this study, most interesting is what these movements reveal in terms of both elite strategy and ideology. Strategically, it has been noted that the attempt to mobilize the masses, through the Village Scouts in particular, marked a drastic departure from the earlier attempt to de-politicize and de-mobilize the population. This may well have been done, as Bowie (1997: 51–2) suggests, primarily out of a sense of despair induced by the absence of good alternatives. Nonetheless, the attempt to popularize reactionary ideology proved resonant with the disaffected, the insecure middle class, and traditional elites threatened by the mobilization of workers and peasants – by some accounts, some 2 million people were involved in the Village Scouts, the Red Gaurs, and *Nawaphon* (see Prajak 2006: 2).[5] Their activities, moreover, proved quite effective in isolating the student movement, in undermining the public's confidence in the democratic government, and in providing the monarchy with a fanatical base of support. On the last point, although the idea that it was the duty of ordinary Thai citizens to kill anyone who threatened or defied the monarchy had been part of the country's official nationalism since the 1910s, it was only in the mid 1970s that civilian mobs were indoctrinated and trained to actually do so. No king or military ruler in Thailand had ever ventured as far.

The 5-day initiation ritual of the Village Scouts described in Bowie (1997: 183–245) provides a clear picture of the state of Thailand's official nationalist ideology in the mid 1970s. Dominating the ritual was the image of a family in which the 'children' (*dek*) owed unquestioned loyalty to their tough-loving parents – the King and Queen. Initiates were encouraged to treat each other like 'brothers and sisters', but this was not the 'brotherhood' of the French Revolution. The emphasis was in fact placed on respecting and heeding one's elders. Even the practice of reducing everyone's age to 8 or 10 years, billed as a way to induce initiates to de-emphasize their diverse backgrounds, was not designed to get them to permanently identify as equals – as was made clear when the age of each participant was restored at the end of the ritual – but in promoting equality only in their submission to father and mother. While the movement ostensibly repudiated politics, Scout leaders clearly conveyed the expectations made of a good subject. Initiates were taught to obey the commands of officials and trust in their ability to discharge their duties wisely. They should also refrain from making any demands of the government, because it was implied that privileges are best accessed through the benevolence of one's superiors, not by 'championing universal laws equally applicable to all' (Bowie 1997: 238). Scouts were

[5] Ostensibly, the Village Scouts sought to mobilize the rural poor to counter efforts by the CPT. Bowie (1997: 248–58), however, found that relatively more affluent people were vastly overrepresented in their ranks, while poorer villagers recruited into the organization tended to lose interest in the organization's activities rather quickly.

advised to keep 'unity' under the King and Queen, without arguing, criticizing, or exhibiting excessive non-conformism. The only domain in which people were required to be politically active was in reporting suspicious behaviour to the authorities and in fighting the foreign governments, agents, and ideologies that threatened Thailand, as well as those Thai-born people placed by their political views outside the bounds of true Thainess.

Concession was made to distinctive regional identities and ethnic differences, as well as the putatively rebellious disposition of the Northeast and the Muslim South, in perpetual danger of falling into the hands of foreigners. In keeping with efforts the authorities had made more recently to secure the loyalty of regional, linguistic, and/or ethnic minorities, initiates were encouraged to be proud of their local traditions, respect those of others, and remember that all Thais were brothers and sisters regardless of their background and provenance. Clearly, all Thai nationals were presented as deserving of membership in the family, at least to the extent that they conformed to the ideological requirements set out for membership. Left unsaid was exactly where each fitted in the familial hierarchy. Indeed, the emphasis placed on preserving the status quo implied that no one should challenge social injustice, unequal treatment under the law, or ethnic discrimination – all of which promised to remain endemic, given that conservatives still regarded northeasterners and most working people as 'stupid, poor, and sick' (*ngo chon chep*) and very much expected them to stay in their place (see Saichol 2005: 534–7). As the King put it in his 1976 birthday address, 'what is more important than suffering itself is that you consent to suffering in order to keep unity' (Bhumibol 1979 [4 December 1976]: 50). On the same occasion the next year, he suggested that, instead of seeking redress for their 'discontentment', which would lead to chaos and disunity, the Thai people should obtain 'satisfaction' simply by 'get[ting] rid of their dissatisfaction' (Bhumibol 1979 [4 December 1977]: 72).

The situation deteriorated rapidly after Prime Minister Kukrit Pramoj announced the dissolution of the House of Representatives in January 1976, in advance of a no confidence vote he had seemed destined to lose. The campaign leading up to elections in April 1976 was marred by unprecedented levels of violence, in which some thirty people were killed as a result of terroristic bombings, grenade attacks on campaign rallies, and assassinations of some of the canvassers, candidates, and leaders of leftist parties. The violence was the work of the Red Gaurs and *Nawaphon*, but was encouraged by the right-wing politicians associated with *Chat Thai* as well as the renegade, extreme faction of the Democrat Party led by Samak Sundaravej, a close advisor and confidant to

Queen Sirikit. *Chat Thai* leader and Defence Minister Praman Adireksan launched the party's campaign with the slogan 'RIGHT KILL LEFT'. Posters appeared in Bangkok screaming that 'all socialists are communists', while a smear campaign was conducted nationwide to accuse leftists and moderates of communism and republicanism. Even politicians with unimpeachable royalist credentials, such as the brothers Pramoj and members of the Democrat Party like Chuan Leekpai, came to be accused of being communists (Morell and Chai-anan 1981: 269). In a climate of hysteria, Village Scout initiations skyrocketed (see Bowie 1997: 23).

The April 1976 election produced a less fragmented legislature. While almost as many parties (nineteen) won seats in the House, the three largest (Democrats, *Chat Thai*, and Social Action) drastically increased their representation at the expense of smaller groups and leftist parties. While more than doubling his party's contingent in the House, Kukrit forfeited his eligibility to serve as Prime Minister after losing his own seat to Samak. The reins of government were taken over by Seni, who led a fractious four-party coalition. Its stability was compromised by conflicts that pitted much of the Democrat Party against its own extreme flank, which was tied to the Village Scout movement (see Bowie 1997: 110), as well as *Chat Thai*, whose leaders Praman Adireksan and Chatichai Chunhavan were involved in the Village Scouts and the Red Gaurs.

Within weeks of the election, Army Commander-in-Chief Krit Siwara died unexpectedly. His death provided an opening for the remnants of the Thanom-Praphat faction, as well as military men close to the leaders of *Chat Thai* and the Queen (see Morell and Chai-anan 1981: 267–73). In mid August, Praphat returned to Thailand, ostensibly to receive medical treatment, but was forced to leave days later, after clashes left two students dead and scores injured. On 19 September 1976, Thanom himself returned, sporting the robes of a Buddhist monk, and was ordained at Wat Boworniwet. The King and Queen made a highly publicized visit to the temple, which was guarded around the clock by the Village Scouts and the Red Gaurs. As the controversy unfolded, Seni resigned and attempted to put together a new coalition that excluded *Chat Thai*, but he had to backtrack after facing the King's opposition. The new cabinet sworn in on 5 October was based on the old coalition, minus two members of the extreme wing of the Democrat Party – Samak, who had travelled to Singapore to convey to Thanom the royal family's approval of his return (see Handley 2006: 234), was among those excluded. In response, the Village Scouts took to the streets to demand that the government drop three progressive Democrats from the executive.

If, as some have suggested (see Thongchai 2002: 249), Thanom's return was a deliberate provocation, it produced the intended effects.

On 24 September, after days of protests, two workers caught passing out handbills against the former dictator were found beaten to death and hanged in Nakhon Pathom. It was revealed soon thereafter that the murders had been the work of the police. On 4 October, students at Thammasat University staged a symbolic protest to demand justice for the killings with a performance that featured the mock hanging of a student. Extreme right-wing newspaper *Dao Sayam* seized on the resemblance between the student-actor and Crown Prince Vajiralongkorn, accusing the students of having hanged the prince in effigy. The subheading under the front-page title 'Country Outraged!' (*Phaendin dueat!*) was: 'The NSCT stomps on the heart of the entire Thai nation' (*Sun . . . yiap hua chai thai thang chat*). As students continued their protests at Thammasat, thousands of *Nawaphon*, Red Gaurs, and Village Scouts converged on the campus to avenge the affront. Some of them were told that the students planned to attack Wat Boworniwet (see Bowie 1997: 26), an idea Queen Sirikit had floated days earlier (see Thongchai 2002: 248), and that the students harboured Vietnamese agents (see Puey 1977: 10), an idea King Bhumibol had hinted at over the previous year (see Somsak 2001: 135), adding to the fabricated insult against the monarchy imminent threats to religion and the nation's sovereignty. Egged on via Army radio, royalist vigilantes and police had the campus surrounded after midnight on 6 October. While the police were under orders to disperse the 4,000 or 5,000 students and arrest their leaders, the message conveyed in radio broadcasts to the Village Scouts and the Red Gaurs was simply: 'Kill them . . . kill them.'

The siege of Thammasat University followed a similar score as the other massacres of civilians that have taken place in Thailand over the past 40 years. Heavily armed officials from the Royal Thai Police and the Border Patrol Police, in concert with the vigilantes who had answered the call to protect 'Nation, Religion, King', attacked the campus with rocket-propelled grenades and automatic weapons. The students defended themselves as best they could, their guards reaching for pistols they had started carrying months earlier after their demonstrations had come under attack. After dawn, some of the NSCT leaders were arrested, having been lured out of the campus by empty promises of a negotiation with the Prime Minister. The students offered to surrender, but found all exits blocked by militants and security forces. At 7.30 a.m., on the pretext that the students were heavily armed, permission was given to the police to 'free fire', supposedly in 'self-defence'.

It is then that the horror for which 6 October 1976 is remembered took place. As the Border Patrol Police called up from Hua Hin's Camp Naresuan stormed the campus, right-wing militants seized a number of unarmed students who were either in police custody or attempting to disperse. Some were shot and hanged from trees, where frenzied mobs cheered the mistreatment of their corpses. Some were tortured to death or burned alive. The police for the most part stood by as the lynchings and mutilations stretched on for hours, in broad daylight (for a detailed timeline, see Puey 1977). Officially, forty-six people died, including two police officers, although it has long been speculated that the casualties may have exceeded one hundred. That evening, it was announced that a new military junta, the National Administrative Reform Council (NARC), had seized power and abrogated the constitution. The coup was justified on the usual grounds, but the junta's statements went so far as to appropriate, almost word-for-word, the *Dao Sayam* headline from the day before, accusing the students of having 'stomped on the hearts of the entire Thai nation' through their act of *lèse majesté* (see NARC 2007 [1976]: 166).

The government formed after the coup was led by a civilian – the former justice of the Supreme Court and palace favourite Thanin Kraivichien. The new strongman was empowered by the new constitution to exercise near-absolute rule, checked only by an appointed legislature packed with military and public administration officials. The new government relentlessly pursued leftists as well as anyone left clamouring for a return to democracy. Thousands of students and intellectuals fled the country or retreated to the jungles – joining the ranks of the communist insurgency. Possibly as many as 8,000 were arrested, and many held without charge because police could now detain people thought to be a 'danger to society' (*phai sangkhom*). Eighteen student leaders were brought before military tribunals to face charges of treason. Under the strict censorship regime imposed by Thanin, secondary schools and universities were forbidden from discussing politics; the police searched libraries, bookstores, and private collections for newly banned literature, some of which went up in flames in 'great Nazi-style public book-burnings' (Klima 2002: 87). Thanin speculated that it would take another 12 years before the Thai people could be made ready for any form of democracy.

A month after the massacre, speaking at a Village Scout oath-swearing ceremony in Chonburi, King Bhumibol showed no sign that the events of 6 October had given him any cause for self-reflection. The King praised the Scouts for, among other things, 'recognizing what's good' (*hen khwam di*), as well as their essential role in defending the nation. Despite what had happened just weeks earlier, the King reminded initiates of their duty to join other units from nearby areas whenever a situation presenting a danger to the nation required their vigilante activities (see Bhumibol 1977 [9 November 1976]: 232). Still far from exhibiting any contrition or regret, moreover, the King explained in his New Year's address that 'the people had made it clear what needed to be done' and that, given that clear statement, it was imperative to 'bring about what needed to be done', despite the hardships it entailed (Bhumibol 1977 [31 December 1976]: 280). Earlier that month, he had told an audience of high-ranking military officers that the country could not afford the luxury of quarrels and dissent in dangerous times. The King added that, if Western newspapers insisted on calling Thai military generals 'dictators', it was the military's responsibility to make sure it would be a 'good dictatorship', given that 'the Thai military has never ruled dictatorially in the manner of Western dictators' (Bhumibol 1977 [14 December 1976]: 275).

A legacy of violence

The conservative 'revolution' carried out by Field Marshal Sarit Thanarat engineered a profound transformation in what could be called Thailand's 'material constitution'. Accompanying the reorganization in the workings of the regime, the expansion of the state's capacity and territorial reach, and the adjustments made to the composition and structure of the ruling coalition was the redefinition of the nationalist ideology that provided the system's legitimacy, reflected in a notion of 'Thainess' that mixed elements of the official nationalism conceived under the absolute monarchy with the same preoccupation for the state's role in enforcing social conformity that had distinguished the first Phibun government. Also designed to maximize the regime's legitimacy were the developmental economic policies, financed by the infusion of foreign funds, which set in motion a thoroughgoing transformation of Thai society, resulting in the integration of all peripheries in the market economy, as well as rising levels of income, education, industrialization, and urbanization.

Few of the innovations introduced in the wake of the 1958 coup survived, intact, the era of mass politics. Indeed, just as the absolutist regime founded by King Chulalongkorn in the late nineteenth century ultimately succumbed to the social transformations set in motion by the rise of an absolutist state (see Kullada 2004), so were the structural foundations of the regime established by Sarit undermined by the effects of measures whose purpose had been to bolster the regime's stability (see also Thak 2007 [1979]: 227). The passage of a semi-democratic constitution in 1968 triggered a sequence of events that would repeat itself several times in the ensuing decades. The resulting intensification of demands for greater political inclusion was met with a conservative reaction designed to restore the pre-1968 status quo, followed in turn by the mobilization of popular forces opposed to the restoration. The massive demonstrations and failed government crackdown of 14 October 1973 aggravated pre-existing divisions within the ruling coalition, eventually inducing the monarchy and the military to cut their losses and give in to demands for the country's democratization, albeit in a way that permitted unelected institutions to remain in control of the transition process.

Thailand's democratization, however, almost immediately led to the renewed intensification of challenges from below, followed by a new conservative reaction aiming to restore a form of dictatorship as repressive as the one in place before 1973. Confronted with the threat to its *power* presented by the liberal-democratic regime that took shape after 1973, as well as the threat to its *legitimacy* presented by the diffusion of popular nationalist ideas, the country's royalist establishment unleashed a wave of vigilante violence that culminated in the student massacre and military coup of 6 October 1976, followed shortly thereafter by the establishment of a 'virtual theocracy' (see Streckfuss 2011: 213), centred on the monarchy, that promised to restore the 'freedom from politics' said to have characterized the period under Sarit. With the fall of Thanin Kraivichien's dictatorship in October 1977 – rooted, once more, in the combination of intra-elite divisions and popular dissatisfaction with the new regime's extreme repression – the workings of 'Thai-style democracy' or 'Democracy with the King as Head of State' underwent a new series of adaptations. Designed to ensure the continuity of the royalist order, by means of tempering the system's authoritarianism, the new set of liberal-democratic reforms granted in the late 1970s set the stage for the cycle to repeat itself yet again.

Owing, in part, to the successive rounds of political struggle it experienced since the death of Field Marshal Sarit, Thailand is no doubt a very different country today from the one it was five decades ago. Still, the legacy of Sarit's conservative revolution is unmistakable in the political crisis into which the country descended with the military coup of 19 September 2006. Beyond the King's cult of personality and extra-constitutional status, the most enduring legacy of the period is the persistence, among royalists, of a world view that conceives the national community in hierarchical as opposed to egalitarian terms. What is left of 'Thai-style democracy', in turn, still functions as a form of 'structural violence' (see Galtung 1969: 171; for a passing reference, see Saichol 2005: 512), because the persistence of (informal) disparities in citizenship status also serves to perpetuate inequalities in income and opportunity far beyond what is strictly unavoidable, given current levels of development and the workings of a market economy (for an overview, see Hewison 2014). Among royalists, moreover, the idea that direct, physical violence against those who challenge 'Nation, Religion, King' is a matter of civic duty or religious merit, or should at any rate be exempt from legal prosecution, is alive and well. Indeed, to the extent that its primary function – aside from its crude reduction of 'Thai' to 'royalist' – is to provide 'cultural' justifications for the forms of direct and structural violence that guarantee the power and privilege of a small minority of 'good people', the official ideology of Thainess lives on, above all else, as a form of 'cultural violence' (see Galtung 1990: 291).

6 Rise of the politicians

With the onset of modernity and mass participation, kings and queens around the world have mostly been reduced to the status of figureheads and tabloid celebrities – those who failed to accept a ceremonial role having often been consigned to far worse fates. At least for a time, not so in Thailand, where the power and prestige of the monarchy soared as the country entered the era of mass politics in the 1970s. The 'direct and open attacks on the monarchy' said to have 'loom[ed] imminently' in the aftermath of the 1976 massacre (see Anderson 1977: 24) did come. Communist insurgents grew more outspoken, as did some of the former student leaders forced by repression to join the CPT (for instance, see Handley 2006: 264). Leaflets and other texts critical of the monarchy, moreover, surfaced in Bangkok with some regularity. Yet the verbal barbs flung from beyond the Thai state's jurisdiction, or from under the cover of anonymity, never really led to the mainstreaming of radical critiques of the monarchy's power and constitutional status. On the contrary, King Bhumibol's popularity would reach new heights in the 1980s and 1990s.

Part of the reason is that, by the time Thailand experienced mass participation in the 1970s, the palace and its allies had had the benefit of a 15-year headstart. While the promotion of the monarchy's image through modern means of mass communication had been a central component of the 'hegemonic project' launched under Sarit (see Connors 2007 [2003]: 44–52), its timing was fortuitous, for the campaign could not only avail itself of a fully implemented system of primary education – where plenty of school hours are still taken up by lessons on morality, religion, and civics heavily imbued with the royalist ideology of Thainess (see Somwung and Siridej 2005) – but also coincided with the rapid diffusion of radios and to a lesser extent televisions in the 1960s and 1970s (see Knodel *et al.* 1987: 42–5). Indeed, it could be said that the longevity of Thailand's 'royal nationalism' has less to do with the country's exceptionalism than it does with the timing of the monarchy's return to political prominence. American assistance and repression made sure that any competition royalists might face for the definition of the country's national identity would find itself badly outmatched.

For most mainstream political actors, the mere appearance of a 'universally revered' monarch was strong enough incentive to frame political demands in a manner that did not challenge the palace or its extra-constitutional prerogatives. Most of the movements and organizations that came onto the scene during that time saw fit not to question the role of the King as sovereign, but rather chose to frame appeals for more rights, freedoms, and opportunities in royal symbolism. Failing that, Thailand's *lèse-majesté* laws – whose enforcement and penalties were doubled after the events of 1976 heightened the monarchy's vulnerability to criticism (see Handley 2006: 259) – effectively restricted the range of political contestation by making an example of the few willing to test the limits of the institution's popularity. Whenever the palace was threatened by events on the streets, moreover, Bhumibol's stage-managed interventions served to steer conflict in less menacing directions. The King's interventions in 1973 and 1992, in turn, further elevated the status of the monarchy, providing some cover for the palace's complicity in the mob violence of the mid 1970s as well as the military coups of 1971, 1976, and 1991.

The extreme repression unleashed by Thanin Kraivichien following the 1976 massacre at Thammasat University was deeply unpopular, so much so that the military felt compelled to remove him in October 1977. King Bhumibol may not have seen it that way at the time, but the generals had acted in the monarchy's best interest, for the institution was forced to come to terms with the fact that the restoration had, once again, failed. Thailand could no longer be governed the way Sarit had ruled it, not without the kind of sustained repression that would ultimately prove self-destructive. The result was an adaptation in both ideology and regime form. On the one hand, the country's official national ideology, as well as the King's own personal efforts, came to be focused on securing the provincial masses' embracement of their subaltern status through renewed emphasis on the familial unity of the peasantry and the monarchy (see Streckfuss 2011: 213–15). On the other hand, the royalist establishment acceded to the urban middle class' demands for a meaningful role in the government of the country. The premiership of General Prem Tinsulanond (1980–8) was marked by the development of functioning representative institutions, as well as the increased salience of electoral participation and competition.

The adaptations, combined with a conspicuous escalation in the state's efforts to 're-mystify' the monarchy, cemented the King's image as a benevolent father and guardian of his subjects' best interests. These measures, however, came short of providing a lasting solution to the problem of regime instability. Indeed, if Thailand had never experienced four consecutive elections without coups or other disruptions in the constitutional order – as it did in 1979, 1983, 1986, and 1988 – the ambition of elected politicians, and their ability gradually to carve out for themselves an increasingly powerful political role, was ultimately the undoing of Thai-style democracy's second incarnation. When Prem stepped down in 1988, the palace, the military, and the bureaucracy once again backed into allowing the country's transition to 'electoral democracy', only to realize soon thereafter that an elected government posed no less of a threat to their prerogatives than it had 15 years earlier.

The coup orchestrated by General Suchinda Kraprayoon in 1991 was an attempt to restore Thailand to the days of 'Premocracy', to turn the clock back to a time when an unelected military man could run the country, legitimized by the existence of a functioning parliament but not exceedingly encumbered by any changes elections might bring to its composition. The failure of Suchinda's restoration, punctuated by a new massacre of demonstrators in the events of 'Black May' 1992, gave way to another adaptation. The military was formally sidelined, the Thai people's wish to elect their own governments begrudgingly granted. Still, as a result of the King's intervention, the palace preserved much of its influence and standing. The network of 'good men' Prem had built in most state institutions was leveraged throughout the 1990s to shape national policy, as well as manipulate or actively undermine elected governments notorious for their weakness and corruption (see McCargo 2005: 507–15). While the inchoateness of Thailand's political system allowed the monarchy to conserve the moral high ground, protect the legitimacy of its routine interferences, and maintain its role as the 'ultimate arbiter of political decisions in times of crisis' (McCargo 2005: 501), its efforts to undermine representative institutions had a crucial unintended consequence: setting the stage for Thaksin Shinawatra's otherwise resistible rise.

Remaking guardianship

The government of Thanin Kraivichien has been called 'the most repressive in Thai history' (Keyes 1987: 100). It is not difficult to see why, in the eyes of its supporters, conditions may have seemed right for a reactionary regime of that kind. The protests of students, workers, and peasants had proven threatening to most elites and unpopular with the urban middle class. In the aftermath of the 1976 coup, moreover, the ranks of the CPT had swelled to over 10,000 fighters (see Morell and

Chai-anan 1981: 294–303). The inroads insurgents were making in their recruitment efforts, the increasingly bold and effective nature of their operations, and the open attacks launched against the royal family, both verbal and physical (see Bowie 1997: 142; Handley 2006: 262–3), stoked fears that the situation might escalate into a full-blown civil war.

Had similar circumstances occurred two decades earlier, when Sarit had to fabricate a similar threat to justify his despotic rule, it is possible that Thailand might have developed an 'authoritarian Leviathan' in the manner of Singapore and Malaysia (see Slater 2010). By the late 1970s, however, three factors militated against this outcome. First, internecine struggles had divided the military as well as royalists outside the state's security apparatus. The divisions haunted Thanin from the start. While the repression alienated moderate royalists, the same policies did not satisfy the extreme right (see Bowie 1997: 134–6) and its allies in the military. The right-wing opposition would soon stage a failed attempt, headlined by General Chalard Hiranyasiri, to seize power in March 1977.

Second, if the development of a strong 'authoritarian Leviathan' requires perhaps above all the willingness of capitalist elites to subject themselves to the kind of taxation needed to support a strong state and a dominant government party, by the late 1970s, Thailand's capitalists were not inclined to bankroll any such endeavour. In the capital city, major business families had grown wealthy and confident enough in their own strength to begin to shake off the patronage of the military and the bureaucracy, looking instead to the electoral and legislative arenas to assert their influence over the state directly (see Pasuk and Baker 2000: 34). In the provinces, where the economic transformation had come later, the 1960s and 1970s had seen the rise of a new class of businessmen, to whom the liberal period had likewise given a taste of the benefits of accessing power directly, through the ballot box (see Anderson 1990: 41–2). While both groups were happy to work with the palace, the military, or the bureaucracy when it suited their interests, neither had any intention to give up sizeable chunks of their wealth to finance the construction of an authoritarian state that would largely have served to limit their own influence and power.

Third, there is much to be said for the argument that the intensification of the communist insurgency actually aggravated divisions within Thailand's ruling class, instead of unifying it, as key constituencies came to the conclusion that the state's reliance on repression was the cause of the continuing unrest, as opposed to a viable solution (see Slater 2010: 24). The urban middle class had welcomed the 1976 coup in the expectation that law and order would be restored, but not the continuing repression (see Bowie 1997: 138–41), perhaps especially given the insurgency's escalation. Giving voice to the educated public's dissatisfaction, Kukrit Pramoj went so far as to argue that the government had given peasants no choice but to join the CPT (see Handley 2006: 266). In addition to the military's internal factionalism, Likhit (1992: 205) points out that the conflict between the military and 'the traditionalists' (i.e., the palace) had resurfaced once the 'imminent danger' presented to both by the liberal regime had been dispatched. The junta's own members, as well as powerful factions within the armed forces, understood that Thanin's policies only aggravated the risk of a 'major civil war' (see Keyes 1987: 101).

The military coup of 20 October 1977 is one of the few coups staged in the post-absolutist period that aimed to make the country more, not less, democratic. The statement by which the new Revolutionary Council (2007 [1977]: 109) justified the operation explicitly promised to hold elections, arguing that Thailand needed greater democracy so as to better address the needs of the people, civil servants, and foreign investors. The 1977 coup was also the first, and to date the only, coup since 1951 to have succeeded despite the opposition of the royal family, which never wavered in its support of Thanin despite the regime's growing isolation.[1] Given that the King was by then Thanin's only major supporter, the Revolutionary Council's (2007 [1977]: 109) statement that the government had done nothing but further divide the country may well have been intended as indirect criticism of the monarchy, particularly in light of the King's rhetoric of unity. This, however, was no anti-royalist coup, but rather one designed, in no small part, to save the monarchy from its own fanaticism. Aside from presiding over the promulgation of a new constitution in December 1978, the new Prime Minister, General Kriangsak Chomanan, relaxed restrictions to freedom of the press, issued amnesties to students caught up in the repression of 1976, gave the youths who had fled to the jungles the opportunity to come back to finish their studies, moved to neutralize extreme right-wing groups, explored political solutions to the insurgency, and pursued more amicable relations with communist regimes in China, the Soviet Union, and mainland Southeast Asia.

The 1978 constitution, which was in force for over 12 years, remains the second most durable constitution Thailand has lived under since 1932. Not unlike the constitution of 1932, the document provided for a system of tutelary democracy. The constitution did not require that the Prime Minister be selected from among the representatives elected by the people; its transitory provisions, set to expire in 1983, allowed

[1] Displeased, the King appointed Thanin to the Privy Council, where he still sits.

members of the cabinet to maintain active civil service posts. The Prime Minister, moreover, was given the power to appoint the Senate, designed to function as the bureaucracy's 'informal political party' (Chai-anan 1989: 333). Aside from exercising control over much of the parliamentary agenda, during the interim period the Senate was granted extensive legislative powers, because the constitution required that motions of no confidence and bills dealing with budgets, economic policy, and national security be deliberated and approved in joint sittings of the two chambers (Article 203). Having realized that the restoration of 'Thai-style democracy' to its earlier, authoritarian form was no longer feasible, but having no intention of returning to the 'open politics' of the 1973–6 period, Kriangsak and his junta fell back on the abortive effort that had been made a decade earlier, in 1968, to establish something of a 'semi-democracy' (*prachathippatai khrueng bai*).[2]

The relative strength of the regime inaugurated in 1978 was precisely that, while it was designed to forestall the emergence of a fully democratic system of government, it reflected lessons that segments of the Thai establishment had learned from the battles of the previous decade. Among the changing circumstances to which it was designed to respond, most important was the emergence of a politically conscious urban middle class. On the one hand, the new regime integrated the urban middle class as junior partner in the ruling coalition, providing its representatives, elected and otherwise, with a voice in the policy-making process (see Chai-anan 1989: 334–5; see also Anderson 1990). On the other hand, it leveraged the middle class' discomfort with the prospect of a fully democratic system of government, which had been at the heart of its shifting posture in the mid 1970s, to justify the tutelage exercised by the palace, the military, and the bureaucracy.

The path-dependent nature of Thailand's trajectory of political development – previously defined, following Page (2006), as the sensitivity of outcomes along the historical sequence to previous outcomes and their temporal ordering – is evident in the regime installed in the wake of Thanin's fall. Not only did the semi-democracy established in 1978 embody the legacies of previous struggles – in Chai-anan's (1989: 334) words, it represented 'the outgrowth of the interplay of social, economic, and political forces in Thai society' – particularly with regard to its inclusion of the urban middle class; the system also reflected the fact that mass mobilization had taken place at a time when the country's royalist establishment, its internal divisions notwithstanding, was firmly entrenched in

[2] The 1978 constitution has been described as a 'marriage' of its two predecessors of 1968 and 1974 (see Nakharin 1991: 64).

the state apparatus. This had not only allowed unelected institutions to undermine and then abruptly terminate the electoral democracy established in 1973, but also to do so in a such a way as to make it possible for relatively minor concessions to effectively co-opt the very group, the urban middle class, whose support had been decisive to the country's democratization.

In the wake of the 1976 massacre, men like General Kriangsak and others appear to have understood that the main challenge for Thailand's ruling class was not the presence of a constituted threat to its power, of the kind that could have been addressed by further repression. The repression, in fact, had already destroyed all forms of organized opposition save for the communist insurgency. The problem was rather one of legitimacy. The emergence of popular nationalist ideas in the mid 1970s had threatened the cultural hegemony of Thailand's official nationalism, disrupting one of the key mechanisms of institutional reproduction that had allowed the alliance of the military and the palace to rule without having recourse to the extreme levels of violence and coercion that sustained authoritarian regimes elsewhere in the region. King Bhumibol's public backing of a measure of repression well in excess of what could be justified in the interest of 'restoring order' had only made matters worse. Even the threat posed by the CPT was still about legitimacy more than power, in that its growth threatened not so much to topple the government but to destroy the public's trust in institutions that claimed to be protecting the country from communism, but whose actions had in fact done nothing except fuel the insurgency's expansion. In the absence of an organized force challenging the power of the military and the palace, the main threat was presented by the acceleration of what Anderson (1977: 24) had referred to as 'secular demystification of Thai politics'.

This interpretation is borne out by evidence of the interest shown by the state's security apparatus in redefining the state's official nationalism. A document produced by the National Security Council in 1976 spoke of the need to rearticulate the country's 'national ideology' (*udomkan khong chat*) – having deemed its present form not only too closely associated with right-wing hysteria and violence, but also too distant from the population to secure its continuing loyalty and facilitate its management – by means of addressing, at least rhetorically, a series of needs and aspirations ascribed to different groups (see Connors 2007 [2003]: 136–8). These recommendations, and others along the same lines, were taken up by Kriangsak's government with the stated intent to 'respond to attacks on the "highest institutions" of the land' (see Connors 2007 [2003]: 139–42). Beginning in 1980, the 're-ideologicization' of both the state and the populace, to be carried out through the state-owned media and other 'socio-political institutions', would be founded on the 'aggressive restoration of the monarchy' through the appropriation of 'the progressive themes of democracy and social development' and their redeployment for hegemonic purposes (Connors 2007 [2003]: 130).

Ironically, the main impediments to the success of the adaptation were the military's continuing fragmentation and King Bhumibol's own opposition. The King eventually came around to the idea, if only after the military's internal divisions had afforded him an opportunity to regain control of the process. While Kriangsak had stayed on as Prime Minister after elections held in April 1979, his position was compromised by the lack of a strong power base in the Assembly, the military, or the bureaucracy. The first military leader since Phraya Phahon to serve as Prime Minister despite no history of troop command (see Morell and Chai-anan 1981: 278), Kriangsak's rise to power in 1977 had been made possible by the 'Young Turks', a group of relatively young colonels who controlled strategic units within the Royal Thai Army. Drawn from Class 7 of the Chulachomklao Royal Military Academy, the Young Turks took an especially self-righteous view of their role as enforcers of justice and morality within the state (see Chalermkiat 1990: 62–70). Dissatisfied with Kriangsak's leadership, in 1980, the Young Turks pressed for his replacement with the new Commander-in-Chief of the Army, General Prem Tinsulanond. Although initially inclined to dissolve the House and call new elections (see Likhit 1992: 210), an audience with King Bhumibol persuaded Kriangsak to resign and allow Prem to form a new government. The King's support was subsequently decisive in saving Prem from coup attempts in 1981 and 1985, and in allowing him to purge from the military individuals and factions, the Young Turks included, who came to challenge his rule.

Through his partnership with Prem, the King found his way back to the moderate course he had abandoned in the 1970s and returned to lead the revitalization of Thailand's national ideology. Unlike the military generals with whom King Bhumibol had previously cohabitated, Prem was not perceived to be animated by greed, lust for power, or ideological extremism. In both form and substance, moreover, the government Prem led was very conspicuously the King's own. Although pushing the limits of good taste, Prem's public displays of submission, including his penchant for grovelling at the King's feet, signalled that the Prime Minister was only the first among the King's subordinates. More substantively, Prem's deference to the King's wishes made Thailand's 'Democracy with the King as Head of State' into the modern-day embodiment of the 'limited monarchy' King Prajadhipok had envisioned in the mid 1920s. While preserving the King's authority to direct the government, assisted by a

Prime Minister tasked with running the country's day-to-day affairs, the system shielded the King from public accountability, particularly given the jail terms attendant on the impudence of questioning the myth of a monarchy 'above', or otherwise not involved in, politics.

Aside from jump-starting the economy, Prem's 8-year tenure in office is perhaps best remembered for ending the communist insurgency. Since its heyday in 1977–9, the CPT had been weakened by the conflict between China and Vietnam that followed the latter's invasion of Cambodia, which led in turn to the CPT's eviction from its bases in Laos. At the same time, China's pursuit of a closer relationship with Bangkok deprived the CPT of its main patron, while the amnesty granted to the former students caused it to haemorrhage personnel and brainpower. Prem's government seized upon these opportunities, offering communist cadres and fighters an amnesty in exchange for turning in their weapons and giving up their struggle. By the mid 1980s, the insurgency was essentially over.

Prime Ministerial Orders 66/2523 and 65/2525, issued in 1980 and 1982, respectively, are not only credited for setting forth a new approach to counter-insurgency, but also for laying out a new vision of a military-led society (see Chalermkiat 1990: 80). While arguing that only 'real democracy' and true 'justice' could assure peace and inspire love for the nation and loyalty to its institutions, the documents reserved for the military and the civilian bureaucracy the tasks of promoting popular participation, educating the public about democracy, suppressing corruption, and regulating the activities of pressure groups and social classes, so as to channel them towards more constructive ends. As for parliament and political parties, the orders explicitly condemned their failure to manage conflicts and offer the people adequate representation, conveniently ignoring the fact that the weakness of both was rooted in the military's constant interference in the political process. The orders' most enduring legacy, however, was the sleight of hand they accomplished in linking the military's criticism of the parliamentary system with its criticism of capitalist exploitation – listed as one of the insurgency's main catalysts – through the identification of political parties with the selfish interests of big business. The association of competitive politics with exploitative capitalism complemented the attempt to use progressive, 'sham-populist' (Anderson 1990: 41) language to strengthen the allegiance of the masses, the peasantry in particular, to the royalist state and its conservative policies.

The monarchy would play a central role in the effort to secure the rural population's continued acceptance of its subaltern status, to be achieved in part through renewed emphasis on its protection of the peasantry (see

Streckfuss 2011: 213–15) and on 'self-sufficient village life' as the defining characteristic of Thai culture (see Handley 2006: 269). Perhaps more than the mobilization of students and workers, most troubling in the eyes of conservatives had been the demonstrations staged in the mid 1970s by peasant groups (see Haberkorn 2011). In response, the state had already begun to shift from taxing to subsidizing the peasantry (see Walker 2012: 49–56). Still, the cultivation of King Bhumibol's image as a benevolent father, wholly dedicated to improving the lives of his 'children', remained essential to the legitimacy of the social hierarchy over which he presided, given the inequality and discrimination the system continued to engender. For that purpose, Prem's government effectuated a tenfold increase in public expenditures on royal projects (see Handley 2006: 290), publicizing the King's philosophy of sustainable development, self-reliance, and contentment in 'sufficiency'.[3] The King himself took to preaching his new gospel of 'plebeian anti-capitalism' (see Moore 1966: 448), emphasizing the monarchy's dual role in 'disciplining' the masses and in protecting ordinary people from the workings of market capitalism (see Connors 2007 [2003]: 132).

The effort made to include the people in the King's 'circle of merit' (Streckfuss 2011: 215) was but a contemporary variant, now festooned with the pious language of localism and community, of a form of conservative reaction Barrington Moore traced all the way back to Cato the Elder (234–149 BC). Specifically, Moore (1966: 491) noted that 'where commercial relationships have begun to undermine a peasant economy, the conservative elements in society are likely to generate a rhetoric of extolling the peasant as the backbone of society'. Often accompanying this rhetoric are calls for a thoroughgoing moral regeneration, to be achieved through continued submission to ostensibly 'traditional' forms of authority and a return to 'a way of life that has supposedly proved its validity in the past' (Moore 1966: 494–6). Most recently, with the 'entrance of the masses on the historical stage', dominant groups intent on protecting their 'traditional' status against the onslaught of modernization have at times sought to earn the masses' support for the conservative reaction through appeals based on the 'plebeian anti-capitalism' Moore (1966: 447–8) identifies as 'the feature that most clearly distinguishes twentieth-century fascism from its predecessors'.

[3] The expression 'sufficiency economy' (*setthakit pho phiang*) was first used in 1997. Its beginnings, however, are traced by the various state agencies dedicated to advertising the idea back to 1974 (see Isager and Ivarsson 2010: 226–7), when the King spoke of achieving development by securing, for the 'majority of the population', 'sufficiency in what they possess, eat, and use' (*khwam pho mi pho kin pho chai*) (see Bhumibol, 18 July 1974). For the genesis of the King's ideas, see Handley (2006: 241–3).

Each of the defining themes of 'Catonism' came to be emphasized repeatedly in King Bhumibol's speeches and in the propaganda campaign launched pursuant to the state's attempt to redefine the country's national ideology. Having long been idealized as the 'backbone of the nation' (see Haberkorn 2011: 39), provincial populations were now urged to resist the lure of 'the City of Extravagance' (see Walker 2010: 241), reject 'borrowed' ideals, values, and tastes (see Handley 2006: 280), refrain from demanding the establishment of a corrupting welfare state (see Handley 2006: 344), and, perhaps above all, ignore promises of economic and social advancement made by evil politicians and their corporate puppetmasters (see Thongchai 2008a: 26). While the great majority of the population has remained, at best, ambivalent about each of these demands, the philosophy has appealed far more effectively to the rich and the urban middle class, from whom it demanded nothing, thanks to its power to justify status inequalities in a reassuringly romanticized image of the country's past. Somewhat improbably, it also made an impression on a great many 'progressive' intellectuals, including former student leaders and radical leftists (see Thongchai 2008b). Some became proponents of a 'community culture' (*watthanatham chumchon*) approach to development that emphasized the need for peasants to withdraw from the market, return to subsistence farming, and focus on reinvigorating local communities instead of pursuing structural changes at the national level (see Chatthip 1991).

The indictment of parliamentary government through its identification with big business interests had an element of truth. By the 1980s, Thailand's erstwhile 'pariah capitalists' sought to play a more active role in politics through the parliamentary system, such that political parties were often identified with the big corporations that funded them (see Nakharin 1991: 73–9). If, moreover, businessmen-turned-politicians had begun to form the largest contingent in the House of Representatives beginning with the 1969 elections, it was not long thereafter that they secured strong representation in the executive as well (see Nakharin 1991: 65). Having said that, refashioning the monarchy and the military as the people's stalwarts against monopoly capitalism was audacious. Through its control of one of the country's largest business conglomerates, the Crown Property Bureau, the monarchy was then, and is now, among Thailand's largest monopoly capitalists, as well as the preferred local partner of large multinational corporations. Military generals, for their part, had long drawn their powers of patronage from corrupt relationships with the business world. Aside from their direct participation in activities against which they now claimed to be defending the people, the monarchy and the military had in fact played a crucial role in facilitating and legitimizing the concentration of most of the country's wealth and capital into the hands of a few dozen families. Nor was the alleviation of inequalities anywhere on the agenda – as Hewison (1996: 81) pointed out, the objective was merely to protect the 'conservative capitalist state' against the onslaught of a 'capitalist revolution' that would have substituted popular participation for authoritarian, technocratic control of the country's political and economic systems.

As Connors (2007 [2003]: 133) has written, reconciling the contrasting roles played by the monarchy – as leading capitalist and anti-capitalist crusader, as agent of 'powerful interests' and bulwark against exploitation, as protector of 'democracy' and critic of alien representative institutions – required an 'iron regime of controlled imagery' as well as the enlistment of much of the media, the education system, and the state in the service of ideological propagation. Once again, the diffusion of television sets and the new expansion in secondary education were critical to that effort, as they now allowed the state to reach directly almost the entirety of the population. With regard to the monarchy, the approach was founded not only on playing up the King's role as 'father of the nation' and agent of the country's development, but also on the monarchy's 're-mystification'. Commenting on an essay written by Thanin Kraivichien in 1977, Kershaw (2001: 139–40, 200) noted that, whereas royalist intellectuals like Kukrit Pramoj had previously 'actively demystified' the monarchy, justifying its role in modern, rationalistic terms, the palace now allowed 'a conservative publicist' like Thanin to 'remystify' the institution by emphasizing 'the more magical side of monarchy'. By 1990, state agencies such as the National Identity Board were no longer squeamish about presenting the King as a 'semi-god' (see Connors 2007 [2003]: 145). Nor was the effort confined to the reigning monarch, for it was during this time that King Chulalongkorn attained 'godlike status' and began to be worshipped as a deity (see Engel and Engel 2010: 83). The effectiveness of the campaign, backed by unprecedented amounts of taxpayer funds, also benefited from the contributions of a 'mediatized and commodified popular religious culture' said to have emerged 'independently of any project of elite hegemony' (see Jackson 2010: 54–5).

The adaptations pursued in the 1980s to the workings of 'Thai-style democracy' and the national ideology of Thainess were extremely successful in stemming the tide of popular nationalism, as well as in forging an emotional bond between much of the population and the King. The adaptations, however, were far less successful in ensuring the regime's stability beyond Prem's tenure as Prime Minister. Yet again, what proved to be the downfall of the 'semi-democracy' established in 1978 was a force that the palace, the military, and the bureaucracy had themselves unleashed through measures designed to bolster the regime's power and legitimacy. Having dismantled the communist insurgency, destroyed the student movement, and demobilized the extreme right, the one threat royalists never conclusively defeated was the ambition of elected politicians, and their ability to tap into aspirations that none of the King's pleas could convince the Thai people to abandon. It would not be long before the rise of the politicians would force another showdown.

Lords of darkness

Thailand's political development provides a compelling illustration for the proposition that military coups tend to increase the likelihood of future military interventions (see Przeworski 2009). By the early 1980s, the military was the beneficiary of as much as one-fifth of annual government expenditures, while the Army remained in control of the most powerful instruments of manufacturing consent, particularly through its ownership and operation of much of the broadcast media (see Chai-anan 1989: 323–4). While both its capacity and its interest in ruling the country dictatorially had been drastically curtailed as a result of modernization, the military retained both the motive and the means to step in whenever its interests were threatened. The opportunity to intervene was also provided by one of the weightiest and most enduring legacies of repeated military coups: the weakness of participatory and representative institutions (see Chai-anan 1989: 325). The fragmentation of Thailand's party system, the absence of programmatic political parties, the tenuousness of the population's attachments to the existing partisan alternatives, and the volatile nature of parliamentary politics had not only undermined the legitimacy of representative institutions, or eroded the capacity of elected politicians to fight back against the military's routine interference, but had also provided the Army with a ready-made excuse to intervene.

Far from reflecting an innate tendency to adopt these kinds of arrangements (for a discussion, see McCargo 1997a), Thailand's failure to develop a 'structured' (see Sartori 1968) or 'institutionalized' (see Mainwaring and Scully 1995) party system is rooted in the role that the palace, the military, and the bureaucracy have played in this aspect of Thailand's political development. Most of the successive coups staged between 1947 and 1976 were accompanied not only by the revocation of the existing parties' registration, but also the dismantlement of their organizations and the confiscation of their assets (see Ockey 2004: 24). The periodic easing of the restrictions placed on the activities of political parties, therefore, had generally led to a proliferation of electoral organizations held together by little more than a big man's popularity and ambition.

Among the over 100 parties registered between 1946 and the mid 1970s (see Kramol 1982: 5), only the Democrat Party managed to achieved a degree of continuity.

Whereas the 1975 elections had not featured the participation of a single government party with the backing of the state, the election results suggested an environment of 'atomization' – in Sartori's (1976: 125) definition, a situation in which the vote is so widely dispersed across a multitude of weak and ephemeral alternatives that 'the number of parties makes little difference'. The 1974 constitution had included measures designed to strengthen political parties – above all by banning independent candidacies and by forcing members of parliament who switched parties between elections to relinquish their seats. Still, the promulgation of the 1974 constitution was followed by the registration of over forty parties. Having no organization in the districts and little time to build one, these parties were highly dependent on local big men, whose networks of power and influence could most effectively be leveraged in the short term to deliver votes in the provinces. Famously, among the local notabilities political parties scrambled to enlist in the mobilization of the provincial electorate were often unsavoury characters referred to as *chao pho*, or 'godfathers'. More generally, parties and candidates for office typically relied on multilayered networks of canvassers – or *hua khanaen* – to deliver votes through a mixture of moral authority, patronage, money, and occasionally coercion. While government parties had previously monopolized access to capable *hua khanaen*, the competition was much fiercer now that no sure-fire winner could be identified *ex ante* as guaranteeing a meaningful return on the investment of time, money, and reputation a local notable would have to put into the election of a given candidate. The situation was rendered more chaotic by the fact that the development funds that had made their way into the periphery during the Vietnam War had created a whole new class of powerful notabilities. While local big men had often previously eschewed elected office, the strengthening of representative institutions increased the position's 'market value' (see Anderson 1990: 46) and rendered political parties 'worth joining' (McVey 2000: 12).

What took place in the aftermath of the 1975 elections served to entrench the inchoateness of Thailand's party system. Confronted with a House of Representatives divided across twenty-two parties, Kukrit Pramoj had only been able to form a coalition government by introducing an elaborate system of quotas, giving the sixteen parties in his coalition, and their internal factions, a share of portfolios and undersecretaries commensurate with their size. Ockey (2004: 26) points out that this method of dividing the spoils of government, born of necessity, had profound consequences on the development of Thai political parties. Most importantly, perhaps, it created an incentive for members of parliament to form factions that could trade their participation in the government's legislative majority for a cabinet post. The most ambitious and resourceful representatives would form factions held together by their ability to bankroll the campaigns of less affluent followers; once in government, the faction leader could use the office to recoup his investment. The logic by which both factions and parties operated generated high levels of instability at both levels (for an extensive overview, see Chambers 2003). The provisions of the 1974 and 1978 constitutions designed to limit party switching between elections did not do much to temper the fluidity in their membership, because the dissolution of the House was regularly followed by an exodus of members of parliament from one party to another.

These limitations notwithstanding, the results of the 1976 elections could be seen as significant progress towards the development of a more streamlined system of parties. The vast majority of the incumbents who jumped the fence in the run-up to the elections migrated to the three largest parties – Democrats, Social Action, and *Chat Thai* (see Somporn 1976: 39–40). As a result, the 1976 elections had witnessed far lesser dispersion in both votes and seats away from the top national contenders, as well as some continuity in the existing parties, demonstrated by the fact that only five seats went to organizations that had won none the year before. Whether or not the 1976 elections could have marked the beginning of the development of a 'structured' party system, any such hopes were dashed by the disruption in party activities that came with the coup staged 6 months thereafter.

The 1978 constitution included even more aggressive provisions to strengthen political parties. In addition to the requirement that sitting legislators would have to relinquish their office upon switching parties, the constitution provided that a member of parliament would lose his or her seat in the event of expulsion from a party (Article 103[7]). Aside from banning independent candidacies, moreover, the constitution aimed to promote the territorial diffusion of political parties by requiring, as a condition for appearing on the ballot, that each must contest at least half the seats in play (Article 95). A new Political Parties Act introduced in 1981 further tightened, along similar lines, the requirements that a party had to meet to obtain and keep its registration.

While these measures were said to have reflected the desire of 'bureaucratic forces' to engineer greater stability (see Nakharin 1991: 66) and more specifically their ambition to create 'real' parties (see McCargo 1997a: 116), the same forces needed no reminders to be careful what they wished for. From the start, 'bureaucratic forces' took measures evincing considerable unease about the threat that political parties could present to their own power, had the reforms produced the intended effects. Indeed, the 1978 constitution included transitory provisions (Article 204) that suspended each of the aforementioned regulations. As a result, the 1979 elections not only permitted independent candidacies, but also allowed candidates merely to run as affiliates of 'political groups', as parties had not yet been formally recognized as legal entities. Nor was the ability of members of parliament to switch parties subject to any restriction throughout the entire legislature elected in 1979. Seeking to profit from the flexibility to divide and conquer, Prem scheduled the 1983 elections 3 days before the expiration of the constitution's transitory provisions, thereby allowing independents as well as small, local parties to remain viable. The contradiction between the introduction of legal measures to strengthen political parties on the one hand, and the continuing attempt to weaken them on the other, suggests that the only thing Thailand's 'bureaucratic forces' abhor more than an inchoate party system is the development of one that is robust enough to challenge their authority.

By the time the transitory provisions of the constitution were allowed to expire, the existing political parties remained loose confederations of financially and organizationally autonomous factions. In turn, the race to the bottom to enlist and maintain the support of local notables effectively prevented parties from coming up with a coherent platform or enforcing any measure of internal cohesion. The dependency of political parties on local notables was further reinforced by the workings of the electoral system in use at the time. In each of the elections held between 1975 and 1996, provinces were subdivided into one-, two-, and/or three-seat constituencies where voters could choose as many candidates as there were seats to be filled, without regard for partisan affiliation. Aside from inducing candidates to campaign against fellow party members, undermining intra-party cohesion, the system increased the primacy of individual candidates over party labels, thereby offering no incentive for local notables to bind themselves more closely to political parties. Indeed, not only were local notabilities increasingly in a position to impose candidacies on their respective political parties; in relatively short order, most major parties also came to be controlled by local business interests and politicians. Only the Democrat Party remained largely under the influence of big business in Bangkok (see Pasuk and Baker 2000: 47).

By the late 1980s, many parties commanded several times the minimum number of members of parliament required to earn the leader a cabinet post and well in excess of the minimum levels of territorial coverage required to maintain their registration. But the only glue keeping such parties together was the prospect of being included in a coalition government, which Ockey (2004: 27) suggests was better for large than it was for small parties. As a result, their membership was extremely fluid. Groups of legislators were constantly 'up for sale'. Faction leaders routinely renegotiated the terms of their membership in a political party, ready to move their contingent of legislators, financial backers, and canvassers to another party any time a better deal might be extended to them in the form of direct monetary incentives or appointments to more lucrative government posts (see Murray 1996: 30). Already widespread as of the mid 1970s (Pasuk and Sungsidh 1994: 3), the use of public office for private gain was transformed into a booming cottage industry in the 1980s. As parliamentary seats and cabinet posts became more profitable in a context of fast-paced economic growth, moreover, competition turned fiercer and correspondently more violent. As Anderson (1990) noted, political assassinations in the 1980s were increasingly related to the competition for public office. Murders of rival candidates and their campaign workers became something of a regular occurrence, as did the killing of canvassers who failed to deliver a number of votes commensurate with the resources to which they had helped themselves (see Klima 2002: 96).

Table 6.1 provides a numerical overview of various dimensions of Thailand's party system in the 1970s and the 1980s. Aside from the relatively large number of 'effective parties', a measure of the fragmentation in the distribution of both votes and seats, perhaps what most jumps out is the share of seats that changed hands in each election, as measured by aggregate seat volatility. Another notable feature is the persistence of rather low levels of nationalization in the vote distributions. Although primarily a symptom of the personalization of elections, the strength of local notabilities, and the weakness of national parties, the system's territorialization was also the expression of some noteworthy regional trends.

Increasingly challenged in its traditional stronghold in Bangkok, it was during this time that the Democrat Party began to assert its dominance in the South. Throughout the 1980s, moreover, *Chat Thai* was consistently the largest party in the Central Region. As for the northern and northeastern constituencies, where the success of liberal, progressive, and socialist parties in 1975 had been interpreted as 'a protest against the economic and political domination of Bangkok' (Race 1975: 378), the repression of the left changed the landscape. Both regions consistently saw the greatest fragmentation and volatility (see Hicken 2009: 126), but each exhibited its own peculiarities. Independent candidates performed especially well in the North in 1979 and 1983; in both 1986 and

Table 6.1 *Thailand's party system, 1975–1988*

	1975	1976	1979	1983	1986	1988
Effective number of parties (votes)	10.23	7.09	11.31	7.06	7.96	9.81
Effective number of parties (seats)	7.58	4.07	8.16	5.58	6.14	7.74
Seats to independents (proportion)	–	–	.20	.07	–	–
Seats to new parties (proportion)	.73	.02	.66	.13	.17	.10
Aggregate seat volatility	.67	.38	.58	.33	.35	.29
Party system nationalization score	.39	.42	.30	.40	.39	.35

Note: The effective number of parties is calculated as $1/\Sigma p_i^2$, where p_i is the proportion of votes/seats garnered by each party (see Laakso and Taagepera 1979). Each independent candidate is considered as one party. Chambers (2005: 497) estimates that the effective number of parties in the legislature decreased to 3.6 after the 1983 elections, when independents were forced to join existing parties.

Aggregate seat volatility (see Bartolini and Mair 1990) is $.5 \times \Sigma\,|\,p_i(t)-p_i(t-1)\,|$, where p_i is the proportion of seats garnered by each party in elections held at time t and $t-1$. It ranges from 0 (seat distribution is unchanged) to 1 in the event that all seats at time t are captured by parties that had won none at $t-1$.

The party system nationalization score (PSNS) (see Jones and Mainwaring 2003) is calculated in two steps. For each party that fielded candidates in a given election, a party nationalization score (PNS) is calculated by subtracting from 1 the Gini coefficient quantifying the inequality in the vote shares garnered by the party across Thailand's provinces, each of which is given equal weight. A PNS of 1 indicates that the party in question received the same vote share in every province, while a PNS of 0 describes a party whose votes came from only one province. The PSNS is then calculated by summing the PNS obtained for each individual party weighted by its national vote share. The measure potentially ranges from 0 (asymptotically, as the number of territorial units goes to infinity), meaning that all parties only won votes in one province, to 1 if all parties received exactly the same vote share in each province.

All calculations were made by the author based on official district-level election returns. The data, originally provided by Allen Hicken (now available at www.electiondataarchive.org), were cross-checked by the author with figures from official election reports (see Ministry of the Interior 1975, 1976, 1983, 1987, 1989). The process resulted in a number of corrections as well as the addition of data missing from the original dataset.

1988, moreover, the largest number of seats in the North were won by parties whose strength was marginal elsewhere. The Northeast, meanwhile, became the country's foremost swing region, as parties that won pluralities of seats in Isan emerged as the top finishers nationally in each of the four elections held between 1979 and 1988.

For all the evidence of its dysfunction, the electoral process asserted a degree of permanency and staying power it had never achieved before. While the 'money politics' that took shape in this period has frequently been stigmatized by progressives and conservatives alike, it should not be forgotten that the system thrived because provincial politicians delivered services that the state refused to provide. Local politicians stepped into the vacuum created by the urban elites' aversion to direct government expenditures on services that could both protect the provincial population from market forces and empower them to make use of the opportunities offered by the workings of the market economy. The system did little to alleviate social and regional inequalities, which continued to grow throughout this period as a consequence of the diminishing contributions made by the agricultural sector to an economy increasingly dominated by the secondary and tertiary sectors (see Walker 2012: 44–9). Still, the panoply of services provincial politicians offered their constituents – roads, bridges, temples, hospital wards, jobs, personal expenses, emergency assistance, and access to credit – made a real difference in the lives of enough people and communities to earn provincial bosses the gratitude and admiration of many. Nishizaki (2005: 185) makes the often overlooked point that provincial voters elected men like Banharn Silpa-archa not because they were bought or coerced, but because they wanted to, and had good reasons to do so given the contemptuous and discriminatory manner in which the state generally treated them.

Quite aside from the fact that the emergence of provincial notabilities in the 1970s would likely have yielded far different results, had a series of palace-backed military interventions staged since 1947 not forestalled the development of a national party system, it should be noted that King Bhumibol himself built up his popularity by diverting public funds that could have been used more productively for the provision of state services towards forms of royal patronage that made little difference in the grand scheme of things. As Nishizaki (2013: 69) puts it, moreover, the monarchy had 'developed a symbiotic, if ambiguous relationship' with politicians like Banharn, who were rewarded for their support of the monarchy's political proxies in Bangkok, as well as their contributions to enhancing the monarchy's popularity in the provinces, with access to the kind of state resources and royal prestige that helped cement their local dominance. Perhaps the real problem, then, was that provincial businessmen and politicians, although mostly suspicious of more participatory forms of democracy (see Pasuk and Baker 1997: 32), had emerged as the modern-day avatar of the local lords King Chulalongkorn decommissioned at the turn of the twentieth century – and that the resurgence of provincial power still threatened the hegemony of a hierarchical, Bangkok-centric political order. Indeed, the palace, the military, the bureaucracy, and Bangkok's *bien pensants* had good reason to detest elected politicians, considering the speed with which their purportedly 'dark influence' (*itthiphon muet*) had come to threaten the power of institutions in which Thailand's national ideology vests all legitimate authority.

The original 'good coup'

Insofar as the 'semi-democracy' that took shape in the 1980s was 'stable' (see Chai-anan 1989), this was a dynamic kind of stability, as opposed to one reflecting a durable pact between elected and non-elected forces. Overmatched in symbolic, financial, and coercive power, elected politicians by and large chose to cooperate with Prem's administration and opted to exploit the opportunities the system presented to gradually subvert 'Premocracy' from the inside. It should be added that the conflict between elected and non-elected officials as it played out throughout the 1980s was less about the formal institutions that made up Thailand's political regime than it was about the enforcement of the existing rules of the game, as various actors sought to take advantage of the ambiguities inherent to the constitutional framework in place at the time. In playing the role of 'subversives' – actors who seek to displace the existing institutional arrangements by working within the system (Mahoney and Thelen 2010: 25–6) – elected politicians promoted institutional change through 'drift' (see Mahoney and Thelen 2010: 19–20), putting up a real fight only to prevent bureaucratic forces from retooling the existing institutions as the balance of power gradually shifted in their favour.

Elected politicians became a constant annoyance for Prem and his administration. The first crisis occurred in 1981, when Prem's extension of his term as Army Commander-in-Chief prompted Kukrit Pramoj's Social Action Party to defect from the government. The coup attempt staged by the Young Turks on 1 April 1981 was also related to this incident, although exactly how is the subject of some dispute. Some accounts cite the Young Turks' own dissatisfaction with the extension of Prem's active military post (see Likhit 1992: 211; Chalermkiat 1990: 69); others contend that the plot had initially enjoyed Prem's support (see Handley 2006: 281–2). At any rate, Prem's job was saved after the King and Queen flew with him to Nakhon Ratchasima, just as the Young Turks began seizing strategic locations around Bangkok, and publicly urged the rebels to stand down. The failure of the coup attempt, in the aftermath of which the Young Turks were amnestied but mostly discharged from the Army, also had the effect of raising the profile of Major-General Athit Kamlang-ek, who led the operations against the rebels. After succeeding Prem as Commander-in-Chief in 1982, Athit went on to become Prem's main rival for power. Whatever the truth behind the 'April Fools' Day Coup', elected politicians had helped aggravate divisions between the military's major factions, exposing the precariousness of the equilibrium upon which the survival of Prem's administration rested.

Recognizing the fact that the effort to forestall the rise of elected politicians was failing, Prem and his allies sought to make permanent the constitution's transitory provisions. The amendment to the constitution, however, was narrowly defeated in its final reading in the National Assembly. The same framing that had benefited the campaign against the amendment, presented as a fight to defend democratic institutions against the onset of a new military dictatorship, also dominated the general elections held weeks later. Prem stayed on as Prime Minister after the 1983 elections thanks largely to the bad blood between the three main parties, which prevented agreement on a common candidate. Still, Prem continued to be haunted by the fractiousness of his coalition as well as the increasingly spirited opposition of *Chat Thai*, which repeatedly sought to muster the votes needed to oust the Prime Minister. Meanwhile, divisions inside the military continued to bedevil the administration. When General Athit threatened a coup in 1984, Prem turned to King Bhumibol to silence the Army chief. The following year, in September 1985, Prem withstood another coup attempt staged by the Young Turks. The military's internal divisions also spilled over to the halls of parliament: when *Chat Thai* finally did manage to get a faction of Social Action to defect from the government in 1986, the manoeuvre was reported to have served Athit's political ambitions (see Chambers 2003: 179).

Prem dissolved the House in May 1986, after losing a vote on a diesel fuel tax, only to have major components of his coalition once again base their election campaigns on the need for a fully elected administration – and be rewarded for it in spades at the ballot box (see Nakharin 1991: 67). Thanks in part to the case made for unseating Prem, the Democrats almost doubled their seat share, winning a plurality of a hundred out of 347 seats. Prem's tenure was extended beyond the 1986 elections owing to the pressure exerted on the main parties by the new Commander-in-Chief of the Army, General Chavalit Yongchaiyudh. When the opposition once more appeared to be on the verge of bringing down the government in April 1987, likewise, Prem's allies in the armed forces got fifteen members of parliament to withdraw their support for the motion of no confidence. Later that year, a disgruntled faction of the Democrat Party, comprised for the most part of southern representatives, took to voting against bills sponsored by the government. Exasperated by the continued fragmentation of his coalition, Prem called new elections for July 1988.

Chat Thai's Praman Adireksan has described the rise to Prime Minister of fellow party leader Chatichai Chunhavan as 'accidental' (see Nakharin 1991: 69). Perhaps a better word for it is 'contingent'. Indeed, it was not an accident that an elected member of parliament was by then in a position to take the office. Not only had elected politicians managed to thwart attempts to create constitutional safeguards against the eventuality; their growing assertiveness, combined with the continuing divisions inside the military, had also forced Prem to spend so much time and effort to defend his position as to effectively prevent him from doing much else. Partially as a result, Prem's government had come under intense criticism from the print media, whose aggressiveness had increased with the ambition of the country's urban bourgeoisie (see Anderson 1990: 41). New social movements representing workers and farmers, moreover, had resumed demonstrating against rising inequality, falling agricultural prices, and the encroachments on local resources threatened by major infrastructural projects (see Pasuk and Baker 2000: 44; Walker 2012: 15–16). While subject to intimidation and harassment, academics also criticized the administration for its listlessness, its lack of accountability, and its disregard for the democratic process (see Thanapol 2006: 108–10). Voters, too, continued to side with parties that vowed to remove Prem. In 1988, the Democrats paid a heavy price at the polls for having failed to make good on their promise, losing over half their seats in parliament.

All that is to say that elected politicians benefited from a series of factors that made it increasingly difficult, under the existing rules, for an unelected, retired general to serve as Prime Minister whatever the composition of the elected legislature. The only real leverage that the palace, the military, and the bureaucracy had on elected politicians was the implicit threat that an elected government would be removed in a military coup, an extreme measure presenting considerable risk. Simply by blocking attempts to change the rules of the game, then, elected politicians had created conditions favourable to rendering the 'tutelary democracy' inaugurated in 1978 a great deal less 'tutelary'. Even so, Chatichai's election was not a foregone conclusion. Still unsure about the viability of an elected, civilian government that would not enjoy the support of the military and the palace, the major parties actually invited Prem to return, if only in exchange for granting elected politicians greater representation in the cabinet and greater influence on policy (see Nakharin 1991: 69).

In more ways than one, Chatichai's government marked a dramatic break with Thailand's recent past. In place of Prem's tendency to muddle through, Chatichai embarked on an ambitious agenda, which featured the promotion of infrastructural 'mega-projects', the pursuit of closer diplomatic and commercial relations with neighbouring Vietnam, Cambodia, and Laos, and a new emphasis on development over security in Thailand's periphery. Chatichai was also not subtle in his attempt to muscle the old 'mandarinate' (see Pasuk and Baker 1997: 22) out of the way. The military's longstanding prerogative to direct foreign and national security policy was usurped as Chatichai transferred those powers to the elected government. So did the military's commercial interests come under attack, especially as the government exhibited greater interest in border regions, where the generals had previously been given a free hand to conduct all manner of semi-legal and illegal dealings, and allowed both the print media and elected members of parliament to expose episodes of corruption in the armed forces. Conservative technocrats in the civil service were ushered out of the cabinet, pressured to carry out the instructions of political appointees, and eclipsed as a source of policy ideas by Chatichai's reliance on an advisory council (*Ban Phitsanulok*) that included several progressive, 'outsider' intellectuals and academics (see Hewison 1993: 175–7). In lieu of Prem's 'statist democracy' (see Chalermkiat 1990: 94), Chatichai gave unprecedented influence to business, courted the support of labour unions, and listened to the concerns of social movements representing the vanguard of an increasingly vibrant and pluralistic civil society (see Hewison 1993).

It is no overstatement to say that Chatichai aimed to carry out something of a silent revolution – one that sought to engineer a whole new regime simply by closing the gaps in the enforcement of the existing rules, as opposed to undertaking major constitutional reforms. For all its transformative ambitions, however, the elected administration's chief vulnerability was to be found in its element of continuity with those that preceded it. Perhaps most important, Chatichai faced a recalcitrant military whose leaders had no intention of submitting to any form of civilian control. Matters got worse when Chavalit retired and briefly joined the cabinet as Defence Minister in March 1990, allowing the rise of General Suchinda Kraprayoon to Commander-in-Chief. With Suchinda's promotion, all major leadership positions in the Royal Thai Army were held by officers belonging to graduates of Class 5 of the Chulachomklao Royal Military Academy, whom Prem had relied upon (and favoured in return) during his power struggles in the 1980s. Handley (2006: 336) refers to Class 5 as 'the most cohesive, ambitious, and corrupt class the school had ever produced' – many of its members having amassed multimillion dollar fortunes by the time Suchinda took charge of the Army. From the beginning, Suchinda unleashed public tirades against elected politicians and issued thinly veiled threats of a military coup. Each time the government was threatened in this fashion, Chatichai emulated Prem by scurrying to confer with King Bhumibol. The King, however, did not do much to hide his contempt for the elected government, or the constitutional provisions from which it derived its authority (see Handley 2006: 337–8).

Not propped up by the military and the crown, the new government was to survive entirely on its own power. Given the fragmentation of Thailand's party system, however, Chatichai's only hope to put together a durable coalition was to indulge the appetite for personal gain and political patronage of the main parties and factions. Once again, Prem had done much the same thing, turning a blind eye to the corruption in his administration and the military. Indeed, while graft is often alleged to have reached new heights under Chatichai, the perception of corruption may have increased simply as a result of the shifting balance of power – as McVey (2000: 13) puts it, 'what had seemed to the Bangkok elites a gentlemanly flow of benefits among those fit to rule appeared less legitimate in the hands of crass outsiders'. If, in particular, Chatichai's coalition relied to a far greater extent on politicians tied to provincial as opposed to metropolitan business interests, the latter were not above using their control of the print media to discredit their provincial rivals through the selective reporting of corruption scandals (see Pasuk and Baker 2000: 40–1).[4]

On the morning of 23 February 1991, Chatichai was abducted at gunpoint while on his way to see the King in Chiang Mai. Later, the National Peace-Keeping Council (NPKC), dominated by Class 5 generals, informed the public that it had seized power from the elected government, issuing an announcement (see NPKC 2007 [1991]: 177–80) that gave five reasons for the coup. First, the NPKC alleged that corruption under Chatichai had been 'unprecedented'. Second, the NPKC claimed that the government had sought to turn 'upright, honest career civil servants' (*kha ratchakan pracham phu sue sat sucharit*) into an 'instrument of politicians' (*khrueang mue khong nak kan mueang*). Third, the NPKC argued that, while the government operated behind a democratic façade, the transfer of powers from unelected to elected officials had made Thailand into a 'parliamentary dictatorship' (*phadetkan ratthasapha*), threatening 'Democracy with the King as Head of State'. Fourth, the NPKC accused the government of trying to 'destroy the military', adding that the armed forces 'would not submit to being under the political control of politicians' (*mai yom tok yu tai itthipon thang kan mueang khong nak*

4 It is typical for owners to regard their newspapers less as a means to make money than as 'vehicles for political lobbying, backstabbing, and rabble-rousing' (see McCargo 2000: 5).

kan mueang). Finally, described as most 'intolerable' was the disloyalty Chatichai had shown for the monarchy in rehabilitating a former Young Turk, Major-General Manoon Rupkhachorn, against whom the generals had dredged up old allegations over plots to assassinate members of the royal family. The NPKC did not leave much to the imagination: the coup had aimed to salvage the pre-eminence of unelected institutions against the onslaught of elected politicians.

While promising reforms, investigations, and a swift return to democracy, the NPKC wasted no time introducing the customary measures called for by these familiar circumstances. After imposing martial law, banning political activities, disbanding the National Assembly, and abrogating the constitution, the junta promulgated an interim charter that provided the new regime with a fig leaf of legality. Ambivalent about the operation, the public acquiesced. King Bhumibol said nothing publicly, but let it be known via Suchinda that the coup had his blessing, at least as long as the NPKC did not 'let the people down'. Eager to keep the conditional support lent to them by the urban electorate and the monarchy, the generals chose Anand Panyarachun, a widely respected former ambassador and chief executive officer – a moderate man with unimpeachable royalist credentials – to serve as Prime Minister until new elections could be held. Anand was given wide latitude to reform the country's economy and reassure foreign investors. On matters other than the economy, however, the scope of his powers was in practice extremely limited.

Much like those that preceded it in 1971 and 1976, the royally sanctioned military coup of 1991 was the beginning of an attempt to roll back the clock to an earlier time – among other things by changing rules of the game that had failed to guarantee unelected institutions the desired degree of control. Despite its public denials, the NPKC's determination to install Suchinda in the Prime Minister's office, to serve in the same capacity Prem did in the 1980s, was evident in the junta's stewardship of the process that led to the promulgation of a new constitution in December 1991. Much like the 1978 constitution, the new charter did not require that the Prime Minister be drawn from the ranks of elected representatives. The NPKC, moreover, was given the power to appoint a 270-member Senate given similar prerogatives to those of the 360-member House. Most importantly, in keeping with the transitory provisions in the 1978 constitution, which the military had failed to make permanent in 1983, no-confidence motions and constitutional reforms would be voted on in joint sittings of the two chambers. In practice, that meant that the Senate and forty-six members (17 per cent) of the House could remove any government and defeat any effort to amend the constitution.

The resistance encountered by the generals throughout the process of drafting the new constitution did not augur well for the longevity of the regime the NPKC sought to install. The press attacked relentlessly. When restrictions to political activities were lifted, new social movements such as the Campaign for Popular Democracy as well as political parties including the Democrats, *Phalang Tham*, and New Aspiration – formed in 1990 by General Chavalit Yongchaiyudh after resigning from Chatichai's cabinet – protested vigorously against the draft, at one point mobilizing up to a hundred thousand people in the streets of Bangkok. The various junta-appointed bodies tasked with drafting the new constitution went back and forth to accommodate the cross-pressures they were operating under (see Murray 1996: 68–84). Eventually, Suchinda was reduced to threatening that no constitution would be granted at all, should the opposition insist on testing his patience. True to form, the Democrats' new leader, Chuan Leekpai, withdrew the party's participation in the movement against the draft. Then, on the occasion of his birthday, King Bhumibol publicly belittled the opposition's objections, reminded them that 'any rule can be changed', and urged them to avoid taking actions that might lead to bloodshed. Within a week, the new constitution had been promulgated.

The NPKC's actions in preparation for new elections, scheduled for 22 March 1992, complemented its efforts on the constitutional front. The party *Samakkhitham* was created in May 1991 with the objective of providing Suchinda with what was hoped would form the core of a legislative majority. Through an aggressive recruitment campaign, *Samakkhitham* enlisted the support of wealthy contributors as well as eighty former members of parliament and eleven former cabinet ministers (see Murray 1996: 41). The best the NPKC could hope for, however, was a strong showing by *Samakkhitham* and the formation of a coalition government with other parties. Ironically, the only major political parties available to form a coalition with *Samakkhitham* were *Chat Thai* and Social Action, which had borne the brunt of the NPKC's anti-corruption rhetoric and investigations. Not surprisingly, some of the politicians and party leaders who agreed to cooperate with the military were exonerated for lack of evidence. Then, the provisional charter was amended to allow ten officials the Assets Examination Committee (AEC) had found guilty of misappropriating funds to appeal their sentences, thereby allowing them to pursue elected office for the foreseeable future. Eventually, Suchinda formed a five-party executive that included eleven of the politicians initially accused of being 'unusually wealthy' and many others with dubious backgrounds and associations (see Murray 1996: 125). He claimed to have gone back on his word for the good of the nation.

Domesticated democracy

Born of the same reactionary animus, the NPKC's attempt to restore the *status quo ante* was no more successful than previous efforts made under Thanom (1971–3) and Thanin (1976–7). Much of the print media saw through what had happened, branding the affair as a 'betrayal' and a 'throwback to a bygone age' (see Murray 1996: 131–3). The business community, with the exception of conglomerates that had profited from their association with the NPKC, opposed Suchinda's assumption of the office of Prime Minister (see Hewison 1993: 180). Far from putting the issue to rest, Suchinda's instalment on 7 April also galvanized the opposition in the streets. Led by retired Major-General Chamlong Srimuang,[5] a former Governor of Bangkok and leader of *Phalang Tham* ('Moral Force' or 'Force of Dharma'), tens of thousands called for Suchinda's resignation in the ensuing weeks, culminating in a large rally at Sanam Luang attended by an estimated 150,000 people on 8 May. Under pressure, the government announced it was prepared to negotiate changes to the constitution.

On 17 May – days after the administration informed the public that coalition parties had failed to come to an agreement on constitutional reforms – the street movement against Suchinda was back in force, as some 200,000 people held another massive demonstration along Ratchadamnoen Avenue. The first violent clashes between police and demonstrators took place at the Phan Fa Bridge after midnight on 18 May. Hours later, the government declared a state of emergency and called in the Army. Despite Chamlong's arrest, pitched battles continued throughout the day on 18 May, as soldiers discharged their automatic weapons into crowds of mostly unarmed demonstrators, while protesters

[5] Once a leader of the Young Turks, Chamlong had distanced himself from his classmates just before they attempted to overthrow Prem's government in 1981, in which he served as Secretary General. An adherent of the fundamentalist Buddhist sect Santi Asoke, Chamlong has since been famous for his ascetic image and his public crusades against abortion, prostitution, alcohol consumption, and other forms of purported immorality. In 1985, Chamlong was elected governor of Bangkok on an anti-corruption platform. Despite a promising start, his first foray into national politics in the 1988 general elections foundered after an associate boasted about the role she had played with Chamlong in the events surrounding the student massacre and coup of 1976. Questions about his involvement have never been properly answered (see McCargo 1997b: 36–41; Thongchai 2002: 257). Having been re-elected overwhelmingly as governor in 1990, Chamlong resigned the post to run in the general elections of March 1992, in which Phalang Tham won forty-one seats, on the strength of a near sweep of metropolitan constituencies. On 4 May 1992, Chalmong went on hunger strike, announcing that he would fast until he died or Suchinda resigned. He reversed himself days later, claiming he needed strength to fight on.

vandalized public property throughout the city, setting vehicles and government buildings on fire. Early the following day, the Army captured the Royal Hotel – the last bastion of resistance on Ratchadamnoen Avenue – savagely beating a group of demonstrators who had taken shelter on its premises, while troops chased smaller groups of protesters assembled in other locations around the city (see *The Nation*, 20 May 1992). As ever, the government claimed it had acted lawfully to suppress a 'riot' and deal with the threat that the demonstrations posed to nation, religion, and King.

On the evening of 20 May, just in time to avoid another confrontation at Ramkhamhaeng University, King Bhumibol summoned Suchinda and Chamlong to a royal audience broadcast on national television (for a transcript of the remarks, see Bhumibol 1992). As the leaders of the opposing sides sat on the floor before him, the King downplayed the significance of the fight over a constitution he described as being 'of sufficiently reasonable quality' (*mi kunnaphap pho chai dai*). Sidestepping the fact that, under the existing rules, amending the constitution required the support of the NPKC-appointed Senate or some 85 per cent of the House, the King chastised Chamlong for disregarding his advice to seek reforms through the parliamentary system, while praising Suchinda for having been open to the possibility all along. Denying agency to the tens of thousands of people who had taken to the streets against the Prime Minister, the King characterized the crisis as a personal vendetta, in which the rest of society had simply become embroiled. Aside from effectively placing the blame for the violence on Chamlong and the protesters – a point made even more forcefully in the months thereafter (see Handley 2006: 360–1) – it is notable that the King, in urging the two to resolve the situation, invited them to seek the guidance of Privy Councillors Sanya Thammasak and Prem Tinsulanond, also in attendance. The conflict that Chamlong and others had 'socialized', mobilizing ordinary people against a military-led government, was to be 'privatized' and brought under the management of the palace.

This time, the protesters heeded the King's words, assembling mostly for the purposes of commemorating the dead. Chamlong was released from custody and disappeared from public view. Suchinda resigned on 24 May, if only after securing the King's signature on a blanket amnesty that guaranteed the armed forces complete impunity for the killing of fifty-two people and the injury of six hundred more. Within 2 weeks, parliament amended the constitution, acceding to the opposition's demand that the Prime Minister be an elected member of parliament, that Senators be stripped of their role in the initiation and approval of no-confidence motions, and that the Speaker of the House be allowed to control the parliamentary agenda by assuming the presidency of the National Assembly ex officio. On 10 June, Anand Panyarachun was selected to serve another brief term as Prime Minister.

With the elections of 13 September 1992, Thailand rejoined the ranks of the world's 'electoral democracies'. For the unelected institutions that had supported the 1991 coup, the failure of Suchinda's restoration was something of a mixed bag. On the one hand, if some of the rules that limited the power of elected politicians had been dismantled in the aftermath of the violence, the task of keeping future elected governments in check was complicated further by the fact that the massacre had thoroughly discredited the Army with the urban middle class, thereby taking the threat of a military coup off the table for the foreseeable future. On the other hand, the King and his men had found a way to turn a situation for which they were co-responsible – through their support of the NPKC, their longstanding promotion of the military's power at the expense of representative institutions, and the impunity they had granted to the perpetrators of all previous massacres – into a matter of domestic and international acclaim. What is more, the palace's management of the transition process had limited the success of 'people power' to a rather modest set of reforms. Most importantly, the 'network monarchy' remained entrenched, because the efforts made by Prem over the previous decade had ensured that leadership positions in most state institutions were filled by trusted royalists (see McCargo 2005: 501), whose resistance to the encroachments of elected officials would continue throughout the 1990s (see Pasuk and Baker 1997:24).

Still, the new environment called for another adaptation, because the 'network monarchy' would have to live with elected governments and find new ways to influence their activities. Aside from stifling the attempt made shortly thereafter to amend the constitution in a more democratic direction – an effort Prem led behind the scenes (see Handley 2006: 371–2) – royalists endeavoured to build a broader coalition, working to co-opt segments of the business community, civil society, and the elected legislature. Stronger relationships were cultivated with both old and new money. The Crown Property Bureau formed partnerships with businesses in most sectors of the urban economy (see Porphant 2008: 174), while Prem and other Privy Councillors took paid positions on the board of directors of companies owned by major conglomerates (see Chai-anan 1997: 55–6; Handley 2006: 376–7). Burned by its experience under Chatichai, the metropolitan business community was by then more inclined to hedge its bets, complementing its interest in electoral politics with investments in closer relationships with the technocrats who had guided economic policy under Prem and Anand (see Pasuk and Baker

1997: 25–9). Meanwhile, royalist intellectuals articulated a new vision for an 'elite civil society' operating in a partnership with, and largely under the direction of, the state (see Somchai 2006: 6–11) – an idea whose appeal extended to 'progressive' civil society organizations that had come to reject 'strategies of mass mobilization and class struggle' (Connors 2002: 48). In the House of Representatives, the network monarchy's chosen partner was Chuan Leekpai's Democrat Party, deemed the most dependable in an array of distrusted alternatives (see McCargo 2005: 508–9).

Even so, the pursuit of working relationships with capitalists, civil society, and politicians was accompanied by a public relations offensive designed to further elevate the King above any potential contenders for the public's loyalty and support, especially in the elected parliament. The glorification of the monarchy continued to benefit from a great deal of inertia. Given the King's existing popularity, private businesses, media organizations, government agencies, and politicians fell over themselves to show their loyalty. Palace officials left little to chance, actively overseeing the monarchy's promotion through the media as well as grand, lavish ceremonies such as those that marked King Bhumibol's 50 years on the throne in 1996 (see Handley 2006: 377–84). In turn, the palace stepped up its ongoing campaign to publicly discredit elected politicians, whom the King took to denouncing with increased frequency and stridency (see Handley 2006: 365–71). In hindsight, the success of the effort to circumscribe the power and limit the autonomy of elected institutions rested on fragile foundations. Succeed it did, however, at least for a time, thanks to the resilience of some of the most dysfunctional aspects of Thailand's electoral and legislative politics.

The events of Black May 1992 had given rise to some hopes that a more streamlined party system organized around two poles could have emerged at last. The campaign for the September elections had been portrayed by the print media as a fight between 'angels' and 'devils'. Cast in the role of 'angels' were political parties whose leaders had backed the demonstrations (*Phalang Tham*, New Aspiration, and Democrats); starring as 'devils' were parties that had supported Suchinda – *Chat Thai*, Social Action, Samak Sundaravej's *Prachakorn Thai*, and Chatichai Chunhavan's *Chat Pattana*. There were at least two reasons, however, why the fight between 'angels' and 'devils' would fail to reconfigure Thailand's party system. The first was simply that the distinction was more about past associations than sharp differences in platforms or ideas. On one side, the alliance that *Chat Thai* and Social Action had formed with Suchinda had been exclusively one of convenience. On the other side, similarly, New Aspiration and *Phalang Tham* opposed Suchinda for reasons that had more to do with Chavalit and Chamlong's disapproval of the military's leadership than their views on the institution's proper role (see Surin 1992: 38; Pasuk and Baker 1997: 25; McCargo 1997b: 64, 244, 271). Even the urban middle class had arguably supported the protests out of disgust for the generals' hypocrisy and mendacity, as opposed to a firm commitment to democracy (see Hewison 1996: 84–5). Partly as a result, while the 'angelic' parties did run on their role in Suchinda's ouster, they did not articulate a vision for the future that clearly set them apart from their rivals. Indeed, the September elections were even freer of programmatic content than those held 6 months earlier, which had already scored quite poorly on that count (see Murray 1996: 211).

Second, the distinction between 'angels' and 'devils' meant little outside Bangkok and some of the major provincial towns. The middle-class character of the anti-Suchinda movement has often since been overstated, but Black May had been for the most part an urban affair. Of the parties at the forefront of the demonstrations, *Phalang Tham* had never ventured far outside the capital. The Democrats, who had played a more passive role, had no real presence in large swathes of the country. New Aspiration was strong in the Northeast, but its candidates, recruited from local notabilities (see McCargo 1997a: 129), ran mostly on local issues. Crucially, moreover, rural voters generally got their news not from the print media but from radio and television, which had operated under strict editorial control. When coverage of the demonstrations, which the broadcast media had initially ignored, finally made it on the air, protesters had been portrayed as rioters, arsonists, and enemies of Buddhism, on whom the military was forced to crack down to save Thailand from anarchy and mob rule (see Murray 1996: 143–6; Klima 2002: 145–50). Even as eyewitness accounts and videotapes of the carnage gradually made their way up-country, it was reported that first impressions often remained most vivid in the minds of villagers (see Murray 1996: 230). For many of them, there were neither angels nor devils.

The general elections of 13 September 1992 produced much the same kind of legislature as previous contests dating back to 1979 (see Table 6.2). Democrat Party leader Chuan Leekpai formed a coalition government that included each of the 'angelic' parties as well as *Ekkaphap* and Social Action, while as many as six opposition parties shared the remaining seats. Predictably, Chuan's government failed to serve out its term, because a corruption scandal involving Agriculture Minister Suthep Thaugsuban prompted *Phalang Tham* to withdraw its support in 1995. The year before, the coalition had withstood the defection of New Aspiration; it had only been saved by Prem's intervention,

Table 6.2 *Thailand's general elections, 1992–1996*

	March 1992	September 1992	July 1995	November 1996
Chat Pattana	–	60	53	52
Chat Thai	74	77	92	39
Democrat Party	44	79	86	123
Ekkaphap	6	8	8	8
Muanchon	1	4	3	2
Nam Thai	–	–	18	–
New Aspiration	72	51	57	125
Phalang Tham	41	47	23	1
Prachakorn Thai	7	3	18	18
Puangchon Chao Thai	1	–	–	–
Ratsadon	4	1	–	–
Samakkhitham	79	–	–	–
Seritham	–	8	11	4
Social Action	31	22	22	20
Tai	–	–	–	1
TOTAL SEATS	360	360	391	393
Effective number of parties (votes)	6.72	6.6	6.83	4.61
Effective number of parties (seats)	6.01	6.11	6.43	4.32
Seats to new parties (proportion)	.42	.19	.05	.003
Aggregate seat volatility	.51	.33	.13	.27
Party system nationalization score	.43	.44	.37	.44

Note: See Table 6.1 for the procedure to calculate the effective number of parties, volatility, and nationalization; all calculations were made by the author based on official district-level election returns. The data for the elections that took place in 1992 were originally provided by Allen Hicken (now available at www.electiondataarchive.org), and then cross-checked by the author with figures contained in official election reports (see Ministry of the Interior 1992; Pollwatch 1992). Data for the results of the 1995 and 1996 elections were gleaned from official election reports (see Ministry of the Interior 1995, 1996).

by which *Chat Pattana* was dragooned into joining the administration (see McCargo 2005: 509; Handley 2006: 372). New elections held in 1995 resulted in the formation of another weak government, this time headed by *Chat Thai*'s Banharn Silpa-archa. Widely criticized for its alleged incompetence and corruption, Banharn's administration lasted a mere 15 months, eventually succumbing to the same internal divisions that had plagued its predecessors.

Somewhat less consistent with previous rounds of voting were the results of the 1996 elections, because the improved performance of the two largest parties led to a marked decrease in the fragmentation of the House of Representatives. New Aspiration more than doubled its seat total, capitalizing on the collapse of *Chat Thai*, which lost almost two-thirds of its legislative contingent, including all but a handful of seats outside its stronghold in the Central Region. The Democrat Party, meanwhile, increased its seat share by almost 50 per cent, benefiting in part from *Phalang Tham*'s implosion. Still, continued factionalism within the main parties in practice rendered the Thai party system more fragmented than the official tallies suggest. New Aspiration, for instance, included as many as ten factions; their jockeying for position was a major factor in the instability of Chavalit Yongchaiyudh's new government, which was reorganized twice before it eventually buckled in late 1997 (see Chambers 2005: 510–11).

By the time Thailand held another general election in 2001, its political system had been thoroughly upended. The first major change – the reform to the country's institutional architecture – came as a result of purposeful action, spearheaded by elite figures often described as 'royal liberals' (Connors 2008). In mid 1994, the Chuan government had appointed a Democracy Development Committee (DDC), chaired by royalist intellectual Prawet Wasi, whose subsequent recommendations had zeroed in on 'curbing' the power of 'bad' (i.e., provincial) politicians (see Prawet 2002: 23). As parliament stalled, Prawet and his supporters mustered the necessary pressure to force its hand, leveraging the distaste that conservative elites, technocrats in the bureaucracy, the metropolitan business community, the Bangkok press, the urban middle class, and some progressive non-governmental organizations shared for 'money politics'. Politicians, whom the reformists had sought to exclude from the process, eventually agreed to establish a ninety-nine member Constitution Drafting Assembly (CDA) after securing the right for parliament to select its seventy-six provincial representatives (one per province, drawn from a list of ten persons elected by each province) and twenty-three other experts. Still dominated by royalist officials and scholars, the CDA produced a document that stuck closely to the principles articulated by the DDC. The new constitution was approved by the National Assembly and promulgated in October 1997.

Ironically, what came to be known as the 'People's Constitution' had been an elite project through and through. In fact, while the reformists held public hearings and consultations with grassroots organizations in an attempt to give themselves the appearance of a 'popular' movement (see Connors 2002: 48), 'royal liberals' had only won the support of the palace and conservative royalists by arguing that the new constitution would have strengthened the authority of the 'network monarchy' (see McCargo 2005: 511–12). This was to be accomplished in two steps.

First, the constitution featured provisions designed to keep provincial politicians out of the cabinet and insulate the executive from the elected legislature, thereby liberating its members from the whims of party/faction bosses. Second, the constitution provided new judicial and administrative bodies – whose composition the network monarchy expected to control through its influence over the Senate, the Supreme Court, and the Supreme Administrative Court – with considerable authority to check the power of the executive and legislative branches. More generally, while the constitution was ostensibly inspired by a host of liberal principles, the rights and freedoms it guaranteed were to remain squarely 'within the elite-defined normative civic culture of "Thainess " ' (Connors 2002: 43). To the extent that the document ever lived up to its billing as the 'People's Constitution', it did so only on account of its unintended consequences.

The new constitution redesigned several of Thailand's political institutions. The appointed Senate was replaced with an upper chamber whose members were to be elected at the provincial level on a non-partisan basis. The Prime Minister was to be drawn from among elected members of parliament, but all cabinet members were now required to resign their seats upon being sworn in. The size of the House of Representatives was increased to 500 deputies, elected through a 'mixed' system that awarded 400 seats in single-member districts (through first-past-the-post) and the remainder through proportional representation to national party lists that cleared a 5 per cent threshold. All candidates were now required to have bachelor's degrees to stand for election, while an Election Commission was given wide-ranging authority to investigate allegations of fraud and vote buying, as well as to disqualify candidates found to have committed infractions. A number of independent agencies – including the National Counter-Corruption Commission, the National Human Rights Commission, the State Audit Commission, and the Office of the Ombudsmen – were instituted as a means to fight corruption, human rights violations, and other abuses of power. A new, fifteen-member Constitutional Court was given the power to review the constitutionality of laws and government decisions.

If the new constitution reshaped the institutional framework that regulated political competition, the financial crisis that brought Thailand's economy to its knees in 1997, quickly spreading through much of East and Southeast Asia, scrambled the country's political landscape. Repeated promises to the contrary notwithstanding, Chavalit's government responded to the sustained attacks on the Thai baht by floating the national currency. In 1 year, the baht lost over half its value, destroying much of the wealth built during the expansion of the previous decade. The stock market plummeted, the banking sector collapsed, and companies that had accumulated significant foreign debt went bankrupt. The gross domestic product shrank by 10 per cent, plunging 3 million people into poverty (see Hewison 2004). Four months after floating the baht, Chavalit was forced to resign and was replaced by a new government headed by Chuan Leekpai – another development attributed to backroom deals brokered by Prem (see McCargo 2005: 510–11). Although ultimately successful in engineering Thailand's economic recovery, Chuan and his cabinet were unpopular because of their perceived subservience to the International Monetary Fund (IMF). Characteristically, the Asian Crisis had been blamed not on its domestic causes, but on the twin bogeymen of international capitalism and globalization, making it all too easy for critics to denounce the structural adjustment policies the IMF attached as a condition for bailing out the Thai economy as further suffering and humiliation inflicted on the country by the same foreign interests responsible for the crisis. With the decline of New Aspiration and the Democrats, the party system of old was left in shambles. And its reorganization was set to take place under a much different set of rules.

On borrowed time

At the turn of the new millennium, Thailand was hailed as a success story, an island of relative freedom in a region where more or less oppressive, corrupt dictatorships are the rule. The country had pulled through a financial crisis that would have brought down many an 'electoral democracy' without succumbing to military rule, while a brand new 'liberal' constitution appeared to have heralded the consolidation of a functioning democratic regime. What is more, the country's democratization had not come at the cost of sacrificing its 'traditional' institutions. Thailand's apotheosized King was widely regarded as a unifying figure, leading his subjects down a middle path that steered them away from the worst excesses of military and parliamentary rule, underdevelopment and unbridled capitalism. It mattered little that the palace and its network clung to extra-constitutional powers. At home, those who questioned the legitimacy of the King's role were reduced to a small and silent minority. For the international press, too, Thailand's 'universally revered' monarchy made for good copy, indulging the orientalism of correspondents, editors, and readers alike. In diplomatic circles, no less given to the soft bigotry of low expectations, it was seen as essential to the country's stability.

The equilibrium was a delicate one. For if the survival of Thailand's 'electoral democracy' was predicated upon the network monarchy's continuing ability to command the deference of elected governments – failing that, as the events since 2006 have shown, it stood ready to dismantle them, even at the cost of pushing the country to the brink of civil war – the network was running on borrowed time. Over the previous three decades, the palace, the military, and the bureaucracy had repeatedly been forced to come to terms with a rapidly changing society, which had rendered fruitless the repeated attempts made to preserve or restore successive status quos, surviving only thanks to timely adaptations that slowed, but did not arrest, the country's political transformation. Having most recently been compelled to accede to popular demands for a fully elected government, under the existing rules the power of the network monarchy hinged entirely on the ageing King's popularity, the hold of its official ideology, and the absence of a majoritarian challenge to its tutelage, guaranteed for the moment by a dysfunctional political system the palace and its allies had a strong hand in creating and a 'vested interest in preserving' (McCargo 2005: 506). Beneath the glistening surface of the 'True-Life Sequel to *The King and I*', as a fawning biography of King Bhumibol described the situation at the time (see Stevenson 1999), the network monarchy was vulnerable.

Perhaps the most profound reason for the system's precariousness was the ongoing nature of the transformations Thailand's social structure had undergone since the 1960s. Possibly more momentous than the rise of new business elites and the growth of the urban middle class, which had powered mass demonstrations in 1973 and 1992, were the transformations taking place at the bottom of Thailand's social hierarchy, undermining its foundations. On the one hand, development and modernization had changed provincial livelihoods, giving rise to a more educated, more worldly, more consumption-minded mass of 'middle-income peasants' (see Walker 2012), 'cosmopolitan villagers' (see Keyes 2012), and 'urbanized villagers' (see Naruemon and McCargo 2012) – an increasingly large percentage no longer involved in agriculture at all – who joined the ranks of the lower-middle class (*chan klang radap lang*) (see Nidhi 2009). On the other hand, the persistence of extreme levels of inequality rendered this vast segment of the population decidedly more receptive to a discourse of empowerment. Although neither political consciousness nor economic grievances automatically translate into political mobilization, the 'struggles for the right to have rights' (see Somchai 2006; see also Missingham 2004) waged by groups representing farmers and workers in the 1990s offered glimpses of the *potential* held by the mobilization of the provincial masses, now far more inclined to regard themselves as 'citizens' than 'children'.

While King Bhumibol's brand of 'plebeian anti-capitalism' had successfully deflected the blame that Thailand's unelected institutions might otherwise have shouldered for the Asian Crisis and a host of other maladies, the renewed emphasis placed on 'sufficiency' after 1997 was evidence of the palace's failure to comprehend, or accept, the implications of the country's socio-economic transformation. The King's rejection of 'progress', his pleas to 'walk backwards into a *khlong*' (canal), his unceasing portrayal of the desire for self-advancement as 'greed', and his articulation of a philosophy that limited the role of the provincial population to 'localized and modest pursuits' (see Walker 2010: 262) were at odds with the aspirations of upward mobility harboured by much of the population. Given the King's fatherly image and well-intentioned presentation, his words engendered no hard feelings; even so, the insistence on this rhetoric placed the palace at a risk of fading rapidly into irrelevance, should someone ever come along with a more empowering vision. To make matters worse, royalists had fallen victim to a measure of overconfidence in spearheading the passage of a new constitution that was far more protective of the executive against the vagaries of Thailand's legislative politics. As long as executives were controlled by, or subservient to the interests of, the network monarchy, these constitutional provisions may have worked, as intended, to reduce the nuisance that elected politicians presented to their smooth functioning. Should a government ever develop the strength to shake off their tutelage, however, the new rules of the game also limited the ability of unelected institutions to deter, undermine, or eject it through means other than brute military force. By the time royalists realized their mistake, it was already too late.

7 Barbarians at the gate

Supporters of Thaksin Shinawatra are apt to compare the deposed Prime Minister to King Taksin the Great, implicitly analogizing their downfall as the story of two great leaders victimized by the Chakri Dynasty (see Prachatai, 2 January 2010). Royalists are less keen on the comparison. The dynasty's founding myth does offer a justification of sorts for the ouster of a popular Prime Minister, as King Taksin's violent demise has long served to illustrate how leaders who abuse their authority may be replaced by men of superior merit. King Taksin, however, is still celebrated as a national hero, credited for the kingdom's reunification. According to official chronicles, moreover, even in defeat, King Taksin demonstrated his greatness and patriotism by accepting the cosmic justice of his fate – at his execution in 1782, moments before he was clubbed to death on the orders of King Rama I, his last words are purported to have been: 'Having exhausted Our merit, We have arrived at Our death' (see Nidhi 2012 [1986]: 503). In the eyes of royalists, conversely, Thaksin Shinawatra's refusal to accept his removal underscores the evil nature of a man determined to subvert, in the name of vanity and greed, the laws of nature upon which the nation's socio-political order is founded.

Rather than a national hero gone astray, royalists have mythologized Thaksin Shinawatra into something of a monster, one worthy of comparisons with no less a genocidal tyrant than Adolf Hitler. Visceral though their hatred may be, the Thaksin phenomenon is a 'monster' of their own making. Aside from openly supporting his rise to power, or authoring the constitutional provisions that allowed him to consolidate his power, Thailand's royalist establishment shoulders much of the responsibility for the historical context in which Thaksin's ascent took place. The Asian Crisis, which wrecked the country's political system, was caused by the failure of an economy built by – and for the benefit of – the palace, the military, the bureaucracy, and their clients in Thailand's banking conglomerates. If the electorate, in those circumstances, was receptive to the appeal of a brash, decisive leader, moreover, it was only because he presented an alternative to the faction-ridden administrations that had resulted from the network monarchy's long-running efforts to forestall the emergence of functioning democratic institutions. It is also hard to miss the fact that Thaksin's most illiberal policies had firm foundations in the ideology of Thainess and the practice of 'Thai-style democracy' – that such measures were popular is little wonder, because the public had long been taught to expect nothing less from a genuine 'Thai-style leader'. But for Sarit, Prem, and Bhumibol, there would have been no Thaksin.

It may well be the case that the defence of private business interests was foremost on the mind of the telecommunications magnate upon entering politics in 1994 (see Pasuk and Baker 2009: 45–57). Thaksin, however, would soon develop greater aspirations, turning to the pursuit of something money cannot buy: a transformative role in the history of the country. One way or the other, his place in the history books is assured, but Thaksin may ultimately prove to be the agent of a transformation quite unlike that to which he once aspired – namely, to lead Thailand's transformation into a developed economy. His model, if he had one, was Sarit Thanarat, not Pridi Banomyong. Insofar as Thaksin came to front a movement for greater 'democracy', which has grown into the most serious challenge ever levelled against the Thai monarchy's authority and power, it was only because Thailand's royalist order no longer had room for a figure as powerful as Sarit.

Prince Damrong Rajanubhab had predicted it all – in 1926. Commenting on the model of 'limited monarchy' under King Prajadhipok's consideration at the time, Prince Damrong warned that the monarchy could find itself in jeopardy should the King have cause to relieve a popular Prime Minister of his duties. The reason it took 80 years for the prediction to come true is twofold. First, Damrong could not have envisioned, given the monarchy's isolation at the time, that in different circumstances a King and his allies could prevent Prime Ministers from becoming all that popular in the first place – certainly not to the extent that the effort to discredit and weaken elected politicians succeeded under Bhumibol. Second, Damrong could not have anticipated that the monarchy would be able to revitalize a world view based on hierarchies of karmic merit and charismatic authority, which was then falling rapidly into disfavour with the educated public. Not only would this aspect of the official ideology of Thainess help render successful coups, especially those with royal sanction, legitimate in the eyes of key segments of the population; Tambiah (1976: 487) also suggests that the persistence of this pre-nationalist world view minimized public opposition to military coups because an incumbent's removal from office, like King Taksin's, was generally assumed to reveal 'loss of merit'. Recent work by Engel and Engel (2010) suggests that similar interpretations of personal injury or misfortune became more, not less, prevalent in parts of Thailand in the second half of the twentieth century.

By 2006, nonetheless, the effectiveness of each of the mechanisms of institutional reproduction by which royalists had kept Prince Damrong's prediction from realization was wearing thin. Thaksin Shinawatra was enormously popular. And while he never openly questioned King Bhumibol's authority to sanction his removal, his supporters were by no means inclined to accept his downfall as proof that his 'merit' had been exhausted, or to acknowledge the authority of self-described 'good men' to overturn their electoral choices. Indeed, the fact that Thaksin's popularity was greatest among constituencies whose self-image no longer comports with the subaltern role to which the ideology of 'Thainess' also consigns them made it possible for the deposed Prime Minister to present the treatment he received at the hands of the King's 'mandarins' (*ammat*) as essentially of a piece with the inequality and discrimination ordinary people endured under the 'rule of the mandarinate' (*ammattayathippatai*).[1] The 2006 coup would thereby accomplish the improbable feat of repackaging the billionaire tycoon's private interests and the aspirations of millions of ordinary people into one and the same cause.

Once again, this is a far cry from what Thaksin Shinawatra had initially set out to do. Thaksin had no quarrel with Thailand's royal nationalism, aside from the implications it had for his own power. In fact, while King Bhumibol often made light of the Prime Minister's corporate babble, Thaksin's governing philosophy was in key respects similar to his own. Like the King's, Thaksin's attempt to win over the affection of the people had been accompanied by a well-publicized expectation that the people would cooperate in their own 'management', even when the government happened to trample on hard-fought constitutional protections. The problem was that Thaksin had mastered the tradecraft of his royalist foes too well – and that, on the wings of his electoral dominance, he had flown too close to the sun, moving aggressively to displace the network monarchy's hold on power. Given the problematic royal succession looming over the horizon, the urgency that the palace and its allies felt to remove the Prime Minister is understandable. Yet the 2006 coup was a mistake all the same, for while it did little to diminish Thaksin's standing with the electorate, or avert the monarchy's prospective return to

[1] Decades earlier, Pridi Banomyong had defined *ammattayathippatai*, in contrast to democracy, as the rule of officials (*kha ratchakan*), courtiers/attendants (*kha fao*), and advisors (*thi prueksa*) appointed by the King (see Pridi 1974: 30).

ceremonial status, it threatened to turn the Chakri Dynasty into a victim of its most durable King's success.

Under new management

By the time Thaksin Shinawatra was re-elected Prime Minister in February 2005, Thailand's political regime, although formally unchanged, had taken on a different character from the one in place before his rise. The country remained an 'electoral democracy' whose workings did not meet the standards generally demanded of a full, liberal democracy. What had changed was the manner in which Thailand's political regime came short. On the eve of general elections held on 6 January 2001, the country retained an element of tutelage that limited, in practice, the authority of elected officials to govern the country. Aside from the influence of the network monarchy and the legitimacy accorded to actions presumed to have been taken on the monarchy's behalf, the anti-majoritarian character of the regime was enabled by the fragmentation of the country's political landscape, as well as the deference shown by Prime Minister Chuan Leekpai and the Democrat Party to unelected institutions. Four years later, the country's electoral democracy had become far more majoritarian or 'plebiscitarian' in nature. But the 'Thaksinization of Thailand', as the phenomenon was referred to at the time (see McCargo and Ukrist 2005), also featured the deterioration of the rule of law and some of the liberal freedoms enjoyed by at least segments of the population. Aside from Thaksin's imperial instincts, the change had been driven by the rearrangement of Thailand's party system, the effects of which spilled over to other institutional realms in such a way as to reshape the workings of the regime as a whole. The 'conversion' of Thailand's political regime was permitted by the erosion in the veto power of unelected institutions, brought about by constitutional provisions that had originally been designed, in a much different context, to accomplish the exact opposite.[2]

The rise of Thaksin Shinawatra would not have been possible without the financial crisis Thailand experienced in 1997. The Asian Crisis opened a 'critical juncture' in the development of Thailand's electoral and legislative politics, because the exogenous shock it inflicted on the system weakened personalities and organizations that had come to dominate

[2] The role that the 1997 constitution played in Thaksin's rise to power has been debated extensively (see Hicken 2009: 126–39; Nelson 2007). While crucial to the eventual streamlining of Thailand's party system, the position articulated here is that the reforms mattered less to Thai Rak Thai's success *in* the 2001 elections than they did to the entrenchment of its dominance *after* the elections.

the country's political scene at both the national and the local levels, generating opportunities for others to take their place. The crisis left the credibility of Thailand's two main parties in ruins. The financial position of their largest business backers suffered a major blow in the economic downturn, as did the finances of candidates, faction bosses, and provincial entrepreneurs who operated local electoral machines. Thaksin's businesses, meanwhile, had managed to escape the brunt of the crisis, because most of the firms under Shin Corporation benefited from lesser exposure to foreign debt. Much as his companies had exploited the weakness of the competition to emerge from the crisis in a position more dominant than before, so did the weakening of established parties, national politicians, and provincial notabilities offer Thaksin a window of opportunity to use his vast financial means, now more than ever at a premium, to effectively corner the electoral market.

Founded on 14 July 1998, Thaksin's political party Thai Rak Thai ('Thais Love Thais') rapidly went on to become the most formidable electoral force in Thailand's history. No one had seen it coming, for while there was no doubting Thaksin's ambition (see McCargo 1997a: 127), his first experience in politics had raised questions about his competence. His spells as Foreign Minister (1994–5) and Deputy Prime Minister (1995–6, 1997) had been brief and undistinguished. Worse, his succession of Chamlong Srimuang as the leader of *Phalang Tham* had coincided with the party's disappearance from Thailand's electoral map.

As it took shape in advance of the 2001 elections, Thai Rak Thai was first and foremost a party of big business. Thaksin put together 'the greatest assemblage of large business groups' (McCargo and Ukrist 2005: 224) ever to coalesce behind a political organization in Thailand, leveraging the metropolitan business community's desire to secure more effective protections from the state. Major conglomerates provided Thai Rak Thai with money, public endorsements, and advisors, raising its profile with incumbent members of parliament. While playing down expectations, Thaksin relied on an army of political consultants, survey researchers, and advertising firms to devise innovative marketing strategies and substantive proposals that could maximize the party's appeal. In the run-up to the elections, Thai Rak Thai announced an economic recovery plan centred on government assistance to small and medium-sized enterprises. As the Asian Crisis continued to take its toll, moreover, Thaksin harnessed the growing dissatisfaction with Chuan and the IMF by placing new emphasis on economic nationalist themes (Pasuk and Baker 2009: 76–80). After extensive market research and consultations with grassroots organizations, Thai Rak Thai also unveiled a rural platform founded on three pillars: an agrarian debt moratorium, the establishment of a revolving THB 1 million fund for every village, and a universal health plan that guaranteed all citizens access to basic medical care for about a dollar (THB 30) a visit. For the first time, a major national party had resolved to appeal to provincial voters directly, an effort that was complemented by a slick advertising campaign that sought to identify Thai Rak Thai constituency candidates with the party's national candidate for Prime Minister. Even as it aimed to nationalize constituency races, however, Thaksin invested considerable effort and resources in the recruitment of candidates known for their influence and popularity in various localities (see Somchai 2008). Thai Rak Thai absorbed a number of politicians who needed external support, but to whom other parties had increasingly little to offer (see Ockey 2004: 45–6). Over a hundred incumbent members of parliament ran under its banner in 2001.

The 2001 elections completely rearranged Thailand's political landscape (see Table 7.1). Thai Rak Thai took 248 seats, just 2 shy of an absolute majority in the House of Representatives. Thai Rak Thai's main rival, the Democrat Party won 128 seats through its continuing dominance of the South. Arguably most notable was the fact that Thai Rak Thai's success had gone well beyond the number of sitting members of parliament it had been able to field. Indeed, Thai Rak Thai's party list did better than its individual candidates in all but sixty-seven constituencies. In its best regions, the North and Northeast, the party received over a million and a half more votes than its candidates. These figures show that what made Thai Rak Thai into an electoral force quite unlike any Thailand had seen before was Thaksin's capacity to combine the old money politics that had traditionally dominated races in the provinces with the nationalization of such elections, accomplished through both charismatic and programmatic appeals to the provincial electorate. Pasuk and Baker (2009: 88) noted that the 2001 elections had been more about parties than any general election ever held before.

Over the ensuing 4 years, Thaksin embarked on a successful effort to make Thai Rak Thai into the dominant force in Thai politics, co-opting the leaders, factions, and politicians of all major parties except the Democrats. New Aspiration and *Seritham* dissolved themselves into Thai Rak Thai within a year; eventually, *Chat Thai* (minus powerful factions based in Chonburi and Buriram) was the sole party in Thaksin's coalition to remain separate from Thai Rak Thai, if only as a 'subsidiary' (see McCargo and Ukrist 2005: 106–7). While as many as fifteen factions operated within Thai Rak Thai, moreover, their power and autonomy were severely curtailed under Thaksin's leadership (see Chambers 2005: 514). Local politicians remained important for mobilizing votes in the

Table 7.1 *Thailand's general elections, 2001–2005*

	2001			2005		
	SMD	PR	TOT.	SMD	PR	TOT.
Thai Rak Thai	200	48	248	310	67	377
Democrat Party	97	31	128	70	26	96
Chat Thai	35	6	41	18	7	25
New Aspiration	28	8	36	–	–	–
Chat Pattana	22	7	29	–	–	–
Seritham	14	–	14	–	–	–
Mahachon	–	–	–	2	–	2
Ratsadon	2	–	2	–	–	–
Social Action	1	–	1	–	–	–
Thin Thai	1	–	1	–	–	–
TOTAL SEATS	400	100	500	400	100	500
Effective number of parties (votes)	4.30	4.01	–	2.57	2.30	–
Effective number of parties (seats)	3.07	2.93	3.05	1.58	1.92	1.65
Seats to new parties (proportion)	–	–	.50	.005	0	.004
Aggregate seat volatility	–	–	.48	.28	.20	.26
Party system nationalization score	.57	.62	–	.69	.71	–

Note: The column 'SMD' reports the number of single-member districts won by each party. The column 'PR' reports the number of seats won by each party's national list in the proportional component of the election.

See Table 6.1 for the procedure to calculate measures of the effective number of parties, volatility, and nationalization. All calculations were made by the author based on official election returns (see ECT 2001 and ECT 2005).

provinces, but they were no longer the locus of the party's financial and organizational resources.

Thai Rak Thai's transformation into a 'predominant party' (see Sartori 1976: 129) was helped by the fact that Thaksin's personal popularity made for long coat-tails, not to mention that members of parliament were compensated generously for their support (see Pasuk and Baker 2009: 192). Even more significant is the assistance that Thaksin was offered by provisions of the 1997 constitution. First, given that ministers were required to resign their legislative seats upon entering the cabinet, exiting the coalition would now require them to give up public office altogether. Second, the Prime Minister could now call elections at 45 days' notice, but the new rules required each candidate to have been a member of a party for at least 90 days prior to the elections. Disloyalty, therefore, now had a price few politicians could afford to pay, because expulsion from a party in the run-up to new elections would mean sitting out an entire legislative cycle. As Thaksin added more components to his party and his coalition, the government's position grew increasingly unassailable. In turn, as the ability of the opposition to lure coalition members out of the government was neutralized, the pressure intensified for the remaining parties to jump on Thaksin's bandwagon, even at the cost of sacrificing the independence they had once enjoyed.

Shrewdly enough, Thaksin capitalized on his dominance of the House of Representatives to implement his campaign promises. Thai Rak Thai's rural platform was enacted within 2 years, supplemented by a host of Keynesian economic measures designed to stimulate demand and investment – whether by reviving the banking sector, providing easier access to credit to small businesses and private citizens, subsidizing some household expenses, attracting foreign capital, or committing the government to large infrastructural projects. While these policies proved controversial because of their cost and, in some cases, their dubious effectiveness, they were popular with provincial voters and the urban working class. The popularity of these programmes, in turn, allowed Thai Rak Thai to 'take credit for improvements in the lives of villagers, at the expense of the provincial and local notables who had previously characterized such resource allocation as personal rather than party patronage' (Ockey 2004: 50). Whereas parties had once depended on notables to deliver votes in the provinces, in much of the country it was now local politicians who could hardly envision winning elections without Thai Rak Thai's endorsement. Thai Rak Thai's bone-crushing victory in the 2005 general elections, in which the party took 377 of 500 seats in the House of Representatives, punctuated the remarkable transformation that Thailand's political system had undergone, in the space of less than a decade, as a result of the rise of Thaksin Shinawatra.

For the 'quality' of Thailand's democracy, the implications were decidedly mixed. On the positive side of the ledger, Thaksin's 5 years in office could be said to have deepened the country's 'electoral democracy'. For the first time, the country had a government specifically chosen by the voters, instead of a patchwork of national parties and local machines cobbled together in smoke-filled rooms after the election. The streamlining of Thailand's party system also enhanced electoral (vertical) accountability, in that voters could now identify with greater certainty what the consequences would be, in terms of national policy, of electing one party or another, as well as who should bear responsibility for the government's successes and failures. So, too, did the political system's responsiveness improve, as Thai Rak Thai's legislative dominance allowed the government to implement the agenda endorsed at the ballot box without being encumbered by the fragmentation and factionalism that had once been rife in the National Assembly. Finally, to the extent that Thaksin was able to shake off the influence of unelected institutions, elections now mattered a great deal more than they ever did in the past.

On the negative side of the ledger, the transformation of Thailand's political system is also what gave Thaksin a licence to pursue a host of illiberal policies. In relatively short order, Thaksin for all intents and purposes neutralized those provisions of the 1997 constitution whose stated goal had been to maximize 'horizontal' or inter-institutional accountability (see O'Donnell 1998). Thanks to its sway over the formally nonpartisan Senate, which controlled their composition, the administration secured the subservience of most of the independent agencies established by the constitution.[3] In addition, while the restrictions placed by Thaksin on freedom of expression would later pale in comparison to the crackdowns enacted by his royalist successors, press freedom suffered as a result of the government's assertion of editorial control over much of the broadcast media, the manipulation of the state's advertising budget to incentivize favourable coverage, the levelling of criminal defamation charges against critics, and other efforts made to intimidate the press into self-censorship. More generally, Thaksin exhibited a great deal of aversion to non-electoral forms of political participation. Aside from publicly delegitimizing civil society organizations pressing demands on the government, or subjecting these groups to legal and bureaucratic harassment, legislation enacted on the subjects of terrorism (2003) and national emergencies (2005) was rightfully criticized for being so broad as to permit the criminalization of most dissent.

Most disturbing, however, were the systematic human rights violations overseen by the administration. In 2003, Thaksin launched a 'War on Drugs' whose stated objective was to eradicate drug trafficking within 90 days. Between February and April, hundreds of people were caught up in a wave of extra-judicial executions.[4] The administration's heavy hand also inflamed long-dormant ethnic tensions in Thailand's Muslim-majority southern provinces of Pattani, Yala, and Narathiwat, which flared up in response to killings committed by security forces during the drug war. Attacks on Army bases and government schools in early 2004 met with

[3] There is considerable merit in the argument that these agencies had been designed less as 'independent' checks on executive power than as an extension of the network monarchy – this is certainly how these bodies have functioned since 2007.

[4] The death toll has since been the subject of much debate, but a commission set up after the coup found that 2,819 murders were committed during the 3-month period, against an average of 1,362 for a comparable period in the years before and after the campaign (see ICID 2008) – the difference, 1,457, is likely close to the actual toll. The ICID found that 1,370 people who may have somehow been linked to the drug trade were killed during that time, without specifying how many deaths had been the work of the military and the police. Only fifty-four deaths were classified as 'extra-judicial executions'.

the state's brutal reprisals, as the military and the police were cited in a number of episodes of torture, kidnapping, and murder of activists and suspected insurgents. On 28 April 2004, 113 people were killed in incidents including the massacre of 28 lightly armed men who had barricaded themselves inside the Kru Ze mosque in Pattani. The following October, the military caused the death by suffocation of seventy-eight among the hundreds of people who had been loaded onto military trucks during a peaceful protest at Tak Bai. Underscoring the plebiscitarian character of the administration, these policies enjoyed overwhelming public support (see Pasuk and Baker 2009: 166; McCargo 2007: 56). What criticism Thaksin did receive, at home and abroad, did nothing to prevent Thai Rak Thai's historic triumph in the 2005 elections.

In fact, there was a great deal of precedent and popular demand for the kind of leadership Thaksin offered, because his illiberal policies had solid foundations in the theory and practice of 'Thai-style democracy'. Thaksin's tolerance of few constraints on his authority, and his tendency to brand his critics as enemies of the nation (see Pasuk and Baker 2009: 157), made him a worthy inheritor to the mantle of 'Thai-style leader' first personified by Field Marshal Sarit. Thaksin's 'War on Drugs' replicated, on a wider scale, the campaign Sarit had undertaken against arsonists and 'hooligans' (*anthaphan*), reflecting the same notion that a paternalistic leader has the right, if not the duty, to deal with miscreants through extra-legal means.[5] The government's refusal to countenance decentralization as a solution to the southern violence, likewise, was consistent with Bangkok's longstanding propensity to equate demands for autonomy with challenges to the nation's integrity and the authority of the state. So, too, did Thaksin's revival of initiatives to promote and enforce social conformity (see Pasuk and Baker 2009: 167–70) draw upon discourse that had long been at the heart of Thailand's official nationalism, as was his argument that a workable social contract required the people to give up their freedoms for the sake of order and stability. Meanwhile, in his routine portrayal of dissent as corrosive, political participation as chaotic, human rights as alien ideas, and constitutional rules as undue constraints on the government's ability to serve the nation, Thaksin read from a script whose lead author and interpreter had been none other than King Bhumibol (for a concise summation of that 'script', see Hewison 1997).

In an essay originally written when Thaksin was still popular with the urban electorate, Thongchai (2013 [2005]: 45–61) discussed the Prime

[5] Pasuk and Baker (2009: 162–3) also noted similarities with the extra-judicial killings that targeted presumed communists during Prem's administration in the early 1980s.

Minister's illiberalism as exemplary of the attitudes towards democracy that developed in Thailand as a result of the monarchy's assertion of über-constitutional status. Indeed, the tendency of Thai respondents to exhibit, in surveys like the 2001 Asian Barometer, weak support for liberal values such as political pluralism, individual liberty, egalitarianism, and separation of powers (see Chu *et al.* 2008: 28), can be attributed directly to the influence of the official ideology of 'Thainess'. It is a testament to the partial success of this ideology in shaping political attitudes that, by 2001, most Thai respondents took no exception to the following statements: 1) 'Government leaders are like the head of a family; we should all follow their decisions'; 2) 'The government should decide whether certain ideas should be allowed to be discussed in society'; 3) 'If we have political leaders who are morally upright, we can let them decide everything'; 4) 'If people have too many different ways of thinking, society will be chaotic'; and 5) 'Harmony of the community will be disrupted if people organize lots of groups.' The popularity of Thaksin Shinawatra's illiberal policies, in this sense, is rooted in political preferences for which the country's royal nationalism was responsible in the first place.

The role of the palace in the 'War on Drugs' and the response to the southern insurgency illustrates the element of continuity embodied in Thaksin's policies. While Thai Rak Thai had long since promised to wage 'wars' on poverty, corruption, and drug trafficking, it is likely no coincidence that the drug campaign started 2 months after King Bhumibol spoke at length, in his 2002 birthday address, of the necessity of waging such a 'war' (see Bhumibol 2002: 1–4) – shortly thereafter, a member of the Privy Council had mused about the need to execute 60,000 drug dealers and users to deliver the nation from 'bad karma' (see Connors 2009: 8). Months after the killings, in his 2003 birthday speech, King Bhumibol not only argued that 'victory in the drug suppression campaign is a good thing', but also went on to note that while some may have faulted the crackdown for the loss of up to 2,500 lives, this was but a 'small matter' (*rueang lek*), as the deaths among users, dealers, officials, and innocent bystanders would have easily exceeded this count had the Prime Minister failed to take action (see Bhumibol 2003: 13). The position of the palace on the situation in the Deep South was a great deal more ambiguous. For while King Bhumibol did urge Thaksin to exercise greater care in addressing the situation, condemning the excesses as counterproductive, Queen Sirikit drummed up support for an increasingly violent and sectarian approach to the insurgency, through actions and public statements whose incitement of militarism and vigilantism hearkened back to the mid 1970s (see McCargo 2007: 57–8; Boyce, 26 April 2005; Marshall 2011: 133–49).

On the whole, it could be said that the idea of Thailand that took shape under Thaksin Shinawatra marked major departures from the country's royal nationalism in only two significant respects. First, Thaksin drew his legitimacy from below, not from above, and justified derogations of constitutional rule not in authority derived from the monarchy but rather in the overwhelming popular mandate he had received. Thaksin needed no prodding to make conspicuous displays of obeisance to the throne, but had equally little compunction about setting out to reduce its extra-constitutional authority. Second, while Thaksin shared with conservative royalists a vision of an essentially passive populace, which owed the government its quiescence between elections, he asked for the people's loyalty not by stressing the virtues of hierarchy, or their duty to accept their station in life, but rather by promising greater equality and opportunities for social and economic mobility (see Hewison 2004: 515). Indeed, while the effort to topple Thaksin's 'electocracy' (see Kasian 2006) was joined by activists and ordinary citizens genuinely interested in a more substantive, liberal brand of democracy, subsequent events show that establishment royalists were troubled less by the government's dictatorial behaviour than they were by the manner such powers had been acquired, through election, and the threat their application presented to the future of Thailand's unelected institutions. It was by design that the military operation some observers found cause to label the 'good coup' ushered in the establishment of a regime a great deal less, not more, democratic.

The downfall

A complete failure in the long run, the military coup staged by the 'Council for Democratic Reform under the King as Head of State' on 19 September 2006 went as well as it could have under the circumstances. Thaksin's absence from the country allowed the generals to seize power without having to place the Prime Minister under arrest. The King's endorsement warded off a potential confrontation between rival factions in the armed forces. Crucially, moreover, the coup was not met with overt public opposition. The residents of Bangkok, who had supported Thai Rak Thai overwhelmingly in the 2005 elections, appeared to breathe a collective sigh of relief. All other constituencies that could have denied the coup's legitimacy seemed willing to be of service. Academics and intellectuals accepted appointments to new bodies tasked with rubberstamping legislation and drafting a new constitution more suitable to the network monarchy's needs. American diplomats went through the motions of expressing concern in public; in confidential communications with Washington, DC, however, they could scarcely contain their satisfaction over Thaksin's ouster, or hide their sympathy for the junta's pleas for 'understanding' (see Boyce, 26 September 2006). While feigning regret over the methods employed to topple the administration, opposition leader Abhisit Vejjajiva (see Boyce, 28 September 2006) and the local staff of international human rights organizations (see Arvizu, 15 December 2006) privately reassured foreign governments that Thailand's democracy needed a reset. Echoing arguments that had been aired by critics of the government in the lead-up to the coup, the junta explained its actions by citing Thaksin's divisiveness, corruption, and abuse of power. The generals did not fail to accuse the government of disrespecting the monarchy 'on frequent occasions'.

Much like Chatichai Chunhavan 15 years earlier, Thaksin Shinawatra's undoing was the zeal with which he had gone about breaking down the extra-constitutional limitations placed on his authority to govern the country. Thaksin had long understood the dangers of doing so, complementing his efforts on the electoral front with an attempt to ingratiate himself with Thailand's unelected ruling class. Aside from initially making the metropolitan business community the centrepiece of his coalition, Thaksin had not neglected, in Handley's (2006: 424) words, to use 'his money to buy off the palace' – contributing to royal projects, subsidizing personal expenses of members of the royal family, and infusing tens of millions of dollars into the Crown Property Bureau (for instance, see *Asia Sentinel*, 1 March 2007). Disillusioned with Chuan Leekpai, whose effectiveness as an administrator never rivalled his wit and pliancy, the palace was at first quite receptive to Thaksin's overtures. Shortly after the 2001 elections, as the Constitutional Court pondered his disqualification from office on asset concealment charges, royalists publicly rallied to Thaksin's defence – bowing to the pressure applied by Prem behind the scenes, the Court acquitted the Prime Minister in an 8–7 ruling (see McCargo 2005: 513). The relationship, however, grew increasingly tense as the influence exerted by the government over the military and civilian bureaucracy began to encroach on some of the palace's prerogatives.

The effort made by Thaksin to win over the support of the military was motivated by the same desire to neutralize a potential threat to the government. In relatively short order, the administration gained control over military reshuffles, at the expense of Prem's authority to install members of his network at the top of the hierarchy. Army Commander-in-Chief Surayud Chulanont was sidelined, while trusted officers including Thaksin's family members and old classmates at the Armed Forces Academy Preparatory School enjoyed preferential treatment in promotions to positions of prestige and strategic importance. The 'repoliticization' of the military (see McCargo and Ukrist 2005: 134–57) also aimed to make high-ranking officers the beneficiaries of the Prime Minister's direct patronage. Aside from approving marginal increases in the military budget, Thaksin took control of defence allocations, using them to cultivate support inside the armed forces. The military, to be sure, remained by no means unified behind the government. Initially, however, Thaksin appeared to have largely earned its backing. Most useful was the enlistment of the Army-owned broadcast media in an increasingly propagandistic effort to promote the administration.

The interest shown in the armed forces and the police, where Thaksin commanded an even more reliable following, contrasted sharply with the treatment reserved for the civilian bureaucrats who had historically dominated Thailand's policy-making process. Aside from frequently drawing unflattering comparisons between civil servants and business entrepreneurs (see Pasuk and Baker 2009: 172), Thaksin moved quickly and on multiple fronts to 'redistribute bureaucratic power to the political executive' (Painter 2006: 28), reversing a practice that had seen technocrats in the bureaucracy exploit the weakness of elected governments to their advantage. Political appointees were placed in top positions within crucial ministries to oversee the drafting of legislation and its implementation – tasks once reserved for career bureaucrats. The bureaucracy was revamped through structural reforms and personnel decisions designed to make it more 'responsive' to the elected leadership (see Pasuk and Baker 2009: 184–8), an effort that proceeded hand in hand with the attempt to stamp out the independence of agencies and courts that had been designed as a counterweight to the power of elected officials. While the process was not without incident, the power of unelected civil servants had sunk to historic lows by the time Thaksin was re-elected in 2005.

None of this escaped the attention of the King's men. Thaksin may have seen himself as a new Sarit, combining the expansion of his government's reach across the machinery of the state with incessant promotion of the monarchy. Five decades on, however, the palace was rather more inclined to consider its prospective return to a ceremonial role as a demotion, and to see the rise of a Prime Minister who would presume to speak for the nation as an intrusion on another prerogative that had long since been the King's. Indeed, while King Bhumibol may have personally disliked Thaksin, and no doubt had cause to view Thaksin's economic vision as a competitor to his own, the palace's opposition stemmed from the fact that the Prime Minister's actions threatened to consign the monarchy, its allies, and its self-described defenders to political irrelevance, disrupting mechanisms of institutional reproduction that had previously allowed them to hold elected politicians in check.

Aside from Thaksin's attempt to disable the network monarchy, which threatened the palace's power to influence the course of events behind the scenes, a major problem was presented by Thaksin's personal popularity and the resonance of his ideas – both of which were unprecedented for a Thai national figure other than King Bhumibol. On the one hand, the emphasis that Thaksin placed on the mandate he received from the electorate implicitly challenged the authority that 'good men' drew from personal service to the King. Thaksin made the challenge explicit in June 2006, when he publicly denounced the machinations of 'persons with *barami* outside the constitution' (*phu mi barami nok ratthathammanun*). On the other hand, the resonance of Thaksin's vision of 'capitalist revolution' and his appeals to the people's aspirations for greater equality not only challenged the King's image as a champion of the downtrodden far more devoted and effective than elected politicians (Hewison and Kengkij 2010: 194–6), but also presented an indirect threat to a hierarchical world view that measures the legitimacy of claims to morality, truth, and power on the basis of an individual's distance from the King, as revealed by social status. Indeed, while Thaksin's message was focused on encouraging ordinary people to work towards their economic advancement, urging them to re-think the inevitability of hierarchies of wealth and status was guaranteed to raise similar questions about the inequalities of power and rights upon which the country's royalist order was founded. Very likely without fully intending to do so (see Jakrapob, 29 August 2007), Thaksin had threatened the hegemony of the official ideology on which the country's royalist order based its legitimacy and power.

In that context, perhaps most troubling to some senior royalists may have been the possibility that Thaksin could have exploited the King's succession – and his replacement with an unpopular Crown Prince thought to be excessively beholden to the Prime Minister – definitively to vanquish the network monarchy and place the monarchy 'under' the constitution. As in all matters involving the Thai royal family, the role that the royal succession has played in the country's political crisis remains opaque and outside the bounds of permissible domestic debate. It is most likely, however, that establishment royalists – some of whom have long wished that King Bhumibol would name a different successor (see John, 25 January 2010) – were determined to prevent Thaksin from presiding over the transition, whether to protect the palace's extra-constitutional authority, guarantee the continuity of their personal networks of influence and power, or, as Marshall (2014) has proposed, perhaps even derail the enthronement of Crown Prince Vajiralongkorn.

Be that as it may, the conservative reaction against Thaksin relied heavily on the moral suasion and charismatic authority of Prem and senior royalists such as Prawet Wasi and Anand Panyarachun, who took to speaking out against the government with increased frequency after the 2005 elections. The effort was accompanied by the activation of military officers who had both instrumental and ideological reasons to resent the elected government's growing influence over the armed forces (see Ukrist 2008). The tide turned during the annual military reshuffle in September 2005, when Prem thwarted Thaksin's attempt to remove high-ranking officers deemed insufficiently loyal to the government. The promotions list eventually signed by the King featured the appointment of General Sonthi Boonyaratglin – a protégé of General Surayud Chulalont, who had been appointed to the Privy Council in 2003 – as Army Commander-in-Chief, while Anupong Paochinda and Saprang Kalayanmitr were appointed commanders of the First and Third Army Regions. It was not long before plans were laid for a military coup, in advance of which Sonthi managed to reassign a number of mid-ranking officers and battalion commanders loyal to Thaksin (see Ukrist 2008: 128–9). Just as efforts were made behind the scenes to secure the support of Queen Sirikit (see Boyce, 3 July 2006) – who had emerged as the palace's most influential figure since Bhumibol took to spending most of his time away from Bangkok in the early 2000s – Prem visited the academies of all major branches of the armed forces, where he gave widely publicized speeches urging soldiers to remember, should push come to shove, that their allegiances should be with the King, not the government.

Another constituency that supported the reaction against Thaksin was drawn from a section of Bangkok's business community, which had grown hostile to the government by the end of Thaksin's first term. On the one hand, Thaksin came to be accused of using his position to favour his own businesses as well as those of relatives and cronies. Given the breadth of Shin Corporation and its satellite companies, Thaksin's competition included much of Bangkok's business elite, including the Crown Property Bureau (see Pasuk and Baker 2009: 229; see also Hewison 2008: 206). On the other hand, Thaksin's negotiation of bilateral free trade agreements with Australia, China, India, and other countries, including the United States, further threatened the interests of business families that had previously dominated commercial banking, agribusiness, and much of the manufacturing sector. These families had initially supported Thaksin expecting greater protection, but the administration's subsequent 'neo-liberal' shift helped turn some of the Prime Minister's earliest backers into some of his most fervent opponents (see Hewison 2008: 202). By Sondhi Limthongkul's own admission, the impetus and funding for the anti-Thaksin street movement that took shape in the second half of 2005 came from this 'feudal elite', who 'were beginning to see their power base decline slowly' and 'got even more scared' when Thaksin meddled 'in areas that no politician [before] dared to intervene' (cited in Crispin, 27 April 2007).[6]

The case through which Sondhi and his allies sought to arouse opposition to Thaksin, primarily among the urban middle class, had four major planks. The first and arguably most important was the call to 'Fight for the King'. Thaksin was accused of having usurped the King's powers, as well as plotting further harm to the monarchy's authority and prestige (see Boyce, 18 November 2005). The second was an attack on Thaksin's democratic legitimacy, allegedly vitiated by vote buying and, more generally, by the provincial electorate's ignorance and stupidity. The third major theme was the corruption of Thaksin's administration. On this count, it should be noted that there exists little evidence to suggest that corruption under Thaksin had been any worse than under his predecessors (or his successors) – ironically, Sondhi would later plead guilty to committing fraud on a far greater scale than anything for which Thaksin has ever been tried, let alone convicted (see *The Nation*, 29 February 2012). Bangkok's elites, however, were quite successful in raising the *perception* of corruption with the urban middle class, which appears to have varied with one's exposure to the print media (see Jäger 2012). Finally, Sondhi's movement took aim at the government's economic policies. While Thaksin's foreign trade policy was presented as a threat to national sovereignty, his domestic initiatives were branded as a ploy by which wealthy capitalists aimed to buy off the provincial electorate through massive transfers of wealth from the urban middle class.

By the end of 2005, Thaksin's position still seemed secure – that the situation would soon become unmanageable was largely the result of his own miscalculations. The Prime Minister's first major blunder turned out to be the sale of his family's shares of Shin Corporation to Temasek Holdings. The USD 2 billion sale – which involved the transfer of assets of some consequence for national security to a company controlled by a

[6] One of his earliest backers, media entrepreneur Sondhi Limthongkul broke with Thaksin as a result of private business conflicts (see *The Nation*, 29 November 2005). Once his television show, which had grown increasingly critical of the government, was taken off the air in September 2005, Sondhi held weekly rallies in Bangkok, while his newspaper (*Phuchatkan*) and satellite television channel ASTV inveighed against the Prime Minister and his policies.

foreign government, made in a way that allowed the Shinawatras not to pay tax – was brandished by the opposition as evidence for its charge that Thaksin's interest in public office was rooted exclusively in its promise of private gain, to be pursued even at the cost of selling out the country to foreign interests. Previously on the verge of giving up the fight, Sondhi Limthongkul parlayed a rally on 4 February 2006 into the birth of a new movement. A crowd 50,000 strong turned out to call on Thaksin to 'get out'; for the first time, Sondhi was joined by Chamlong Srimuang and his 'Dharma Army'. Within days, the movement coalesced into the People's Alliance for Democracy (PAD), whose membership included academics, government officials, labour leaders, civil society organizations, professionals, and ordinary citizens of every extraction (see Pye and Schaffar 2008). In the following 2 months, tens of thousands of people wearing yellow shirts joined anti-Thaksin demonstrations, pleading with the King to invoke Article 7 of the constitution to appoint a new Prime Minister (see Connors 2008).

It was at that point that Thaksin made another crucial mistake. As if to challenge his critics to produce evidence for their contention that the people had lost trust in his leadership, Thaksin dissolved the House of Representatives and scheduled a snap general election for 2 April 2006. Certain of defeat but determined to deny the Prime Minister any legitimacy, the new leader of the Democrat Party, Abhisit Vejjajiva, announced a boycott of the elections, joined by the leaders of *Chat Thai* and *Mahachon*. For Thaksin and his allies, the election would be an unmitigated disaster. Deprived of a real opposition, Thai Rak Thai was awarded 460 seats. Forty seats, however, remained vacant because Thai Rak Thai candidates failed to garner the 20 per cent vote share required to be certified the winners in almost every southern constituency; in the South, Thai Rak Thai's vote percentage was dwarfed by 'No' votes, cast by almost one in three voters nationwide. Worse, Thai Rak Thai executives were soon implicated in efforts to bribe small parties into contesting the election, while Democrat Party officials were also caught buying politicians into fabricating charges of bribery against Thai Rak Thai. Publicly, Thaksin declared victory. His decision to take a leave of absence, however, indicated that he understood otherwise.

What Thaksin and his allies had expected would solidify the government's position had backfired so badly that, by late April 2006, King Bhumibol felt comfortable enough to publicly take sides in the controversy. Speaking to a batch of newly appointed judges, the King urged the judiciary to 'solve' the 'problem' and reminded them of their oath to 'work for democracy'. He then asked a rhetorical question: 'Should the elections be nullified?' While His Majesty would not say, he volunteered the opinion that the election had been 'undemocratic'. Sensing that the winds had shifted, the Constitutional Court voided the election on a technical flaw. Within weeks, a number of other proceedings related to the elections led the Attorney General to bring party dissolution charges against both Thai Rak Thai and the Democrats, while three members of the Election Commission who refused to resign were tried, convicted, and sentenced to 4 years in prison. Even still, Thaksin was far from defeated. Having resumed his duties as 'caretaker' Prime Minister in late May 2006, he gradually withdrew his promise to sit out the next election. As the country approached a new round of voting – initially scheduled for 15 October 2006, but likely to be delayed a few weeks pending the instalment of a new Election Commission – it became increasingly clear that the only way to deny Thai Rak Thai another landslide victory was to make sure the elections did not take place at all.

The wrecking crew

As effortlessly as the military operation was executed on the night of 19 September 2006, the task before the generals and their supporters was a great deal more complex than the Prime Minister's removal from office. The Council for National Security (CNS) – as the junta became known upon the appointment of General Surayud Chulanont as Prime Minister – dedicated its 15 months in office to the pursuit of two objectives. The first was to correct the unintended consequences of the 1997 constitution, with a view to strengthening the tutelage of unelected institutions. The second was to return Thailand's political system to the fragmentation and volatility of the pre-1997 period, pursued through constitutional reforms as well as both judicial and extra-judicial efforts to neutralize the sources of Thaksin's strength: his popularity, his wealth, and his organization. In the days after the coup, the junta initiated the process that would lead to Thaksin's criminal prosecution and the eventual confiscation of his assets, impanelling an Assets Examination Committee (AEC) to investigate episodes of corruption. The measure was accompanied by orders that disbanded the Constitutional Court and replaced it with a smaller Constitutional Tribunal, newly endowed with broad powers to suspend the electoral rights of officials belonging to political parties subject to dissolution. The legality of these measures was sanctioned in the interim charter promulgated on 1 October 2006.

The efforts to discredit Thaksin, however, quickly ran into trouble, as the AEC struggled to find evidence linking Thaksin to clear-cut episodes of corruption. Before disbanding, the AEC froze the proceeds that Thaksin's family had reaped from the sale of Shin Corporation. Over half the USD 2.1 billion was eventually seized by the state in late February 2010, after a division of the Supreme Court with jurisdiction over political cases ruled that Shin Corporation had profited from the administration's policies – significantly, the assessment of 'unusual wealth' and 'policy corruption' did not require the Court to establish the commission of specific crimes. Indeed, while a number of cases continue to languish in the courts, the only offence for which Thaksin has been convicted thus far is a charge he incurred for signing off on his wife's purchase of a plot of public land along Bangkok's Ratchadaphisek Road in 2003. Having been acquitted of charges of corruption and abuse of power, Thaksin was sentenced to 2 years in prison, without suspension, for violating a law barring public officials from doing business with agencies subject to their authority.

The inquiries into the human rights violations committed during Thaksin's tenure proved even more problematic, likely because holding members of the administration accountable for laying out the policies pursuant to which the abuses were committed required exposing the role that members of Thailand's security forces along the chain of command had played in the policies' execution. The worst episodes of repression in the South were whitewashed by the courts – with regard to the Tak Bai incident, a provincial court in Songkhla ruled that 'army and police officials had acted according to the law, used sound judgment and done their best given the circumstances' (see *The Nation*, 30 May 2009; see also AHRC, 11 May 2007). The investigation into the 'War on Drugs' was outsourced to an 'independent commission' whose report recommended the case's referral to the International Criminal Court, but failed to uncover evidence of the administration's direct involvement (see *The Nation*, 16 January 2008).

The disaggregation of Thaksin's coalition faced similar obstacles. In late May 2007, the Constitutional Tribunal ordered the disbandment of Thai Rak Thai over the conduct of two of its executives in the 2006 election campaign, sparing the Democrat Party. Upon ordering Thai Rak Thai dissolved for having attempted to 'seize power through unconstitutional means', the Tribunal retroactively applied rules introduced by the junta to disqualify all 111 members of Thai Rak Thai's executive board from public office for 5 years, banning Thaksin and most of the party's lead politicians from participating in future elections. The People Power Party (*Phak Phalang Prachachon*), where the surviving Thai Rak Thai politicians migrated in the months that followed the ruling, was never the juggernaut its predecessor had been. But the resilience of Thaksin's support in the provinces guaranteed a strong showing in elections the junta had promised to hold within a year of the coup.

Clear evidence of the junta's failure to dent Thaksin's electoral base was provided by the results of the non-binding referendum held in August 2007 to approve the constitution drafted under its supervision. The generals had relied on a number of stratagems, threats, and repressive measures to secure the appearance of a popular endorsement (see AHRC, 20 August 2007). Heavy restrictions had been placed on the campaign against the draft, as the military government excluded dissenting voices from much of the broadcast media, banned the opposition from advertising its views, and seized campaign material advocating 'No' votes. Meanwhile, thousands of officials from the Interior Ministry and the Internal Security Operations Command (ISOC) were mobilized to 'educate' the public about the draft, at times urging the population to vote 'Yes' as a means to show their loyalty to the monarchy. Even so, the result was humiliating. Aside from the low turnout (58 per cent), Thailand's Northeast and Upper North voted against the draft. The fifteen-point margin that separated the 'Yes' and 'No' votes overall was rooted in the strong support the draft constitution had earned in the Central Region and the South.

Its dubious legitimacy notwithstanding, the 2007 constitution proved one of the military coup's few notable achievements (for an account of the deliberations, see Nelson 2013). The principal modifications it made to Thailand's political regime can be grouped under three headings. First, the constitution included new provisions, such as Article 237, that expanded the power of the courts to remove governments and dissolve political parties. Other provisions minimized the potential for the new Constitutional Court to act in ways contrary to the framers' intent: its membership was reduced to nine members, while new selection procedures maximized the network monarchy's control over its composition.[7] Second, whereas Thaksin's ability to bend independent agencies to his will had been facilitated by his influence over the elected Senate, the new constitution provided that the Senate would be composed, in addition to the representatives elected by each province, of an almost equal number of appointees selected by a panel dominated by the judiciary and 'independent' agencies. Third, the 2007 constitution featured rules designed to increase the fragmentation of the House of Representatives and weaken the Prime Minister. The new electoral system scrapped most single-member districts in favour of the old two- and three-seat constituencies. The number of seats to be allocated based on the votes cast for party lists was reduced to eighty, ten for each of eight provincial

[7] Compare Articles 204, 206, and 221 of the 2007 constitution with Articles 255, 257, and 274 of the 1997 constitution.

clusters. Meanwhile, the Prime Minister's ability to punish defections and disloyalty was greatly reduced. Cabinet members were no longer required to resign their seats in parliament. In the event of an election called as a result of an early House dissolution, Article 101(3) lowered the number of days a candidate was required to have been a member of a party before the election from 90 to 30, thereby allowing incumbents to freely switch parties once a new election was called at 45 days' notice.

Under the circumstances, the People Power Party's victory in the general election held on 23 December 2007 was a remarkable achievement. The disqualification of Thai Rak Thai's national leadership had rendered the People Power Party far more dependent on local electoral machines. Indeed, some old Thai Rak Thai politicians had felt confident enough in their own prospects to form separate parties, which by and large stood ready to support governments of any colour and stripe. To make matters worse, Thaksin's choice of a 'nominee' – former Bangkok governor Samak Sundaravej – had not been especially felicitous, for while it did little to reverse the party's decline in Bangkok, it earned the People Power Party few votes in the provinces. Against the odds, the party still managed to take 233 of 480 seats (see Table 7.2). The Democrat Party rebounded from its disastrous performance in 2005, but Abhisit Vejjajiva's first shot at the premiership underscored his lack of national electoral appeal, considering the lengths to which the generals had gone to tilt the playing field in his favour (see Freedom House 2008). As intended, the elections produced a House of Representatives a great deal more fragmented than it had been in 2005. Still, it was not difficult for Samak to form a coalition government, because the People Power Party came close enough to a majority to virtually pre-empt any other outcome, absent a major shake-up.

The efforts to engineer the required shake-up began almost immediately, as the Election Commission investigated the possible dissolution of the People Power Party and three of its coalition partners for violations that four party executives (one per party), including the new House Speaker, had committed during the campaign. Unwilling to let the results stand, but mindful of the risks of staging another military coup, the judicial strategy to overturn the 2007 elections held great promise for royalists (see Dressel 2010). The strategy, however, had two major limitations. First, the process was to take time, because it required the Election Commission to investigate the cases and refer them to the Constitutional Court, which would in turn hold a full trial. Second, a judicial intervention could always backfire; not unlike a military coup, it required a context in which the judiciary's actions would be accepted as the way

Table 7.2 *Thailand's general elections, 2007–2011*

	2007			2011		
	KHET	PR	TOT.	SMD	PR	TOT
People Power Party	199	34	233	–	–	–
Pheu Thai	–	–	–	204	61	265
Democrat Party	131	33	164	115	44	159
Chat Thai	30	4	34	–	–	–
Chat Thai Pattana	–	–	–	15	4	19
Pheu Phaendin	17	7	24	–	–	–
Chat Pattana Pheu Phaendin	–	–	–	5	2	7
Matchimathippatai	11	–	11	–	–	–
Ruam Jai Thai Chat Pattana	8	1	9	–	–	–
Pracharat	4	1	5	–	–	–
Bhum Jai Thai	–	–	–	29	5	34
Rak Prathet Thai	–	–	–	–	4	4
Mataphum	–	–	–	1	1	2
Phalangchon	–	–	–	6	1	7
Others (3 parties)	–	–	–	–	3	3
TOTAL SEATS	400	80	480	375	125	500
Effective number of parties (votes)	4.02	2.96	–	3.12	2.76	–
Effective number of parties (seats)	2.75	2.77	2.77	2.51	2.73	2.57
Seats to new parties (proportion)	.60	.54	.59	.69	.65	.68
Aggregate seat volatility	.78	.66	.75	.70	.66	.67
Party system nationalization score	.56	.66	–	.59	.66	–

Note: The column 'KHET' (for 2007) reports the number of seats won by each party in one-, two-, and three-seat constituencies. 'SMD' (for 2011) reports the number of single-member districts won by each party. The column 'PR' reports the number of seats won by each party's national list in the proportional component of the election.

See Table 6.1 for a description of measures of the effective number of parties, volatility, and nationalization. All calculations were made by the author based on official election returns (see ECT 2007 and ECT 2011) supplemented, for the 2007 elections, by provincial-level data from news reports (see NNA, 2 March 2011).

out of a crisis of some kind. In practice, that meant that the People Power Party was guaranteed to spend at least several months in office, in which it was expected to push through amnesties and constitutional amendments designed to countermand the legacy of the 2006 coup. Thaksin Shinawatra's return to Thailand in February 2008 did not augur well for the longevity of the country's new tutelary democracy.

Once again, it fell upon the PAD to engineer circumstances conducive to Samak's removal. By the time it began holding rallies in May 2008, however, the PAD had taken on a much different character. While attendance was far weaker than it had been in 2006, what the PAD lacked in crowd size it more than made up for in incendiary rhetoric and ideological extremism. Gone, in particular, were the paeans to 'royal liberalism' (see Connors, 7 July 2008), replaced by demands that democracy be scrapped in favour of a system dominated by appointed men, calls for executing enemies of the monarchy, xenophobic rants against the country's neighbours, and the dehumanization of provincial voters guilty of having brought Thaksin's flunkies back into power. Samak's bluster only served to further inflame the crisis. Indeed, while Samak's historical ties with the military and the palace earned the new government no sympathy from generals and palace insiders, his record in support of brutal crackdowns in 1976 and 1992 – which he continued to defend as justified and proportionate – gave the PAD and its allies in the press an opening to portray the fight against Thaksin as the continuation of previous struggles against dictatorship, even as the Yellow Shirts implored the military to stage a coup and adopted the ultra-nationalist ideology, the violent rhetoric, and the hateful propaganda songs of the royalist vigilantes with whom Samak had been affiliated in the 1970s.

The first major success in the PAD's new campaign came in July 2008, when Foreign Minister (and Thaksin's personal lawyer) Noppadon Pattama resigned his office in the wake of a ruling of the Constitutional Court. The Court found that the government had exceeded its authority when it signed a memorandum of understanding in support of Cambodia's request to have UNESCO list the Preah Vihear temple as a World Heritage Site. The PAD seized on the chance to accuse the government of treason and call on the armed forces to 'recover' the thousand-year-old Khmer ruin, which the International Court of Justice awarded to Cambodia in 1962. In the weeks that followed, Thaksin skipped bail and left the country in anticipation of his criminal conviction in the Ratchadaphisek Road land case, giving his opponents a chance to brand him a 'fugitive from justice'.

It is around this time that the PAD also stepped up its activities in the streets. In the space of a few days at the end of August 2008, PAD activists briefly took over government buildings and the offices of the National Broadcasting Services of Thailand (NBT), temporarily shut down airports in three southern cities, and placed the Government House under indefinite occupation. The increasingly confrontational approach seemed to have borne fruit on 9 September, when the Constitutional Court unanimously voted to remove Samak from office, on the pretext that his appearance as the host of two television cooking shows violated a conflict of interests provision in the constitution. The ruling caused so little public outcry that the People Power Party eventually declined to renominate Samak as Prime Minister; its choice instead fell upon Somchai Wongsawat, Thaksin's brother-in-law, whose soft-spokenness was in clear contrast to Samak's bombast. Any hope that Somchai's assumption of the office might have cooled things down proved unfounded, however, as the Court's verdict did far more to embolden than it did to pacify the PAD.

On 7 October 2008, violence erupted outside the National Assembly between the police and thousands of PAD activists. Its officers having come under attack by the PAD's armed guards, the police responded by shooting tear-gas canisters into the crowds, causing serious injuries among protesters. The PAD also accused the police of killing two of its supporters, although questions remain about the circumstances of their deaths.[8] Whatever the truth behind the incidents, the violence prompted key royalists to openly show their support of the PAD. Army Chief Anupong Paochinda publicly requested the government's resignations. Democrat Party leader Abhisit Vejjajiva joined Anand Panyarachun at the funeral of PAD guard Methi Chatmontri, while Queen Sirikit pledged large donations for hospitals treating injured PAD supporters and presided over the funeral of slain protester Angkana Radabpanyawut. Her statement that Angkana had died in the defence of the nation and the monarchy, moreover, affixed the palace's imprimatur on the PAD's cause – something that rank-and-file Red Shirts frequently credit for 'opening their eyes' (*ta sawang*) to the partisan role of the monarchy. According to insiders, King Bhumibol sought to avert further damage, ordering Anupong not to stage a coup (see John, 6 November 2008). Perhaps confident in the support they enjoyed from the Queen (see Marshall 2011: 174), however, PAD leaders reacted indignantly when two of the King's confidants publicly urged them to suspend the protests (see John, 23 November 2009).

The deaths also spurred the PAD to further escalate its offensive. After their leaders publicly disavowed 'non-violence', thousands of PAD supporters placed Bangkok's international airports under occupation in late November, shutting down most air traffic in and out of Thailand. The government reacted by declaring a state of emergency, but could not count on the Army to enforce it. As the stand-off continued to take its toll on Thailand's economy and expose the government's powerlessness, the stage was set for the execution of what Anand Panyarachun had

[8] Police Lieutenant-Colonel Methi Chatmontri most likely died after mistakenly setting off a bomb he was transporting in his car. As for the young woman killed in clashes with police, Angkana Radabpanyawut, investigations reached different conclusions: one, that she was hit in the torso by a tear gas canister; the other, that her injuries were more consistent with the accidental blast of an explosive device.

privately described weeks earlier as 'not [. . .] a coup in the traditional sense of the word' (see Entwistle, 18 October 2008). On 2 December, the Constitutional Court dissolved the People Power Party, *Chat Thai*, and *Matchimathippatai*, disqualifying over a hundred of their executives from office and forcing the Prime Minister's resignation. As in the Samak decision, the Constitutional Court's former President later admitted that the ruling was based not on the merits of the case, but on the Court's desire to restore 'order' in society (see Matichon, 16 March 2013).

Other initiatives to restore 'order' quickly followed. The PAD suspended its activities almost immediately after the verdict. In the days thereafter, the Democrat Party made a deal with banned Thai Rak Thai politician and infamous provincial strongman Newin Chidchob, who led his faction of thirty members of parliament to part ways with the bulk of the People Power Party's membership, now reconstituted in *Pheu Thai* – the 'Friends of Newin' would later join the new party *Bhum Jai Thai*. Newin's break with Thaksin was followed by a meeting held at the home of the Army Commander-in-Chief, attended by the leaders of small parties whose support was required to provide Democrat Party leader Abhisit Vejjajiva with a narrow majority in the House of Representatives (for accounts of the meeting, see *The Nation*, 10 and 29 December 2008; Bangkok Post, 9 June 2011). When Abhisit became the Prime Minister on 17 December 2008, the natural 'order' of things seemed to have been restored at last.

The sequence of events that ushered Abhisit Vejjajiva into the Prime Minister's office provides a compelling illustration of the network monarchy's *modus operandi*. As in the mid 1970s, privileged constituencies that have long grounded their claim to power in the imperative to safeguard 'order' and 'unity' had little hesitation in fomenting disorder and disunity when the voters selected the wrong government. Indeed, it was only through the funding of business elites, the inaction of the military, and the public backing of personalities in the Democrat Party and the palace that the PAD was able to deny the elected government's capacity to govern. Once the disorder had succeeded in highlighting, in the eyes of enough voters, the futility of insisting that the election results be allowed to stand, the Constitutional Court stepped in, in the name of restoring 'order', by selectively enforcing rules introduced under military rule for the benefit of those who had engineered the disorder.[9] In the aftermath of

[9] At the conclusion of scandal-plagued proceedings, in late 2010, the Constitutional Court spared the Democrat Party from dissolution on a technicality (see Horn, 29 November 2010). In 2009, the Election Commission had declined to bring charges against two of its new allies on similarly dubious grounds (see Ferrara 2011: 82–3).

the court decision, business elites, the military, and the palace mustered the financial resources, the coercive power, and the moral authority, respectively, required to put together a new government that featured some of the old one's most corrupt and opportunistic politicians (see Chang Noi, 22 December 2008; Ferrara 2011: 90–2). Undertaken in the name of fighting corruption and upholding 'good government', the series of machinations initiated with the 2006 coup had in fact served a different agenda: make democracy so dysfunctional as to both legitimize and materially enable the tutelage offered by the palace, the military, the bureaucracy, and the courts. There was only one problem: in the haste to remove Thaksin and his nominees, the 'invisible hand' had slipped its cloak of invisibility.

The politics of identity

The existing work on the subject is divided over the nature and significance of the 'Red Shirt' movement that rapidly gathered strength following the instalment of Abhisit Vejjajiva as Prime Minister. Some writers have emphasized economic disparities between classes and regions, pointing to the fact that Thaksin and the Red Shirts are strongest among the urban working class and in Thailand's North and Northeast, while political parties and movements aligned with the royalist 'Yellow' cause tend to be more popular with Bangkok's middle and upper-middle class as well as in the relatively affluent South. An often-cited finding in support of this argument is that the income per capita of provinces that voted for the Democrat Party in 2007 was, on average, twice as large as that of provinces that went with the People Power Party (see UNDP 2010: 78). Others have questioned this interpretation, identifying in the mobilization of patronage networks the Red Shirts' main strength (see Crispin 2012; McCargo 2012b). These works generally point to the finding that, on the whole, there appear to be only minor differences in the class status of 'Reds' and 'Yellows' at the individual level (see Ammar and Somchai 2012), particularly as both camps enjoy the sympathy and support of people from all walks of life. McCargo (2012a) also cited the delayed reaction to the 2006 military coup as evidence that the Red Shirt movement is not as spontaneous as previous movements for democracy, reflecting its primary nature as a vehicle through which Thaksin and his allies wage a largely private battle for power.

The argument made here is that the Red Shirt movement is all that and more. It is 'all that' because the elements emphasized in these writings are hardly incompatible. Indeed, sophisticated analyses of the movement's class and regional dimensions are by no means blind to the importance of conflicts at the elite level (for instance, see Pasuk and Baker 2012; Hewison 2012). As for the movement's spontaneity, work on the collective action problem from Olson (1965) on down has shown that in most circumstances common interests or grievances are not enough for rational individuals to come together and take action; the fact that it might take time, resources, or 'patronage networks' to mobilize a mass movement, therefore, says little about the underlying concerns. The Red Shirt movement, however, is all that 'and more' because the apparent contradiction in the empirical evidence of the importance of socio-economic factors can be explained by supplementing the focus on elite conflict and class/regional inequalities with an emphasis on collective identities that are as much the reflection of 'objective' demographic differences as they are a result of political mobilization. As Przeworski and Sprague (1986: 7–8) explained, demographic traits do not spontaneously (or inevitably) lead to particular attitudes; to the extent that such traits correlate with certain preferences or behaviours, they do so only as a result of 'a process of creating images in society, of forging collective identities, of mobilizing commitments' among citizens who share a varying set of characteristics, led by agents vying with one another 'to impose a particular form of organization upon the life of society'.

Supporters and opponents of Thaksin Shinawatra may disagree on whether his economic policies were designed to unshackle the population's entrepreneurial spirit or ensnare it in a relationship of dependency with the state, but they generally agree that Thaksin's enduring popularity is the result of material benefits his government delivered to various constituencies. True enough, Thai Rak Thai's administration presided over the recovery of Thailand's economy well past where it had been before the Asian Crisis. A great many people, moreover, personally benefited from the 'populist' policies introduced by the administration (for instance, see Selway 2011: 188–93). Thaksin's success, however, would have been easy to replicate, had it been rooted in a purely monetary calculus. Indeed, that is just what some of his enemies believed (for Sondhi Limthongkul's rendition, see Shah, 22 November 2006). Even as they railed against the immorality of Thaksin's 'populism', therefore, the administrations of Surayud Chulanont and Abhisit Vejjajiva kept many of his policies in place – in some cases rebranding them as a way to promote the 'sufficiency economy' (see Walker, 15 February 2007) or as a form of *noblesse oblige* (see Sopranzetti, 7 February 2011) – and unveiled their own sets of 'populist' measures (for instance, see Achara, 16 January 2011). Yet they failed to win over most of Thaksin's supporters – for whom, as it turns out, the packaging in which the policies came was at least as important as the 'gifts' they bore.

The reality is that Thaksin's popularity with provincial voters has never been exclusively, or perhaps even primarily, about material benefits. Rather, Thaksin remains popular with these voters for reasons of a more affective or emotional nature. Perhaps, above all, Thaksin was the beneficiary of a psychological mechanism that is well known to professional election consultants: the idea that the loyalty of others is more effectively secured by getting them to do something for you, as opposed to doing something for them (the 'Ben Franklin Effect'). Thaksin was the first Prime Minister whom much of the provincial electorate and the urban working class had expressly chosen. That these voters stuck with Thaksin through thick and thin, and in some cases saw their commitment grow as the result of the adversities he endured, is rooted in the simple fact that he was 'their' Prime Minister.

Thaksin's rhetoric and policies reinforced the identification between himself and his supporters. It may well be the case that the primary beneficiaries of Thaksinomics had been large corporations, particularly those in his own network (see McCargo and Ukrist 2005: 218). In fact, as one observer recognized early on, Thaksin's 'pluto-populism' was founded on the premise that 'the plutocrats make big money, and the people don't make big trouble' (see Chang Noi, 18 February 2002). Under his tenure, moreover, no serious attempt was made to enshrine into law any notion of 'social rights', establish a genuine welfare state, or tackle vast disparities in income and access to services perpetuated by a 'pro-rich' tax system heavily reliant on regressive forms of indirect taxation (see Pasuk and Pornthep 2012: 21–2) and biased patterns of government expenditures that see the city of Bangkok gobble up almost three-quarters of the national budget, despite accounting for only a quarter of its gross domestic product and one-sixth of the population (see World Bank 2012: 7). Thaksin's economic vision, however, did not lecture voters to stay in their place, but encouraged them to imagine a different future for themselves and their families. Indeed, while his suggestion that everyone could be wealthy may have been facile or disingenuous, the appeal to 'unfulfilled capitalist desires' (see Sopranzetti 2012) was powerful in a context where the ambitions ordinary people came to harbour as the result of modernization were frustrated by the persistence of extreme inequalities and delegitimized by a discourse that urged them never to aspire beyond 'sufficiency'. By explicitly grounding his authority in the mandate he received from ordinary people, moreover, Thaksin's rhetoric recast the majority of the electorate as Thailand's true sovereign power, in fulfilment of a promise that most of the country's constitutions had failed to keep. Whether such authority was exercised for good or ill, it is hard to fault Thaksin's supporters for feeling that they mattered.

In the months that followed Thaksin's ouster, a Thai academic reasoned that the military coup of 19 September 2006 had 'turned citizens into subjects' (*tham hai phonla mueang klai pen phrai*) – stripping away, with Thaksin's office, the people's right to govern themselves (see Pitch 2007: 63–6). Aside from anticipating the historical imagery the Red Shirt movement would later embrace, Pitch identified the reason why voters had cause to interpret the actions taken against Thaksin as having denied *them* full membership in Thailand's national community. The arguments made by royalists in support of the coup only deepened the undercurrent of anger and frustration that Thaksin and his allies would successfully harness in their fight against the royalist establishment. The invalidation of such clear electoral choices, and its justification in terms as offensive, elitist, and occasionally dehumanizing, that is, rendered a sizeable number of Thaksin's supporters receptive to arguments denouncing the fundamental injustice of Thailand's traditional hierarchies of status and power. The illiberal measures designed to obliterate Thaksin's influence, too, not only exposed a less benevolent side to the royalist world view but also revealed the hypocrisy of much of the criticism directed at Thaksin's own administration.

There is little doubt that the establishment of the United Front for Democracy against Dictatorship (UDD) constituted an attempt by Thaksin and his network to 'socialize' their private struggle for power by involving constituencies that could tip the balance in their favour. Founded in the months that followed the 2006 coup, the UDD initially struggled to get off the ground. Crowds of Thaksin supporters numbering a few thousand people, at that point still wearing yellow to show allegiance to the monarchy, began to stage anti-junta demonstrations days after the dissolution of Thai Rak Thai, culminating several weeks later in violent clashes outside the residence of General Prem Tinsulanond. At the end of June 2007, however, royalists were confident that the UDD was already 'a spent force' (see Boyce, 25 June 2007). By then, it seems, even Thaksin's most fervent supporters pinned their hopes on the upcoming elections, far more so than the floundering street movement mobilized through the networks of big men like Newin Chidchob.

The UDD only began to catch on once it became clear, in mid 2008, that the same forces that had backed the coup in 2006 were determined not to let the results of the 2007 elections stand. Now wearing red for contrast, UDD activists staged counterdemonstrations to the PAD beginning in June 2008, at times engaging in violent confrontations with their Yellow Shirt counterparts. The real turning point, however, was Abhisit Vejjajiva's rise to Prime Minister, which catalysed the movement's growth well beyond the networks of patronage upon which it had initially relied.

As the movement expanded, UDD leaders also demonstrated a growing capacity to communicate a message – broadcast throughout the country by the Red Shirts' satellite television channel and dozens of community radio stations – that appealed to their supporters' desire to be considered full members of the national community, irrespective of wealth, status, or karmic stock, and to be treated equally under the law without 'double standards'. By far most memorable was UDD core leader Nattawut Saikuea's invocation of a rather unambiguous metaphor during a speech delivered in late 2008, in which he addressed 'the sky' to inform its celestial dwellers that the men and women whose feet are firmly planted in 'the earth' are also 'Thai people'. What is more, by training its sights on the so-called *ammat* – the king's mandarins, courtiers, and praetorian guards – for the first time in decades the UDD complemented calls for 'democracy' with the demand that no unelected institution, no matter how close to the palace, should have the authority to substitute its own judgement for that of the electorate.

Given the issues at stake, it is not altogether surprising that the fight came to be presented through imagery harking back to the days of the absolute monarchy. Dismissed by pundits as anachronistic, the adoption of the word *phrai* as an identifier was designed to foster among a diverse mix of Red Shirt supporters and sympathizers a collective identity as *de facto* second-class citizens, called upon by history to complete a century-old struggle for self-determination and equal rights. Its invocation was not unprecedented, because similar imagery recurs in radical texts written on the subject of structural inequalities well after 1905 – even the 'First Announcement of the People's Party', drafted over a quarter-century after the status of *phrai* was abolished, had promised 'equal rights and freedom from being the *phrai*, servants, and slaves of the royal class'. The Red Shirts' appropriation of the term stood for the idea that, while the abolishment of the status of *phrai* in 1905 may have formally recognized the legal personhood of the majority of the population, in practice ordinary men and women remained far from being acknowledged as equal and collectively sovereign citizens, because the informal hierarchies of citizenship status at the heart of the ideology of 'Thainess' in practice still rendered ordinary people less than fully 'Thai'. One need not be poor and downtrodden to wear a shirt emblazoned with the word *phrai*, because the peasantry and the working class are not the only groups the official ideology of Thainess relegates to a subordinate political role. Northeasterners and other ethnic minorities have long been considered less than fully 'Thai', while individuals whose convictions challenge the country's royal nationalism are deemed 'un-Thai' regardless of social status or regional origin. The power of the word *phrai* was its inclusiveness, because it suggested that anyone denied an equal political role, irrespective of class or regional background, was still treated as less than a full citizen or person.

The Red Shirts' embracement of their identity as *phrai* also underscored the radical nature of the challenge the movement presented to the country's royalist order. The usage of the word *phrai* to mean 'not yet acknowledged as fully Thai', in fact, was a rather thinly disguised attack on an official ideology that combines pre-nationalist cosmological hierarchies with modern nationalist discourse. The juxtaposition of *phrai* with 'Thai', in particular, evoked the old, pre-nationalist usage of the word *tai/thai* as the designation for an elite, as opposed to the entire population. Recall, for instance, that the Ramkhamhaeng Inscription (whether it is a thirteenth-century document or nineteenth-century forgery matters little in this context) described the general population not only as the King's subjects or serfs *(phrai fa),* but also as 'servants/slaves of the *tai*' (*kha tai*) – as in *phrai fa kha tai*. Indeed, Nidhi (2010: 28–33) suggests that the word *phrai* is most usefully contrasted with *phu di* ('gentry': literally, 'good person') – a designation that can now apply to anyone, regardless of birth, whose behaviour, speech, and morality conform with Bangkok's elite culture. In this sense, the demand that self-identified *phrai* be recognized as fully 'Thai' challenged the existence, or the legitimacy, of a single model of 'Thainess' (and hence full personhood or citizenship) based on a Bangkok-centric, elite-defined ideal.

In a social and political order founded on the belief that one's access to power reveals 'merit' and 'goodness', and that 'merit' and 'goodness' in turn legitimize one's access to power, those without power are not supposed to take pride in their own powerlessness, which reveals absence of merit, nor do they have any business demanding more power. Not unlike the word 'villain' ('villein') in English, the word *phrai* has remained in the Thai lexicon not just as the designation for an archaic legal status, but also as a synonym for 'ignoble', 'villainous', or 'vulgar'. Indeed, some royalists were quick to call attention to the Royal Institute Dictionary's entry for the word *phrai* and highlight 'bad/evil person' (*khon leo*) as one of its possible meanings, perhaps without fully grasping that this was precisely the point. The embracement of their identity as *phrai*, that is, not only affirmed the Red Shirts' new-found sense of pride in their status as commoners, but also their rejection of a social order founded upon 'natural' hierarchies of merit and goodness, as well as their dismissal of an official historical narrative that has long cast those who challenge their 'natural' superiors in the role of villains and enemies of the nation. Whereas the northeastern rebels who fought the Siamese state in the early 1900s had fundamentally upheld beliefs in hierarchies of karmic merit, coalescing behind self-styled 'holy men', a century later the Red Shirts chose to flaunt their own unholiness, implicitly repudiating the entire world view at the heart of Thailand's royal nationalism.

The emphasis placed in this account on the construction and mobilization of collective identities resolves the apparent contradiction between empirical findings showing that support for Thaksin-backed parties (and the Red Shirt movement itself) is strongest in some of the country's less affluent provinces but does not appear to be strongly related to class at the individual level. Most of Thailand's least affluent provinces are located in the northern and northeastern regions (see Figure 7.1), where Thaksin's 'populist' policies have been shown to have measurably improved standards of living – partly as a function of their relative underdevelopment and partly as a result of specific targeting for electoral purposes (see Carsten and Pairat, 16 June 2013). As Figure 7.1 shows, however, while the northern and northeastern regions have witnessed, on the whole, greater economic growth than the Central Region since 2000, other parts of the country (like provinces east and southeast of Bangkok, as well as a number of southern provinces) have done even better. A comparison between Figures 7.1 and 7.2, moreover, reveals that within the North and Northeast, the support of Thaksin-backed political parties is geographically clustered in provinces that vary considerably in economic performance. Thaksin-backed parties have done especially well in most of the Upper North, an area that includes some of the region's wealthier provinces (Chiang Mai, Lampang, and Lamphun) as well as some of the provinces that have experienced relatively weak growth (Lampang, Lamphun, Phrae, Nan) compared with the Lower North. In the Northeast, likewise, Thaksin-backed parties tend to be weaker in the region's lower portion along the Cambodian border – provinces that have benefited just as much from economic growth since 2000.

Within the northern and northeastern regions, Thaksin-backed political parties (and, at least anecdotally, the Red Shirt movement itself) are most strongly supported, not necessarily in the poorest provinces, or the provinces that have benefited the most from 'populist' policies, but in those provinces whose populations have been considered 'less than perfectly Thai' on account of their geographic and ethno-linguistic distance from Bangkok (see Streckfuss 2012: 313). With the Malay South, these are the regions that were integrated into the country's national territory most recently and with the greatest difficulty – the former northern principalities and the area on the Khorat Plateau due north and northeast of Nakhon Ratchasima. Curiously, moreover, what the red strongholds in the Upper North share with the red strongholds in the Northeast is that they are inhabited for the most part by ethnic Tai

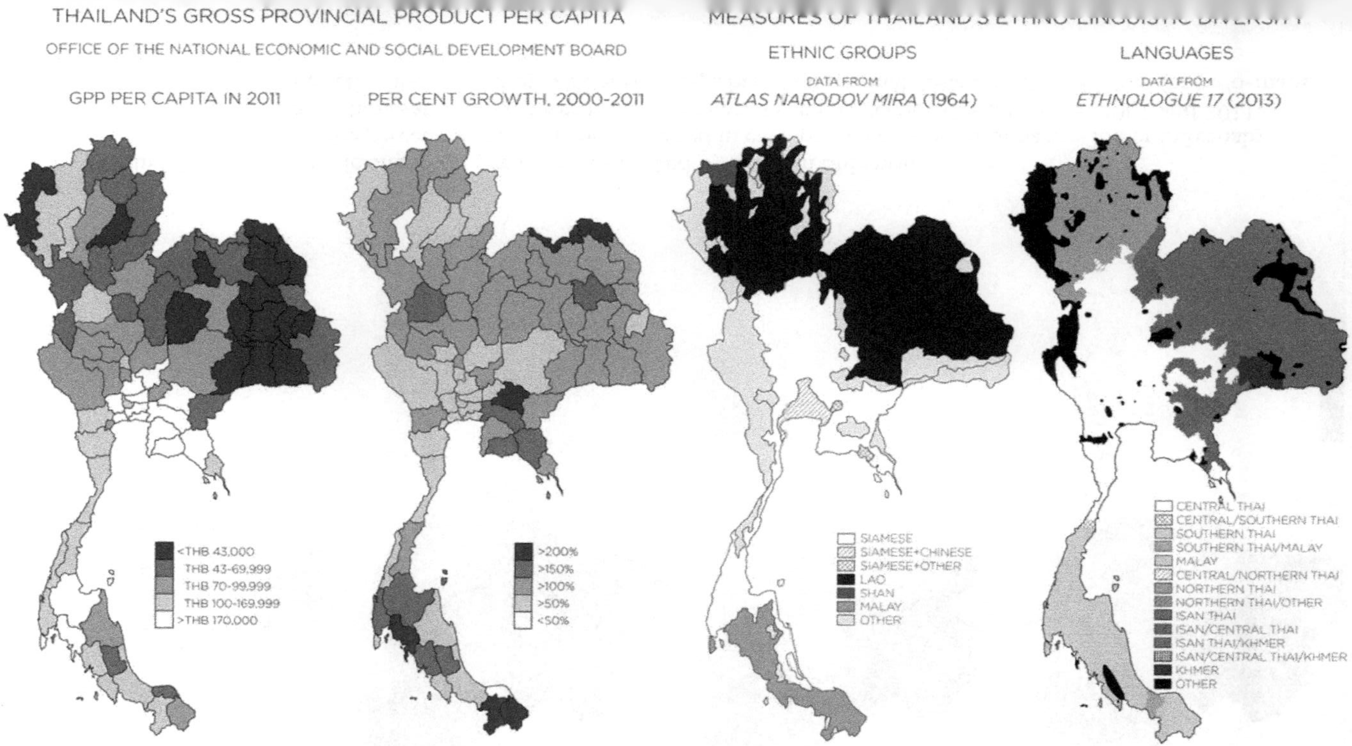

Figure 7.1 Provincial income per capita and ethno-linguistic diversity
Note: GDP per capita figures are available at www.nesdb.go.th/Default.aspx?tabid=96. The third map from the left was generated using shapefiles contained in the 'Geo-Referencing for Ethnic Groups' (GREG) dataset (see Weidmann, Rød, and Cederman 2010), which relies on data/maps from the Soviet-era *Atlas Narodov Mira* (Bruk, Solomon, and Apenchenko 1964). The fourth map from the left was generated using data on linguistic groups contained in Lewis, Simons, and Fennig (2013), which cites as its source Mahidol University's Institute of Languages and Culture for Rural Development.

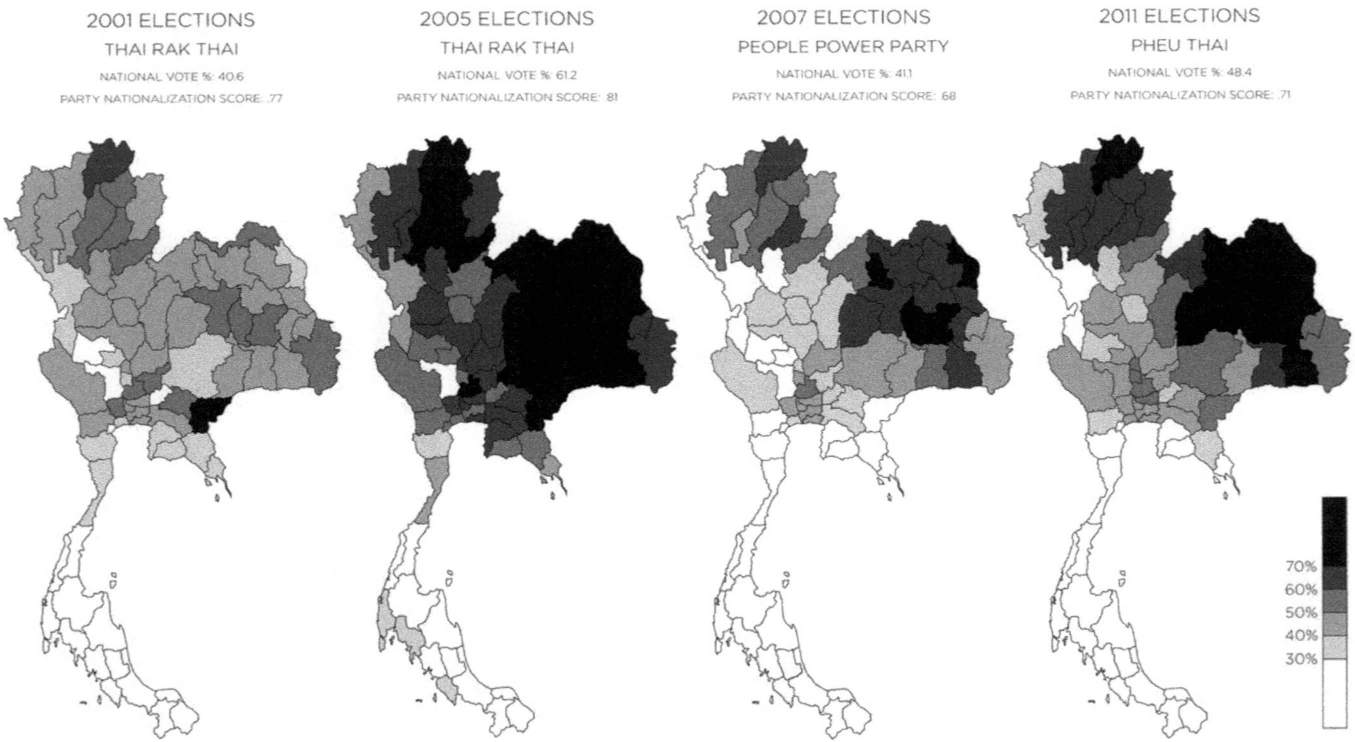

Figure 7.2 Election performance of parties led or backed by Thaksin Shinawatra
Note: Figures refer to the percentage of valid votes received in each province by political parties led or informally supported by Thaksin Shinawatra in the party-list component of general elections held between 2001 and 2011, excluding the 2006 election invalidated by the courts. Maps based on original design by Daniel Dalet (http://d-maps.com).

peoples whom the authorities had jointly referred to as 'Lao' until the early twentieth century (*khon mueang* or Yuan/Northern Thai and *khon isan* or Lao/Northeastern Thai). It is notable, in particular, that Thaksin-backed political parties have done rather poorly in the relatively backward northwestern province of Mae Hong Son, where non-Tai tribal groups are a majority, while their performance has been, by the standards of the region, most uneven (across time and space) in lower northeastern provinces with a Central Thai presence (Nakhon Ratchasima, Buriram) and/or a mixture of Lao and Northern Khmer populations (Buriram, Surin, and Sisaket) (see Figure 7.2).

The strong support that Thaksin-backed parties have garnered in the Upper North and much of the Northeast, from voters of all socio-economic backgrounds,[10] suggests that these provinces are most solidly red because Thaksin Shinawatra and his allies have successfully harnessed pre-existing ethno-regional identities. At the individual level, the relative underdevelopment of these regions matters primarily because it has come to form part of local identities, serving as an emblem of their less than full inclusion in Thailand's national community. What these voters got from the shift that Thaksin's policies marked in 'the nation's most important power bargains' towards 'the rural electorates of northern and northeastern Thailand' (see Walker 2012: 222–3), was not just more development, or a more 'secure relationship with the state', but also an affirmation of their ethno-regional pride and yearning for recognition. The extensive usage that the Red Shirts have made of regional dialects in their mobilization efforts, challenging Central Thai's position as the language of politics and administration (see Nidhi 2010: 150–5), served a similar purpose. For while it has long been common for members of ethno-regional groups afflicted by what some have called 'Thai deficiency syndrome' – *khon isan* among them – to tone down their distinctiveness to avoid prejudice and scorn (see Kasian 2009; McCargo 2012a: 88), the Red Shirts encouraged their supporters to assert themselves as equal by proudly expressing aspects of their identities once de-emphasized out of fear that others might judge them inferior.

It is perhaps no wonder, in this sense, that the support of Thaksin-backed political parties has grown more concentrated in these provinces over time (see Figure 7.2), as Thailand's political crisis has intensified, given the extent to which royalists have relied on offensive portrayals of northern and (especially) northeastern voters to blame Thaksin's electoral success on his supporters' purported moral inferiority and

[10] Of course, there are also plenty of voters in these regions, of all class backgrounds, who are indifferent or hostile to Thaksin and the Red Shirts (see Nishizaki 2014).

'un-Thainess'. Indeed, Thaksin's enemies have arguably done even more than his supporters to favour the convergence of northern and northeastern regional identities into a 'red' collective identity, through their frequent invocation (or invention)[11] of debasing cultural stereotypes. It is also not surprising that those most inclined to identify as 'red' and actively participate in the movement's activities are *not* the regions' poorest inhabitants (see Naruemon and McCargo 2012), but men and women who have been lifted by economic development into the ranks of a new provincial middle class. Aside from likely being more aware of the scope and significance of regional disparities, these are precisely the kinds of people the literature expects would press demands for greater self-expression and individual equality (see Inglehart and Welzel 2005).

A similar reasoning helps explain the attitudes common in the country's non-Muslim South among voters regardless of socio-economic status. Much like Thaksin's base in the North and the Northeast, the South's loyalty to the Democrats – and its alignment on the royalist side of the country's political divide – is less a reflection of its residents' affluence, sophistication, or longstanding ideological proclivities,[12] than it is the result of the party's effectiveness in constructing, affirming, and mobilizing regional identities, kept politically relevant by playing up the distinctiveness of southern political culture and the threat that 'outsiders' pose to southern 'moral ideals' (see Askew 2008: 12). In fact, while Thaksin and his allies have been successfully cast by Democrats in the South as a 'demonic' other (see Askew 2008: 11), in the final analysis southerners are not so different from Thaksin's own supporters: for reasons of both interest and affect, the Democrat Party is 'their' party.

Only in Bangkok and its surroundings does there appear to be a clear class divide, something that may be attributed to two factors. The first is that Bangkok is the place where inequalities are most extreme and where, therefore, the 'unfulfilled capitalist desires' of the urban working class are also most 'burning', to use Sopranzetti's (2012) formulation. The second is that class disparities in Bangkok tend to overlap with differences in ethno-regional background, because individuals whose families migrated

[11] Despite having long been viewed 'rather more positively' (Keyes 1987: 127), northerners were not spared the denigration of their regional identities. In 2011, for instance, famous Ponzi schemer and anti-Thaksin activist Akeyuth Anchanbutr, now deceased, attacked Prime Minister Yingluck Shinawatra in these terms: 'But the fact is, uneducated or lazy and stupid northern women will happily do work that normal women wouldn't do, like prostitution. So should a northern woman, who is unintelligent and stupid, but happens to have the position, know what job is suitable for her?' (see Prachatai, 6 November 2011).

[12] Up to the 1970s, when the Democrats first became dominant in the region, the South had actually been known for its progressivism (see Morell and Chai-anan 1981: 296).

from the country's most economically depressed regions, especially the Northeast, make up the lion's share of the urban working class. These people are not only more likely to be economically deprived, but also to be most directly affected by overt racism in personal interactions, as well as the negative portrayals that elite discourse and popular culture generally reserve for northeasterners, based on their appearance, speech, and purported ignorance or stupidity. As for the city's middle and upper-middle class, similarly, opposition to Thaksin and his 'nominees' has far less to do with this constituency's purported enlightenment and concern for good government than the success with which royalists have deployed the so-called 'clean politics discourse' (see Thongchai 2008a: 24–7) to reinforce the sense of moral superiority of middle-class voters, provide a narrative that gives a principled spin to positions grounded in interest, resentment, or fear, and effectively transform hatred of Thaksin into a marker of middle-class identity, backed by a great deal of social pressure.

As Montesano (2010: 280) has written, 'insecurities' over status have 'haunted the rank and file of the yellow camp' to a far greater extent than the 'red' camp. Indeed, there is both anecdotal and statistical evidence suggesting that while 'Yellow Shirt' sympathizers generally enjoy somewhat higher levels of income and job/life security – largely because, compared with the lower-middle-class citizens who make up the bulk of the Red Shirt movement, a greater proportion are employed in the formal sector of the economy – they are more likely to *feel* economically deprived and insecure (see Aphichat 2010). Given the emphasis that Thaksin's populism placed on the informal sector, these citizens are said to have feared being forced to bear the cost of the advancement of others, even as their own economic situation stagnates or deteriorates (see Nidhi 2010: 132–7). Conversely, while Red Shirt sympathizers tend to be more optimistic about their prospects of social mobility, they were given ample reason to suspect that Thaksin's removal reflected the royalist establishment's determination to hold them back (see Sopranzetti 2012).

Once again, these attitudes are as much a reflection of an objective reality as they are by-products of the manner the conflict was framed. In the months and years that followed the 2005 election, in which Thai Rak Thai had dominated every region except the South, the leaders of what would become the PAD and their allies among politicians, military generals, royalist academics, and parts of the national press were perhaps most effective in arousing the insecurities and fears of urban middle-class voters, warning that Thaksin's populism would come at the expense of *their* economic well-being and social status (see Pasuk and Baker 2009:

253, 264–6). More generally, royalists have proven especially skilled at the politics of resentment – an emotion Elster (2007: 149) fittingly describes as 'caused by the reversal of a prestige hierarchy, when a formerly inferior group or individual emerges as dominant' – tapping into urban middle-class anxieties over the former peasantry's ongoing transformation into a large and politically assertive 'new middle class'. As Nidhi (2010: 60–5) has noted, urban dwellers have tended to regard much of the provincial population as 'lovely' (*na rak*) and worthy of compassion (*songsan*), but not as entitled to any rights. The former peasantry's economic and political rise, in turn, has not only fuelled, among segments of the urban middle class, insecurities over the prospective loss of their superior status, but also a more generalized, visceral feeling – magnified by the impending royal succession – that social change and 'populist' policies are robbing them of 'their' country.

Indeed, the success with which royalists have played up the notion that the provincial electorate's ignorance, credulousness, and corruption requires the placement of the majority of the electorate – routinely branded 'water buffaloes' (*khwai*) – under the tutelage of 'good people' is likely owed to the therapeutic and motivating functions served by these cultural stereotypes, especially when combined with the invocation of the monarchy as the symbol of social hierarchies threatened by the forces of modernization, globalization, and electoralism (see Nidhi 2010: 137–43). For while this image of the provincial electorate may well be 'dangerous nonsense' (see Pasuk and Baker, 6 December 2013), its reaffirmation of the urban middle classes' wounded sense of moral superiority also arms them with a righteous reason, in the words of American conservative William F. Buckley, to stand 'athwart history, yelling Stop'.

This reasoning might also shed some light on why much of the Central Region and Lower North remains a patchwork of political machines dominated by the cliques of local big men. The fact that the Central Plains, roughly comprised between the northern town of Sukhothai and the capital Bangkok, have long served as the core of the kingdom and the model of Thai language and culture precludes appeals based on either the affirmation of vilified regional identities or the endangerment of regional cultural values. The underdevelopment once found in provinces like Suphanburi, to be sure, was an important factor in the rise of politicians like Banharn Silpa-archa, who affirmed provincial identities by promoting local development and giving local electorates influence over policy making in Bangkok (see Nishizaki 2011). Still, underdevelopment does not define regional identities to the extent it does elsewhere, nor does it fuel resentments against the capital city shared quite as widely. The result is that voting decisions and partisan orientations lack the homogeneity, across provinces, found in other regions. At the same time, the fact that the Central Plains lack the opulence that characterizes parts of Bangkok – and the extreme inequalities that go along with it – mitigates the intensity of class divisions, facilitating the assemblage of local coalitions that include citizens of all classes.

Crashing the gates

The Red Shirts staged their first series of large demonstrations in April 2009. On 8 April, tens of thousands joined a rally outside the Government House, where the Red Shirts had been protesting for 2 weeks to demand Abhisit's resignation and, they claimed, end the rule of the *ammat*. It was then that Thaksin Shinawatra addressed the crowds on video and called for a 'people's revolution'. Three days later, hundreds of protesters led by former pop star Arisman Pongruangrong broke into a hotel in Pattaya where an ASEAN summit was taking place, forcing its cancellation. The Red Shirts only dispersed after the government declared a state of emergency and sent in the Army to crack down on protesters still assembled in Bangkok. Surrounded by the military, UDD leaders called off their rally at the Government House on 14 April 2009.

In the months that followed the failure of the 2009 uprising, the UDD redoubled its efforts to recruit followers, educate sympathizers, and build an organization in the provinces. Less than a year later, its leaders unveiled an ambitious plan to bring a million people to Bangkok and force Abhisit to resign. As thousands of Red Shirts converged on the capital on 12 March 2010, the situation was rendered particularly explosive by the fact that the UDD and the government had similar game plans. The UDD had strength in numbers, but numbers alone would not suffice to bring down the government. Rather, the Red Shirts had to launch a series of provocative and disruptive actions that would expose Abhisit's inability to control the situation; the country's increased ingovernability would then force the Prime Minister to resign, as the Red Shirts demanded, or invite a backlash by cracking down violently. The government's strategy was similar. The administration used legislation such as the Internal Security Act as well as the deployment of thousands of security forces in an attempt to depress the number of demonstrators, while the government-controlled media and the royalist press presented the Red Shirts as 'rural hordes' hell-bent on laying waste to the capital city. Their numbers dwindling and image discredited, the Red Shirts would then be forced to go home or attempt to stay relevant by resorting to greater confrontation and violence, which would in turn facilitate their repression. Both strategies were dangerous insofar as their success was predicated upon fomenting disorder and blaming it on the other side. As ever, the problem was that conditions of disorder are inherently unpredictable, especially in circumstances where both sides do not fully control their own forces.

While neither side got exactly what it wanted, both got enough of what they wanted to cause a great deal of blood to be spilled, particularly among protesters. Over the first month of the protests, in which demonstrations reached peaks of at least 150,000 people, the Red Shirts executed their game plan effectively. From the rally sites set up at symbolically charged locations in downtown Bangkok – at the Phan Fa Bridge and later at the Ratchaprasong Intersection – the Red Shirts carried out a number of provocations in defiance of the Internal Security Act, pursuant to which various locations in the city had been declared off-limits to their marches. Brahmanical cursing rituals were staged at the Prime Minister's residence, at the Government House, and at Democrat Party headquarters, where the Red Shirts spilled gallons of their own blood. Perhaps most vexing for the government, the Red Shirts had been peaceful and good-natured, notwithstanding the property damage caused by a series of night-time bombings whose perpetrators went largely unidentified. Security forces were frequently seen fraternizing with the demonstrators, whose forays around the city regularly attracted the sympathy of throngs of local residents.

Even the first military crackdown staged on 10 April 2010, 2 days after the government claimed emergency powers, appeared to have emboldened the movement. Thousands of Red Shirts confronted the Army at various locations surrounding the Phan Fa Bridge, causing the soldiers' advance to stall. The stalemate was broken after nightfall, when a group of unidentified men dressed in black – likely active-duty military officers, possibly animated by support for the Red Shirts, intra-Army rivalries, or a combination of both – attacked the troops at two locations, assassinating their commander, Colonel Romklao Thuwatham, and four other soldiers before vanishing back into the shadows. As they staged a panicky retreat, troops opened fire on the crowds of protesters. One foreign journalist and ten demonstrators were killed in the melee; ten other protesters killed by live ammunition on 10 April were shot *before* the troops had come under attack, or in incidents not directly related to the confusion caused by the actions of 'men in black' (for an accounting of the circumstances of each death, see PIC 2012: 92–117). While the Red Shirts had taken by far the most casualties, the success with which they had held off the Army was an embarrassment for the administration. A few days later, the Red Shirts abandoned their encampment at the Phan Fa Bridge and moved all protest activities to Ratchaprasong.

The tide turned at the end of April, as the government seized control of the narrative and gradually won the backing of the fight's principal audience, the urban middle class, for a more incisive crackdown. Crowds of 'multicolour' protesters mobilized by royalist groups were permitted to attack the Red Shirts at the edge of their sprawling encampment. After a few evenings of taunting and sporadic fighting, five grenades went off at the Sala Daeng intersection, killing one 'multicolour' protester. A few days later, a dramatic evacuation of patients at the nearby Chulalongkorn Hospital was staged after Red Shirt activists had breached the premises in search of 'snipers' they claimed to have spotted on the rooftop. These public relations victories for the government were accompanied by an increasingly successful media campaign that accused the Red Shirts of sheltering 'terrorists' (*phu ko kan rai*). The government also touted the confession of a man (recently acquitted of all charges; see Khao Sod, 9 August 2013) apprehended for shooting a rocket-propelled grenade at the Defence Ministry, who now claimed his real target had been the revered Temple of the Emerald Buddha (*Wat Phra Kaeo*). Meanwhile, its spokesperson announced the discovery of a plot orchestrated by Thaksin to topple the monarchy. Like others before them, the Red Shirts had been made into enemies of the nation, Buddhism, and the King.

At the beginning of May, Abhisit offered the Red Shirts a compromise that included a promise to dissolve the House and call early elections by the end of 2010. Widely regarded as a reasonable solution to the stand-off, the proposal split the leadership of the movement. As moderate leaders abandoned the site of the protests, the government retracted its proposal. Soon thereafter, a sniper assassinated Major-General Khattiya Sawasdipol ('Seh Daeng'), who had been responsible for organizing security at the Red Shirt barricades. Between 14 and 19 May, the Army advanced on all sides of Ratchaprasong, firing tens of thousands of live rounds into scattered groups of demonstrators who defended themselves with slingshots, firecrackers, and heaps of burning tyres, while perhaps a few dozen men wielding handguns and grenade launchers fought unsuccessful running battles with the armed forces. Some fifty-five civilians were killed in and around 'live fire zones', where soldiers operated under exceedingly broad rules of engagement (see PIC 2012: 1340–5) permitting the use of live ammunition against any protester, armed or unarmed, whose actions could be deemed threatening to soldiers, civilians, or property. An additional six died in an attack on the Buddhist temple at Wat Pathum Wanaram, where hundreds of Red Shirts had sought refuge after UDD leaders surrendered to police in the early afternoon of 19 May. As the Red Shirts dispersed, fires were started in some thirty buildings in downtown Bangkok.

In the end, neither side had scored a clear victory. Abhisit had swept the Red Shirts from the streets of Bangkok without alienating the usual swing constituency, the city's middle class, whose potential support for the Red Shirts had been compromised by the intransigence of their leaders, their portrayal as terrorists and enemies of the monarchy, and the property damage inflicted in the wake of their surrender. The movement's capacity to mobilize was also severely curtailed by the arrest of hundreds of people and the filing of terrorism charges against UDD leaders, most of whom were now in prison, in hiding, or silenced by the conditions attached to their bail. Even so, reports of the Red Shirt movement's demise were greatly exaggerated. If anything, the death of dozens of people, and the manner in which the killings were justified, served to harden the Red Shirts' base of support – their collective identity as *de facto* second-class citizens reinforced by the knowledge that people like them could be massacred by the state with impunity, amid the indifference of the palace and the urban middle class.

Demonstrations held months after the killings featured spontaneous outbursts that showed just how badly the violence had backfired, among the Red Shirts' supporters, on the institution of the monarchy, in whose name the crackdown had been executed. In a commemoration staged on 19 September 2010 at the Ratchaprasong intersection, thousands of Red Shirts erupted in chants of *hia sang kha* – the expression, perhaps best rendered in English as 'the fucking low life (*hia*: literally, "monitor lizard") ordered the killings', was widely believed to have referred to King Bhumibol. When the demonstrators left, the barriers outside the partially destroyed Central World shopping complex were found plastered with anti-monarchy graffiti (see Ünaldi 2014). While the UDD took measures to contain open expressions of anti-monarchy sentiment, including the appointment of seasoned activist Thida Thawornset as its leader, the anger was thinly disguised in a speech that Jatuporn Prompan delivered on the first-year anniversary of the 10 April crackdown (see Buchanan 2013). To rapturous applause, Jatuporn shredded the idea of Thai exceptionalism and the familial imagery at the heart of the state's royal nationalism, observing that Thailand must be the only country in the world where the family's children are routinely murdered 'for' or 'on behalf of' (*phuea*) the nation's 'father' and 'mother'.

What electoral advantage Abhisit and the Democrat Party might have drawn from the dispersals was squandered by the government's hesitation to lift the repressive measures imposed pursuant to the emergency decree, which had featured the closing of much of the Red Shirt media (see HRW 2011: 136–46) and an unprecedented wave of arrests on charges of *lèse majesté*. When elections were eventually held on 3 July 2011 – under rules, similar to those in place before the coup, that restored single-member districts and the single national constituency for party lists (without the 5 per cent threshold) – Abhisit and his backers were administered a clear rebuke. Aided by the selection of Yingluck Shinawatra as its leader, Pheu Thai won a majority of 265 out of 500 House seats – its national party list outdistancing the Democrats by over 4 million votes. Pheu Thai won overwhelming victories in the Upper North and the Northeast, where candidates running under the banner of *Bhum Jai Thai* were punished for their collaboration with Abhisit by mostly being trounced outside Newin Chidchob's stronghold in Buriram. Despite the inclusion of much of the UDD leadership on its party list, Pheu Thai also made significant inroads in Bangkok, where it carried almost a third of all constituencies and came within 70,000 votes of the Democrat Party on the proportional side of the ballot. In the city, the Democrats actually outperformed their polling numbers, possibly as a result of a last-ditch appeal for voters to reject those who had 'burned down the city'. Still, as Yingluck Shinawatra took the office of Prime Minister, with the backing of over 60 per cent of the House, it was clear that the holy war on Thaksin had accomplished very little.

Running on empty

Thailand's royalists have long understood the gravity of the threat posed by Thaksin Shinawatra and his supporters. Months before the Red Shirts streamed into Bangkok in March 2010, Privy Council President Prem Tinsulanond was reported to have urged top military officers to read an article that placed Thailand in the early stages of a civil war (see *Bangkok Post*, 29 December 2009). By and large misunderstood was the nature of the threat. While ridiculing the idea that a billionaire former Prime Minister would lead a 'people's revolution', royalists publicly emphasized underdevelopment as the root cause of Thaksin's success in mobilizing support in the provinces – whether because of genuine grievances resulting from 'social injustice' (see *MFA*, 4 May 2010) or because the rural population's dependency on the state makes for solid 'foundations for populist democracy' (Anek 2006: 198; see also Pasuk and Baker 2008: 78–9). Public rationalizations of this kind were no doubt reassuring, in that they contemplated a paternalistic solution to the crisis centred on improving the lot, morality, and intellect of those who challenged the status quo, as opposed to granting any of their demands for structural change. The drawback was that they missed the point entirely. For if the issue of inequality is at the heart of Thailand's ongoing political conflict, the rise of the Red Shirt movement is rooted less in the economic deprivation of provincial voters – let alone their backwardness – than it is in their modernization.

The conflict between hierarchical and egalitarian conceptions of the Thai nation explosively resurfaced in the wake of the military coup of 19 September 2006 for reasons of both a structural and contingent nature. Indeed, while the Red Shirts came together as a result of contingencies related to Thaksin's rise and fall, the emergence of the largest popular movement in Thailand ever to press demands for popular sovereignty, equal citizenship, and 'real' democracy represents the culmination of a historical process that Vandergeest (1990) traced back to the abolition of the status of *phrai* in 1905, the introduction of a universal civil law in 1925, and the collapse of the absolute monarchy in 1932 – developments credited for setting in motion the secular decline in the legitimacy of pre-nationalist social hierarchies based on 'levels of being'. The popularity of King Bhumibol, the royal nationalism articulated during his reign, and the strategic adaptations pursued by royalists in response to pressures from below have served to slow down, arrest, or even reverse the country's National Revolution. By the onset of the twenty-first century, however, modernization had reached so wide across the national territory, and had transformed the lives of so many, as to make appeals to the ambition of ordinary people to be recognized as full and equal members of Thailand's national community more resonant than they had ever been. It is no wonder, in this sense, that the Red Shirts see themselves as the inheritors of the legacy of Pridi Banomyong and the People's Party, far more so than to the mass movements of 1973 or 1992 (see Streckfuss 2012: 322). For their primary objective, as they see it, is to complete a mission the Promoters left unfinished and previous movements for democracy largely shirked from – namely, to subordinate the monarchy, the unelected institutions that ground their authority in the monarchy's defence, and the 'good people' who base claims to special rights and powers on their purported proximity to the monarchy, to the letter of the law and the will of the electorate.

In this endeavour, Thaksin and his supporters have something the People's Party had only dreamed of assembling: the support of a solid plurality of the voting public, which has time and again expressed its preference for 'popular' over 'elite' forms of democracy. The resilience of their popular backing, in turn, has allowed them to disrupt each of the mechanisms of institutional reproduction that had previously sustained the primacy of unelected institutions. Their strength at the ballot box, in parliament, and in the streets has undermined the power of the royalist establishment, which can no longer count on the political system's fragmentation and the indifference of the population routinely to impose its will on elected governments. Meanwhile, the resonance of their counter-hegemonic vision of the Thai nation's structure and future has broken down the royalist consensus that had once allowed unelected institutions to exert power and influence without sustained recourse to repression. Whatever royalists in Bangkok might think, the demands put forth by the Red Shirts, and the Promoters before them, are likely to intensify as a result of further development, and perhaps especially as a consequence of the ongoing efforts effectively to disenfranchise most of the electorate. Eight decades on, as Thailand comes full circle, the choice before the country's royalists remains limited to the two options King Prajadhipok was presented with on 24 June 1932 – in the final analysis, the triumphs of the Ninth Reign have served only to delay a decision that cannot be put off much longer. Should the nation's self-appointed guardians fail to see the past as mere prologue, they could soon find their own 'merit' to have definitively run dry.

8 State of unexception

Giovanni Sartori once articulated the rationale for comparative political analysis by noting that 'comparing is "learning" from the experience of others and that, conversely, he who knows only one country knows none' (Sartori 1991: 245). The journey Thailand has travelled since the days of the absolute monarchy illustrates the point quite compellingly. In 1932, the leadership of the People's Party justified its seizure of power in a blistering assessment of where Siam stood relative to countries that had already dispensed with absolutist regimes and most vestiges of feudalism. With Field Marshal Sarit's conservative 'revolution', the universal values in which the People's Party had initially framed its vision for Siam's future were repudiated as useless or damaging foreign imports, while the Promoters' cosmopolitan outlook was replaced with one emphasizing the uniqueness of Thailand's history and culture. Based on the country's purported exceptionalism, authorities have since championed the notion that Thailand has little to learn from the experience of other countries – which is typically drawn upon only insofar as it can be miniaturized into grim cautionary tales – and have urged Thai scholars, activists, students, and ordinary people to refrain from 'tagging along with foreigners' (see Thongchai 2004 [1994]: 7) incapable of grasping what sets the country apart from the rest of the world. The 'theology of Thai exceptionalism' (Paisarn, 16 July 2011) not only renders many Thais, in the words of Thongchai Winichakul (cited in Prachatai, 22 July 2013), 'ignorant and narcissistic' in their attitudes towards other countries, but also robs them of a chance to genuinely understand their own. The uncritical acceptance of the mantra that Thailand has been a 'democracy' since 1932, as recited in school textbooks and other official publications, is only one example of the limitations that the blinders of exceptionalism impose on one's capacity to make sense of Thailand's historical experience.

On the face of it, Thailand is something of an unlikely candidate for claims to exceptionalism and uniqueness. Most aspects of Thailand's national culture – including models of kingship, religious practices, legal traditions, literary classics, artistic forms, and architectural styles – are local adaptations of foreign imports, reflecting the country's nature as a decidedly 'worldly' place (see Peleggi 2007). Only Thailand's avoidance of direct colonization renders its historical experience distinctive by the standards of the region. Even on this count, however, the difference between Thailand and its neighbours is in some ways more about form than substance, given the country's subjection to forms of indirect colonization, and its application of colonial models of governance in territories that were brought under its jurisdiction in the late nineteenth century (see Anderson 1978; for a more recent discussion, see Harrison 2010). The fact that the country was never formally annexed by European colonial empires, in this sense, does more to explain the historical genesis of its claims to uniqueness – as an excuse for forms of internal rule that have long been out of style in countries with which Thailand may otherwise compare unfavourably – than it does to substantiate any such pretence. Today, Thailand's performance on most political, social, and economic indicators remains decidedly middling. Compared with other upper-middle-income countries, it is probably fair to say that Thailand only stands out for its number of military coups, its extreme levels of economic inequality, its abysmal education system, and (more recently) the enforcement of its draconian *lèse majesté* law – four by-products of the decades-old struggle waged by royalists to forestall the country's democratization.

Despite the efforts and resources expended by the authorities to convince the country of its own incommensurability, the Thai public could be said never to have fully internalized these attitudes. Commenting on literary standards, Phillips (1987: 16) pointed out that 'what is important from a Thai point of view is that literature clarify or reveal that which is obviously real but unrecognized; that it make people think about what previously was improper (or dangerous or irrelevant) to think about; that it give shape, meaning, and identities to things'. Writings of this kind are often at least implicitly comparative. Somewhat improbably, however, this posture did find its way into the work of both local and foreign scholars, some of whom have proven quite willing to concede the axiom that the uniqueness of Thailand's historical experience places it beyond meaningful comparisons (for an overview, see Anderson 1978: 197; Phillips 1976). Certainly, other works have been criticized for doing the exact opposite – that is, for failing 'to give adequate stress to the importance of historical and cultural constraints on the nature of [Thailand's] development' (Thak 2007 [1979]: 1). Then again, the call to acknowledge the importance of context can only be taken as a plea for better comparisons, as opposed to an excuse for giving up comparative ambitions altogether.

Its illusions of exceptionalism notwithstanding, over the past century, Thailand has faced challenges that have clear parallels in the history of developed and developing nations alike. Indeed, the approach taken in this study was founded on the premise that, while no general theory is sufficiently attuned to local realities to properly explain the experience of any one country, placing Thailand in its proper comparative context yields insights not available to those willing to assume its uniqueness. This concluding chapter reflects on the implications that this book's comparative historical analysis has for the study of regime instability in Thailand and beyond – contrasting its explanation of the country's political development with major alternatives, as well as situating the Thai case in the comparative literature on political regimes and democratization. A final note is reserved for a discussion of the events that have taken place in Thailand since the 2011 elections – one designed to interpret, through the prism of the theory developed in this study, what these events portend about the country's future.

Thailand and beyond

At least since Lakatos (1970) published his seminal essay on the methodology of scientific research programmes, it has been broadly accepted that the validity of any explanatory theory can only be evaluated against existing alternatives, with a view to establishing whether it 'offers any novel, excess information compared with its predecessor[s] and whether some of this excess information is corroborated' (Lakatos 1970: 120). Accordingly, the appraisal of the explanation put together in this book for Thailand's regime instability – and its ongoing political crisis – begins here with an assessment of how it matches up against three of its principal rivals. The discussion highlights the failure of each of these narratives to provide a satisfactory explanation for Thailand's trajectory of political development; following Lakatos (1970), it seeks to demonstrate how the theory built in this study explains facts generally adduced in support of its main competitors as well as facts that cannot be squared with any of its rivals.

The first lesson to be drawn from this study is that the regime instability Thailand has experienced since 1932 is not the result of the transplantation of 'Western' political institutions that are incompatible with 'Thai' culture, history, and tradition. In Thailand, arguments prefiguring the 'Asian Values' thesis are as old as the debate over constitutionalism. King Chulalongkorn warned that the introduction of 'Western ideas' and 'Western political institutions' would be tantamount to 'cultivat[ing] rice in Siam using European agricultural textbooks about wheat'. His sons and successors, King Vajiravudh and King Prajadhipok, responded in similar fashion to the growing demands for reform, describing parliamentary government as unsuited to the cultural or racial characteristics of the Siamese people. A few decades later, it is in cultural terms that the government of Field Marshal Sarit explained the failure of the 1932 revolution, attributing it to the departure it marked from homegrown practices and values Sarit purported to restore (see Hewison and Kengkij 2010: 187–8; Thak 2007 [1979]: 100). This line of reasoning has since featured regularly in the work of royalist politicians and academics. Over his long reign, King Bhumibol has often commented on the threat that 'Western' constitutionalism poses to the country's order and unity, as well as the incompatibility of democratic institutions with Thailand's 'national culture' (see Hewison and Kengkij 2010: 190–2; see also Handley 2006: 201, 251–2, 319, 337, 343, 429–31, 439–41). Most recently, royalists have been heard describing the fight against Thaksin Shinawatra as Thailand's last stand in defence of local values besieged by the forces of globalization (see Seaton and Wehrfritz, 6 September 2008).

Its long and noble lineage notwithstanding, this narrative is not of much use in explaining the regime instability that Thailand has experienced over the past eight decades. It might be worth noting upfront that the traditions generally cited as obstacles to the country's democratization – Buddhist models of kingship/authority and Buddhist conceptions of an 'ideal politico-social order' (see Tambiah 1976: 431) – are hardly unique to Thailand. The notion that a righteous leader would represent the will of an entire people better than its members can express it, through elections or other forms of public deliberation, has deep roots in Western political thought dating back to Plato, as does the belief in 'natural inequalities' that stigmatizes the failure by any member of society to keep his place, and perform the attendant 'duties', for threatening the 'disorder of the parts' that leads to anarchy and social disintegration (see Walzer 1982: 153–4; 171–5). There is a great deal of evidence, moreover, to suggest that these ideas have come to form an integral part of Thailand's national consciousness, not because of their historical rootedness but as a result of their modern-day inculcation. Indeed, while the twentieth-century ideology of Thainess draws upon genuine traditions people could 'recognize in their daily lives' (see Reynolds 2002: 10), its cultural hegemony has far less to do with its greater compatibility with local culture than it does with differentials of power and resources between actors who have historically attempted to advance different conceptions of what it means to be Thai, grounded in equally plausible claims to cultural appropriateness.

The point is not that culture – or, perhaps more accurately, ideology – does not matter. As shown throughout this book, modern adaptations of traditional ideas of authority and socio-political order are core components of Thailand's royal nationalism, which has shaped the values, beliefs, and behavioural norms shared by a great many people. Still, to say that references to culture have often helped legitimize the subversion of constitutional regimes is not to say that culture was the *cause* of their instability. Certainly, the fact that the putatively more 'Thai-style' regimes established along the way have not proven appreciably more stable would appear to suggest that the 'culture' they embodied was never as widely shared or as deeply felt as royalists might have wished. Likewise, the resources expended by the state to educate the public to the official version of Thainess – and suppress viable alternatives – would seem to indicate that its core principles did come especially naturally to much of the country's population. In the final analysis, the case of Thailand shows that 'culture is destiny' only in the sense that a country's 'destiny' is subject to constant reinvention, and that any 'culture' is ambiguous enough to be retrofitted accordingly, in support of arrangements of power it may later be claimed to have brought into being.

Turning the cultural argument on its head, it is perhaps more accurate to say that Thailand's political instability is rooted not in the transplantation of alien institutions, but rather in the efforts made by Thai authorities to enforce, in defiance of the country's cultural diversity and ongoing cultural change, the 'unity' of all behind a modern ideology they have sought to dress up as the expression of timeless ethno-cultural traits, uniformly innate to peoples across its national territory. Owing in part to the success of Thailand's royal nationalism, departures from constitutional rule have often enjoyed a modicum of support among certain segments of the population. But the continuing pressure for representative institutions and liberal freedoms, exerted over the past century by increasingly large and varied constituencies, speaks rather clearly to the failure of the royalist project of unity in hierarchy and social conformity. At no time has that failure been more apparent than it is now.

The second lesson to be drawn from this study is that the regime instability Thailand has experienced since 1932 is not the result of irreconcilable differences between 'modern' urban middle-class voters and 'backward' provincial voters. The most influential version of this narrative appeared in Anek (1996), who identified the root cause of the country's instability in the fundamentally different conceptions of democracy espoused by the urban and provincial electorates. Famously, Anek (1996) argued that provincial voters pay little heed to debates over national policy or ideology, using their votes to reward politicians who attend to tangible improvements to the lives of their communities. Given the overwhelmingly rural and small-town make-up of the country's population, elected legislatures tend to be stacked with provincial representatives whom civic-minded voters in Bangkok despise for their incompetence and corruption; the inept, predatory nature of elected administrations, in turn, periodically renders urban voters available to support military interventions promising to wipe the slate clean. Originally, Anek (1996: 220–3) had argued that building a stable democracy would require a synthesis of the two visions, as opposed to the imposition of urban middle-class values on provincial voters. It only took the rise of Thaksin Shinawatra, however, for Anek to take to the moral barricades and endorse reforms designed to increase the weight of urban middle-class votes at the expense of the provincial electorate's representation, on the conceit that Thaksin's populism would otherwise 'destroy the nation' (Anek 2006: 202). This argument has since become a constant refrain in the rhetoric of royalist thinkers and pressure groups, whose proposals to restrict or dismantle electoral democracy revolve around the idea that voters in the provinces, particularly the Northeast, must first learn to cast their ballots for 'good people'.

The account offered in this book provides a very different picture of the interests, aspirations, and psychology of urban and provincial voters alike. Provincial Thais, for their part, are a great deal more sophisticated than they are often given credit for. Indeed, over the past several electoral cycles, the provincial electorate has not only voted 'very consistently and very rationally' (Chang Noi, 1 September 2008), but has also exhibited attitudes that combine 'pragmatic' or instrumental orientations to politics with more principled and more affective orientations – a balance that Almond and Verba (1963: 354–5) identified long ago as conducive to a functioning democracy. Likewise, while Anek was right to identify in the urban middle class the key swing constituency in Thailand's oscillation between democracy and non-democracy, the reality is that Bangkok's middle class does not instinctively turn on governments that engage in corrupt, predatory practices. As shown by the lead-up to the royalist military coups of 1947, 1976, 1991, 2006, and 2014, it is rather more often the case that the issues of corruption and good government become politically activated when democracy begins to work as intended – that is, when elected governments begin to promote greater popular participation, expand their authority over matters, such as policy making and appointments, traditionally reserved for officials in the military and civilian bureaucracy, and/or weaken the hold that informal networks of power loosely linked to the palace have come to exercise on much of the state. While the provincial electorate is often accused of falling all too easily for the promises of 'immoral' politicians, the urban middle class is no less susceptible to the role that elites play, on both sides, in shaping the political preferences of their target constituencies.

There are, of course, differences between the values prevalent among Bangkok's middle and upper-middle class, or for that matter southern voters, and those prevalent in Thailand's North and Northeast. Broadly speaking, if the latter tend to favour a highly majoritarian form of 'popular democracy', the former appear to be more comfortable with a less inclusive form of 'elite democracy' protective of the rights and freedoms of some electoral minorities (i.e., themselves). A recent survey conducted by the Asia Foundation (2011: 35–6) bears out this interpretation, finding significant regional differences in understandings of democracy. Voters in Bangkok and its surroundings (26 per cent) are less likely to say that democracy is primarily about 'elections/majority rule/participation' than voters in the North/Northeast (37 per cent). Conversely, more voters in the South (57 per cent) and Bangkok (55 per cent) defined democracy on the basis of 'rights and freedoms' than northeastern voters (42 per cent). The survey, however, does not provide much indication that higher education, higher income, or self-identification as a royalist ('Yellow') is correlated with more liberal, enlightened, or 'modern' attitudes. In fact, several items suggest quite the opposite. While illiberal, 'post-democratic' attitudes are not exclusive to any group (see Glassman 2010), nothing in the available data suggests that southerners or Bangkokians hold views that are any more 'modern' or 'sophisticated' than anyone else.

Indeed, Bangkok's middle and upper-middle class is, on balance, rather deficient on some of the characteristics that classic modernization theory (see Inkeles 1966: 141–4) identifies as the by-product of economic development, urbanization, education, and exposure to mass media (for a similar argument, see Anderson, 5 August 2011; see also Englehart 2003; Thongchai 2008a). On the contrary, throughout the country's ongoing political crisis, urban middle-class citizens and personalities have distinguished themselves for their reactionary dispositions, their transcendental hero worship, their support for draconian restrictions to freedom of speech, their witch-hunts against citizens who stray from royalist orthodoxy, their intolerance of foreigners and progressives, their utopian longings for a past that never was, their abandonment of rational argument in favour of magical thinking and nationalist mythology, their wholesale rejection of individual equality, their dehumanizing portrayals of provincial voters, and their embracement of hierarchical world views based on superstitions of merit and karma. In this respect, Thailand's urban middle class is far from an isolated case. The history of the past century, particularly as it relates to the genesis of fascism and other extreme right-wing movements, provides ample evidence for just how anxious, flighty, and impressionable creatures members of the urban middle class can be, when made to feel squeezed from above and from below.

Just as in the discussion about culture, the point is not to suggest that modernization does not matter. On the contrary, modernization matters a great deal to Thailand's history of regime instability. But the profound socio-economic transformations the country has experienced since the 1960s did not so much give rise to a cleavage between a 'modern' urban middle class and a 'backward' provincial population, as much as it transformed the aspirations and self-image of citizens at *all levels* of Thailand's social hierarchy. While the urban middle class was the first to demand a seat at the table, the middle-class electorate has also exhibited considerable nervousness about the threat to its social status and economic position presented by more inclusive political systems that confer upon provincial voters the power to choose the country's government. This insecurity and ambivalence, in turn, have facilitated the effort of the royalist establishment to turn much of the urban middle class against democracy when necessary. On occasion, the 'moral panic' instigated by royalists has led segments of the urban middle class to adopt reactionary stances antithetical to the enlightened views so often said to set them apart from the general public. Once again, Thailand's regime instability has less to do with the 'backwardness' of provincial voters than their progressive modernization – and the actions that the palace, the military, and urban elites have periodically taken to fend off the increasingly serious threat that social change presents to their status and power.

The third lesson to be drawn from this study is that the regime instability Thailand has experienced since 1932 is not exclusively, or even primarily, the result of class conflict. Before elaborating on this point, it is worth stipulating that the literature on the social/economic origins of dictatorship and democracy *does* offer valuable insights into various aspects of Thailand's political development. Barrington Moore's classic study, for instance, can help make sense of the alliance formed under Field Marshal Sarit in the late 1950s, shedding light on why a 'commercial and industrial class which is too weak and dependent to take power and rule in its own right' (Moore 1966: 437) would agree to support a regime dominated by the palace, the military, and the bureaucracy. Similarly, Rueschemeyer *et al.* (1992: 63) provide clues about the scarce cohesiveness subsequently exhibited by *authoritarian* coalitions, rooted in the absence of a serious enough revolutionary threat from below (see also Slater 2010), as well as the fragility of *democratic* coalitions, rooted in the opposition of Thailand's elites to 'extending political inclusion to the lower classes' (see Rueschemeyer *et al.* 1992: 8). The fact that democratization has since been complicated by Thailand's extreme levels of economic inequality (see Montesano 2010: 277–80), moreover, is consistent with the proposition that inequality tends to undermine democratic regimes because elites have more to lose from the redistributive policies that tend to result from majority rule (see Acemoglu and Robinson 2006: 35–8). These works also help put into some perspective the behaviour of the urban middle class, and its frequent oscillations between supporting democracy and opposing it, which happens to be entirely consistent with the ambiguous role middle classes have played in the democratization process elsewhere (for an overview, see Mahoney 2003: 148).

Highlighting the importance of class structure and class disparities, however, does not require one to subscribe to the notion that Thailand's ongoing political crisis is above all the expression of 'class conflict'. First, and perhaps most obviously, the conflict cannot be reduced to a fight between dominant and subordinate classes, with the middle class cross-pressured into swinging back and forth between different positions. While it is equally simplistic to describe the crisis exclusively as an elite affair, Thailand's regime instability has always been caused, in various measures, by intra-elite divisions. Indeed, although the focus on class structure and inequalities illuminates a fundamental tension, which has been emphasized repeatedly throughout this study, between the demands for greater democracy from below, which have grown increasingly insistent as a consequence of modernization, and elite interest in preserving Thailand's existing social structure, intra-elite divisions are crucial to the manner in which social cleavages become politically activated and mobilized. Second, if Thaksin Shinawatra's continuing strength and popularity are in part functions of his ability to appeal to class interests – as are the strength and popularity of his enemies with Bangkok's middle and upper-middle class – this study has shown that class interest is not enough to explain the preferences and behaviour of supporters and opponents alike, as reflected in the cross-class profile of both the Red and Yellow movements, as well as the varying significance of class in different parts of the country.

It is for this reason that Thailand's recent political conflict is best described as an 'identity conflict'. Individual preferences over alternative regime types do not simply flow, unmediated, from one's socio-economic status; rather, they are the product of political commitments established and mobilized through appeals made by different sides to various aspects of their target constituencies' self-image and identities – aspects that include, but are not limited to, class. Visions of 'popular' and 'elite' democracy, moreover, appeal to different constituencies not just for their instrumental value, estimated on the basis of their expected distributive consequences for various classes or regions, but for what these alternative regime types represent, intrinsically, about the structure of the Thai nation and one's place in it: the abandonment or preservation, respectively, of the different moral valuations and legitimate political roles the ideology of Thainess assigns to various groups based on their social status, regional origin, and political ideas.

Having established what Thailand's regime instability is *not* about, this book's explanation can be summarized as follows. The notion that political regimes, democratic or otherwise, are 'contingent outcomes of conflict' suggests that their instability is the result of: 1) the unresolved nature of conflicts over the organization of state and society, which this study has traced back to the 'unfinished business' of the 1932 revolution; and 2) the failure of any of the institutional arrangements adopted over the years to either elicit the compliance of all major political actors or confer upon any of them the capacity definitively to impose their will on the others. Beginning with Sarit's conservative revolution, the alliance formed by the palace, the military, the bureaucracy, and parts of the business community did manage to entrench itself, relying on rules of the game that criminalized all forms of opposition as well as the aggressive promotion of an official ideology crafted in support of its hegemonic project. That initial advantage, and its reproduction over time, is what has allowed these institutions to exercise, with a degree of legitimacy, powers well in excess of what most of the constitutions adopted since have provided, generally for the purposes of circumscribing, undermining, or overthrowing governments that threatened their prerogatives. The tendency of asymmetries of power and legitimacy to expand over time, however, was countervailed by social transformations – resulting in part from developmental policies and political accommodations that had been originally designed to strengthen the stability of successive royalist regimes – that would later lead to the system's destabilization. The instability generally stemmed from a combination of: 1) growing intra-elite divisions, caused by the shifting balance of power in the ruling political coalition that led to pressures for institutional change to reflect new realities; and 2) intensifying pressures for greater inclusion coming from below, whose mobilization was typically favoured by the presence of intra-elite divisions.

In the decades since Field Marshal Sarit killed off the 1932 revolution, Thailand's royalist political order has experienced three major disruptions comparable to the one marked by the rise of Thaksin Shinawatra. Much like the current one, such crises originated in reforms made to the country's institutional architecture – leading to the promulgation of new constitutions in 1968, 1974, and 1978 – in response to latent or constituted challenges to the status quo. While designed to appease various constituencies, inside and outside the ruling circle, by partially granting their demands for greater influence or inclusion, each of these adaptations actually emboldened oppositional forces to step up their activities (1968–71), press for a variety of new demands (1973–6), or gradually subvert the existing institutional arrangements from the inside (1979–91). Much like the current one, each such crisis was met with a conservative reaction that featured, in varying order, a military coup, the proscription of organized oppositions, a massacre of street demonstrators, and an attempt to restore the *status quo ante*, retrofitted with new safeguards designed to remedy the structural flaws blamed for the previous regime's downfall. Sooner or later, however, the restoration's failure led to new adaptations that accommodated, in exchange for preserving prerogatives reserved for the monarchy, the military, and the bureaucracy, some of the demands of disgruntled elites and newly mobilized groups, sowing the seeds of a new round of crisis by providing constituencies singled out for co-optation, as well as those left out by the arrangement, with opportunities to grow stronger and more assertive.

Over successive iterations of the cycle, the electorate's growing politicization, fuelled in part by socio-economic change, has rendered authoritarian and semi-democratic regimes increasingly unsustainable. As a result of the rising costs attached to the suspension or denial of electoral democracy, Thailand's royalist establishment – although still willing to resort to brute force whenever its back is against the wall – was gradually reduced to exercising informal powers behind the façade of a weak formal democracy. Even this, nonetheless, has proven increasingly problematic, thanks to the growing assertiveness of elected governments and their constituents' rejection of more 'guided' or 'elite' forms of democracy. In this sense, the severity of Thailand's ongoing political crisis is rooted not only in the secular decline of the royalist establishment's power and legitimacy, but also in the rise of a political force – the first of its kind since the days of Sarit – whose alternative, 'counterhegemonic' vision of the nation's structure and future has earned the backing of a solid plurality of the electorate, which has proven largely impervious to repression and co-optation. If history is any guide, the threat is likely to become all the more serious as a result of ongoing socio-economic change, or the deployment of measures taken in the past to deal with lesser challenges.

While this explanation lacks the abstraction and parsimony of the three alternatives described earlier, its greater concreteness and complexity render it capable of explaining facts cited in support of each, as well as other facts that cannot be reconciled with any of its rivals. Its emphasis on mechanisms of institutional reproduction explains the longevity of the country's royalist order, often claimed to be rooted in culture and tradition, while accounting for the fact that the said political order has faced constant challenges from actors and constituencies socialized into the same 'culture'. Its emphasis on the social and political construction of identity, resulting from a competitive process in which various actors seek to draw advantage from social, economic, and cultural change, explains differences in political attitudes often attributed to different levels of modernization, while also accounting for the fact that more educated or affluent voters have periodically embraced rather more obscurantist positions. Its emphasis on the historical genesis of social cleavages, as well as on the mechanisms by which social divisions are politically activated and mobilized, explains the latent tensions rooted in Thailand's processes of state formation, nation building, and industrialization, while also accounting for the fact that such cleavages have found expression in very different ways across time and space.

The fact that this explanation is, on the whole, not especially unorthodox reaffirms a fundamental point: with regard to its travails with democracy and non-democracy, Thailand is only as 'exceptional' as any other country. Indeed, while this book disavowed any attempt to build a theory sufficiently simple or abstract to warrant pretensions of universal validity, in the interest of accommodating the idiosyncrasies of the case, the resulting 'middle-range theory' does lend itself to 'complex and contingent generalizations' (see George and Bennett 2005: 144) that might inform the literature on regime instability more broadly.

One such general insight is that the logic of path dependence, based on the tendency of asymmetries of power and legitimacy to reproduce themselves over time, provides a causal mechanism for the workings of the 'military legacy' blamed by the literature for rendering democracies previously disrupted by military coups more vulnerable to future authoritarian reversals (see Przeworski 2009: 27–8). As it is generally understood, military coups tend to be followed by the repression of civil society organizations and the expansion of the military's domestic prerogatives and budgets. Even in situations where the generals overthrow a constitutional regime with the 'transitional mission of "re-establishing order"' (Przeworski 2009: 28), moreover, their formal return to the barracks may be preceded by the establishment of institutions designed to help the military protect its newly acquired powers and resources, limit the range of action of civilian governments, and keep civil society organizations, like political parties, weak and fragmented. The weakness of civil society, in turn, reduces the costs of future military interventions – minimizing, with the potential of encountering serious opposition, the need for repression. At the same time, the dysfunction likely to plague democracies with a history of coups justifies the military's ongoing tutelage, up to and including the removal of elected governments that fail to guarantee the requisite degree of 'order'. All else being equal, each military coup widens asymmetries of power and legitimacy that elevate the military and its allies above weak and discredited civil society organizations, rendering future democratic regimes more prone to collapse, easier to overthrow, and less likely to assert themselves as the 'only game in town'.

When a country's transition to democracy is undertaken 'early' (relative to levels of development) and collapses at the hands of the military, successive iterations of the cycle of transition and reversal may lead the armed forces to become, in Tilly's (1985: 186) words, 'powerful, unconstrained organizations that easily overshadow all other organizations within their territories', thereby presenting the generals with an opportunity to exploit the weakness of 'mutual constraints between rulers and ruled' to govern in a despotic fashion – all the more so in client states, like Thailand, whose security forces have been showered with money and equipment by foreign powers. The focus on ever-expanding asymmetries of power and legitimacy, however, does not explain how civil society, although badly outmatched in coercive power and moral authority, could ever acquire the strength to challenge military rule or, in periods of civilian rule, threaten the prerogatives of the military and its allies so severely as to precipitate another reversal.

The solution, which may be abstracted into another general insight, is that the conflictual logic of the process of institutional reproduction provides institutions, even those that benefit from self-reinforcement, with a 'dynamic of potential change' (see Mahoney 2000: 523). Measures taken to strengthen a military regime seeking to rule indefinitely, that is, may also trigger dynamics that eventually threaten its reproduction, exacerbating each of the problems that define authoritarian politics (see Svolik 2012: 2–13): the problems of *authoritarian power sharing* and *authoritarian control* (of the population).

With regard to the issue of *authoritarian power sharing*, the military's desire to broaden the ruling coalition, in the interest of greater stability, may feature accommodations that eventually lead to challenges from within the ruling circle. In keeping with previous work on the subject (see Rueschemeyer *et al.* 1992; Slater 2010), this dynamic of potential change should most concern cases in which the revolutionary threat posed by disenfranchised groups advocating communism or other visions of radical reorganization of society is not sufficiently strong, or emerges too late, to produce stable elite coalitions in support of authoritarianism. With regard to the issue of *authoritarian control*, similarly, the military's desire to exercise power legitimately, with minimal recourse to physical force, by securing the support or acquiescence of the population at large – or, conversely, its failure to muster the wherewithal to impose heavy enough levels of repression (for reasons that may have to do with its lack of internal cohesiveness, the tenuousness of its support among other elites, and/or its dependency on foreign sources of patronage) – may induce it to stop well short of eliminating all potential oppositions, permitting, in time, the reorganization of groups disadvantaged by the status quo. In addition, it is for good reason that military officers are 'modernizers par excellence' (Huntington 1965: 423), because military-led regimes are often heavily dependent on performance for legitimation. The promotion of development, however, also engenders socio-political transformations that encourage, in combination with intra-elite divisions, challenges from below.

In these situations, subject to the (contingent) success of oppositional forces in mobilizing the population to their cause, the military may respond to challenges by cracking down violently, as it has multiple times in Thailand. Episodes of repression that prove unpopular with the constituencies upon which the military and its allies rely for support, however, may aggravate divisions within the ruling coalition, or the armed forces themselves, as did the massacres of demonstrators carried out in Thailand in 1973 and 1992. Even when the state violence is met with these constituencies' approval, as in the case of the 1976 and 2010 crackdowns, the costs and risks associated with the sustained levels of repression required to suppress oppositions on an ongoing basis may eventually induce the military and its allies to shift from repression to co-optation. Co-optation, in turn, may take the form of accommodations designed to further restructure or broaden the ruling coalition, and possibly grant some of the demands of newly mobilized constituencies, as well as renewed efforts to promote development – setting in motion the same familiar processes that lead to new challenges from within and from below. Based on Thailand's experience, one could also venture the hypothesis that, all else being equal, the cycle of regime instability is likely to last longer in the presence of high levels of economic inequality, activated social cleavages cutting across class divisions, and official ideologies, like Thailand's royal nationalism, that prove effective in legitimizing the power of unelected institutions on grounds other than performance.

In the long run, economic development should still render the denial of electoral democracy increasingly untenable. In this scenario, however, the tendency of electoral democracy to become more stable as incomes rise does not necessarily reflect the impact that economic development has on the *benefits* elites expect to draw from authoritarian reversals, but rather the effect that modernization has on the *costs* of staging a military coup, having fuelled successive rounds of struggle that ended up sanctioning demands for greater inclusion, having facilitated the emergence of organized forces more capable of opposing future seizures of power, and having therefore predicated the success of authoritarian reversals on the application of ever more extreme levels of repression. Prior to the illegal seizure of power staged by General Prayuth Chan-ocha on 22 May 2014 – a development many observers had thought improbable – the violence that took place on the streets of Bangkok in April and May 2010 appeared to have given the men leading the Royal Thai Army a clear enough sense of the dangers and likely futility of staging another coup. One can only hope that it will not take a tragedy of even worse proportions before Thailand consigns its history of military coups to the place where it belongs – in the history books.

Democracy without qualifiers

The comparative data on regime instability presented by Przeworski (2009) suggest that Thailand may have experienced its last coup d'état – given current rates of economic growth, it will not be long before the country's income per capita crosses a threshold beyond which there are no examples of authoritarian reversals. It is, of course, seldom wise to predict a country's future based on other countries' past, all the more so given the recent dismantlement of electoral democracy, to say nothing of the climate of censorship and intimidation that has enveloped Thailand since the military took action ostensibly to 'bring back happiness' to its people. As worrisome as the present situation is, however, circumstances warrant a measure of optimism in the prospect that the cycle of coups and constitutions might one day soon be broken, if perhaps only in the next reign. Thailand's unelected institutions still have means and motives in abundance to deny the country its electoral democracy. But a key lesson to be drawn from Thailand's contemporary political development is that efforts to deny the electorate the right to choose its own governments have grown increasingly unsustainable and counterproductive. As damaging as the events of 2006, 2008, and 2010 were for the authority of the monarchy, and the unelected institutions that draw their extra-constitutional powers from the monarchy's protection, the attempt currently underway to reverse decades of democratic development could turn out a great deal worse.

The period of relative stability and calm that followed the election of Prime Minister Yingluck Shinawatra was not the result of a deal struck by the government with royalist forces. It was rather the reflection of a fragile equilibrium, kept in place by the royalist camp's caution not to risk its own destruction and the care taken by the government not to push royalists so far as to leave them with no other option. At the same time, efforts made by each side to wear down the other threatened constantly to upset the delicate balance. For its part, the administration had taken pains not to openly defy the monarchy, the military, or the courts. It did not pursue, as its supporters demanded, reforms to legislation that criminalizes criticism of the royal family, preferring instead quietly to reduce the number of prosecutions. It did not move to cut the military's oversized budget and hold military officers accountable for the killings of Red Shirt protesters, even as murder charges were filed against Abhisit Vejjajiva and Suthep Thaugsuban. And it was careful not to fall afoul of the Constitutional Court's rulings, taking time-consuming legislative detours around the obstacles the judiciary placed in its way to block the constitutional amendment process. While keen to avoid a showdown, the government nonetheless seemed intent on gradually divesting unelected institutions of their powers, methodically dismantling the legal means at their disposal to resist, while relying on the Red Shirts to make extra-legal, coercive remedies less and less attractive.

Royalists, meanwhile, had sought to undermine the government through a variety of means, assisted by the provisions of the 2007 constitution. Shortly after the 2011 elections, the Democrat Party and a group of appointed senators took to filing a barrage of complaints with 'independent' agencies and courts, seeking the impeachment of the Prime Minister, the dissolution of Pheu Thai and its coalition partners, and several injunctions against legislative efforts said to threaten 'Democracy with the King as Head of State'. While generally willing to consider the petitions, regardless of their substantive and procedural soundness, the judges shied away from staging another 'judicial coup'. The Constitutional Court only took the risk of clearly overstepping the bounds of its authority to stall the constitutional reform process. Most notably, the Court issued a ruling in July 2012 that cautioned the legislature against amending the constitution to permit the election of a new constituent assembly, on the grounds that it might be construed as an attempt to overthrow 'Democracy with the King as Head of State', in violation of Article 68 of the constitution. In doing so, the Court itself flouted the letter of Article 68, which only empowered it to act upon a motion of the Attorney General, thereby establishing a precedent that would later see the Court agree repeatedly to investigate and rule on whether measures taken by the executive and the legislature constituted, as the opposition alleged, acts of sedition.[1] But if the Constitutional Court was prepared to fight to guard the legacy of the 2006 coup, not to mention keep the government under the proverbial Sword of Damocles, the justices passed on multiple chances to dissolve Pheu Thai and remove the Prime Minister.

For some royalists, that was not good enough. Indeed, no special insight was required to recognize that, in this war of attrition, time and the structural forces at play favoured the government and its supporters. Queen Sirikit's disappearance from public view, upon suffering a debilitating stroke in July 2012, and King Bhumibol's increasingly evident physical and mental decline were only the most conspicuous signs of the imminence with which Thailand was destined to turn the page. While many in the royalist camp could ultimately be reconciled with the rollback of measures imposed in the aftermath of the 2006 coup – and, more generally, the country's gradual transformation into a genuine constitutional monarchy – others were less prepared to accept it. It is no coincidence, in this sense, that the group leading the conservative reaction this time would be the Democrat Party, which had only played a supporting role in the events of 2006 and 2008. On the one hand, the failure on the part of other royalist groups to rally impressive crowds in repeated anti-government demonstrations staged since 2011 left the Democrat Party as the only organization with the capacity to engineer circumstances conducive to the removal of Yingluck Shinawatra, through the mobilization of its support base in Bangkok and the South. On the other hand, few had as much to lose as the leaders of the Democrat Party from the restoration of Thaksin Shinawatra's electoral and legislative dominance. Given the party's proven inability to win elections, at least in its current guise, its leaders faced a stark choice: keep losing, and eventually be sacrificed once the party got serious about winning again, or earn themselves a chance to come back to power by leading the effort to dismantle the 'Thaksin System' through extra-constitutional means, in a throwback to the counter-revolutionary struggle some of the party's founders had waged in the 1930s.

Amid reports that more incisive attempts to suspend electoral democracy would be staged by the end of the year (see *The Nation*, 21 September 2013), it is as yet unclear what prompted the government, in late October 2013, suddenly to rush through the House of Representatives

[1] While the Constitutional Court remains in office at the time of writing, thus far the justices have said nothing about the military's assumption of absolute power and suspension of much of the constitution, their oft-repeated concern for 'checks and balances' having apparently been exhausted with the unlawful termination of an elected government.

a blanket amnesty covering most of the offences committed by political actors since the beginning of Thailand's crisis. Whatever the truth behind it, the amnesty bill would soon join the series of blunders, miscalculations, and self-inflicted wounds that punctuate the political career of Thaksin Shinawatra. The Red Shirt movement, which remained the single greatest deterrent against any form of coup d'état, refused to endorse a bill that guaranteed the principles of the 2010 crackdown the same impunity enjoyed by their predecessors. For those royalists most opposed to the government, meanwhile, the amnesty created both a motive and an opportunity to act. The prospect of Thaksin's exoneration and return to Thailand, combined with the National Assembly's final passage of an amendment to the constitution establishing a fully elected Senate, heralded the undoing of the 2006 coup, complete with the retrenchment of most of the powers the 2007 constitution vested in unelected institutions. At the same time, the distancing of the Red Shirts and the amnesty's broad-based unpopularity gave royalists a chance to pounce. Given the pre-planned nature of the operation, it is no surprise that street protests did not stop when the government announced it would no longer pursue the amnesty, which the Senate proceeded to vote down unanimously, or when the Constitutional Court struck down the reform to the Senate's composition – again, without dissolving Pheu Thai – ruling it an attempt to overthrow 'Democracy with the King as Head of State'. For the Democrats and their powerful backers among members of the royal family, palace officials, retired military generals, and some business elites, it was now or never.

Weeks earlier, few could have predicted that as many people would turn out to join the start of the 'People's Revolution' called by the leaders of the Democrat Party on 24 November 2013 – and again on 9 and 22 December – in massive rallies at least as large as those staged by the Red Shirts in 2010 (between 100,000 and 200,000 people) and two to three times as large as anything the People's Alliance for Democracy (PAD) had managed in 2006 and 2008. But for the size of its crowds, however, there was nothing new about the 'People's Committee to Change Thailand into an Absolute Democracy with the King as Head of State' (PCAD) fronted by former Deputy Prime Minister Suthep Thaugsuban.[2] The demand that power be handed over to an unelected 'People's Council', which would hold it for a period long enough to enact vaguely specified 'reforms' promising to 'uproot' the 'Thaksin System',

[2] The movement wants to be called by the international media the 'People's Democratic Reform Committee' (PDRC), but the title used here is a more accurate translation of the Thai original: *Khana Kamma Kan Prachachon Phuea Plian Plaeng Prathet Thai Hai Pen Prachathippatai Thi Sombun An Mi Phra Maha Kasat Pen Pramuk.*

was similar to the PAD's earlier proposal that the country be shut down for a few years in order to 'cleanse dirty things' (see Prachatai, 22 March 2011). The definition provided for the 'Thaksin System', equated to 'the dictatorship of capitalist political parties through the parliamentary system', borrowed rhetoric that had featured in royalist efforts to discredit the electoral and legislative process since the Prime Ministerial Orders issued under Prem Tinsulanond in 1980 and 1982. The PCAD's rallying cry of 'corruption' – rendered emptier than usual by the fact that the movement had coalesced behind one of Thailand's most transactional, unprincipled politicians – echoed the same argument royalists have made to overthrow elected governments since 1947. Also reminiscent of that era was the Democrat Party's implicit claim that the establishment of a 'perfect' or 'absolute' democracy required first and foremost the elimination of opponents they could not defeat at the ballot box – as if their model of a fair fight was still the only election in which the party ever won a majority, held in January 1948 after the military was done with 'uprooting' Pridi Banomyong's influence. Finally, as already noted, the claim that the defence of the constitution – whose honour had been outraged by Pheu Thai's attempt to amend it in parliament – required its suspension to make room for 'good people' to hold power had even deeper historical roots, in the demands made by Prince Boworadet's 'National Salvation Council' in October 1933.

Most revealing of the PCAD's world view and sense of historical mission, however, was the case articulated by its leaders and supporters for the 'lawfulness' of its proposals, as well as the symbolism in which the movement framed its demands. Aside from claiming the right to 'peaceful resistance' under Article 69 of the constitution against the government's alleged attempt to hold power unlawfully – presumably, the administration's illegality stemmed from its refusal to resign once the PCAD had declared it 'null and void' – and aside from citing the duty of all Thais under Article 70 to 'protect Democracy with the King as Head of State', the PCAD asserted its authority to seize the state based on Article 3 of the constitution, which vested sovereign power in 'the people' (see ASTV-Phuchatkan, 1 December 2013). It is important to note that the PCAD made no claim to represent the majority of the population, something that would have been easy enough to verify through an election. As Nidhi (31 December 2013) pointed out, the movement's reference to its supporters as 'the great mass of the people' (*muan maha prachachon*) was meant self-consciously to elevate a minority of 'good' men and women, endowed by their special properties with the right to speak on everyone's behalf, to the role of the country's true demos, in keeping with the hierarchical world view of Thailand's royal nationalism. Of course, the PCAD's right to exercise the sovereignty Article 3 reserved for 'the people' was subject to the endorsement of an even higher power, King Bhumibol, who would be asked to sanction the appointment of an unelected Prime Minister and the establishment of the 'People's Council' under Article 7 of the constitution. In spelling out this argument in support of the PCAD, the official Lawyers Council of Thailand adduced as 'legal' precedent the series of royally endorsed military coups staged since 1932 (see LCT, 16 January 2014) – summoning, yet again, the law of the jungle.

The rejection of individual equality implicit in this reasoning was made rather more explicit in the speeches and public statements of PCAD leaders, who openly argued against 'one person one vote' on the grounds that a few hundred thousand 'quality' votes in Bangkok should trump the 15 million votes 'without quality' cast for Yingluck Shinawatra in 2011 (see Khao Sod, 20 December 2013). Among their supporters, too, this view is widespread – of the hundreds interviewed by the Asia Foundation (2014: 18) at PCAD rallies in late 2013, for instance, 70 per cent agreed with the statement that 'Thais are not ready for equal voting rights'. Indeed, while the label 'fascist' has been applied to several aspects of the movement's agenda, rhetoric, and tactical repertoire, the label best describes the PCAD's outlook on nationhood and democracy – in Mussolini's (2001 [1932]: 85) own words: 'Fascism is opposed to Democracy, which equates the nation to the majority, lowering it to the level of that majority; nevertheless it is the purest form of democracy if the nation is conceived, as it should be, qualitatively and not quantitatively'. The insignia ubiquitous at PCAD rallies sent a similar message. For if the appropriation of Thailand's tricolour flag stood for the notion that 'the great mass of the people', not the electorate, was the truest expression of the nation's will, the whistles its supporters blew in unison to call foul on the administration's purported illegalities signified the PCAD's intention to seize from the electorate the role of arbiter of a government's fitness for office. Rather unambiguously, the movement presented itself as the last stand in defence of Thailand's 'monarchy-centred hierarchical political order' (see Thitinan, 15 February 2013) – or, as this study has characterized it, against the completion of its National Revolution.

Having mobilized a great number of people against the government, the PCAD's numbers were neither large nor sustained enough to topple it outright. For all the talk of 'People's Revolution', then, the game plan was ultimately the same as the PAD's in 2008 – to engineer the conditions of paralysis, chaos, and violence necessary for the military, the courts, and 'independent' agencies to remove the administration. In pursuit of this objective, the PCAD attacked a gathering of some 80,000 Red Shirts on 30 November, resulting in five deaths, and staged daily incursions on government buildings, some of which were temporarily placed under occupation. Refusing to be drawn into a confrontation, the government put up virtually no resistance, allowing the PCAD and its conspicuously armed 'guards' free rein over the city. The situation escalated further when the government dissolved the House of Representatives and scheduled new elections for 2 February 2014, which the Democrat Party proceeded to boycott and the PCAD vowed to stop. For that purpose, the PCAD successfully blocked the registration of candidacies in most of southern Thailand and attacked the candidate registration site in Bangkok, leaving one policeman and one protester dead. Having largely failed in its endeavour to 'shut down Bangkok' from 13 January onwards, the PCAD obstructed advance absentee voting in much of the city on 26 January, forcing the closure of most polling stations, and then disrupted the distribution of ballots in parts of the country, in defiance of restrictions imposed by the government pursuant to the Emergency Decree. On election day, PCAD supporters blocked voting completely in nine southern provinces and partially in nine other provinces in the South and the Central Region, denying over 10 million voters the chance to cast their ballots.

Not surprisingly, the elections failed to bring the situation any closer to a resolution. The protesters, for their part, remained far from achieving their goals. The military continued to provide covert material support and overt expressions of sympathy, warning the government against dispersing the demonstrations, but the generals baulked at the demands for a coup. The Constitutional Court offered legal cover to the PCAD and the Democrat Party, finding their attempt to overthrow the government consistent with 'Democracy with the King as Head of State', but the justices declined to order the election's postponement. The Election Commission did nothing to prevent the disruption of the candidate registration process, but its members were ultimately compelled to organize the polls. As the international media, moreover, took to reporting with some insistence on the PCAD's hateful rhetoric and anti-democratic agenda, the scenes of armed guards blocking voters from accessing polling stations, or shooting their assault rifles into crowds of pro-election protesters, earned the movement few new supporters. Stretched thin over several locations in Bangkok, PCAD rallies often came under attack by unknown assailants firing pistols and grenades – in total, similar attacks staged in Bangkok and Trat caused the death of a dozen people, some of them children. The rallies, in turn, visibly shrank in size, down to just a few thousands on most evenings, leaving the movement to be increasingly defined by the thuggish behaviour of the armed men in its midst. In recognition of the public's growing impatience with the PCAD's 6-week occupation of several major intersections in central Bangkok, by then mostly deserted, at the end of February, Suthep Thaugsuban announced the end of the 'Bangkok Shutdown' and the rallies' consolidation in a single location in Lumphini Park.

The elections, however, also failed to provide the government with the desired boost. While Pheu Thai is estimated to have received at least 10 million votes, lack of campaigning, absence of competition, fear of violence, and declining confidence in the administration caused turnout to sink below 50 per cent. Worse, the fact that races could not be organized in twenty-eight constituencies ensured that parliament would remain shuttered in the absence of a quorum – possibly for months on end, given the Election Commission's determination to delay the by-elections required to fill vacant seats – leaving the administration in place in a limited, caretaker capacity. The impasse grew more intractable after the Constitutional Court declared the election null and void, citing the fact that the voting could not be completed in one day, because the ensuing dispute between the government and the Election Commission prevented the issuance of the Royal Decree required to set a new election day. Most dangerous to the government, from a public relations standpoint, were the restrictions that its caretaker status placed on its authority to dispose of funds appropriated in the 2014 budget, which were needed to pay thousands of rice farmers amounts owed to them under a controversial subsidy scheme. When it was announced that the administration had secured a THB 5 billion emergency loan from the Government Savings Bank for a small portion of the payments, PCAD supporters rushed to withdraw their deposits, compelling the loan's cancellation and the resignation of the bank's chief executive officer (see *Bangkok Post*, 20 February 2014).[3]

Left stranded in a political no-man's land – at once constitutionally limited in the exercise of its powers and prevented from organizing the election of a new government – Yingluck Shinawatra's embattled administration was left vulnerable to the coordinated assault mounted by the PCAD, the courts, and 'independent' agencies. Just as the police moved to reclaim some of the areas occupied by the PCAD, coming under heavy fire from the professional gunmen in its ranks – one such incident on 18 February left two policemen and four protesters dead – the Civil Court not only issued an injunction against any attempt to disperse the

[3] It goes without saying that the military junta, established months later, had not the slightest trouble securing the funds needed to make the outstanding payments. Now that the suspension of the constitution had removed all restrictions to the executive's power, the generals were eager to receive the 'gratitude' of the aggrieved farmers (see *The Nation*, 25 May 2014).

rallies, citing a weeks'-old finding by the Constitutional Court that the PCAD had demonstrated 'peacefully and without weapons', but also prohibited the government from doing anything to prevent or stop the occupation of roads and buildings (see Khao Sod, 19 February 2014). Meanwhile, the noose around the administration's neck continued to tighten in preparation for a possible judicial coup. Having already issued a ruling that established a prima facie case for the impeachment of over 300 legislators, whose 'crime' had been to vote in favour of a fully elected Senate, the National Anti-Corruption Commission (NACC) agreed to fast-track an investigation that might lead to the Prime Minister's own impeachment. Yingluck was accused of dereliction of duty over the government's failure to address the corruption alleged to have plagued the rice subsidy scheme, despite the fact that no episode of corruption had been established in court. Seizing upon a ruling by the Supreme Administrative Court, which had recently ordered the reinstatement of royalist civil servant Thawil Pliensri as Secretary General of the National Security Council, the Constitutional Court also agreed to examine the implications that the reversal of his 2011 transfer had for the entire cabinet's fitness to remain in office.

The hammer fell on 7 May 2014, when the Constitutional Court dismissed Yingluck Shinawatra from office as well as nine other ministers and deputy ministers who had been members of the executive at the time of Thawil's transfer. The Constitutional Court found that the transfer had constituted an abuse of power, rendered more egregious by the suspicion that the measure had formed part of a broader scheme to manoeuvre Yingluck's former brother-in-law into the position of National Police Chief.[4] The next day, the NACC also referred Yingluck for impeachment by the Senate.

After all this, however, the achievement of the PCAD's objectives remained elusive. Contrary to the expectations of some, the Constitutional Court found no grounds to remove the remaining twenty-four members of the caretaker government, while the NACC similarly declined to recommend the impeachment of the entire cabinet. The combined result of the two decisions, therefore, was to deny the PCAD the constitutional crisis it hoped would pave the way for the application of Article 7 of the constitution and the establishment of its 'People's Council'. What hopes the PCAD still had to overthrow the government,

[4] To date, the courts have raised no similar objection to the fact that the country's new military dictator, as Commander-in-Chief of the Army, managed to have his brother General Preecha Chan-ocha appointed Commander of the Third Army Region, to say nothing of the dozens of officials General Prayuth's junta has transferred to inactive posts since seizing power.

now led by Niwatthamrong Boonsongpaisan, were pinned on the half-appointed Senate, whose new Acting President was asked to act in lieu of the House of Representatives to select a new government. It only took days, however, for this option to also prove impracticable. Having reopened briefly to complete a narrow agenda following the election of a new batch of Senators, the upper house ended its extraordinary session on 10 May without taking up the PCAD's demands. Perhaps more than the time at their disposal, the main obstacle faced by the PCAD's supporters in the Senate was the fact that Article 7 required that Thailand be in a situation to which no provision of the constitution was applicable before royalists could claim to have carte blanche to decide the matter as they wished, ostensibly 'in accordance with the constitutional practice of Democracy with the King as the Head of State'. For the present circumstances, however, the constitution contained applicable provisions that unambiguously pointed to an election as the solution. Barring a military coup, an option that remained as fraught and unattractive as ever, the PCAD had lost.

When General Prayuth Chan-ocha appeared on television in the early morning of 20 May 2014, unilaterally to announce the imposition of martial law throughout the country, it was not immediately clear what his intent was. Having previously resisted the pressure applied on him to stage a coup, even at the height of the violence around the February election, it was not unreasonable to wonder whether the general had intervened to provide Suthep Thaugsuban an opportunity to make a graceful exit before the time came to admit defeat and turn himself in, as he had promised to do if 'victory' had not been achieved by 26 May. It was perhaps for this reason that Red Shirt leaders ordered their supporters, assembled on the other side of the Chao Phraya River since the previous weekend, to take no action. Even the fact that Prayuth had declared martial law in violation of the constitution – Article 188 only gave the King, whose assent had not been sought, the authority to 'declare and lift martial law' nationwide – went almost unnoticed. The truth would only emerge on the second day of the 'negotiations' in which representatives of the government, the United Front for Democracy against Dictatorship (UDD), the Democrat Party, and the PCAD agreed to participate under the military's auspices, which came down to an attempt by the military to strong-arm the caretaker administration into submitting to the PCAD's demands. Having failed to do so, General Prayuth placed all attendees under arrest and took charge of the country's administration. Once again, 'order' would be restored – courtesy of the law of the jungle – in accordance with the designs of those responsible for the disorder.

As this book goes into production, less than 1 month into Thailand's new season of military dictatorship, it remains too early to tell exactly what General Prayuth's 'National Council for Peace and Order' (NCPO) will ultimately seek to accomplish. What has happened since the coup, however, offers little indication that the generals have learned much from the last century of Thailand's political development. Aside from appropriating the PCAD's rhetoric lock, stock, and barrel – among other things, blaming the country's troubles on the failure of representative democracy ('parliamentary dictatorship') to assure the requisite levels of 'happiness', peace, morality, and reverence for the monarchy – the junta has filled key positions with hardliners such as retired generals Anupong Paochinda and Prawit Wongsuwan, long reported to have been behind the PCAD in the first place (see Szep and Lefevre, 13 December 2013). Its campaign of censorship, arbitrary detentions, searches, and seizures has focused almost entirely on disrupting the Red Shirts' leadership, media, and organizational structure in the provinces, as well as on silencing independent journalists, activists, and academics critical of the establishment. Meanwhile, the NCPO is conducting a wholesale purge of the police and the civil service, one that aims to root out officials deemed to have cooperated too eagerly with the previous government. When, or on what conditions, the country will be returned to civilian rule remains uncertain – what reform measures have been announced or floated in the press suggest that the NCPO plans to do so only once it is satisfied than no civilian government will be in a position to challenge a revitalized royalist order.

In this endeavour, there is no reason to believe that the NCPO will be any more successful than the men who headlined royalist coups in 1971, 1976, 1991, and 2006. For the time being, General Prayuth appears to have consolidated the junta's control of the state, no part of which has put up any resistance against its illegal takeover. Having effectively immobilized the Red Shirts' opposition, moreover, the NCPO enjoys the same benefit of the doubt that the urban middle class has historically extended to military regimes that promised to 'restore order', not to mention the enthusiastic support of those – drawn primarily from the Democrat Party's support base in Bangkok and the South – who have come to believe that drastic measures are required conclusively to deal with Thaksin Shinawatra and his allies. General Prayuth, however, will be presented with a likely insoluble dilemma much sooner than his plan to teach the nation's schoolchildren greater 'love of [the] establishment' (see ThaiPBS, 13 June 2014) has a chance to bear fruit. On the one hand, the prosecution of the PCAD's agenda to 'eradicate' the so-called 'Thaksin System' without facing mass opposition probably requires levels of repression harsh and sustained enough eventually to compromise middle-class support, aggravate divisions known to exist within the palace and the military, and send the junta's allies and enablers scrambling for the exits. On the other hand, relaxing repression is almost guaranteed to lead to a new round of mass protests, of the kind that will force the military either to reverse course or crack down violently, probably to no greater avail than the crackdowns staged in 1973, 1976, 1992, and 2010. In the likely event that the armed forces either lack the stomach or the cohesiveness to follow through with uprooting the 'Thaksin System', or are forced to relent upon facing mounting opposition, the conservative restoration will fail just as miserably as previous attempts made under Thanom (1971–3), Thanin (1976–7), Suchinda (1991–2), and Sonthi/Surayud (2006–7).

Either way, it is difficult to envision a scenario in which the current suspension of electoral democracy extends the life of Thailand's fading royalist order by more than a few years. Indeed, while the PCAD's selective outrage over the 'corruption' of (some) elected politicians had, at least for a time, successfully shifted the terms of the debate, the removal of another government chosen by the voters is bound eventually to return the spotlight onto Thailand's real problems: an unaccountable monarchy, a bloated military not subject to civilian control, a system of justice that works as the extension of the will of a privileged elite, a conception of the 'rule of law' founded on the principle that 'good people' can do exactly what they want, an array of repressive legislation that stifles debate over some of the most pressing questions surrounding the country's future, an education system that rewards conformity over independent thought, endemic inequalities in income, opportunity, and treatment under the law, and an official ideology that still denies the majority of the population an equal political role. While the Red Shirt movement, moreover, has thus far been prevented from mobilizing in opposition to the coup, it is unlikely that provincial voters will take kindly to measures designed to deny them a chance freely to choose their own governments – justified on the usual grounds that they are not 'educated' or 'Thai' enough to be trusted with the responsibility – no matter how much re-education or populism (see *Bloomberg News*, 12 June 2014) is directed at them. Even if the military eventually agrees to impose the unprecedented levels of repression required to 'uproot' a political force that has won every election held in the past 15 years, when the dust settles, the demands for individual equality that made Thaksin Shinawatra successful in the first place will not only still be there, but can also be expected to grow as a result of further economic development. As noted, modernization threatens the status quo far more severely than Thaksin or the Red Shirts ever did. Unless the NCPO is willing (and able) to set up a regime along the lines of Burma's old military dictatorship, it will not be long before the Bangkok establishment is confronted with much the same challenge.

The reality is that the political instability Thailand has experienced since 2006, which has been extreme even by its own standards, is rooted in the simple fact that the country's royalist order has all but lost the authority it once had to exercise power without force. If royalists were still able to steer the course of events behind the scenes, through the network monarchy's vaunted 'invisible hand', they would not have relied on censorship, *lèse majesté*, street violence, military firepower, and outlandish court rulings as heavily or as frequently as they have over the past 8 years, at the cost of seeing their authority decline even further. More than a sign of confidence and strength, the repressive measures through which the NCPO has sought to suppress even the most isolated expressions of public opposition to the coup – the likes of which Thailand has not seen in the wake of military coups dating back to 1976 – reflects an awareness that the situation could rapidly spiral out of its control, given the breakdown in the cultural hegemony that had once allowed royalists to minimize their recourse to legal and physical coercion. In 2014, no one harboured any illusions that the ideological and symbolic arsenal deployed in 2006 would prove nearly as effective in forestalling immediate mass resistance.

The monarchy, upon which the tenuous legitimacy of the country's hierarchical order rests, has sustained the most damage on this count, because the constant invocation of the need to 'protect the institution' in the service of conspicuous anti-democratic measures has weathered down its once glistening façade. Having long been described as a 'stabilizing influence', it has become increasingly clear, in Thailand and abroad, that the monarchy bears a large share of the responsibility for the country's failure to consolidate a functioning democracy – an assessment rendered all the more widespread by the crackdown on freedom of expression undertaken in recent years in a vain quest to shield the institution from the ensuing surge of scrutiny and criticism. As the Ninth Reign has slowly been coming to a close, the Thai monarchy has grown to resemble the white elephant that has long served as one of its symbols – an institution that combines a lack of clear practical purpose with exorbitant costs of protection and maintenance, as measured in blood, treasure, and individual freedoms.

In these circumstances, it is notable that the monarchy's endorsement of the 2014 coup only came several days after the fact, in the form of a

Royal Command released to the public without the King's handwritten signature. Judging by his recent public appearances, King Bhumibol may be in no condition to approve or disapprove of the coup, but he was well enough to sign a document or take part in a photo opportunity with General Prayuth. Whether it was decided by Prayuth himself, or at the insistence of the King's handlers, the minimization of the monarchy's involvement in the process signals nervousness about the possibility that the institution might risk signing its own death sentence by providing unambiguous support to another act staged in defiance of the law and the will of the electorate. In turn, the monarchy's diminished standing and the desultory character of its endorsement introduce an additional element of vulnerability for the NCPO, on top of the recalcitrance of much of the public, the presence of an organized (if, for the time being, dormant) opposition, the disapproval of the international community, the precariousness of the economic situation, and the dubious sustainability of current levels of repression.

Beyond the NCPO's likely failure to force the good people of Thailand permanently to relinquish the right to choose their own governments, the succession of King Bhumibol – however traumatic and contentious it may turn out to be – will offer the country its best chance yet to build a stable democratic regime. Indeed, the fact that the monarchy's authority was allowed, over decades, to grow ever more dependent on one man's charisma and popularity promises to consign what legitimacy Thailand's hierarchical order still commands to the same funeral pyre in which the remains of its longest-serving monarch will turn to ashes. At that point, there will be no one left in Thailand under whose 'royal feet' enough people will still 'wish to be enslaved for all eternity' – as recited in a vow of submission royalists can still be heard making to King Bhumibol.[5] Whether or not the excuse of 'protecting the monarchy' is still serviceable, it goes without saying that the military will continue to resist any attempt made by civilian authorities to rationalize its internal organization, reduce the incongruous number of generals within its ranks, slash its resources to a level commensurate with Thailand's external threats, or relieve it of the domestic role that has been the source of so much wealth and power. Even so, as the monarchy's protection ceases to provide a workable justification for authoritarian reversals, and as the potential for military interventions to backfire continues to rise as a result, the generals' propensity for

[5] There are several variants of the expression, brought to the author's attention by a Thai academic who shall remain unnamed. One such variant is *kho pen kha tai fa phrabat thuk chat pai* – literally, 'I wish to be a serf under the royal feet for all future rebirths.'

hedging their bets in defence of personal and corporate interests will facilitate the management of the threat presented by the armed forces, if not their immediate subjection to civilian control.

Even in the event that it ushers in the military's lasting confinement to barracks, the demise of Thailand's royalist order will not suffice to bring about a 'real', liberal democracy: a system of government where the majority rules, through elected representatives, without trampling on the rights of minorities. The illiberalism of Thaksin Shinawatra's tenure in office, in particular, raises serious concerns about the prospective revival of similar forms of plebiscitarian rule, all the more so given the state of the opposition. Openly contemptuous of the electoral process, the Democrat Party has continued to ignore calls for internal reforms, increasingly pinning its ambitions of power on the military and the courts. On this point, however, it is worth underscoring that there is nothing natural or permanent about Thaksin Shinawatra's electoral dominance. The said dominance is only assured as long as one side appeals to the majority of the voters and the other considers itself above doing so, or as long as elections can be framed as a choice between 'popular' and 'elite' forms of 'democracy'. Should royalists find it in themselves to disavow an idea of the nation founded on hierarchies of superior and inferior beings, give up on defining for everyone else what it means to be 'Thai', and embrace a process of reform aiming to chart a pluralistic future, as opposed to preventing one from being born, they would not only provide the country with the benefit of a viable constitutional opposition, a real choice between two plausible governing alternatives, and a liberal counterweight against Thaksin and his allies; they would also give those in the Red Shirt movement whose concerns transcend Thaksin's restoration a partner with whom to work towards the founding of a system of government, the first of its kind in Thailand, that combines majority rule with the respect of minority rights.

Thailand's long journey to the development of a consolidated democracy may feature yet more twists, turns, and tragedies. What can be said with some certainty is that the only promise of stability is held by the establishment of a political regime that grants demands for full political inclusion, individual equality, and a form of 'democracy' stripped of the qualifiers that have long stood for limitations to the authority vested in the people and their elected representatives. Indeed, no illusion of exceptionalism can change the fact that Thailand's royalists have now arrived at the same crossroads before which Western European conservatives stood around a century ago, at the conclusion of their own countries' National Revolutions. The sooner they reconcile themselves to the constitutional role King Prajadhipok was forced to accept, at the barrel of a gun, on 24 June 1932, the better the chances that the completion of Thailand's unfinished National Revolution will not entail the birth of a new republic. Monarchies with a longer 'history' than Thailand's, after all, were doomed by the obstinacy with which their supporters stood in the way. Having spent the Ninth Reign lecturing ordinary people to renounce earthly ambitions for the sake of national unity, the onus is now on royalists to demonstrate their commitment to king and country, by way of pledging some of their own vanities to the bonfire.

Bibliography

NEWS ARTICLES

1932. 'The New Siam: The King Signs the New Constitution', *Bangkok Times Weekly Mail*, 28 June.

1932. 'The New Regime: Committee of Defence', *Bangkok Times Weekly Mail*, 3 August.

1932. 'The New Regime in Siam: The Princes' Fall from Power', *Bangkok Times Weekly Mail*, 29 August.

1932. 'The People's Association', *Bangkok Times Weekly Mail*, 30 August.

1932. 'Bangkok's First Trade Union', *Bangkok Times Weekly Mail*, 25 October.

1933. 'A New Association', *Bangkok Times Weekly Mail*, 9 January.

1933. 'People's Assembly Dissolved: Appointment of New State Council', *Bangkok Times Weekly Mail*, 3 April.

1933. 'Luang Pradit's Scheme: An Official Statement', *Bangkok Times Weekly Mail*, 13 April.

1933. 'The People's Association', *Bangkok Times Weekly Mail*, 22 April.

1933. 'The New Revolution in Siam: The Men Concerned', *Bangkok Times Weekly Mail*, 21 June.

1933. 'The New Order: The King to the Assembly', *Bangkok Times Weekly Mail*, 6 July.

1933. 'Luang Pradit on His Way Back', *Bangkok Times Weekly Mail*, 1 September.

1933. 'The Situation: Translations of Official Communiqués', *Bangkok Times Weekly Mail*, 17 October.

1934. 'Siam To-Day: Luang Bipul's [sic] Broadcast', *Bangkok Times Weekly Mail*, 30 June.

1934. 'Siam To-Day: These Last Two Years', *Bangkok Times Weekly Mail*, 6 July.

1934. 'Siam To-Day: What the Constitutional Government Has Done', *Bangkok Times Weekly Mail*, 7 July.

1934. 'The Assembly: The Inheritance Tax Act', *Bangkok Times Weekly Mail*, 6 August.

1934. 'The Assembly: An Important Meeting', *Bangkok Times Weekly Mail*, 29 September.

1934. 'Constitution Day', *Bangkok Times Weekly Mail*, 15 December.

1935. 'The Assembly: Yesterday's Debate', *Bangkok Times Weekly Mail*, 25 January.

1936. 'Siam's Administration To-Day: A Sturdy Viewpoint', *Bangkok Times Weekly Mail*, 16 June.
1936. 'The New Siam: Luang Bipul's [sic] Broadcast', *Bangkok Times Weekly Mail*, 25 June.
1939. 'The Land of the Thai: The Proper Name', *Bangkok Times Weekly Mail*, 29 May.
1940. 'A New Year Address by the Premier', *Bangkok Times Weekly Mail*, 2 April.
1940. 'Premier Addresses the Thai Nation', *Bangkok Times Weekly Mail*, 21 October.
1941. 'Terms of Truce Agreement', *Bangkok Times Weekly Mail*, 3 February.
1941. 'The National Assembly: Press Act Passed', *Bangkok Times Weekly Mail*, 12 September.
1941. 'The National Assembly: Unemployment Bill Discussed', *Bangkok Times Weekly Mail*, 17 September.
1946. 'Sahacheep Gets 28, Constitution Front Gets 29 of 75 Seats', *Bangkok Post*, 9 August.
1947. 'Democrat Party Leaders Will Not Join Any Coalition Government', *Bangkok Post*, 29 January.
1947. 'Ex Premier Ready for Comeback', *Bangkok Post*, 22 March.
1947. 'November 8 Coup D'État Identifies 1947 as Year of Counter Revolution', *Bangkok Post*, 31 December.
1948. 'Campaign for Phibun Speeds Up', *Bangkok Post*, 5 February.
1948. 'MPs Beleaguer Phibun on Khuang Resignation', *Bangkok Post*, 21 April.
1949. '2 MPs Cause Commotion During Vote', *Bangkok Post*, 28 January.
1949. 'MP Majority Shows Up at Phibun Rally', *Bangkok Post*, 22 June.
1950. 'Democrats to Call General Debate: Assistance Pledged by Other MPs', *Bangkok Post*, 12 January.
1950. 'Democrat Chiefs Oppose Foreign Policy Debate', *Bangkok Post*, 14 January.
1950. 'New Party Formed to Back Gov't', *Bangkok Post*, 23 January.
1950. 'Democrats Delay Action on General Debate', *Bangkok Post*, 2 June.
1951. 'Democrat Boycott Declared', *Bangkok Post*, 29 December.
1952. 'Opposition Northeasteners Ready to Join General Sarit', *Bangkok Post*, 1 September.
1952. 'Sarit Outlines Developments for Northeast', *Bangkok Post*, 26 September.
1952. 'Gov't Party Organizing', *Bangkok Post*, 30 October.
1953. 'Opposition MPs Give Up Fight', *Bangkok Post*, 13 January.
1953. 'Pro-Gov't MPs' Rules Arranged', *Bangkok Post*, 8 July.
1956. 'Pibul Wins Party Vote 50–32 – But 32 Walk Out', *Bangkok Post*, 21 January.
1956. 'Special Pay to Pro-Gov't MPs Halted', *Bangkok Post*, 24 January.
1956. 'S.-M. Party Unanimously Backs Pibul', *Bangkok Post*, 25 January.
1956. 'Labour Board Planned Here', *Bangkok Post*, 18 June.
1956. 'Regulations "to Protect All Sides" ', *Bangkok Post*, 21 August.
1956. 'New Labour Decrees Approved by Cabinet', *Bangkok Post*, 13 December.
1957. '"Thai People Never Will Go Red" – Pibul', *Bangkok Post*, 5 February.

1957. 'Sarit "Will Try to Help N.E."', *Bangkok Post*, 13 April.
1957. 'Democrats, Sahabhum Raise Questions of King and Constitution in Interviews', *Bangkok Post*, 7 July.
1992. 'Chronology of Events', *The Nation*, 20 May.
2005. 'The Truth About Thaksin, Sondhi', *The Nation*, 29 November.
2006. 'Military "Must Back King"', *The Nation*, 15 July.
2006. 'Coup as It Unfolds', *The Nation*, 21 September.
2007. 'Royal Wealth', *Asia Sentinel*, 1 March.
2008. '"War on Drugs" Probe Draws a Blank', *The Nation*, 16 January.
2008. 'Democrat Govt's Shotgun Wedding?' *The Nation*, 10 December.
2008. 'Masters of the Game', *The Nation*, 29 December.
2009. 'Court Clears Security Officials over Tak Bai Deaths', *The Nation*, 30 May.
2009. 'Read All about It – It's a "Civil War"', *Bangkok Post*, 29 December.
2010. 'T(h)aksin?', *Prachatai*, 2 January.
2011. 'Yon Roi Truat Sop Khanaen Luektang So.So. Baeb Sat Suan Muea 23 Thanwakhom 2550 (Yaek Rai Changwat)', *Nation News Agency (NNA)*, 2 March.
2011. 'Sondhi Calls for Thailand's Closure for 3–5 Years to "Cleanse Dirty Things"', *Prachatai*, 22 March.
2011. 'Abhisit Strongly Chided by Chumpol', *Bangkok Post*, 9 June.
2011. 'Gen. Prayuth Urges Voters to Back the "Good People"', *Bangkok Post*, 15 June.
2011. 'Discussing Lèse Majesté Law', *Prachatai*, 28 June.
2011. 'Akeyuth Anchanbutr Curses Northern Women, Slams Yingluck', *Prachatai*, 6 November.
2012. 'Sondhi Gets 85 Years over Business Fraud', *The Nation*, 29 February.
2013. 'Wasan Soipisut Kham to Kham San Ratthathammanun Phalat', *Matichon*, 16 March.
2013. 'Thongchai: Thai-Style History Education Makes Thais Ignorant and Narcissistic', *Prachatai*, 22 July.
2013. 'Court Acquits Policeman Accused of Launching RPG Attacks', *Khao Sod English*, 9 August.
2013. 'Group of 40 Senators Denies Gov't Ouster Plot', *The Nation*, 21 September.
2013. '"Suthep" Thalaeng Ko.Po.Po.So. Prakat Chettana Lang Rabop Thaksin – Pithak Ratthathammanun – Sang 2 Thanwakhom Yut Ratchakan', *ASTV-Phuchatkan*, 1 December.
2013. '2 Siang "Sombat-Seri" Kap 1 Siang Khong Khon Thai', *Khao Sod*, 20 December.
2014. 'Court Strips Gov't of Various Emergency Powers', *Khao Sod English*, 19 February.
2014. 'GSB Staff Expel Board Director', *Bangkok Post*, 20 February.
2014. 'Rice Payments Tomorrow', *The Nation*, 25 May.
2014. 'Thai Army Adopts Thaksin-Style Populist Steps to Spur Growth', *Bloomberg News*, 12 June.
2014. 'Military Junta to Revise School Curricula to Stimulate Greater Patriotism and Love of Establishment', *ThaiPBS*, 13 June.

Anderson, Benedict 2011. 'Outsider View of Thai Politics', *Prachatai*, 5 August.

Achara Ashayagachat, 2011. 'Abhisit's Populist Promises Falling on Deaf Ears', *Bangkok Post*, 16 January.

AHRC (Asian Human Rights Commission) 2007. 'UPDATE (Thailand): General Responsible for Killings Not Prosecuted but Reinstated', AHRC Update on Urgent Appeal, 11 May. Accessed on 20 August 2013 at: www.humanrights.asia/news/urgent-appeals/UP-069-2007

2007. 'THAILAND: A Long Road Back to Human Rights and the Rule of Law', *AHRC Document AS-196-2007*, 20 August. Accessed on 20 August 2013 at: www.humanrights.asia/news/ahrc-news/AS-196-2007

Carsten, Paul and Pairat Temphairojana 2013. 'Thailand's Boom: To the Northeast, the Spoils', *Reuters*, 16 June.

Chang Noi (pseud.) 2002. 'Understanding Thaksin's Pluto-Populism', *The Nation*, 18 February.

2008. 'The Facts about Vote-Buying and Patronage', *The Nation*, 1 September.

2008. 'When the Beauty of Democracy is not so Beautiful', *The Nation*, 22 December.

2010. 'Witness the Death of Deference', *The Nation*, 22 March.

2010. 'Whatever Happened to the Gold-Legged Frog?' *The Nation*, 19 April.

Connors, Michael K. 2008. 'Thailand's "New Politics' Charade", *Asia Sentinel*, 7 July. Accessed on 20 August 2013 at: www.asiasentinel.com/opinion/thailands-new-politics-charade

Crispin, Shawn W. 2007. 'Recollections, Revelations of a Protest Leader', *Asia Times*, 27 April. Accessed on 20 August 2013 at: www.atimes.com/atimes/Southeast_Asia/ID27Ae01.html

Horn, Robert 2010. 'Thai Ruling Party Keeps Power – For Now', *Time*, 29 November.

Lintner, Bertil 2009. 'The Real Thai Crisis: A Conflict Between Old Money and New Money', *Wall Street Journal Asia*, 15 April.

McCargo, Duncan 2013. 'The Last Gasp of Thai Paternalism', *New York Times*, 19 December.

Nidhi Eoseewong 2013. 'The Great Mass of the People', *Prachatai*, 31 December.

Paisarn Likhitpreechakul 2011. 'Karma Confusion and the Theology of Thai Exceptionalism', *The Nation*, 16 July.

Pasuk Phongpaichit and Chris Baker 2013. 'Vote-Buying Claims Nothing but Dangerous Nonsense', *Bangkok Post*, 6 December.

Praphon Angsukasikorn 1947. 'Dramatic Political Story Behind November Coup', *Bangkok Post*, 31 December.

Schiller, Bill 2011. 'King's Failing Health, and his $30B Fortune, Puts Thailand in Jeopardy', *Toronto Star*, 3 August.

Seaton, Jaimie and George Wehrfritz 2008. 'All Politics isn't Local: The Real Enemy of Demonstrators Threatening to Shut Down the Country is Globalization', *Newsweek*, 6 September.

Shah, Angilee 2006. 'Transcript: Interview with Sondhi Limthongkul', *Asia-Media*, 22 November. Accessed on 20 August 2013 at: http://archive-edu.com/page/660303/2012-11-14/ http://www.asiamedia.ucla.edu/article.asp?parentid=58318

Sopranzetti, Claudio 2011. 'Abhisit's Gift', *New Mandala*, 7 February. Accessed on 20 August 2013 at: asiapacific.anu.edu.au/newmandala/2011/02/07/abhisits-gift

Streckfuss, David 2010. 'The Spring of Thailand's Ethnic Discontent', *Wall Street Journal*, 24 May.

Szep, Jason and Amy Sawitta Lefevre 2013. 'Powerful Forces Revealed Behind Thai Protest Movement', *Reuters*, 13 December.

Thitinan Pongsudhirak 2013. 'Thailand's Stalemate and Uneasy Accommodation', *Bangkok Post*, 15 February.

Walker, Andrew 2007. 'Sufficiency Makeover', *New Mandala*, 15 February. Accessed on 20 August 2013 at: asiapacific.anu.edu.au/newmandala/2007/02/15

PRIMARY SOURCES AND DOCUMENTS

Adams, John 1851 [1777]. 'Novanglus Papers, No. 7', in Charles Francis Adams (ed.), *The Works of John Adams, Vol. 4*. Boston: Charles C. Little and James Brown.

Arvizu, Alexander A. 2006. 'DAS John Meeting with Human Rights Watch', *US Embassy Cable 06BANGKOK7447*, 15 December.

Assembly of the People's Representatives 1935. 'Rai Ngan Kan Prachum Lap Sapha Phu Thaen Ratsadon Khrang Thi 16/2477, 31 Mokkarakhom 2477', in *Thalaengkan Rueang Phrabat Somdet Phra Poramintharamaha Prajadhipok Phra Pokklao Chao Yu Hua Song Sala Ratcha Sombat*. Bangkok: Rong Phim Prajant.

Bhumibol Adulyadej 1957. 'Prakat Phra Borommaratcha Ongkan Tang Phu Raksa Phra Nakhon Fai Thahan', 16 September.

1974. 'Phra Barommaratcha Owat Nai Phithi Phraratchathan Parinyabat Khong Mahawitthayalai Kasetsart Na Hong Prachum Mahawitthayalai Kasetsart, Wan Pharuehat Thi 18 Karakadakhom 2517', 18 July.

1977 [1976]. 'Phra Ratcha Damrat Phraratchathan Nai Phithi Phraratchathan Thong Pracham Run Luk Suea Chao Ban Changwat Chonburi Na Rong Rian Atsasamchan Sriracha Changwat Chonburi Wan Phut Thi 9 Phruetsachikayon Pho.So. 2519', in Office of His Majesty's Principal Private Secretary, *Pramuan Phra Ratcha Damrat Lae Phra Barommaratcha Owat Thi Phraratchathan Nai Okat Tang Tang Pi Pho.So. 2519*. Bangkok: Krom Phaenthi Thahan.

1977 [1976]. 'Phra Ratcha Damrat Phraratchathan Nai Phithi Pradap Yot Nai Thahan Chan Nai Phon Na Phra Thi Nang Boromphiman Wan Angkhan Thi 14 Thanwakhom 2519', in Office of His Majesty's Principal Private Secretary, *Pramuan Phra Ratcha Damrat Lae Phra Barommaratcha Owat Thi Phraratchathan Nai Okat Tang Tang Pi Pho.So. 2519*. Bangkok: Krom Phaenthi Thahan.

1977 [1976]. 'Phra Ratcha Damrat Phraratchathan Kae Prachachon Chao Thai Nai Okat Wan Khuen Pi Mai Wan Suk Thi 31 Thanwakhom 2519', in Office of His Majesty's Principal Private Secretary, *Pramuan Phra Ratcha Damrat Lae Phra Barommaratcha Owat Thi Phraratchathan Nai Okat Tang Tang Pi Pho.So. 2519*. Bangkok: Krom Phaenthi Thahan.

1979 [1974]. 'Royal Speech Given to Representatives of Associations, Religious Organizations, Teachers, Students from Schools, Colleges and Universities on the Occasion of the Royal Birthday Anniversary at the Dusidalai Hall, Chitralada Villa, Dusit Palace, on Wednesday, 4 December 1974', in Royal Speech [sic] *Given to the Audience of Well Wishers on the Occasion of the Royal Birthday Anniversary at the Dusidalai Hall, Chitralada Villa, Dusit Palace, on 4 December 1974, 1975, 1976, 1977, 1978*. Bangkok: Amarin.

1979 [1975]. 'Royal Speech Given to the Audience of Well Wishers on the Occasion of the Royal Birthday Anniversary at the Dusidalai Hall, Chitralada Villa, Dusit Palace, on Thursday, 4 December 1975', in Royal Speech [sic] *Given to the Audience of Well Wishers on the Occasion of the Royal Birthday Anniversary at the Dusidalai Hall, Chitralada Villa, Dusit Palace, on 4 December 1974, 1975, 1976, 1977, 1978*. Bangkok: Amarin.

1979 [1976]. 'Royal Speech Given to the Audience of Well Wishers on the Occasion of the Royal Birthday Anniversary at the Dusidalai Hall, Chitralada Villa, Dusit Palace, on Saturday, 4 December 1976', in Royal Speech [sic] *Given to the Audience of Well Wishers on the Occasion of the Royal Birthday Anniversary at the Dusidalai Hall, Chitralada Villa, Dusit Palace, on 4 December 1974, 1975, 1976, 1977, 1978*. Bangkok: Amarin.

1979 [1977]. 'Royal Speech Given to the Audience of Well Wishers on the Occasion of the Royal Birthday Anniversary at the Dusidalai Hall, Chitralada Villa, Dusit Palace, on Sunday, 4 December 1977', in Royal Speech [sic] *Given to the Audience of Well Wishers on the Occasion of the Royal Birthday Anniversary at the Dusidalai Hall, Chitralada Villa, Dusit Palace, on 4 December 1974, 1975, 1976, 1977, 1978*. Bangkok: Amarin.

1992. 'Phra Ratcha Damrat Nai Okat Thi Nai Sanya Thammasak Prathan Ongkhomnatri Lae Phon-Ek Prem Tinsulanond Ongkhomnatri Nam Phon-Ek Suchinda Kraprayoon Lae Phon-Tri Chamlong Srimuang Fao Thun La Ong Thuli Phrabat Na Phratamnak Chitrlada Rahothan, Wan Phut Thi 20 Phruetsaphakhom 2535 Wela 21:30 Nalika', 20 May.

2002. 'Phra Ratcha Damrat Phraratchathan Kae Khana Bukkhon Tang Tang Thi Khao Fao Thuai Phraphon Chai Mongkhon Nai Okat Wan Chaloem Phrachonmaphansa Na Sala Dusidalai Suan Chitralada Wan Phut Thi 4 Thanwakhom 2545', 4 December.

2003. 'Phra Ratcha Damrat Phraratchathan Kae Khana Bukkhon Tang Tang Thi Khao Fao Thuai Phraphon Chai Mongkhon Nai Okat Wan Chaloem Phrachonmaphansa Na Sala Dusidalai Suan Chitralada Wan Pharuehat Thi 4 Thanwakhom 2546', 4 December.

Boyce, Ralph L. 2005. 'Thailand: Queen Calls for Unity and Vigilance in the Face of Continuing Southern Violence', *US Embassy Cable 05BANGKOK2837*, 26 April.

2005. 'The King and Him; The Opposition Plays Their King against the Prime Minister', *US Embassy Cable 05BANGKOK7197_a*, 18 November.

2006. 'What's Thaksin Up To?' *US Embassy Cable 06BANGKOK3916*, 3 July.

2006. 'Thai Officials Plea for Understanding', *US Embassy Cable 06BANGKOK5929*, 26 September.

2006. 'Democrat Party Leader Discusses Coup Aftermath', *US Embassy Cable 06BANGKOK5972*, 28 September.

2007. 'Weekend Protests in Bangkok Fizzle Again', *US Embassy Cable 07BANGKOK3501*, 25 June.

Chulalongkorn 1989 [1887]. 'Phra Ratcha Damrat Nai Phrabat Somdet Phra Chulachomklao Chao Yu Hua Song Thalaeng Phra Borommaratcha-Thibai Kae Khai Kan Pokkhrong Phaendin', in Chai-anan Samudavanija and Khattiya Kansut (eds.), *Ekkasan Kan Mueang Kan Pokkhrong Thai Pho.So. 2417–2477*. Bangkok: Sathaban Sayam Sueksa Samakhom Sangkhomsat Haeng Prathet Thai.

1989 [1903]. 'Phra Borommaratcha-Thibai Wa Duai Khwam Samakkhi Kae Khwam Nai Khata Thi Mi Nai Am Phaendin', in Chai-anan Samudavanija and Khattiya Kansut (eds.), *Ekkasan Kan Mueang Kan Pokkhrong Thai Pho.So. 2417–2477*. Bangkok: Sathaban Sayam Sueksa Samakhom Sangkhomsat Haeng Prathet Thai.

Damrong Rajanubhab 1974 [1926]. 'Memorandum, 1 August 1926', in Benjamin A. Batson (ed.), *Siam's Political Future: Documents from the End of the Absolute Monarchy*. Cornell University Southeast Asia Program.

Direk Chaiyanam 1935. 'Banthuek Yo Kan Pai Fao Phrabat Somdet Phrachao Yu Hua Khrang Thi 1 Muea Wan Thi 12 Thanwakhom Pho.So. 2477' [12 December 1934], in *Thalaengkan Rueang Phrabat Somdet Phra Poramintharamaha Prajadhipok Phra Pokklao Chao Yu Hua Song Sala Ratcha Sombat*. Bangkok: Rong Phim Prajant.

1935. 'Banthuek Yo Kan Pai Fao Phrabat Somdet Phrachao Yu Hua Khrang Thi 3 Muea Wan Thi 20 Mokkarakhom Pho.So. 2477' [20 January 1934], in *Thalaengkan Rueang Phrabat Somdet Phra Poramintharamaha Prajadhipok Phra Pokklao Chao Yu Hua Song Sala Ratcha Sombat*. Bangkok: Rong Phim Prajant.

1935. 'Banthuek Yo Kan Pai Fao Phrabat Somdet Phrachao Yu Hua Khrang Thi 4 Muea Wan Thi 24 Mokkarakhom Pho.So. 2477' [24 January 1934], in *Thalaengkan Rueang Phrabat Somdet Phra Poramintharamaha Prajadhipok Phra Pokklao Chao Yu Hua Song Sala Ratcha Sombat*. Bangkok: Rong Phim Prajant.

ECT (Election Commission of Thailand) 2001. *Kho Mun Sathiti Lae Phon Kan Lueaktang Samachik Sapha Phu Thaen Ratsadon Pho.So. 2044*. Bangkok: ECT.

2005. *Kho Mun Sathiti Lae Phon Kan Lueaktang Samachik Sapha Phu Thaen Ratsadon Pho.So. 2048*. Bangkok: ECT.

2007. *Sarup Kho Mun Sathiti Kan Chai Sitthi Lueaktang So.So.23 Thanwakhom 2550*. Bangkok: ECT.

2011. *Sarup Kho Mun Sathiti Kan Chai Sitthi Lueaktang So.So.3 Karakadakhom 2554*. Bangkok: ECT.

Entwistle, James F. 2008. 'Thai Prime Minister Somchai Disregards Army Commander's Suggestion He Resign', *US Embassy Cable 08BANGKOK3143*, 18 October.

ICID (Independent Committee for the Investigation, Study and Analysis of the Formulation and Implementation of Narcotic Suppression Policy) 2008.

'Preliminary Report (unofficial translation)'. Accessed on 20 August 2013 at: prachatai.com/english/node/551

Jakrapob Penkair 2007. 'Transcript of Remarks Given at the Foreign Correspondents' Club of Thailand', Bangkok, 29 August.

John, Eric G. 2008. 'Palace Insider Tells Ambassador of the King's Opposition to a Coup and to PAD Protests', *US Embassy Cable 08BANGKOK3317*, 6 November.

2009. 'Thailand: Circles of Influence Inside the Institution of the Monarchy in King Bhumibol's Twilight', *US Embassy Cable 09BANGKOK2967*, 23 November.

2010. 'Thailand: Ambassador Engages Privy Council Chair Prem, Other "Establishment" Figures on Year Ahead', *US Embassy Cable 10BANGKOK192*, 25 January.

LCT (Lawyers Council of Thailand) 2014. 'Thalaengkan Khong Sapha Thanai Khwam Rueang Cha Chai Matra 3 Lae Matra 7 Khong Ratthathammanun Na Wela Dai Lae Doi Khrai', 16 January.

Leng Srijant 2007 [1912]. 'Banthuek Wa Duai Khwam Sueam Sam Lae Khwam Charoen Khong Prathet', in Thamrongsak Phetchlert-anan (ed.), *'Kho Ang' Kan Patiwat-Ratthaprahan-Kabot Nai Mueang Thai Patchuban: Bot Wikhro Lae Ekkasan*. Bangkok: The Foundation for the Promotion of Social Sciences and Humanities Textbooks Project.

Lindgren, Mattias 2013. 'Income per person (GDP/cap, PPP$ inflation-adjusted), Version 13'. Accessed on 11 January 2014 at: www.gapminder.org/data/documentation/gd001

MFA (Ministry of Foreign Affairs) 2010. 'PM Proposes Five-Point Roadmap for Reconciliation towards Elections by Year-End', 4 May. Accessed on 20 August 2013 at: www.thaiembassy.org/athens/th/news/591/18295-PM-proposes-five-point-roadmap-for-reconciliation.html

Ministry of the Interior 1975. *Raingan Phon Kan Lueaktang Samachik Sapha Phu Thaen Ratsadon, 26 Mokkarakhom 2518*. Bangkok: Krom Kan Pokkhrong Krasuang Mahatthai.

1976. *Raingan Phon Kan Lueaktang Samachik Sapha Phu Thaen Ratsadon, 4 Mesayon 2519*. Bangkok: Krom Kan Pokkhrong Krasuang Mahatthai.

1983. *Raingan Kan Wichai Kan Lueaktang Samachik Sapha Phu Thaen Ratsadon Pho.So. 2526*. Bangkok: Krom Kan Pokkhrong Krasuang Mahatthai.

1987. *Raingan Wichai Kan Lueaktang Samachik Sapha Phu Thaen Ratsadon Pho.So. 2529*. Bangkok: Krom Kan Pokkhrong Krasuang Mahatthai.

1989. *Raingan Wichai Kan Lueaktang Samachik Sapha Phu Thaen Ratsadon Pho.So. 2531*. Bangkok: Krom Kan Pokkhrong Krasuang Mahatthai.

1992. *Raingan Phon Kan Lueaktang Samachik Sapha Phu Thaen Ratsadon, 22 Minakhom 2535*. Bangkok: Krom Kan Pokkhrong Krasuang Mahatthai.

1995. *Kho Mun Sathiti Lae Phon Kan Lueaktang Samachik Sapha Phu Thaen Ratsadon 2 Karakadakhom 2538*. Bangkok: Krom Kan Pokkhrong Krasuang Mahatthai.

1996. *Kho Mun Sathiti Lae Phon Kan Lueaktang Samachik Sapha Phu Thaen Ratsadon 17 Phruetsachikayon 2539*. Bangkok: Krom Kan Pokkhrong Krasuang Mahatthai.

NARC (National Administrative Reform Council) 2007 [1976]. 'Thalaeng Kan Khong Khana Patirup Kan Pokkhrong Phaendin', in Thamrongsak Phetchlert-anan (ed.), *'Kho Ang' Kan Patiwat-Ratthaprahan-Kabot Nai Mueang Thai Patchuban: Bot Wikhro Lae Ekkasan*. Bangkok: The Foundation for the Promotion of Social Sciences and Humanities Textbooks Project.

NPKC (National Peace-Keeping Council) 2007 [1991]. 'Thalaeng Kan Khong Khana Raksa Khwam Sangop Riaproi Haeng Chat Chabap Thi 1 Rueang Kham Chi Chaeng Hetphon Kan Khao Yuet Lae Khuap Khum Amnat Nai Kan Pokkhrong Prathet', in Thamrongsak Phetchlert-anan (ed.), *'Kho Ang' Kan Patiwat-Ratthaprahan-Kabot Nai Mueang Thai Patchuban: Bot Wikhro Lae Ekkasan*. Bangkok: The Foundation for the Promotion of Social Sciences and Humanities Textbooks Project.

Phahon Phonphayuhasena 1935. 'Kho Khwam Thua Nai Kan Top Phra Ratcha Banthuek' [9 January], in *Thalaengkan Rueang Phrabat Somdet Phra Poramintharamaha Prajadhipok Phra Pokklao Chao Yu Hua Song Sala Ratcha Sombat*. Bangkok: Rong Phim Prajant.

Phibun Songkhram 1978 [1945]. 'Co-operation with and Resistance against Japan during the War', in Thak Chaloemtiarana (ed.), *Thai Politics: Extracts and Documents 1932–1957*. Bangkok: The Social Science Association of Thailand.

Pollwatch 1992. *Raingan Kan Lueaktang Samachik Sapha Phu Thaen Ratsadon, 13 Kanyayon 2535*. Bangkok: Khana Kammakan Ongkon Klang Kan Lueaktang.

Prajadhipok 1935 [1933]. 'Letter from the King to Phraya Manopakorn Nitithada, 31 January 1933', in *Thalaengkan Rueang Phrabat Somdet Phra Poramintharamaha Prajadhipok Phra Pokklao Chao Yu Hua Song Sala Ratcha Sombat*. Bangkok: Rong Phim Prajant.

1935 [1934]. 'Phra Ratcha Banthuek 1' [dated 26 September 1934], in *Thalaengkan Rueang Phrabat Somdet Phra Poramintharamaha Prajadhipok Phra Pokklao Chao Yu Hua Song Sala Ratcha Sombat*. Bangkok: Rong Phim Prajant.

1935 [1934]. 'Phra Ratcha Banthuek 2' [dated 26 September 1934], in *Thalaengkan Rueang Phrabat Somdet Phra Poramintharamaha Prajadhipok Phra Pokklao Chao Yu Hua Song Sala Ratcha Sombat*. Bangkok: Rong Phim Prajant.

1935 [1934]. 'Letter from the King to the Royal Secretary in Bangkok, 27 October 1934', in *Thalaengkan Rueang Phrabat Somdet Phra Poramintharamaha Prajadhipok Phra Pokklao Chao Yu Hua Song Sala Ratcha Sombat*. Bangkok: Rong Phim Prajant.

1935 [1934]. 'Phra Ratcha Banthuek: Kho Khai Tang Tang Phuea Sanoe To Khana Ratthaban Lae Sapha Phu Thaen Ratsadon' [dated 20 December 1934], in *Thalaengkan Rueang Phrabat Somdet Phra Poramintharamaha Prajadhipok Phra Pokklao Chao Yu Hua Song Sala Ratcha Sombat*. Bangkok: Rong Phim Prajant.

1974 [1926]. 'Problems of Siam', in Benjamin A. Batson (ed.), *Siam's Political Future: Documents from the End of the Absolute Monarchy*. Cornell University Southeast Asia Program.

1974 [1927]. 'Democracy in Siam', in Benjamin A. Batson (ed.), *Siam's Political Future: Documents from the End of the Absolute Monarchy*. Cornell University Southeast Asia Program.

Pridi Banomyong 1974. *Prachathippatai Lae Ratthathammanun Bueang Ton Kap Kan Rang Ratthathammanun*. Bangkok: Rong Phim Nitiwet.

2000 [1972]. 'Some Aspects of the Establishment of the People's Party and the Democracy', in Chris Baker and Pasuk Phongpaichit (eds.), *Pridi by Pridi: Selected Writings on Life, Politics, and Economy*. Chiang Mai: Silkworm Books.

2000 [1973]. 'Uphold the Aim for Full Democracy of the Heroes of 14 October', in Chris Baker and Pasuk Phongpaichit (eds.), *Pridi by Pridi: Selected Writings on Life, Politics, and Economy*. Chiang Mai: Silkworm Books.

2000 [1981]. 'Establishment of the Anti-Japan Resistance Movement and Seri Thai', in Chris Baker and Pasuk Phongpaichit (eds.), *Pridi by Pridi: Selected Writings on Life, Politics, and Economy*. Chiang Mai: Silkworm Books.

2000 [1982]. 'The People's Party and the Revolution of 24 June', in Chris Baker and Pasuk Phongpaichit (eds.), *Pridi by Pridi: Selected Writings on Life, Politics, and Economy*. Chiang Mai: Silkworm Books.

Prisdang (ten additional signatories) 1989 [1885]. 'Chao Nai Lae Kha Ratchakan Krap Bangkhomthun Khwam Hen Chatkan Kan Plian Plaeng Rabiab Ratchakan Phaendin Ro.So. 103', in Chai-anan Samudavanija and Khattiya Kansut (eds.), *Ekkasan Kan Mueang Kan Pokkhrong Thai Pho.So. 2417–2477*. Bangkok: Sathaban Sayam Sueksa Samakhom Sangkhomsat Haeng Prathet Thai.

Revolutionary Council 1958a. 'Prakat Khong Khana Patiwat Chabap Thi 1', *Royal Thai Gazette (Special Issue)* 75(81): 3–4.

1958b. 'Prakat Khong Khana Patiwat Chabap Thi 2', *Royal Thai Gazette (Special Issue)* 75(81): 5–6.

1958c. 'Prakat Khong Khana Patiwat Chabap Thi 4', *Royal Thai Gazette (Special Issue)* 75(81): 10–16.

2007 [1977]. 'Thalaeng Kan Khong Khana Patiwat' [dated 20 October 1977], in Thamrongsak Phetchlert-anan (ed.), *Kho Ang' Kan Patiwat-Ratthaprahan-Kabot Nai Mueang Thai Patchuban: Bot Wikhro Lae Ekkasan*. Bangkok: The Foundation for the Promotion of Social Sciences and Humanities Textbooks Project.

Royal Thai Army 1964. *Anuson Phanathan Chomphon Sarit Thanarat*. Bangkok: Thanakan Phim.

Sarit Thanarat 1964 [1959]. 'Kham Prasai Nai Wan Khrop Rop Pi Haeng Kan Patiwat, 20 Tulakhom Pho.So. 2502', in Council of Ministers (ed.), *Pramuan Sunthonphot Khong Chomphon Sarit Thanarat, Pho.So. 2502–2504*. Bangkok: Rong Phim Samnak Thamniap Nayok Ratthamontri.

Siwisan Waja 1974 [1932]. 'Memorandum, 9 March 1932', in Benjamin A. Batson (ed.), *Siam's Political Future: Documents from the End of the Absolute Monarchy*. Cornell University Southeast Asia Program.

Thianwan 1989 [1904–5]. 'Wa Duai Khwam Fan Lamoe Tae Mai Chai Non Lap', in Chai-anan Samudavanija and Khattiya Kansut (eds.), *Ekkasan Kan*

Mueang Kan Pokkhrong Thai Pho.So. 2417–2477. Bangkok: Sathaban Sayam Sueksa Samakhom Sangkhomsat Haeng Prathet Thai.

1989 [1906]. 'Wa Duai Samai Rue Wela', in Chai-anan Samudavanija and Khattiya Kansut (eds.), *Ekkasan Kan Mueang Kan Pokkhrong Thai Pho.So. 2417–2477*. Bangkok: Sathaban Sayam Sueksa Samakhom Sangkhomsat Haeng Prathet Thai.

1989 [1907]. 'Praiwet Kham Nae Nam', in Chai-anan Samudavanija and Khattiya Kansut (eds.), *Ekkasan Kan Mueang Kan Pokkhrong Thai Pho.So. 2417–2477*. Bangkok: Sathaban Sayam Sueksa Samakhom Sangkhomsat Haeng Prathet Thai.

Vajiravudh 1914 [1911]. *Pluk Chai Suea Pa*. Bangkok: Rong Phim Sophonphiphattanakon.

1989 [1905]. 'Raingan Kan Prachum Paliment Sayam', in Chai-anan Samudavanija and Khattiya Kansut (eds.), *Ekkasan Kan Mueang Kan Pokkhrong Thai Pho.So. 2417–2477*. Bangkok: Sathaban Sayam Sueksa Samakhom Sangkhomsat Haeng Prathet Thai.

BOOKS AND JOURNAL ARTICLES

Acemoglu, Daron and James A. Robinson 2006. *Economic Origins of Dictatorship and Democracy*. Cambridge University Press.

Akin Rabibhadana 1969. *The Organization of Thai Society in the Early Bangkok Period, 1782–1873*. Cornell University Southeast Asia Program, Data Paper No. 74.

Akira, Suehiro 1996. *Capital Accumulation in Thailand, 1855–1985*. Chiang Mai: Silkworm Books.

Aldrich, John H. 1995. *Why Parties? The Origin and Transformation of Political Parties in America*. University of Chicago Press.

Almond, Gabriel A. and Sidney Verba 1963. *The Civic Culture: Political Attitudes and Democracy in Five Nations*. Boston: Little, Brown and Company.

Ammar Siamwalla and Somchai Jitsuchon 2012. 'The Socio-Economic Bases of the Red/Yellow Divide: A Statistical Analysis', in Michael J. Montesano, Pavin Chachavalpongpun, and Aekapol Chongvilaivan (eds.), *Bangkok, May 2010: Perspectives on a Divided Thailand*. Singapore: ISEAS.

Anchali Susayan 2003. *Phrai Samai Ro. 5: Khwam Plian Plaeng Khong Rabop Phrai Lae Phon Krathop To Sangkhom Thai Nai Ratchasamai Phrabat Somdet Phra Chulachomklao Chao Yu Hua*. Bangkok: The Foundation for the Promotion of Social Sciences and Humanities Textbooks Project.

Anderson, Benedict 1977. 'Withdrawal Symptoms: Social and Cultural Aspects of the October 6 Coup', *Bulletin of Concerned Asian Scholars* 9: 13–30.

1978. 'Studies of the Thai State: The State of Thai Studies', in Eliezer Ayal (ed.), *The Study of Thailand: Analyses of Knowledge, Approaches, and Prospects in Anthropology, Art History, Economics, History, and Political Science*. Ohio University Center for International Studies, Southeast Asia Series No. 54.

1990. 'Murder and Progress in Modern Siam', *New Left Review* 181: 33–48.

1991 [1983]. *Imagined Communities: Reflections on the Origin and Spread of Nationalism*. London: Verso.

Anek Laothamatas 1996. 'A Tale of Two Democracies: Conflicting Perceptions of Elections and Democracy in Thailand', in Robert H. Taylor (ed.), *The Politics of Elections in Southeast Asia*. Cambridge University Press.

2006. *Thaksina-Prachaniyom*. Bangkok: Matichon.

Anuman Rajathon 1954. 'Kingship in Siam', *Journal of the Siam Society* 42: 1–10.

Aphichat Sathitniramai 2010. 'Suea Daeng Khue Khrai: Mob Tem Ngoen Rue Chon Chan Klang Mai Kap Thang Phraeng Sangkhom', in various authors, *Red Why, Daeng... Thammai*. Bangkok: Open Books.

Arendt, Hannah 1990 [1963]. *On Revolution*. London: Penguin Books.

Asia Foundation 2011. *2010 National Survey of the Thai Electorate*. Bangkok: Asia Foundation.

2014. *Profile of the 'Bangkok Shutdown' Protestors*. Bangkok: Asia Foundation.

Askew, Marc 2008. *Performing Political Identity: The Democrat Party in Southern Thailand*. Chiang Mai: Silkworm Books.

Barmé, Scot 1993. *Luang Wichit Wathakan and the Creation of a Thai Identity*. Singapore: ISEAS.

2002. *Woman, Man, Bangkok: Love, Sex, and Popular Culture in Thailand*. Chiang Mai: Silkworm Books.

Bartolini, Stefano, and Peter Mair 1990. *Identity, Competition, and Electoral Availability: The Stabilization of European Electorates 1885–1985*. Cambridge University Press.

Batson, Benjamin A. 1974a. *Siam's Political Future: Documents from the End of the Absolute Monarchy*. Cornell University Southeast Asia Program.

1974b. 'The Fall of Phibun's Government, 1944', *Journal of the Siam Society* 62: 89–120.

1984. *The End of the Absolute Monarchy in Siam*. Oxford University Press.

Battye, Noel A. 1974. *The Military, Government and Society in Siam, 1868–1910: Politics and Military Reform During the Reign of King Chulalongkorn*. PhD dissertation: Cornell University.

Bennett, Andrew and Colin Elman 2006. 'Complex Causal Relations and Case Study Methods: The Example of Path Dependence', *Political Analysis* 14: 250–67.

Bowie, Katherine A. 1997. *Rituals of National Loyalty: An Anthropology of the State and Village Scout Movement in Thailand*. Columbia University Press.

Bruk, Solomon I. and V.S. Apenchenko (eds.) 1964. *Atlas Narodov Mira*. Moscow: Glavnoe Upravlenie Geodezii I Kartografi.

Buchanan, James 2013. 'Translating Thailand's Protests: An Analysis of Red Shirt Rhetoric', *ASEAS – Austrian Journal of South-East Asian Studies* 6: 60–80.

Capoccia, Giovanni and R. Daniel Keleman 2007. 'The Study of Critical Junctures: Theory, Narrative, and Counterfactuals in Historical Institutionalism', *World Politics* 59: 341–69.

Caramani, Daniele 2004. *The Nationalization of Politics: The Formation of National Electorates and Party Systems in Western Europe*. Cambridge University Press.

Chai-anan Samudavanija 1981. *Chiwit Lae Ngan Khong Thianwan Lae K.S.R. Kulap*. Bangkok: Bannakit.

1989. 'Thailand: A Stable Semi-Democracy', in Larry Diamond, Juan Linz, and Seymour Martin Lipset (eds.), *Democracy in Developing Countries*. London: Lynne Rienner Publishers.

1997. 'Old Soldiers Never Die, They are Just By-Passed: The Military, Bureaucracy, and Globalization', in Kevin Hewison (ed.), *Political Change in Thailand: Democracy and Participation*. London: Routledge.

2002. 'State-Identity Creation, State-Building and Civil Society, 1939–1981', in Craig J. Reynolds (ed.), *National Identity and Its Defenders: Thailand Today*. Chiang Mai: Silkworm Books.

Chalermkiat Phionuan 1990. *Prachathippatai Baep Thai: Khwam Khit Thang Kan Mueang Khong Thahan Thai*. Bangkok: Thammasat University Press.

Chambers, Paul 2003. *Factions, Parties, Coalition Change, and Cabinet Durability in Thailand: 1979–2001*. PhD dissertation: Northern Illinois University.

2005. 'Evolving Toward What? Parties, Factions, and Coalition Behaviour in Thailand Today', *Journal of East Asian Studies* 5: 495–520.

Charnvit Kasetsiri 2000. *2475 Kan Patiwat Sayam*. Bangkok: The Foundation for the Promotion of Social Sciences and Humanities Textbooks Project.

2001. '14 Tula: Banthuek Prawatsat', in Charnvit Kasetsiri and Thamrongsak Phetchlert-anan (eds.), *Chak 14 Thueng 6 Tula*. Bangkok: The Foundation for the Promotion of Social Sciences and Humanities Textbooks Project.

2008. *Prawat Kan Mueang Thai-Sayam Pho.So. 2475–2500*. Bangkok: The Foundation for the Promotion of Social Sciences and Humanities Textbooks Project.

2010. *Kabot Phrai Samai Ayutthaya Kap Naeo Khwam Khit Phu Mi Bun – Phra Si Ariya – Phra Malai*. Bangkok: The Foundation for the Promotion of Social Sciences and Humanities Textbooks Project.

Chatthip Nartsupha 1984. 'The Ideology of Holy Men Revolts in North East Thailand', in Andrew Turton and Shigeharu Tanabe (eds.), *History and Peasant Consciousness in South East Asia*. Osaka: National Museum of Ethnology.

1991. 'The "Community Culture" School of Thought', in Manat Chitakasem and Andrew Turton (eds.), *Thai Constructions of Knowledge*. School of African and Oriental Studies, University of London.

1999. *The Thai Village Economy in the Past*. Chiang Mai: Silkworm Books.

Chu Yun-Han, Larry Diamond, Andrew J. Nathan, and Doh Chull Shin 2008. *How East Asians View Democracy*. Columbia University Press.

Coedès, George 1966. *The Making of South East Asia*. University of California Press.

1968. *The Indianized States of Southeast Asia*. University of Hawaii Press.

Cohen, Stanley 2002 [1972]. *Folk Devils and Moral Panics: The Creation of the Mods and the Rockers*. London: Routledge.

Connors, Michael K. 2002. 'Framing the "People's Constitution"', in Duncan McCargo (ed.), *Reforming Thai Politics*. Copenhagen: NIAS Press.

2007 [2003]. *Democracy and National Identity in Thailand*. Copenhagen: NIAS Press.

2008. 'Article of Faith: The Failure of Royal Liberalism in Thailand', *Journal of Contemporary Asia* 38: 143–65.

2009. 'Ambivalent about Rights: "Accidental" Killing Machines, Democracy and Coups d'État', Southeast Asia Research Centre Working Papers Series No. 102.

2011. 'When the Walls come Crumbling Down: The Monarchy and Thai-Style Democracy', *Journal of Contemporary Asia* 41: 657–73.

Copeland, Matthew P. 1993. *Contested Nationalism and the 1932 Overthrow of the Absolute Monarchy in Siam*. PhD dissertation: Australian National University.

Crispin, Shawn 2012. 'Thailand's Classless Conflict', in Michael J. Montesano, Pavin Chachavalpongpun, and Aekapol Chongvilaivan (eds.), *Bangkok, May 2010: Perspectives on a Divided Thailand*. Singapore: ISEAS.

Crosby, Josiah 1945. *Siam: The Crossroads*. London: Hollis & Carter.

Cushman, Richard D. (ed. David K. Wyatt) 2000. *The Royal Chronicles of Ayutthaya: A Synoptic Translation*. Bangkok: The Siam Society.

Dahl, Robert A. 1991. *Democracy and its Critics*. Yale University Press.

Damrong Rajanubhab 1927. *Laksana Kan Pokkhrong Prathet Sayam Tae Boran*. Bangkok: Rong Phim Sophonphiphattanakon.

1955 [1935]. *Nithan Boranna Khadi Bang Rueang*. Bangkok: Krom Sinlapakon.

Darling, Frank C. 1965. *Thailand and the United States*. Washington, DC: Public Affairs Press.

David, Paul A. 2007. 'Path Dependence: A Foundational Concept for Historical Social Science', *Cliometrica* 1: 91–114.

Dhani Nivat 1946. 'The Old Siamese Conception of the Monarchy', *Journal of the Siam Society* 36: 91–106.

Dressel, Björn 2010. 'Judicialization of Politics or Politicization of the Judiciary? Considerations from Recent Events in Thailand', *Pacific Review* 23: 671–91.

Elster, Jon 1990 [1983]. *Explaining Technical Change: A Case Study in the Philosophy of Science*. Cambridge University Press.

2007. *Explaining Social Behaviour: More Nuts and Bolts for the Social Sciences*. Cambridge University Press.

Engel, David M. and Jaruwan S. Engel 2010. *Tort, Custom, and Karma: Globalization and Legal Consciousness in Thailand*. Stanford University Press.

Englehart, Neil A. 2001. *Culture and Power in Traditional Siamese Government*. Cornell Southeast Asia Program, Series No. 18.

2003. 'Democracy and the Thai Middle Class: Globalization, Modernization, and Constitutional Change', *Asian Survey* 43: 253–79.

Fearon, James D. 1999. 'What is Identity (as We Now Use the Word)?' Stanford University: unpublished manuscript.

Ferrara, Federico 2011. *Thailand Unhinged: The Death of Thai-Style Democracy*. Singapore: Equinox.

2012. 'The Legend of King Prajadhipok: Tall Tales and Stubborn Facts on the Seventh Reign in Siam', *Journal of Southeast Asian Studies* 48: 4–31.

Fineman, Daniel M. 1997. *A Special Relationship: The United States and Military Government in Thailand, 1947–1958*. University of Hawaii Press.

Flood, Thadeus 1975. 'The Thai Left Wing in Historical Context', *Bulletin of Concerned Asian Scholars* 7: 55–67.

Freedom House 2008. 'Thailand', in *Freedom in the World 2008*. Lanham, MD: Rowman & Littlefield. Accessed on 20 August 2013 at: www.freedomhouse.org/report/freedom-world/2008/thailand

2012. 'Thailand', in *Freedom in the World 2012*. Lanham, MD: Rowman & Littlefield. Accessed on 20 August 2013 at: www.freedomhouse.org/report/freedom-world/2012/thailand

Galtung, Johan 1969. 'Violence, Peace, and Peace Research', *Journal of Peace Research* 6: 167–91.

1990. 'Cultural Violence', *Journal of Peace Research* 27: 291–305.

Gay, Bernard 2002. 'Millenarian Movements in Laos, 1895–1936: Depictions by Modern Lao Historians', in Mayoury Ngaosrivathana and Kennon Brezeale (eds.), *Breaking New Ground in Lao History: Essays on the Seventh to Twentieth Centuries*. Chiang Mai: Silkworm Books.

George, Alexander L. and Andrew Bennett 2005. *Case Studies and Theory Development in the Social Sciences*. MIT Press.

Giles Ungpakorn 2010. *Thailand's Crisis and the Struggle for Democracy*. Bangkok: WD Press.

Glassman, Jim 2010. '"The Provinces Elect Governments, Bangkok Overthrows Them": Urbanity, Class and Post-Democracy in Thailand', *Urban Studies* 47: 1301–23.

2011. 'Cracking Hegemony in Thailand: Gramsci, Bourdieu, and the Dialectics of Rebellion', *Journal of Contemporary Asia* 41: 25–46.

Goldstone, Jack A. 1991. *Revolution and Rebellion in the Early Modern World*. University of California Press.

1998. 'Initial Conditions, General Laws, Path Dependence, and Explanation in Historical Sociology', *American Journal of Sociology* 104: 829–45.

2003. 'Comparative Historical Analysis and Knowledge Accumulation in the Study of Revolutions', in James Mahoney and Dietrich Rueschemeyer (eds.), *Comparative Historical Analysis in the Social Sciences*. Cambridge University Press.

Grabowsky, Volker 1995a. 'Introduction', in Volker Grabowsky (ed.), *Regions and National Integration in Thailand 1892–1992*. Wiesbaden: Harrassowitz Verlag.

1995b. 'The Isan up to Its Integration into the Siamese State', in Volker Grabowsky (ed.), *Regions and National Integration in Thailand 1892–1992*. Wiesbaden: Harrassowitz Verlag.

Haberkorn, Tyrell 2011. *Revolution Interrupted: Farmers, Students, Law, and Violence in Northern Thailand*. University of Wisconsin Press.

2013. 'Getting Away with Murder in Thailand: State Violence and Impunity in Phatthalung', in N. Ganesan and Sung Chull Kim (eds.), *State Violence in East Asia*. University of Kentucky Press.

Hall, Peter A. and Rosemary C.R. Taylor 1996. 'Political Science and the Three New Institutionalisms', *Political Studies* 44: 952–73.

Handley, Paul M. 2006. *The King Never Smiles: A Biography of Thailand's Bhumibol Adulyadej*. Yale University Press.

Harrison, Rachel V. 2010. 'The Allure of Ambiguity: The "West" and the Making of Thai Identities', in Rachel V. Harrison and Peter A. Jackson (eds.),

The Ambiguous Allure of the West: Traces of the Colonial in Thailand. Cornell University Southeast Asia Program.

Hewison, Kevin 1993. 'Of Regimes, State and Pluralities: Thai Politics Enters the 1990s', in Kevin Hewison, Richard Robison, and Garry Rodan (eds.), *Southeast Asia in the 1990s: Authoritarianism, Democracy and Capitalism*. St. Leonards: Allen & Unwin.

1996. 'Political Oppositions and Regime Change in Thailand', in Garry Rodan (ed.), *Political Oppositions in Industrializing Asia*. London: Routledge.

1997. 'The Monarchy and Democratization', in Kevin Hewison (ed.), *Political Change in Thailand: Democracy and Participation*. London: Routledge.

2004. 'Crafting Thailand's New Social Contract', *Pacific Review* 17: 503–22.

2008. 'A Book, the King and the 2006 Coup', *Journal of Contemporary Asia* 38: 190–211.

2012. 'Class, Inequality, and Politics', in Michael J. Montesano, Pavin Chachavalpongpun, and Aekapol Chongvilaivan (eds.), *Bangkok, May 2010: Perspectives on a Divided Thailand*. Singapore: ISEAS.

2014. 'Considerations on Inequality and Politics in Thailand', *Democratization* 21: 846–66.

Hewison, Kevin and Kengkij Kitirianglarp 2010. ''Thai-Style Democracy': The Royalist Struggle for Thailand's Politics', in Søren Ivarsson and Lotte Isager (eds.), *Saying the Unsayable: Monarchy and Democracy in Thailand*. Copenhagen: NIAS Press.

Hicken, Allen 2009. *Building Party Systems in Developing Democracies*. Cambridge University Press.

Hong Lysa 1984. *Thailand in the Nineteenth Century: The Evolution of the Economy and Society*. Singapore: ISEAS.

HRW (Human Rights Watch) 2011. *Descent into Chaos: Thailand's 2010 Red Shirt Protests and the Government Crackdown*. New York: HRW.

Huntington, Samuel P. 1965. 'Political Development and Political Decay', *World Politics* 17: 386–430.

Inglehart, Ronald and Christian Welzel 2005. *Modernization, Cultural Change, and Democracy: The Human Development Sequence*. Cambridge University Press.

Ingram, James C. 1971. *Economic Change in Thailand 1850–1970*. Stanford University Press.

Inkeles, Alex 1966. 'The Modernization of Man', in Myron Weiner (ed.), *Modernization: The Dynamics of Growth*. New York: Basic Books.

Isager, Lotte and Søren Ivarsson 2010. 'Strengthening the Moral Fibre of the Nation: The King's Sufficiency Economy as Etho-Politics', in Søren Ivarsson and Lotte Isager (eds.), *Saying the Unsayable: Monarchy and Democracy in Thailand*. Copenhagen: NIAS Press.

Ivarsson, Søren 2008. *Creating Laos: The Making of a Lao Space between Indochina and Siam, 1860–1945*. Copenhagen: NIAS Press.

Jackson, Peter A. 2002. 'Thai Buddhist Identity: Debates on the Traiphum Phra Ruang', in Craig J. Reynolds (ed.), *National Identity and Its Defenders: Thailand Today*. Chiang Mai: Silkworm Books.

2010. 'Virtual Divinity: A 21st-Century Discourse of Thai Royal Influence', in Søren Ivarsson and Lotte Isager (eds.), *Saying the Unsayable: Monarchy and Democracy in Thailand*. Copenhagen: NIAS Press.

Jäger, Kai 2012. 'Why Did Thailand's Middle Class Turn against a Democratically Elected Government? The Information-Gap Hypothesis', *Democratization* 19: 1138–65.

Jit Phumisak 1976. *Khwam Pen Ma Khong Kham Sayam Thai Lao Lae Khom Lae Laksana Thang Kan Sangkhom Khong Chue Chat*. Bangkok: Social Sciences Association of Thailand.

Jones, Mark P. and Scott Mainwaring 2003. 'The Nationalization of Parties and Party Systems. An Empirical Measure and an Application to the Americas', *Party Politics* 9: 139–66.

Kasian Tejapira 2006. 'Toppling Thaksin', *New Left Review* 39: 5–37.

2009. 'The Misbehaving Jeks: The Evolving Regime of Thainess and Sino-Thai Challenges', *Asian Ethnicity* 10: 263–83.

Kershaw, Roger 2001. *Monarchy in South-East Asia: The Faces of Tradition in Transition*. London: Routledge.

Keyes, Charles F. 1967. *Isan: Regionalism in Northeastern Thailand*. Cornell University Southeast Asia Program, Data Paper No. 65.

1977. 'Millennialism, Theravada Buddhism, and Thai Society', *Journal of Asian Studies* 36: 283–302.

1987. *Thailand: Buddhist Kingdom as Modern Nation-State*. Boulder: Westview Press.

2012. '"Cosmopolitan" Villagers and Populist Democracy in Thailand', *South East Asia Research* 20: 343–60.

Kingshill, Konrad 1991. *Ku Daeng – Thirty Years Later: A Village Study in Northern Thailand 1954–1984*. Northern Illinois University Center for Southeast Asian Studies Special Report No. 26.

Klima, Alan 2002. *The Funeral Casino: Meditation, Massacre, and Exchange with the Dead in Thailand*. Princeton University Press.

Knodel, John E., Aphichat Chamratrithirong, and Nibhon Debavalya 1987. *Thailand's Reproductive Revolution: Rapid Fertility Decline in a Third-World Setting*. University of Wisconsin Press.

Kobkua Suwannathat-Pian 1995. *Thailand's Durable Premier: Phibun through Three Decades, 1932–1957*. Oxford University Press.

1996. 'Thai Wartime Leadership Reconsidered: Phibun and Pridi', *Journal of Southeast Asian Studies* 27: 166–78.

2003. *Kings, Country, and Constitutions: Thailand's Political Development 1932–2000*. London: Routledge/Curzon.

Kramol Tongdhamachart 1982. *Toward a Political Party Theory in Thai Perspective*. Singapore: ISEAS Occasional Paper No. 43.

Kruger, Rayne 1964. *The Devil's Discus: An Enquiry into the Death of Ananda, King of Siam*. London: Cassell.

Kullada Kesboonchoo Mead 2004. *The Rise and Decline of Thai Absolutism*. London: Routledge/Curzon.

Laakso, Markkuu and Rein Taagepera 1979. 'Effective Number of Parties: A Measure with Application to West Europe', *Comparative Political Studies* 12: 3–27.

Lakatos, Imre 1970. 'Falsification and the Methodology of Scientific Research Programmes', in Imre Lakatos and Alan Musgrave (eds.), *Criticism and the Growth of Knowledge*. Cambridge University Press.

Landon, Kenneth Perry 1939. *Siam in Transition: A Brief Survey of Cultural Trends in the Five Years since the Revolution of 1932*. University of Chicago Press.

Lewis, M. Paul, Gary F. Simons, and Charles D. Fennig (eds.) 2013. *Ethnologue: Languages of the World, Seventeenth Edition*. Dallas: SIL International.

Likhit Dhiravegin 1992. *Demi Democracy: The Evolution of the Thai Political System*. Singapore: Times Academic Press.

Linz, Juan J. and Alfred Stepan 1996. *Problems of Democratic Transition and Consolidation*. Johns Hopkins University Press.

Lipset, Seymour Martin and Stein Rokkan 1967. 'Cleavage Structures, Party Systems, and Voter Alignments: An Introduction', in Seymour Martin Lipset, and Stein Rokkan (eds.), *Party Systems and Voter Alignments: Cross-National Perspectives*. New York: Free Press.

Loos, Tamara 2002. *Subject Siam: Family, Law, and Colonial Modernity in Thailand*. Chiang Mai: Silkworm Books.

Mahoney, James 2000. 'Path Dependence in Historical Sociology', *Theory and Society* 29: 507–48.

2003. 'Knowledge Accumulation in Comparative Historical Research: The Case of Democracy and Authoritarianism', in James Mahoney and Dietrich Rueschemeyer (eds.), *Comparative Historical Analysis in the Social Sciences*. Cambridge University Press.

Mahoney, James and Kathleen Thelen 2010. 'A Theory of Gradual Institutional Change', in James Mahoney and Kathleen Thelen (eds.), *Explaining Institutional Change: Ambiguity, Agency, and Power*. Cambridge University Press.

Mainwaring, Scott and Timothy Scully 1995. *Building Democratic Institutions: Party Systems in Latin America*. Stanford University Press.

Marshall, Andrew MacGregor 2011. *Thailand's Moment of Truth: A Secret History of Twenty-First Century Siam*. Accessed on 20 August 2013 at: www.scribd.com/doc/58516989/thaistory

2012. *The Tragedy of King Bhumibol*. Accessed on 20 August 2013 at: www.zenjournalist.com

2014. *A Kingdom in Crisis: Royal Succession and the Struggle for Democracy in 21st Century Thailand*. London: Zed Books.

Marshall, T.H. 1964 [1949]. 'Citizenship and Social Class', in T.H. Marshall (ed.), *Class, Citizenship and Social Development*. New York: Doubleday.

McCargo, Duncan 1997a. 'Thailand's Political Parties: Real, Authentic and Actual', in Kevin Hewison (ed.), *Political Change in Thailand: Democracy and Participation*. London: Routledge.

1997b. *Chamlong Srimuang and the New Thai Politics*. London: Hurst & Co.

2000. *Politics and the Press in Thailand: Media Machinations*. London: Routledge.

2004. 'Buddhism, Democracy, and Identity', *Democratization* 11: 155–70.

2005. 'Network Monarchy and Legitimacy Crises in Thailand', *Pacific Review* 18: 499–519.

2007. 'Thaksin and the Resurgence of Violence in the Thai South', in Duncan McCargo (ed.), *Rethinking Thailand's Southern Violence*. Singapore: NUS Press.

2008. *Tearing Apart the Land: Islam and Legitimacy in Southern Thailand*. Cornell University Press.

2010. 'Thailand's Twin Fires', *Survival* 52: 5–12.

2012a. 'Informal Citizens: Graduated Citizenship in Southern Thailand', in Michelle Ann Miller (ed.), *Ethnic and Racial Minorities in Asia: Inclusion or Exclusion?* London: Routledge.

2012b. 'Two Cheers for Rally Politics', in Michael J. Montesano, Pavin Chachavalpongpun, and Aekapol Chongvilaivan (eds.), *Bangkok, May 2010: Perspectives on a Divided Thailand*. Singapore: ISEAS.

McCargo, Duncan and Ukrist Pathmanand 2005. *The Thaksinization of Thailand*. Copenhagen: NIAS Press.

McVey, Ruth 2000. 'Of Greed and Violence, and Other Signs of Progress', in Ruth McVey (ed.), *Money and Power in Provincial Thailand*. University of Hawaii Press.

Missingham, Bruce D. 2004. *The Assembly of the Poor in Thailand: From Local Struggles to National Protest Movement*. Chiang Mai: Silkworm Books.

Montesano, Michael J. 2010. 'Four Thai Pathologies, Late 2009', in Marc Askew (ed.), *Legitimacy Crisis in Thailand*. Chiang Mai: Silkworm Books.

2012. 'Introduction: Seeking Perspective on a Slow-Burn Civil War', in Michael J. Montesano, Pavin Chachavalpongpun, and Aekapol Chongvilaivan (eds.), *Bangkok, May 2010: Perspectives on a Divided Thailand*. Singapore: ISEAS.

Moore, Barrington 1966. *Social Origins of Dictatorship and Democracy: Lord and Peasant in the Making of the Modern World*. Boston: Beacon Press.

Morell, David and Chai-anan Samudavanija 1981. *Political Conflict in Thailand: Reform, Reaction, Revolution*. Cambridge, MA: Oelgeschlager, Gunn & Hain.

Murashima, Eiji 1988. 'The Origin of Official State Ideology in Thailand', *Journal of Southeast Asian Studies* 19: 80–96.

1991. 'Democracy and the Development of Political Parties in Thailand 1932–1945', in Eiji Murashima, Nakharin Mektrairat, and Somkiat Wanthana (eds.), *The Making of Modern Thai Political Parties*. Tokyo: Institute of Developing Economies.

Murray, David 1996. *Angels and Devils: Thai Politics from February 1991 to September 1992 – A Struggle for Democracy?* Bangkok: Orchid Press.

Mussolini, Benito 2001 [1932]. 'The Doctrine of Fascism', in Stanislao Pugliese (ed.), *Italian Fascism and Antifascism: A Critical Anthology*. Manchester University Press.

Nakharin Mektrairat 1991. 'The Economic Base and Power of Modern Thai Political Parties', in Eiji Murashima, Nakharin Mektrairat, and Somkiat Wanthana (eds.), *The Making of Modern Thai Political Parties*. Tokyo: Institute of Developing Economies.

1992. *Kan Patiwat Sayam Pho.So. 2475*. Bangkok: Khrongkan 60 Pi Prachathippatai.

2006. *Phra Phu Song Pokklao Prachathippatai: 60 Pi Si Ratcha Sombat Kap Kan Mueang Kan Pokkhrong Thai*. Bangkok: Thammasat University Press.

Naruemon Thabchumpon and Duncan McCargo 2012. 'Urbanized Villagers in the 2010 Thai Redshirt Protests: Not Just Poor Farmers?' *Asian Survey* 51: 993–1018.

Nattapoll Chaiching 2009. *Kan Mueang Thai Samai Ratthaban Chomphon Po. Phibun Songkhram Phai Tai Rabiap Lok Khong Saharat Amerika Pho.So. 2491–2500*. PhD dissertation: Chulalongkorn University.

2010. 'The Monarchy and the Royalist Movement in Modern Thai Politics, 1932–1957', in Søren Ivarsson and Lotte Isager (eds.), *Saying the Unsayable: Monarchy and Democracy in Thailand.* Copenhagen: NIAS Press.

2011. 'Chak "Khana Ro. So. 130" Thueng "Khana Ratsadon:" Khwam Pen Ma Khong Khwam Khit "Prachathippatai" Nai Prathet Thai', *Sinlapa Watthanatham* 32: 80–99.

2013. *Kho Fan Fai Nai Fan An Luea Chuea: Khwam Khluean Wai Khong Khabuankan Kan Pati Pak Patiwat Sayam (Pho. So. 2475–2500)*. Bangkok: Fa Diao Kan.

Neher, Clark D. 1970. 'Constitutionalism and Elections in Thailand', *Pacific Affairs* 43: 240–57.

Nelson, Michael H. 2007. 'Institutional Incentives and Informal Local Political Groups (Phuak) in Thailand: Comments on Allen Hicken and Paul Chambers', *Journal of East Asian Studies* 7: 125–47.

2013. 'Elite Political Culture in Contemporary Thailand: Voters, Members of Parliament, and Political Parties in the Debates of the 2007 Constitution Drafting Committee', Southeast Asia Research Centre, Working Papers Series No. 141.

Nidhi Eoseewong 2009. 'Patirup Sangkhom', in Wutthichai Wachiramethi, Anand Panyarachun, Nidhi Eoseewong, Seksan Prasertkul, and Suphawut Saichuea (eds.), *Prachathippatai Nai Raya Plian Phan.* Bangkok: Open Books.

2010. *Kan Mueang Khong Suea Daeng*. Bangkok: Open Books.

2012 [1986]. *Kan Mueang Thai Samai Phrachao Krung Thonburi.* Bangkok: Matichon.

Nishizaki, Yoshinori 2005. 'The Moral Origin of Thailand's Provincial Strongman: The Case of Banharn Silpa-archa', *South East Asia Research* 13: 184–234.

2011. *Political Authority and Provincial Identity in Thailand: The Making of Banharn-buri.* Cornell Southeast Asia Program.

2013. 'The King and Banharn: Towards an Elaboration of Network Monarchy in Thailand', *South East Asia Research* 21: 69–103.

2014. 'Peasants and the Redshirt Movement in Thailand: Some Dissenting Voices', *Journal of Peasant Studies* 41: 1–28.

Ockey, James 2002. 'Civil Society and Street Politics in Historical Perspective', in Duncan McCargo (ed.), *Reforming Thai Politics*. Copenhagen: NIAS Press.

2004. *Making Democracy: Leadership, Class, Gender, and Political Participation in Thailand.* Chiang Mai: Silkworm Books.

O'Donnell, Guillermo 1994. 'Delegative Democracy', *Journal of Democracy* 5: 55–69.

1998. 'Horizontal Accountability in New Democracies', *Journal of Democracy* 9: 112–26.

Olson, Mancur 1965. *The Logic of Collective Action.* Harvard University Press.
Orren, Karen and Stephen Skowronek 2004. *The Search for American Political Development.* Cambridge University Press.
Page, Scott E. 2006. 'Path Dependence', *Quarterly Journal of Political Science* 1: 87–115.
Painter, Martin 2006. 'Thaksinisation or Managerialism? Reforming the Thai Bureaucracy', *Journal of Contemporary Asia* 36: 26–47.
Pasuk Phongpaichit and Chris Baker 1997. 'Power in Transition: Thailand in the 1990s', in Kevin Hewison (ed.), *Political Change in Thailand: Democracy and Participation.* London: Routledge.
2000. 'Chao Sua, Chao Pho, Chao Thi: Lords of Thailand's Transition', in Ruth McVey (ed.), *Money and Power in Provincial Thailand.* University of Hawaii Press.
2008. 'Thaksin's Populism', *Journal of Contemporary Asia* 38: 62–83.
2009. *Thaksin.* Chiang Mai: Silkworm Books.
2012. 'Thailand in Trouble: Revolt of the Downtrodden or Conflict among Elites?', in Michael J. Montesano, Pavin Chachavalpongpun, and Aekapol Chongvilaivan (eds.), *Bangkok, May 2010: Perspectives on a Divided Thailand.* Singapore: ISEAS.
Pasuk Phongpaichit and Pornthep Benyaapikul 2012. *Economy of Tomorrow. Locked in the Middle-Income Trap: Thailand's Economy between Resilience and Future Challenges.* Bangkok: Friedrich Ebert Stiftung.
Pasuk Phongpaichit and Sungsidh Piriyarangsan 1994. *Corruption and Democracy in Thailand.* Chiang Mai: Silkworm Books.
Peleggi, Maurizio 2007. *Thailand: The Worldly Kingdom.* London: Reaktion Books.
Phillips, Herbert P. 1976. 'Some Premises of American Scholarship on Thailand', in Clark D. Neher (ed.), *Modern Thai Politics.* Cambridge: Schenkman.
1987. *Modern Thai Literature: With an Ethnographic Interpretation.* Hawaii University Press.
PIC (People Information Centre) 2012. *Khwam Ching Phuea Khwam Yuttitham: Hetkan Lae Phon Krathop Chak Kan Salai Kan Chumnum Mesa-Phruetsapha 53.* Bangkok: Fa Diao Kan.
Pickerell, Albert and Daniel E. Moore 1957. 'Elections in Thailand', *Far Eastern Survey* 26: 92–6.
Pierson, Paul 2004. *Politics in Time.* Princeton University Press.
Pitch Pongsawat 2007. 'Kan Ratthaprahan 19 Kanyayon 2549 Khue Kan Tham Hai Phonla Mueang Klai Pen Phrai', in Thanapol Eawsakul (ed.), *Ratthaprahan 19 Kanya: Ratthaprahan Phuea Rabob Prachathippatai An Mi Phramahakasat Song Pen Pramuk.* Bangkok: Fa Diao Kan.
Porphant Ouyyanont 2008. 'The Crown Property Bureau in Thailand and the Crisis of 1997', *Journal of Contemporary Asia* 38: 166–89.
Prajak Kongkirati 2006. 'Counter-Movements in Democratic Transition: Thai Right-Wing Movements after the 1973 Popular Uprising', *Asian Review* 19: 1–33.
2013 [2005]. *Lae Laeo Khwam Khluean Wai Ko Prakot: Kan Mueang Watthanatham Khong Nak Sueksa Lae Panyachon Kon 14 Tula.* Bangkok: Fa Diao Kan.

Pramuan Ruchanaseri 2005. *Phra Ratcha Amnat.* Bangkok: Sumet Ruchanaseri.

Prawet Wasi 2002. 'An Overview of Political Reform Issues', in Duncan McCargo (ed.), *Reforming Thai Politics.* Copenhagen: NIAS Press.

Przeworski, Adam 1988. 'Democracy as a Contingent Outcome of Conflict', in Jon Elster and Rune Slagstad (eds.), *Constitutionalism and Democracy.* Cambridge University Press.

1991. *Democracy and the Market.* Cambridge University Press

2006. 'Self-Enforcing Democracy', in Donald Wittman and Barry Weingast (eds.), *Oxford Handbook of Political Economy.* Oxford University Press.

2009. 'The Mechanics of Regime Instability in Latin America', *Journal of Politics in Latin America* 1: 5–36.

Przeworski, Adam and Fernando Limongi 1997. 'Modernization: Theories and Facts', *World Politics* 49: 155–83.

Przeworski, Adam and John Sprague 1986. *Paper Stones: A History of Electoral Socialism.* University of Chicago Press.

Puey Ungphakorn 1977. 'Violence and the Military Coup in Thailand', *Bulletin of Concerned Asian Scholars* 9: 4–12.

Pye, Oliver and Wolfram Schaffar 2008. 'The 2006 Anti-Thaksin Movement in Thailand: An Analysis', *Journal of Contemporary Asia* 38: 38–61.

Race, Jeffrey 1975. 'The January 1975 Thai Elections: Preliminary Data and Inferences', *Asian Survey* 15: 375–81.

Ramsay, J. Ansil 1979. 'Modernization and Reactionary Rebellions in Northern Siam', *Journal of Asian Studies* 38: 283–97.

Renard, Ronald D. 2006. 'Creating the Other Requires Defining Thainess Against Which the Other Can Exist: Early-Twentieth Century Definitions', *Southeast Asian Studies* 44: 295–320.

Reynolds, Craig J. 1987. 'Jit Poumisak in Thai History', in Craig J. Reynolds (ed.), *Thai Radical Discourse: The Real Face of Thai Feudalism Today.* Cornell University Southeast Asia Program.

2002. 'Introduction', in Craig J. Reynolds (ed.), *National Identity and Its Defenders: Thailand Today.* Chiang Mai: Silkworm Books.

2006. *Seditious Histories: Contesting Thai and Southeast Asian Pasts.* University of Washington Press.

Reynolds, Craig J., Yoshinori Nishizaki, Jim Glassman, Nicholas Farrelly, Pongphisoot Busbarat, Samson Lim, Tyrell Haberkorn, and Pavin Chachavalpongpun 2011. *Time's Arrow and the Burden of the Past: A Primer on the Thai Un-State.* Australian National University: unpublished manuscript.

Reynolds, E. Bruce 2004a. 'Phibun Songkhram and Thai Nationalism in the Fascist Era', *European Journal of East Asian Studies* 3: 99–134.

2004b. *Thailand's Secret War: OSS, SOE, and the Free Thai Underground During World War II.* Cambridge University Press.

Riggs, Fred 1966. *Thailand: The Modernization of a Bureaucratic Polity.* Hawaii University Press.

Rueschemeyer, Dietrich, Evelyne Huber Stephens, and John D. Stephens 1992. *Capitalist Development and Democracy.* University of Chicago Press.

Rujaya Abhakorn and David K. Wyatt 1995. 'Administrative Reforms and National Integration in Northern Thailand, 1892–1932', in Volker Grabowsky (ed.), *Regions and National Integration in Thailand 1892–1992*. Wiesbaden: Harrassowitz Verlag.

Saichol Sattayanurak 2003. *Somdet Krom Phraya Damrong Rajanubhab Kan Sang Atta Lak 'Meuang Thai' Lae 'Chan' Khong Chao Sayam*. Bangkok: Matichon.

2005. *Kan Mueang Lae Kan Sang 'Khwam Pen Thai' Doi Mom Ratchawong Kukrit Pramoj*. Chiang Mai University.

2006. 'Si Phaendin: "Khwam Pen Thai" Lae Khwam Mai Thang Kan Mueang', in Thanet Wongyannawa (ed.), *Chakrawanwitthaya: Bot Khwam Phuea Pen Kianti Kae Nidhi Eoseewong*. Bangkok: Matichon.

2008a. 'Ratchakan Thi 5: Kan Sang Withi Khit Kiao Kap Sangkhom Lae Watthanatham Thai (1)', Midnight University Document Number 1455. Accessed on 27 September 2014 at: http://v1.midnightuniv.org/midnight2544/0009999472.html

2008b. 'Ratchakan Thi 5: Kan Sang Withi Khit Kiao Kap Sangkhom Lae Watthanatham Thai (2)', Midnight University Document Number 1456. Accessed on 27 September 2014 at: http://v1.midnightuniv.org/midnight2544/0009999471.html

2008c. 'Krom Phraya Damrong Rajanubhab: Manothat 'Mueang Thai Lae Khwam Pen Thai' (1)', Midnight University Document Number 1524. Accessed on 27 September 2014 at: http://v1.midnightuniv.org/midnighttext/0009999970.html

2008d. 'Krom Phraya Damrong Rajanubhab: Manothat 'Mueang Thai Lae Khwam Pen Thai' (2)', Midnight University Document Number 1525. Accessed on 27 September 2014 at: http://v1.midnightuniv.org/midnighttext/0009999969.html

Saneh Chamrik 2001. 'Kan Mueang Thai Kap Patiwat Tulakhom', in Charnvit Kasetsiri and Thamrongsak Phetchlert-anan (eds.), *Chak 14 Thueng 6 Tula*. Bangkok: The Foundation for the Promotion of Social Sciences and Humanities Textbooks Project.

Sartori, Giovanni 1968. 'Political Development and Political Engineering', in J.D. Montgomery and A.O. Hirschman (eds.), *Public Policy, Vol. XVII*. Harvard University Press.

1976. *Parties and Party Systems*. Cambridge University Press.

1991. 'Comparing and Miscomparing', *Journal of Theoretical Politics* 3: 243–57.

Schattschneider, E.E. 1988 [1960]. *The Semisovereign People: A Realist's View of Democracy in America*. Boston: Wadsworth.

Scott, James C. 1976. *The Moral Economy of the Peasant: Rebellion and Subsistence in Southeast Asia*. Yale University Press.

Selway, Joel Sawat 2011. 'Electoral Reform and Public Policy Outcomes in Thailand: The Politics of the 30-Baht Health Scheme', *World Politics* 63: 165–202.

Sidel, John T. 2008. 'Social Origins of Dictatorship and Democracy Revisited: Colonial State and Chinese Immigrant in the Making of Modern Southeast Asia', *Comparative Politics* 40: 127–47.

Sivaram, M. 1981 [1936]. *The New Siam in the Making: A Survey of the Political Transition in Siam 1932–1936*. New York: AMS Press.

Skinner, G. William 1957. *Chinese Society in Thailand: An Analytical History*. Cornell University Press.

1960. 'Change and Persistence in Chinese Culture Overseas: A Comparison of Thailand and Java', *Journal of the South Seas Society* 16: 86–100.

Skocpol, Theda 1979. *States and Social Revolutions: A Comparative Analysis of France, Russia and China*. Cambridge University Press.

Slater, Dan 2010. *Ordering Power: Contentious Politics and Authoritarian Leviathans in Southeast Asia*. Cambridge University Press.

Slater, Dan and Erica Simmons 2010. 'Informative Regress: Critical Antecedents in Comparative Politics', *Comparative Political Studies* 43: 886–917.

Somchai Phatharathananunth 2006. *Civil Society and Democratization: Social Movements in Northeast Thailand*. Copenhagen: NIAS Press.

2008. 'The Thai Rak Thai Party and Elections in North-Eastern Thailand', *Journal of Contemporary Asia* 38: 106–23.

Somporn Sangchai 1976. *Some Observations on the Elections and Coalition Formation in Thailand, 1976*. Singapore: ISEAS Occasional Paper No. 43.

Somsak Jeamteerasakul 2001. *Prawatsat Thi Phoeng Sang: Ruam Bot Khwam Kiao Kap 14 Tula Lae 6 Tula*. Bangkok: Samnak Phim 6 Tula Ram Luek.

2005. '50 Pi Kan Prahan Chiwit 17 Kumphaphan 2498', *Fa Diao Kan* 3: 64–80.

Somwung Pitiyanuwat and Siridej Sujiva 2005. *Civic Education in Thailand: Policies and Practices in Schools*. Bangkok: Chulalongkorn University Press.

Sopranzetti, Claudio 2012. 'Burning Red Desires: Isan Migrants and the Politics of Desire in Contemporary Thailand', *South East Asia Research* 20: 361–79.

Stevenson, William 1999. *The Revolutionary King: The True-Life Sequel to The King and I*. London: Constable.

Stowe, Judith A. 1991. *Siam Becomes Thailand: A Story of Intrigue*. University of Hawaii Press.

Streckfuss, David 1993. 'The Mixed Colonial Legacy in Siam: Origins of Thai Racialist Thought, 1890–1910', in Laurie J. Sears (ed.), *Autonomous Histories, Particular Truths: Essays in Honor of John R. W. Smail*. University of Wisconsin Center for Southeast Asian Studies Monograph Number 11.

2011. *Truth on Trial in Thailand: Defamation, Treason, and Lèse-Majesté*. London: Routledge.

2012. 'An "Ethnic" Reading of "Thai" History in the Twilight of the Century-Old Official "Thai" National Model', *South East Asia Research* 20: 305–27.

Sulak Sivaraksa 2002. 'The Crisis of Siamese Identity', in Craig J. Reynolds (ed.), *National Identity and Its Defenders: Thailand Today*. Chiang Mai: Silkworm Books.

Surin Maisrikrod 1992. *Thailand's Two General Elections in 1992: Democracy Sustained*. Singapore: ISEAS Research Notes and Discussion Papers No. 75.

Svolik, Milan W. 2012. *The Politics of Authoritarian Rule*. Cambridge University Press.

Tambiah, Stanley J.R. 1976. *World Conqueror and World Renouncer: A Study of Buddhism and Polity in Thailand against a Historical Background*. Cambridge University Press.

Tanabe, Shigeharu 1984. 'Ideological Practice in Peasant Rebellions: Siam at the Turn of the Twentieth Century', in Andrew Turton and Shigeharu Tanabe (eds.), *History and Peasant Consciousness in South East Asia*. Osaka: National Museum of Ethnology.

Tanter, Raymond and Manus Midlarsky 1967. 'A Theory of Revolution', *Journal of Conflict Resolution* 11: 264–80.

Tarling, Nicholas 1978. 'Atonement Before Absolution: British Policy Towards Thailand During World War II', *Journal of the Siam Society* 66: 22–65

Tej Bunnag 1977. *The Provincial Administration of Siam, 1892–1915: The Ministry of the Interior under Prince Damrong Rajanubhab*. Oxford University Press.

2008. *Khabot Ro.So. 121*. Bangkok: The Foundation for the Promotion of Social Sciences and Humanities Textbooks Project.

Thak Chaloemtiarana (ed.) 1978. *Thai Politics: Extracts and Documents 1932–1957*. Bangkok: The Social Science Association of Thailand.

2007 [1979]. *Thailand: The Politics of Despotic Paternalism*. Chiang Mai: Silkworm Books.

Thamrongsak Phetchlert-anan (ed.) 2007. *'Kho Ang' Kan Patiwat-Ratthaprahan-Kabot Nai Mueang Thai Patchuban: Bot Wikhro Lae Ekkasan*. Bangkok: The Foundation for the Promotion of Social Sciences and Humanities Textbooks Project.

Thanapol Eawsakul 2006. 'Sao Lak Thang Chariyatham Chue Prem', *Fa Diao Kan* 4: 99–112.

Thawatt Mokarapong 1972. *History of the Thai Revolution: A Study in Political Behaviour*. Bangkok: Chalermnit.

Thelen, Kathleen 1999. 'Historical Institutionalism in Comparative Politics', *Annual Review of Political Science* 2: 369–404.

2004. *How Institutions Evolve: The Political Economy of Skills in Germany, Britain, the United States, and Japan*. Cambridge University Press.

Thitinan Pongsudhirak 2008. 'Thailand since the Coup', *Journal of Democracy* 19: 140–53.

Thompson, Virginia 1967 [1941]. *Thailand: The New Siam*. New York: Paragon.

Thongchai Winichakul 2000a. 'The Quest for "Siwilai": A Geographical Discourse of Civilizational Thinking in the Late Nineteenth and Early Twentieth-Century Siam', *Journal of Asian Studies* 59: 528–49.

2000b. 'The Others Within: Travel and Ethno-Spatial Differentiation of Siamese Subjects 1885–1910', in Andrew Turton (ed.), *Civility and Savagery: Social Identity in Tai States*. Richmond, Surrey: Curzon.

2001. 'Prawatsat Thai Baeb Rachachatniyom', *Sinlapa Watthanatham* 23: 56–65.

2002. 'Remembering/Silencing the Traumatic Past: The Ambivalent Narratives of the October 6, 1976 Massacre in Bangkok', in Charles F. Keyes and Shigeharu Tanabe (eds.), *Cultural Crisis and Social Memory: Modernity and Identity in Thailand and Laos*. London: Routledge/Curzon.

2004 [1994]. *Siam Mapped: A History of the Geo-Body of a Nation*. Chiang Mai: Silkworm Books.

2008a. 'Toppling Democracy', *Journal of Contemporary Asia* 38: 11–37.

2008b. 'Nationalism and the Radical Intelligentsia in Thailand', *Third World Quarterly* 29: 575–91.

2013 [2005]. 'Kham Hai Phon Prachathippatai Baeb Lang 14 Tulakhom', in Thongchai Winichakul, *Prachathippatai Thi Mi Kasat Yu Nuea Kan Mueang*. Bangkok: Fa Diao Kan.

Tilly, Charles 1985. 'War Making and State Making as Organized Crime', in Peter Evans, Dietrich Rueschemeyer, and Theda Skocpol (eds.), *Bringing the State Back In*. Cambridge University Press.

2007. *Democracy*. Cambridge University Press.

Toem Wiphakphochanakit 2003 [1970]. *Prawatsat Isan*. Bangkok: The Foundation for the Promotion of Social Sciences and Humanities Textbooks Project.

Turton, Andrew 2000. 'Introduction', in Andrew Turton (ed.), *Civility and Savagery: Social Identity in Tai States*. Richmond, Surrey: Curzon.

Ukrist Pathmanand 2008. 'A Different Coup d'État?', *Journal of Contemporary Asia* 38: 124–42.

Ünaldi, Serhat 2014. 'Working Towards the Monarchy and Its Discontents: Anti-Royal Graffiti in Downtown Bangkok', *Journal of Contemporary Asia* 44: 377–403.

UNDP (United Nations Development Programme) 2010. *Human Security, Today and Tomorrow: Thailand Human Development Report 2009*. Bangkok: UNDP.

Vandergeest, Peter 1990. *Siam into Thailand: Constituting Progress, Resistance, and Citizenship*. PhD dissertation: Cornell University.

Vella, Walter F. 1957. *Siam under Rama III: 1824–1851*. Locust Valley: J.J. Augustin.

1978. *Chaiyo! King Vajiravudh and the Development of Thai Nationalism*. University of Hawaii Press.

Vickery, Michael 1970. 'Thai Regional Elites and the Reforms of King Chulalongkorn', *Journal of Asian Studies* 29: 863–81.

Von Feigenblatt, Otto F. 2009. 'The Thai Ethnocracy Unravels: A Critical Cultural Analysis of Thailand's Socio-Political Unrest', *Journal of Alternative Perspectives in the Social Sciences* 1: 583–611.

Walker, Andrew 2010. 'Royal Sufficiency and Elite Misrepresentation of Rural Livelihoods', in Søren Ivarsson and Lotte Isager (eds.), *Saying the Unsayable: Monarchy and Democracy in Thailand*. Copenhagen: NIAS Press.

2012. *Thailand's Political Peasants: Power in the Modern Rural Economy*. University of Wisconsin Press.

Walzer, Michael 1982. *The Revolution of the Saints: A Study in the Origins of Radical Politics*. Harvard University Press.

Warangkana Niyomrit 2003. *Khwam Tuen Tua Thang Kan Mueang Khong Samanchon Nai Samai Ratchakan Thi Ha*. MA thesis: Ramkhamhaeng University.

Weidmann, Nils B., Jan Ketil Rød, and Lars-Erik Cederman 2010. 'Representing Ethnic Groups in Space: A New Dataset', *Journal of Peace Research* 47: 491–9.

Wenk, Klaus 1968. *The Restoration of Thailand under Rama I: 1782–1809*. University of Arizona Press.

Wilson, Constance 1997. 'The Holy Man in the History of Thailand and Laos', *Journal of Southeast Asian Studies* 28: 345–65.

Wilson, David A. 1962. *Politics in Thailand.* Cornell University Press.

Wilson, David A. and Herbert P. Phillips 1958. 'Elections and Parties in Thailand', *Far Eastern Survey* 27: 113–19.

Worawit Baru 1995. 'Tradition and Cultural Background of the Patani Region', in Volker Grabowsky (ed.), *Regions and National Integration in Thailand 1892–1992.* Wiesbaden: Harrassowitz Verlag.

World Bank 2012. *Improving Service Delivery. Thailand: Public Finance Management Report.* Bangkok: World Bank.

Wyatt, David K. 1969. *The Politics of Reform in Thailand: Education in the Reign of King Chulalongkorn.* Yale University Press.

2003. *Thailand: A Short History.* Yale University Press.

Index

Lightning Source UK Ltd.
Milton Keynes UK
UKHW02f0635190418
321322UK00016B/253/P

9 781107 657298